STORIES *from the* SAMURAI FRINGE

STORIES *from the* SAMURAI FRINGE

Hayashi Fusao's Proletarian Short Stories and the Turn to Ultranationalism in Early Shōwa Japan

JEFF E. LONG

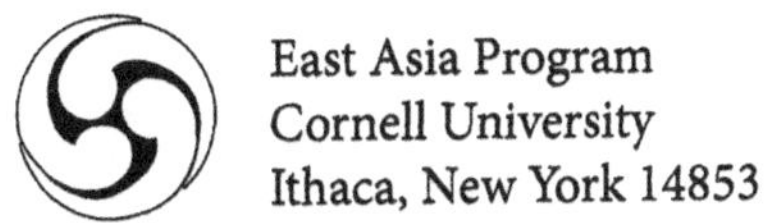

East Asia Program
Cornell University
Ithaca, New York 14853

The Cornell East Asia Series is published by the Cornell University East Asia Program (distinct from Cornell University Press). We publish books on a variety of scholarly topics relating to East Asia as a service to the academic community and the general public. Standing Orders, which provide for automatic notification and invoicing of each title in the series upon publication, are accepted. Address submission inquiries to CEAS Editorial Board, East Asia Program, Cornell University, 140 Uris Hall, Ithaca New York 14853-7601.

Number 190 in the Cornell East Asia Series.

ISSN: 1050-2955
ISBN: 978-1-939161-70-3 hardcover
ISBN: 978-1-939161-90-1 paperback
ISBN: 978-1-942242-90-1 e-book
Library of Congress Control Number: 2018957339

Cover image: Hiroshige (1797–1858). "Fujikawa," from the series Fifty-three Stations of the Tōkaidō Road (Tōkaidō gojūsan tsugi), also known as the Kyōka Tōkaidō.
『東海道五十三次（狂歌入東海道）藤川』「行過る 旅人とめて 宿引の 袖にまつはる ふぢ川の駅　常盤園繁窮」
Accessed: https://en.wikipedia.org/wiki/53_Stations_of_the_T%C5%8Dkaid%C5%8D#/media/File:Tokaido53_Fujikawa.jpg
Cover design: Mai
Interior: Sheryl Rowe-Holland

The paper in this book meets the requirements for permanence of ISO 9706:1994.

Contents

Acknowledgments

This monograph builds on my research while a graduate student, so to start, I would like to thank the many scholars who shared their professional expertise on modern Japanese history and literature with me over the years. At the doctoral level, I benefited greatly from Sharon A. Minichiello's gracious mentorship. She was an inspirational teacher, a consummate professional in navigating the administration of the Center for Japanese Studies, and I learned much from her research on Taishō era politics. Lucy Lower was generous with her time in our discussions regarding the intricacies of modern Japanese literature and the relevance of literary theory to the study of history. In reading my dissertation on Hayashi Fusao's *tenkō*, Patricia G. Steinhoff urged me to take Hayashi seriously as a Marxist writer. Professors Yong-ho Choe and Harry J. Lamley encouraged me to clarify my definitions of key terms, and discussions with both of them helped me to consider the development of the Japanese socialist movement within the larger historical framework of colonial Korea and the politically riven state of 1930s' China. In St. Louis, Marvin Marcus pushed me to read and think about Meiji and Taishō literature as a cultural foundation for Japanese literature of the 1930s, and the late Eugene Soviak spent many hours talking with me about the historical and intellectual context of Japanese nationalism during the Meiji years and beyond. I had recently returned from three years of language study, and a year working for a Japanese company, in a Japan at the peak of its economic miracle. Professor Soviak suggested reading Hayashi Fusao's works as an entry point for examining the revived nationalist discourse that was so evident from my experiences in Japan.

My research could not have been completed without the help of many other organizations and their professional and financial support. Bloomsburg University of Pennsylvania awarded a sabbatical leave, release time, and a research grant enabling me to conduct research in Japan and affording the time to write this book. The Blakemore Foundation provided a

Refresher Grant to attend a summer session of the Inter-University Center for Japanese Language Studies in Yokohama Japan, where I was not only able to improve my Japanese language skills but was also able to access the research materials available at the Kanagawa Museum of Modern Literature, a beautiful facility overlooking the port at Yokohama. In addition, I also conducted research for this manuscript at the following institutions: the National Diet Library and the Museum of Modern Literature in Tokyo, the Kumamoto University Library, the Ōita Prefectural Library, the University of Tokyo's Institute of Social Science Library, the Van Pelt Library at the University of Pennsylvania, and the Harvard-Yenching Library. I would like to thank the staff at each of these libraries for their help in procuring the needed materials, and at the Yenching Library for a travel grant to fund my visit in 2015. In addition, I would like to thank the staff at Andruss Library for directing me through the inter-library loan process and for identifying available resources at other libraries when needed. Much of this research was presented at several academic meetings where I benefited from the panelists and audience's comments and questions to improve the monograph. As such, I would like to recognize those venues: the Annual Midwest Conference on East Asian Thought, the Rocky Mountain Modern Language Association's Annual Convention, the Association for Asian Studies' Annual Meeting, the Modern Language Association's Annual Meeting, and the Midwest Japan Seminar. I would also like to thank Taylor & Francis for allowing me to include some of the content from an earlier article: "Songs that cannot be sung: Hayashi Fusao's 'Album' and the political uses of literature during the early Shōwa years," *Japan Forum* 19, no. 1 (March 2007): 69–88, in this monograph. At the Cornell East Asia Series press, Mai Shaikhanuar-Cota has been a wonderful editor, and I appreciate her guidance in seeing this monograph through its publication. In Bloomsburg, I would like to thank Gayle Decker for copyediting and Jillian Lashmett for indexing the monograph. Finally, this work has been significantly improved by the close reading and thoughtful suggestions for revision by two readers for the press.

Personally, my parents, JC and Charlene Long, and my sister and niece, Debbie and Keely Baldridge, have always provided a haven from the stress of preparing this manuscript, as has my wife's family on Cheju Island. Much of the reading for and the writing of the manuscript was conducted in the public libraries in Cheju-city, and I would like to thank the Mun

and the Im families for allowing me to stay with them during my sabbatical leave to prepare several chapters of the monograph. My oldest son Cody has accompanied me on several of these trips to Japan and South Korea, and it has been a joy to watch him and my younger son, Somkiet, grow up during this time, and to Hyun Jung who has been through this whole process with me, I express my gratitude for her support and her many sacrifices to see this project through to its completion.
Sarang hae yo, goma wŏ yo!

INTRODUCTION

The *Tenkō* Experience, Hayashi Fusao, and Ideology

Few events have symbolized the interwar Japanese intellectual community's inability to put up a principled resistance to the Japanese government's growing authoritarianism like the *tenkō* phenomenon of the 1930s.[1] Instead of deporting, exiling, or executing its political dissidents, the state placed them in solitary confinement. Then, as Patricia Steinhoff has documented, the state used a number of social pressure inducements to encourage them to sign *tenkō* statements in an attempt to rehabilitate them for their return back into Japanese society.[2] Academic studies of the 1950s through the 1970s focused first on the institutional use of *tenkō* as a means to repress communism and the Japanese Left. In the 1970s and 1980s, scholars turned to studies of individual members of the intellectual community, largely to confirm that these individuals maintained their commitment to Marxism at some intellectual level, despite having renounced the Communist Party while imprisoned. From the 1990s onward, scholars have been examining the *tenkō* phenomenon as one of the jumping off points for the rise of a romanticized ethnic nationalism in interwar Japan. While acknowledging the contributions of these works to our social, political, and our ideological understanding of early Shōwa Japan (1926–1937), these studies often fail to prioritize the agency of the individuals

1. Literally the two characters that compose the ideogram for *tenkō* 転向 mean "a change of direction," but in this specific historical context, scholars have translated the term as a political and/or ideological renunciation of the Communist Party and its affiliated organizations and activities. Here the term will remain untranslated, and further discussion of *tenkō* within the context of early Shōwa Japan follows in Chapter 8.

2. See Patricia G. Steinhoff's classic study of the *tenkō* phenomenon, *Tenkō: Ideology and Societal Integration in Prewar Japan* (New York: Garland Publishing, 1991).

involved. Thus, we are often presented with a long list of oppressors and victims, heroes and turncoats, hawks and doves for the "dark valley" narrative of Japan's prewar years, a narrative that emphasizes the stark choices the intellectual community faced and either confirms their complicity with serving the goals of the wartime Japanese state or lauds their resistance to the authorities.

This monograph, then, is an attempt to engage the *tenkō* phenomenon from the intellectual's perspective by examining the *tenkō* of writer and literary critic Hayashi Fusao (1903–1975). Hayashi's turn to ultranationalism in the 1930s and 1940s was so extreme that scholars often discount altogether his time in the radical student movement and his participation in the proletarian literature movement. Flipping the mirror on this interpretation, here we examine Hayashi's *tenkō* through a study of his proletarian fiction. Taking seriously his Marxist turn in the 1920s reveals first the political nature of Hayashi's literature, particularly his struggle with the leaders of the Socialist movement to define the role of literature in the movement. Hayashi's turn to Marxism was predicated on his negative interpretation of the Meiji state's support for the ideas of modernity that in practice had adversely affected his family situation. Sheldon Garon has argued that "the ideas of modernity—progress, science, and rationality—meant a great deal to the Japanese people" during Japan's modern period and that these ideas were also pivotal in "cement[ing] several key alliances between various social groups and the state" during the prewar period.[3] Garon's research emphasizes "the appeal of modernization" as one of the main motivating factors in bringing members of society and the Meiji state together.[4] Likewise, modernity is a significant background theme for this monograph, since Hayashi spent the greater part of his life engaged in an attempt to condemn the influence of the Japanese state's modernization policies on Japan's traditional social structure.

Garon in his work does not deny the existence of conflict in these complex relationships between members of the state and members of society. Still, his attempt to show how the state turned "the Japanese people into active participants in the state's various projects" does stress consensus

3. Sheldon Garon, "Rethinking Modernization and Modernity in Japanese History: A Focus on State-Society Relations," *The Journal of Asian Studies* 53, no. 2 (May 1994): 350.

4. Sheldon Garon, *Molding Japanese Minds: The State in Everyday Life* (Princeton: Princeton University Press, 1997), 18.

over conflict in the Japanese state's ability to "manage" society.[5] In contrast, Kevin Doak, in an essay exploring the intersection between nationalism and religion in early Shōwa Japan, finds that the state often had to deal with antagonistic social forces that openly contested its political and cultural hegemony over society.[6] He concentrates on the ethnic (*minzoku*) nationalist challenge to state (*kokka*) nationalism and shows how the Japanese state responded to this challenge. Doak's ironical point is that in blurring the lines between these different conceptions of the "nation" and "nationalism," the Japanese state "engag[ed] in a moral critique of modernity itself—the very foundation of an earlier, Meiji, national pride."[7]

Where Garon views modernity as a positive goal that the state encouraged so as to involve members of society in state-led campaigns, Doak's more contentious reading of this process asserts that modernity was a politically and culturally contested issue in the 1930s. Doak argues that those individuals who regarded modernity as a concept corrupted by Western notions of "civilization" pressured the state to criticize the whole modernization process, the very process that the state considered one of its greatest achievements. From Garon's standpoint, the state's efforts to gain the support of Japanese society were gradual and reciprocal. While the state used the "carrot" of modernization to motivate the societal forces at work in modernizing Japan, the negotiation process also challenged the state to adjust its modernizing policies and programs to take into consideration the concerns of two increasingly significant social forces in Japanese society: the rising middle class and women. We consider how this negotiation process affected Hayashi's family directly in Chapter 1 and then in Chapters 2, 3, and 4, we examine how the negative impact of modernization on Hayashi's family became a theme that he explored in his earliest proletarian short stories.

In contrast to Garon's social history, in which the state sanctions the ideas of modernity to gain public support, Doak focuses on a critical cultural and intellectual moment of negotiation between the state and the

5. Garon, *Molding Japanese Minds*, 6.

6. Kevin M. Doak, "Nationalism as Dialectics: Ethnicity, Moralism, and the State in Early Twentieth-Century Japan," in *Rude Awakenings: Zen, the Kyoto School, & the Question of Nationalism*, ed. James W. Heisig and John C. Maraldo (Honolulu: University of Hawai'i Press, 1994), 174–196.

7. Ibid., 187.

Japan Romantic School (Nihon Rōmanha) coterie. He contends that, from 1937 to 1943, the writers in the Japan Romantic School with their moralistic and idealistic use of ethnicity in their literature forced the state to criticize Western notions of modernity.[8] Ultimately, the state co-opted the ethnic nationalist challenge, Doak notes, but not before those who posed this challenge obliged the Japanese state to condemn the very foundation on which it rested: the idea of the modern nation-state. These writers, for their part, urged the state to condemn the idea of "a Japanese modernity" based on Western notions of "civilization." However, as Doak argues, in so doing, they also lost their critical position from which they had opposed the state's definitions of modernity in the 1930s.

According to Garon's assertion, we find that the desire for the "ideas of modernity" brought the members of state and society together. However, from Doak's research we also discover that some writers and intellectuals intensely contested the state's definition of modernity. One of the main social groups involved in this dialogue with the state over modernity was middle-class Japanese intellectuals, a group that scholars call the intelligentsia, or *interi* in Japanese.[9] They worked mainly in the field of journalism and, alongside academics in the universities, comprised the largest part of the intellectual community during the prewar years. Germaine Hoston has argued that the ideas of Marxism—"its claim to scientific truth and universality"—attracted some of this group because it "empowered the critique of their own society from without."[10] While the ideas of Marxism permitted some of the intelligentsia to distance themselves from their own "Japaneseness," and to analyze modernity from a position radically different from that offered by liberals, conservatives, and the Japanese state, the Marxist organizations themselves offered structural support and even protection for those ideas. Thus, here we will refer to Marxism in its broadest sense: both as a set of ideas based on Marx's

8. Doak, "Nationalism as Dialectics," 187.

9. Masakazu Yamazaki, "The Intellectual Community of the Showa Era," in *Showa: The Japan of Hirohito*, ed. Carol Gluck and Stephen R. Graubard (New York: W.W. Norton & Company, 1992), 248.

10. Germaine A. Hoston, "Emperor, Nation, and the Transformation of Marxism to National Socialism in Prewar Japan: The Case of Sano Manabu," *Studies in Comparative Communism* 18, no. 1 (Spring 1985): 38.

teachings and practice, and as a set of institutions that provided support for Marxist political and cultural activities.

At the start of the twentieth century, the state began to view Marxism and other forms of socialism as dangerous and began to suppress them. By the 1930s, the state considered most left-wing thought and activities illegal. In search of alternatives, some Japanese intellectuals turned to cultural nationalism as a means of political and social criticism. To discuss the development of this in prewar Japan, this monograph draws on Harumi Befu's definition of East Asian cultural nationalism as "a third type of nationalism, which emerges once national sovereignty has been achieved, [and which] focuses on the creation, crystallization, and expression of the cultural identity of the nation."[11] Kevin Doak has further refined our understanding of cultural nationalism as more of an "umbrella" term, one that suggests "... how ethnic, civil and even statist variants of nationalism are mobilized through cultural discourse."[12] The Japanese intelligentsia produced a considerable range of cultural nationalist responses during the 1930s, as Kevin Doak and Roy Starrs have shown previously, and these responses became meaningful in the postwar years as possible alternatives for envisioning postwar Japan after its prewar and wartime legacy of militarism at home and expansion abroad.[13]

Hayashi Fusao was one of these intellectuals who produced a cultural nationalist vision of Japan during the 1930s. However, unlike the more subdued, refined cultural nationalism of renowned writers such as Kawabata Yasunari and Tanizaki Jun'ichirō, Hayashi infused his cultural nationalism with the emotional appeal of patriotism. He celebrated the beauty of the Japanese land and people in his works, yet he also endeav-

11. Harumi Befu, "Introduction," in *Cultural Nationalism in East Asia: Representation and Identity*, ed. Harumi Befu, Research papers and policy studies, no. 39 (Berkeley: Institute of East Asian Studies University of California, 1993), 2.

12. Kevin M. Doak, *A History of Nationalism in Modern Japan: Placing the People*, Handbook of Oriental Studies (Leiden and Boston: Brill, 2007), 3.

13. Kevin M. Doak, *Dreams of Difference: The Japan Romantic School and the Crisis of Modernity* (Berkeley: University of California Press, 1994), and Kevin M. Doak, "Ethnic Nationalism and Romanticism in Early Twentieth-Century Japan," *The Journal of Japanese Studies* 22, no. 1 (Winter 1996): 77–103. Roy Starrs, "Writing the National Narrative: Changing Attitudes toward Nation-Building among Japanese Writers, 1900–1930," in *Japan's Competing Modernities: Issues in Culture and Democracy 1900–1930*, ed. Sharon A. Minichiello (Honolulu: University of Hawai'i Press, 1998), 206–227.

ored to protect that beauty from those who would exploit it. In this way, Hayashi's cultural nationalism provided an alternative view of Japan that combined an appreciation for Japan's genteel past with an extremism grounded in Japan's bushido legacy. We will explore this turn to cultural nationalism during the mid-to-late 1930s in Chapters 7 and 8 in this monograph.

When he began to identify his desire to protect the beauty of the Japanese nation with an overriding loyalty to the Japanese emperor after the start of the Sino-Japanese War in 1937, Hayashi's cultural nationalist image of Japan became an ultranationalist one. In this sense, as scholars such as Maruyama Masao, Richard Storry, and George M. Wilson have concluded, ultranationalism was not so much a departure from nationalism as it was an extreme, overt form of nationalism.[14] In Hayashi's case, it involved the extreme nationalist expression of his loyalty for the nation and his desire to protect Japanese traditions against foreign influences, two of the common characteristics in distinguishing ultranationalist thought, as recognized by Maruyama.[15] Kawabata's and Tanizaki's cultural nationalism in the 1930s, as Starrs has suggested, became important during the immediate postwar years, and their views acted as models showing that Japan need not discard all of its native traditions while recovering physically and emotionally from the devastation of the war.[16] The postwar intellectual community rejected Hayashi's cultural nationalist position during the early 1930s, recognizing only his cooperation with the state and his ultranationalistic discourse during the late stages of the early Shōwa years.

Still, as a writer in the proletarian literature movement of the 1920s, Hayashi sought an organizational means through which to express his desire for social justice, to struggle against the source of that repression—the Japanese state—and to develop a concept of proletarian literature with an emotional appeal that would inspire others to join the movement. Here

14. Maruyama Masao, "Introduction," in *Nationalism and the Right Wing in Japan: A Study of Post-War Trends* (New York: Oxford University Press, 1960), xvii–xviii; see the preface in Richard Storry, *The Double Patriots: A Study of Japanese Nationalism* (Chatto & Windus, Ltd., 1957; reprint, Westport, CT: Greenwood Press, Publishers, 1976; page citations are to the reprint edition); and George M. Wilson, "ultranationalism," in *Kodansha Encyclopedia of Japan*, 144–146.

15. Maruyama Masao, "Introduction," xvii–xviii.

16. Starrs, "Writing the National Narrative," 224.

in Chapters 4, 5, and 6, the focus on Hayashi's proletarian short stories is the most fruitful, as we trace his idealization of the movement, his struggle with his fellow writers to define the movement, and finally his memorialization of the movement. In the end, first, Hayashi interpreted the fall of the proletarian cultural movement as an organizational casualty because it was sacrificed to demands by the Communist Party's leadership that all proletarian writers should join the party first and then prioritize the political needs of the party over aesthetic concerns in their writing. Then, second, he blamed the Japanese state and its authoritarian push toward homefront unity for narrowing the proscription on any ideology deemed to be critical of the Emperor system.

After the start of the second Sino-Japanese War in 1937, Hayashi's politics of *tenkō* turned to ultranationalism, which aligned him with the state rhetoric of national oppression at the hands of Western imperialists. Thus, the compilation of his last set of proletarian short stories, which he turned into a biographical novel entitled *Taiyō to Bara* (Sun and Roses) in 1938, marked his break with the proletarian literature movement and the end of his Marxist-inspired short stories. In the final chapters of that novel, which we will scrutinize how, in Chapter 8, Hayashi attempts a labored, but extremely political reconfiguration of his *tenkō* experience. Ultimately, Hayashi reveals his positive support for the Japanese land and the Japanese people in those chapters of *Sun and Roses*, even as he bitterly recounts the sacrifice of intellectuals like himself at the hands of figures representing imperial authority.

This is as far as our study of Hayashi's proletarian short stories will take us, but it does allow the reader to glimpse the onset of his turning his *tenkō* experience into an ideology. Here, David Pollack's broader definition of ideology in *Reading Against Culture* is useful. He delineates ideology as "the contending webs of economic, political, social, religious, and cultural relations through which power is distributed and exercised, and within which our lives are lived." Pollack's corollary to this definition is to acknowledge that humans construct these relations and endow this created "reality" with a sense of permanence.[17] Drawing on Pollack's concep-

17. David Pollack, *Reading Against Culture: Ideology and Narrative in the Japanese Novel* (Ithaca, NY: Cornell University Press, 1992), 89–90. Here, Pollack's constructs this definition out of his reading of Dominick LaCapra's *Soundings in Critical Theory* (Ithaca: Cornell University Press, 1989), and from Terry Eagleton's works on ideology: *Ideology:*

tual framework for ideology, this work argues that Hayashi employed his proletarian short stories as a political means to engage his fellow writers in an extended discussion about the place and the role of the writer and literature in the Socialist movement. When it became apparent that the leaders of the left-wing literary movement did not agree with him, he used his proletarian short stories to create a new narrative of social, economic, and political relationships in which to place his creative efforts and to denounce the leaders of the movement.

Next, Hayashi turned his physical and mental experience of *tenkō* into a way of life, which we can view in the completion of his final proletarian novel *Sun and Roses* between 1937 and 1938. Here, he turned to the older *shishōsetsu* form of narrative to establish the authenticity of his new life as a cultural nationalist writer. While Hayashi wanted his readers to view these works as autobiographical (indicating the genuine commitment of his *tenkō* to cultural nationalism) his fellow writers like Miyamoto Yuriko, as Brett de Bary notes, realized quickly the contradiction in the use of the *shishōsetsu* form to "invoke" sincerity in *tenkō* literature.[18] Thus, we will follow Edward Fowler's reading of the *shishōsetsu* writers from the Meiji period whose claims of "sincerity" and "authenticity" Fowler treats as a "formal convention."[19] Using this framework, in Chapter 8 we explore Hayashi's assertion of his sincere "change of direction" in *Sun and Roses*. Subsequently, as I have discussed elsewhere, Hayashi endeavored to make this *tenkō* ideology permanent during the wartime years. He developed new political and social relationships with extreme nationalist groups in the 1940s and through different types of writings such as his historical novels and his biographies of historical figures, which he started writing in the early 1930s and continued reworking to fit the new political context of wartime Japan.[20]

An Introduction (London: Verso, 1991) and *The Ideology of the Aesthetic* (London: Blackwell, 1990).

18. Brett de Bary, "'Credo Quia Absurdum': *Tenkō* and the Prisonhouse of Language," in *Culture and Identity: Japanese Intellectuals during the Interwar Years*, ed. J. Thomas Rimer (Princeton, NJ: Princeton University Press, 1990), 156.

19. Edward Fowler, *The Rhetoric of Confession: Shishōsetsu in Early Twentieth-Century Japanese Fiction* (Berkeley: University of California Press, 1988), x.

20. Specifically, see Chapter 5 in my examination of the different ways Hayashi wrote and then reworked his first major historical novel *Seinen* (*Youth*) in Jeff E. Long, "Over-

THE STATE AND HAYASHI FUSAO

In this way, Hayashi's political use of literature and his *tenkō* represented his response to the internal "Japanification" of those members of the Japanese intelligentsia who had experimented with "red" ideas and organizations during the 1920s and 1930s. Benedict Anderson argues in his work *Imagined Communities* that the Meiji leaders, when fashioning the Japanese state during the late nineteenth and early twentieth centuries, employed the "official nationalism" model as a means to establish rule over the Japanese people.[21] Anderson asserts that, based on the idea of preserving the preeminent interest of the state, the leadership of the Japanese state undertook the imperialist enterprise as part of a political legitimization process designed to create "the general impression that the conservative oligarchy was an authentic representative of the nation of which Japanese were coming to imagine themselves members."[22] Anderson then focuses his study on the Japanese state's cultural and linguistic attempts to "Japanify" those ethnically and racially distinct members of its colonial empire through the modern education system and the medium of print. He ends his discussion by stressing the process through which the Japanese leadership employed the official nationalist model to incorporate Koreans, Taiwanese, and Manchurians into Japan's "nationally-imagined" imperial system, without giving them the opportunity for upward political mobility within that system.[23] Thus, Anderson's focus is on the colonial enterprise and the Japanese state's attempt to bring members of its empire into the imperial fold. This strategy of official nationalism is part of the Meiji oligarchs' desire to avoid being marginalized in their own "emerging nationally-imagined community," Anderson asserts.[24]

In Japan of the 1930s, the elite political leadership groups faced a simi-

---

coming Marxism in Early Shōwa Japan: Hayashi Fusao's *Seinen* and the Turn to Ultranationalism" (Ph.D. diss., University of Hawai'i, 2000), 158–201.

21. Benedict Anderson, *Imagined Communities: Reflections on the Origin and Spread of Nationalism*, Revised Edition (New York: Verso, 1991), 94–99. Anderson borrows the notion of "official nationalism" from the work of Hugh Seton-Watson, *Nations and States: An Enquiry into the Origins of Nations and the Politics of Nationalism* (Boulder, CO: Westview Press, 1977). Anderson, *Imagined Communities*, 86.

22. Anderson, *Imagined Communities*, 97.

23. Ibid., 99.

24. Ibid., 101.

lar predicament in their relationship with those parts of the intellectual community influenced by the Left. The development and employment of the *tenkō* policy thus illustrates the Japanese state's endeavor to Japanify, to use Anderson's words, its domestic dissidents in the early Shōwa period. In her discussion of the *tenkō* phenomenon's significance for 1930s' Japan, sociologist Patricia Steinhoff charges that the *tenkō* policy established by the Japanese government not only aided in gathering patriotic support for the war effort on the Asian continent but more notably "eroded one of the last forces of resistance to nationalism, the Japan Communist Party" and its affiliated organizations.[25]

Though Hayashi Fusao was not a member of the party, he drew the attention of the authorities because he was active in groups such as the radical student movement and the left-wing literary movement where he associated with communist writers and activists. Steinhoff identifies Hayashi's *tenkō* as a "spiritual *tenkō*," signifying that he recanted his belief in Leftist ideology when he found that those ideas could no longer give meaning to his existence.[26] Steinhoff explains that exploration into the Japanese cultural tradition was one way that many spiritual *tenkōsha*, including Hayashi, found a sense of immortality; thus, "by immersing themselves in ancient cultural history, by identifying with the historically continuous Japanese people, and by participating in the national goals and destiny of Japan, the spiritual *tenkōsha* were able to establish that precious sense of connection."[27]

In Hayashi's case, the search for meaning would eventually converge on the Japanese people and land, leading him to the foremost symbol of Japanese national culture, the Emperor. He joined what Kevin Doak has termed the populist nationalist efforts of intellectuals during the interwar years to develop a nationalism centered on the people in order to express their opposition to the Japanese state's overriding concern to protect its

25. Steinhoff, *Tenkō*, 209.

26. Steinhoff has changed the English translation of *shūkyō-teki tenkō* from its more literal meaning, religious *tenkō*, to spiritual *tenkō* to "encompass the search for meaning in nationalistic and philosophic as well as religious frames of reference." In addition to the spiritual *tenkō*, Steinhoff in this chapter also discusses the "common-man" *tenkō* (*shimin-teki*) and the "political" *tenkō* (*seiji-teki*), terms that she has borrowed from the main Welfare and Rehabilitation Organization that worked with the *tenkōsha* (Teikoku Kōshin-kai). Steinhoff, *Tenkō*, 129–130.

27. Steinhoff, *Tenkō*, 169.

authority over the interests of the Japanese people.[28] Drawing on either or both ethnic (*minzokushugi*) and civic (*kokuminshugi*) definitions of nationalism, Doak maintains that these intellectuals asserted a difference that the Japanese state could not tolerate. During the 1930s and through the Asia-Pacific War, the Japanese state worked to close the gap between the state and the nation. Under the signifier of "nation-state" (*kokumin-kokka*), the state made conscious efforts to incorporate the intellectuals into a common endeavor to mobilize the Japanese populace for war.

As Doak notes, Hayashi became an integral part of that war effort during the summer of 1937.[29] As such, technically Hayashi and all members of the intellectual community who committed *tenkō* did join the nationally imagined community sponsored by the leaders of the Japanese state. However, each found ways to reconnect with that national community and participate in it on many different levels and to various degrees as Steinhoff makes clear in her chapter delineating the three types of *tenkō*.[30] Hayashi also worked to redefine himself as a writer through his *tenkō* during the 1930s. Since he made use of both ethnic and civic nationalism "through [a] cultural discourse" to criticize the Japanese state during the early 1930s, here we will refer to his nationalist expressions of dissent as cultural nationalism.[31]

This monograph's initial three chapters build on scholar Mizuno Yukiko's assertion that Hayashi Fusao's early turn to Marxism should be examined through his literature of the time. Scholars writing about Hayashi's *tenkō* predominantly make use of his post-*tenkō* theoretical essays, his polemical statements, his historical novels and biographies, and

---

28. Kevin M. Doak, *A History of Nationalism in Modern Japan: Placing the People*, Handbook of Oriental Studies (Leiden and Boston: Brill, 2007), 202.

29. In this discussion, Doak builds on the earlier work of Thomas Havens to explicate this tension between nation and state during the interwar years. Doak, *A History of Nationalism in Modern Japan*, 200–202. He is also drawing on his own work in Kevin M. Doak, "Nationalism as Dialectics: Ethnicity, Moralism, and the State in Early Twentieth-Century Japan," in *Rude Awakenings: Zen, the Kyoto School, & the Question of Nationalism*, ed. James W. Heisig and John C. Maraldo (Honolulu: University of Hawai'i Press, 1994), 174–196.

30. Steinhoff, *Tenkō*, 129–173.

31. As noted earlier, Doak defines cultural nationalism as more of an "umbrella" term, one that "reminds us of how ideologies mobilize identity within various forms of nationalism." Doak, *A History of Nationalism in Modern Japan*, 3. While he eschews the term for more precise definitions of ethnic, civic, or statist nationalism in his own work, here the emphasis is on Hayashi's use of a cultural means to express his nationalist sentiments.

his postwar reflections on his youth to describe his interest in Leftist thought. These works often depict a naive youth who was duped by an intellectual trend of the times before coming to his senses and embracing the State's patriotic rhetoric as typified in the late 1930s into the 1940s. Hayashi, particularly in his postwar memoirs, encouraged this reading of his Marxist youth. In contrast, Mizuno has argued in her 1999 and 2001 journal articles that reading Hayashi's short stories written during his youth is a much more effective means to investigate his turn to Marxism.[32] Her point is that these short stories more accurately reflect the idealism and dynamism of the radical student movement that captured Hayashi's interest as well as depicting his contempt for authority figures that also continued through his life. More significantly, her analysis also refutes Hayashi's own postwar attempts to downplay the role that his Marxist past had in shaping his understanding of state-society relations and the relationship of politics and literature. As such, one of this monograph's main goals is to restore Hayashi's turn to Marxism and his literary and theoretical contributions to the proletarian literature movement as essential components of his overall *tenkō* experience.

Thus, the first three chapters build on Mizuno's research, examining Hayashi's humanist short stories written in 1918 when he was a middle school student in Ōita, and then extending this analysis to his first socialist literature produced in 1921 and 1922 while studying at the Kumamoto Fifth Higher School. This section of the monograph ends with the first review of his earliest proletarian fiction. Influenced by his reading of the Austrian countess Hermynia Zur Mühlen's Marxist fairytales, Hayashi translated some of her work in 1924 and then began writing his own proletarian children's stories from 1925 to 1926 while he was an undergraduate at Tokyo Imperial University. These chapters highlight the idealism in his short stories and his evident love for writing fiction that contained a healthy dose of ambivalence toward and skepticism of authority figures, not only those associated with the State but also for those peer leaders of the radical student movement during the 1920s. As such, we find Hayashi to be writing literature that not only inspires and entertains, but also cen-

32. Mizuno Yukiko, "Hayashi Fusao kenkyū: 'E no nai ehon' wo chūshin ni," *Shōwa Bungaku Kenkyū* 38 (March 1999): 1–13; Mizuno Yukiko, "Hayashi Fusao kenkyū: yōshōnenki saikentō," *Tsuru University Graduate School Review* 5 (2001): 50–64.

sures the intellectuals and the leaders of the Socialist movement of his time. This challenges both Hayashi's memories of his move from politics to literature, and Mizuno's assertion that Hayashi was always a writer first and a political radical second.

From this point, university officials expelled Hayashi Fusao from Tokyo Imperial University for his involvement in radical student activities, and he joined the proletarian literature movement full time during what scholars are beginning to refer to as Japan's experience of the international "red decade" (1925–1935).[33] To explore Hayashi Fusao's move from a Marxist to a nationalist understanding of what it means to be a Japanese subject, the next five chapters of the monograph trace Hayashi's interaction with other proletarian writers and the Marxist cultural organizations supporting them. Through an analysis of his proletarian short stories from 1926 up to 1938, these chapters examine Hayashi's open struggle with other members over the place of literature in this political movement, up to the point where he stopped writing Marxist-themed literature. In this book most of these stories are receiving their first analytical treatment since during the postwar years both the Japanese Communist Party and Hayashi himself attempted to erase these works from the canon of proletarian literature.[34] Other critical studies typically emphasize, in a linear fashion, Hayashi's ideological problems with the left-wing literature movement's leadership group that led to an emotional and sudden conversion to Japanese romanticism and his "return to Japan" (*Nihon e no kaiki*) in the late 1930s. Nevertheless, as Hayashi moved from "romanticizing" to "defining," and then eventually to "remembering and memorializing" the movement and the decade in his short stories, we find a

33. See Norma Field and Heather Bowen-Struyk's brief history of the "red decade" in their Introduction to *For Dignity, Justice, and Revolution: An Anthology of Japanese Proletarian Literature*, ed. Heather Bowen-Struyk and Norma Field (Chicago: University of Chicago Press, 2016), 3–8.

34. Samuel Perry in his recent work, *Recasting Red Culture in Proletarian Japan: Childhood, Korea, and the Historical Avant-Garde* (Honolulu: University of Hawai'i Press, 2014), xi–xii, notes that one of his goals in writing this work was to reintroduce certain authors and certain texts that the Japanese Communist Party and those groups associated with it have left out of the canon of proletarian literature. In some small way, I hope to build on and contribute to Perry's success in "recasting red culture" by taking seriously Hayashi Fusao as a Marxist and by treating his proletarian short stories as integral to the development of the red decade.

far more personal and political rationale for his eventual turn to ultra-nationalism than is presented in previous studies. This section of the monograph concludes with a reflection on Hayashi's attempt in 1938 to deliberately use the last of his "proletarian" stories to rewrite, rework, and re-remember his Marxist youth as a more nostalgic time and a more genteel place; even as, instead, we see a young Japanese cultural nationalist who was budding and maturing in the provincial port town of Ōita.

In the final two sections, this monograph places Hayashi's political use of literature and then his political use of his *tenkō* experience within two interpretive contexts. We start with a historiography of previous studies examining the Japanese intellectual community in the early Shōwa years to provide the broader framework for a more concentrated study of the *tenkō* experience itself. Once we have a more informed understanding of how scholars have viewed the intellectual community in this period, we examine the scholarly interpretations of the *tenkō* experience in the 1930s, and finally consider those works specifically focused on Hayashi Fusao. With this analytical structure in place, the epilogue briefly outlines Hayashi's desperate and anguished acquiescence to defeat during the American Occupation of Japan. After that, the epilogue highlights Hayashi's new lease on his intellectual life during Japan's economic recovery of the 1960s. During that decade, some Japanese began to insist that it was time for a more positive reassessment of the Asia-Pacific War within the context of Japan's modern history. This time Hayashi became a champion of wartime nationalism during the 1960s, and then of the culture of Emperor-worship during the 1970s, finding, at last, a postwar home for his *tenkō* ideology of the war years.

1

A Sullied Lineage in Modernizing Japan

Hayashi Fusao's Marxist Turn in Memory

Takeo tried to wash off the mud at a small stream. Instead, he was soaked through and through by the time he got home. He told his Dad that he had slipped and fallen in the water. "Idiot!" his father screamed, flinging a bundle of straw at Takeo. The straw missed him, but Takeo started crying anyway. Sobbing, he was hiding in the shade of a hedgerow when his mother came home from the factory and gently reminded him that a samurai's son doesn't blubber like that. Remembering the storage room filled with antique spears and a container full of traditional samurai armor at his old home in the port of Ōita, Takeo stopped crying, and his mother pulled out a clean kimono for him to wear. The samurai armor and spears were handed down from his mother's family.

—"Arubamu"

Hayashi Fusao's childhood was marked by the reduction of his family's social status and the loss of their economic security—a common story among former samurai families during the Meiji period. Hayashi was born May 30, 1903, in the port city of Ōita on the northeastern coast of Kyūshū. His maternal grandfather was Gotō Noritake, a samurai of the Oka (also known as the Takeda) *han*, and his mother, Hidé, was the heiress (*ietsuki musume*) of the Gotō household. Hayashi was raised as a member of his mother's family, and his given name was Gotō Toshio. From an early age, Hidé raised her son to inherit the Gotō mantle, often showing him the swords and armor handed down from his samurai grandfather.

Hayashi Fusao, "Arubamu," *Kaizō* 18, no. 10 (October 1936): 71.

She intended to raise him as the son of a samurai family (*shizoku no musuko*), so she told him stories about the ancestry of the Gotō house and had him try on the traditional clothing of the samurai from time to time. In this way, Hayashi's mother attempted to impress upon her son his Kyūshū roots and his *shizoku no chi*, or "samurai lineage."[1] However, Hidé's marriage to Nagata Ryūtarō, the son of a small landowner in a village bordering Ōita, contributed to the Gotō family's already declining fortunes in several ways. First, Ryūtarō married into the Gotō family as an adopted son-in-law (*irimuko*) and managed a general store in the Ōita port area. As Isoda Kōichi notes, Hayashi's family must have viewed the marriage as an embarrassment, especially if considering the pairing from the perspective of Tokugawa-era (1600–1867) social norms, from which the marriage of a higher-ranking samurai's daughter to a farmer's son was unthinkable.[2]

Still, Hayashi was Ryūtarō's and Hidé's only child, and they treated him as a *botchan*, their cherished son.[3] Safe in this sense of security where all who lived around him acknowledged his "samurai lineage," Hayashi recalls that with his forceful personality, he picked fights with other children on the playground, emerging as the big bully (*gaki daishō*) of the neighborhood. As he matured, he became an excellent student at Ōita Kenritsu Ōita Shihan Fuzoku Elementary School. Despite a problem with stammering (which developed when he entered elementary school) and

1. Isoda Kōichi, "Hayashi Fusao, Dan Kazuo: sakka to sakuhin," in *Hayashi Fusao, Dan Kazuo shū*, vol. 66, Nihon bungaku zenshū, ed. Itō Sei (Tokyo: Shūeisha, 1969), 409. *Shizoku* is a social class distinction that has its origins in early Meiji efforts of social reform. In 1869, the social class of *shizoku* included the upper and middle samurai, and ranked second behind the *kazoku* that included the daimyo and the court aristocrats. In 1872, the Meiji government amalgamated the two classes below the *shizoku*, the *sotsu* composed of lower samurai and the *heimin* or common people. By the time of Hayashi's birth, the *shizoku* was no longer a privileged position by law, but the prefectural government still used this designation to keep track of one's legal address (*honseki*) for the family registry. In 1947, the Occupation government abolished this social class distinction.

2. Ibid., 409.

3. Hayashi Fusao, "Fu: Hayashi Fusao nenpu," in *Hayashi Fusao chosakushū*, vol. 1 (Tokyo: Tsubasa shoin, 1968), 446. Albert Craig has given an excellent definition of *botchan*—"a boy of good family, without great virtues or special vices, raised carefully without a knowledge of privation or hardship"—in his essay "Kido Kōin and Ōkubo Toshimichi: A Psychohistorical Analysis," in *Personality in Japanese History*, ed. Albert M. Craig and Donald H. Shively (Berkeley: University of California Press, 1970; reprint, Michigan Classics in Japanese Studies, no. 13, Ann Arbor: Center for Japanese Studies at The University of Michigan, 1995), 277 (page citations are to the reprint edition).

his less than stellar behavior, Hayashi indicates that the other students selected him to become the classroom monitor (*kyūchō*). He remembers the school administration choosing him to represent grades one to three at a nighttime ceremony, held "to venerate the Meiji emperor from afar" (*yōhaishiki*) upon the emperor's death in 1912.[4] Hayashi was nine years old and in his third year of elementary school at the time. Besides the respect he garnered in the classroom for being such a good student, he began to read voraciously. He read youth magazines, collections of children's stories from around the world, and adventure stories, so much so that his mother began to call him a bookworm (*hon no mushi*), he notes.[5] Up until the age of ten, he lived in a secure home and school environment. School officials and his teachers acknowledged his academic prowess, while his parents' love for him and the respect given him by others, he writes, validated his sense of privilege derived from his maternal family's *shizoku* background.

Hayashi's *botchan* life soon came to a devastating halt. He notes in his biographical sketch (*nenpu*) that, from 1913, his father Ryūtarō's bouts of drinking and debauchery became increasingly excessive; and in two years' time, his family received notice that their businesses had gone bankrupt.[6] Isoda argues that this is the second way in which Ryūtarō embarrassed the Gotō family's samurai lineage. Nevertheless, literary scholar Mizuno Yukiko paints a more sympathetic picture of Ryūtarō's extreme behavior. She notes that Ryūtarō expanded his business, adding a *ryokan* (Japanese-style inn) to the general store just before the ongoing industrial development in Ōita port shifted to the port's eastern side.[7] As his business fortunes sank, Ryūtarō moved his family in 1915 to the village of Kita Taiheiji on the outskirts of Ōita. There, he rented from a local farmer a mud-walled storehouse (*dozō*) with no indoor kitchen or bathroom.[8] Mired in debt, Ryūtarō increasingly turned to alcohol as a means to drown his worries;

4. Kawamori Yoshizō, "Hayashi Fusao den," in *Hayashi Fusao, Shimaki Kensaku*, vol. 28, Gendai Nihon bungakukan, ed. Kobayashi Hideo (Tokyo: Bungei shunjū, 1969), 4.

5. Hayashi, "Fu: Hayashi Fusao nenpu," 446.

6. Ibid.

7. Mizuno Yukiko, "Hayashi Fusao kenkyū: yōshōnenki, saikentō," *Tsuru University Graduate School Review* 5 (2001): 52.

8. Mōri Toshio, "Hayashi Fusao no shōgai oyobi bungakuteki sōzō," *Tsurumi daigaku kiyō: dai'ichibu, kokugo kokubungaku hen* 31 (March 1994): 133.

moreover, he began to threaten his family with violence.[9] Isoda asserts that not only was Hide's marriage to someone perceived to be of lower class a disgrace to the Gotō family, but Ryūtarō also eventually cost the family their livelihood and forced them to live in humbling, even demeaning circumstances. Hayashi also recalls putting up with every sort of degradation one might imagine while living in the village.[10] Still, Mizuno suggests that instead of blaming Ryūtarō personally for all the family's problems, we should consider the economic situation that pushed him over the edge.[11] Building on Hayashi's reflections on his boyhood, however, Isoda insists that Ryūtarō's downward spiral was the third and final humiliation to the Gotō family's samurai lineage. Hayashi records that, because Ryūtarō was frequently inebriated and able to do little more than make straw sandals (*waraji*) that Hayashi helped to sell in the local marketplace, Hidé found a job in a nearby silk mill. She became the primary breadwinner, and the family relied on her income to make ends meet.[12]

A SULLIED LINEAGE IN MODERNIZING JAPAN

Although the *shizoku* status in the early twentieth century was little more than a title of honor indicative of a bygone age, the Gotō family pride rested on memories of when that status meant something more tangible in Japanese society.[13] In a sense then, Hayashi's childhood is symbolic of the *shizoku* experience, especially during the greater historical transition between the Tokugawa and the Meiji (1868–1912) years. The *shizoku* made up about five percent of the total population in 1873, and for the government who paid their hereditary stipends, this group was an immense burden. More than a fourth of the Meiji government's budget went to pay these stipends. Thus, in order for the government to put into practice its

9. Mizuno, "Hayashi Fusao kenkyū: yōshōnenki," 52.

10. Hayashi Fusao, "Fu: Hayashi Fusao nenpu," 447.

11. Mizuno, "Hayashi Fusao kenkyū: yōshōnenki," 52.

12. Kawamori, "Hayashi Fusao den," 4. In explaining his qualifications to write proletarian literature, Hayashi recounts his childhood experiences, particularly the humiliation he endured while attempting to sell Ryūtarō's straw sandals in his "Hihyō ni tsuite" *Bungei sensen* 3, no. 12 (December 1926): 29.

13. Matsumoto Keiko, *Higanbana: miryoku aru otokotachi e no chinkonka* (Tokyo: Seiga shobō, 1989), 119.

policy of "civilization and enlightenment" (*bunmei kaika*), most of the Meiji leaders believed that the social and economic privileges accorded the *shizoku* needed to be curtailed and then eliminated as quickly as possible. As Sidney DeVere Brown has suggested: "The story of the *shizoku* ... is largely the tale of the *liquidation* [emphasis mine] of their special samurai privileges. By 1882 their legal rights were gone, by 1914 the government ended the use of the term *shizoku* in the household registers (*koseki*), and in 1947, following the end of World War II, the very title was abolished along with all other distinctions."[14]

The Meiji government attempted to help the *shizoku* through this difficult transition by promoting economic policies such as the *shizoku jusan* transition program. Meiji officials designed this program to familiarize the *shizoku* with the workings of Western commercial practices and to financially support their new endeavors in business. Nevertheless, like Hayashi's family, "on the whole 'the way of the samurai in business,' became synonymous with failure."[15] After watching the banks, industries, and other business ventures run by members of the *shizoku* either fail or go bankrupt, the Meiji government suspended the program in 1889. Clearly, many members of the *shizoku* and their families were having a difficult time making the transition from Tokugawa to Meiji Japan. Still, we must also remember that a large group of the *shizoku* did excel in their new surroundings and comprised part of the new Japanese elite. They joined the bureaucracy, the military, the police force, and some were even successful in the business world.

In contrast, many of those *shizoku* who were having a difficult time used violence to express their discontent with the changes taking place in Japan through violence. They assassinated some of the Meiji leaders, most notably Ōkubo Toshimichi in 1878, and participated in several rebellions and riots. The culmination of these violent acts was the Satsuma Rebellion (*Seinan sensō*) of 1877, led by Saigō Takamori. Saigō was the samurai that most disaffected *shizoku* of the 1870s looked to for leadership. From the end of the rebellion in 1877 to the present, in the minds of the Japanese people, Saigō would also become the personage most often associated with the unyielding spirit of those disaffected *shizoku*, the more so be-

14. Sidney DeVere Brown, "Shizoku," in *Kodansha Encyclopedia of Japan*, 151.
15. Brown, "Shizoku."

cause his rebellion was the final revolt against the state. The Meiji government survived these outbursts of violence, mainly because they were localized in the provinces, were not highly organized, and addressed principally the specific grievances of the *shizoku*, which drew the sympathy, but not the support, of the larger populace.

With armed revolt no longer a viable option, *shizoku* dissent increasingly took political form. Itagaki Taisuke, from the Tosa *han* in Shikoku, was one of several *shizoku* who led the challenge to the Meiji state's factional politics through the Freedom and People's Rights Movement (*Jiyū minken undō*) between 1874 and 1890. In this movement, the discontented *shizoku* joined with the *gōnō*, wealthy farmers, who were also prominent village leaders and demanded the formation of a National Assembly and the promulgation of a democratic constitution. Western notions of popular sovereignty and expansion of liberty, taken from Rousseau, Locke, Spencer, and others became the weapons the *shizoku* used to push for government reform. Their responses to the Meiji government's modernizing policies took a variety of forms ranging from the extreme of resisting these policies using physical force, to a pro-government position of active participation in those policies. Members of the *shizoku* also advocated the use of political means to resist and change government policies. Hayashi would make his own choices, but these early *shizoku* responses provided a rich historical legacy to draw upon later when forming his response to the perceived humiliation of his *shizoku* roots.

Isoda Kōichi has suggested that Hayashi interpreted the humiliation of his mother—who for him was the very symbol of his "*shizoku no chi*," his samurai lineage—within the larger historical context of the *shizoku* liquidation described above.[16] Watching his mother work in a silk mill that paid little in return, Hayashi witnessed firsthand the results of government attempts at leveling Japanese society (*shimin byōdō*). The same government policies that fostered the growth of industrial capitalism and stressed the accumulation of wealth as the basis for social and economic status did so to the detriment of the *shizoku*, whose status was based on a combination of military and bureaucratic skills. Moreover, though the leaders of the Meiji government shared the same *shizoku* roots, when they encouraged the development of industrial capitalism in Japan, in effect

16. Isoda, "Hayashi Fusao, Dan Kazuo," 409–410.

they were supporting the elimination of the *shizoku*'s special privileges and the toppling of the *shizoku* class.

Isoda argues that, for Hayashi, the extrapolation from local reality to a greater historical perspective was a straightforward one. He watched his mother work herself to physical exhaustion every day at a silk mill, which was run by an owner who made profits off the labor of women. His mother stood for the samurai lineage of traditional Japan; she symbolized the "*Nihonteki mono*," or "Japanese things" of the Tokugawa period that persisted in Meiji Japan.[17] The owner of the mill represented the industrial capitalists who gained social and economic privilege from the accumulation of wealth, a concept disdained by the *shizoku* in Tokugawa Japan. In Hayashi's mind, the mill and the industrial capitalists would come to signify "*kindai*," or "the modern age," which supported and encouraged the industrial capitalists.[18] Consequently, Hayashi associated the Meiji state with "the modern," namely with the historical process and the historical figures leading the Meiji government. The Meiji state, which had introduced the industrial capitalist economic system into Japan, had also directed the development of a "modern" social system. In due course, Hayashi blamed this social system for the Gotō family's humiliation and thus, the disgrace of his samurai lineage.

Hayashi's mother resigned herself to menial labor despite their family's background, because it was evident that unless one was born into wealth, the chief means of raising one's status in Japanese society was through the education system. Meiji Japan was not to be a world where society valued the military skills and genealogy of the samurai as much as one's *gakureki* (educational background) or one's success in this world (*risshin shusse*).[19] Isoda concludes that he doesn't "know how conscious Hayashi was during his youth of the shape that his family fortunes had taken (*unmei no kōzu*). However, Hayashi's samurai lineage (*shizoku no chi*) concealed deep in his heart would lead him, in due course, to seek revenge against [those who

17. Isoda, "Hayashi Fusao, Dan Kazuo," 418. Isoda does not make the actual connection between Hayashi consciously perceiving his samurai lineage as a *Nihonteki mono* until he discusses Hayashi's *Seinen* later in the essay, but he anticipates this connection from the beginning of the essay.

18. Ibid., 410.

19. Ibid.

had contributed to] the direction that his family fortunes had taken."[20] The direction that Isoda refers to here was the dishonor of his mother's samurai lineage. She sacrificed herself in a silk mill where, at least in Hayashi's mind, industrial capitalists were overseeing the construction of the "modern" age, while deliberately destroying the "Japanese things" he grew up cherishing the most. Yamashita Etsuko, in her work on the role of the mother in Japanese literature, asserts that the mother rather than the father signifies the home for most Japanese writers from the Meiji period onward.[21] She suggests that Japanese writers associate the mother with a specific time and place that precedes any later ideological commitments. Thus, Yamashita explains that the *tenkō* literature (*tenkō bungaku*) written by Hayashi and other proletarian writers wrote during the 1930s represents is "a return to 'the mother'" (*'haha' e no kaiki*), which is a play on "a return to Japan" (*Nihon e no kaiki*), the popular rallying cry of writers from the Japan Romantic School in the late 1930s.[22]

Hayashi took his mother's sacrifice and humiliation personally, and he blamed the Meiji government for sullying his samurai lineage. He then turned to Marxism as an alternative and antistatist theory of social and economic development. Hayashi's pending involvement in radical student groups gave him an organizational means to oppose the Japanese government and its imposition of the industrial capitalist economic system upon Japanese society in general. However, as Isoda argues, Hayashi accepted Leftist radicalism to protest the lowering of the Gotō family's social status, a specific historical circumstance resulting from the Meiji government's attempts to "modernize" the Japanese economy and society.

HAYASHI FUSAO'S MARXIST TURN IN MEMORY

Most scholars have studied Hayashi's embrace of Marxism through either his "Bungakuteki kaisō" ("Literary reminiscences," prepared in 1955) or

20. Isoda, "Hayashi Fusao, Dan Kazuo," 410.

21. Yamashita Etsuko, *Mazakon bungakuron: jubaku toshite no 'haha'* (Tokyo: Shinyōsha, 1991), 167.

22. See Yamashita, *Mazakon bungakuron*, 164, for usage of the phrase "'*haha' e no kaiki*" as the title of that section of the chapter and page 166 for Yamashita's discussion of the importance of the mother in *tenkō* literature overall.

his "Fu: Hayashi Fusao nenpu" ("Biographical sketch," prepared in 1968), which affords us the aging Hayashi's perspective on those years.[23] However, beginning with Kumamoto literary scholar Shutō Motosumi's research on the short stories Hayashi submitted to the Kōyūkai (the Fifth Higher School's alumni association) journal *Ryūnan* (Southern dragon), recent scholarship has focused on analyzing Hayashi's Marxist turn through his early literature.[24] Building on Shutō's work, Mizuno Yukiko has demonstrated with her meticulous research that, although Hayashi's "Biographical Sketch" includes much information on his Marxist transformation while in Kumamoto, it also includes the pitfalls of memory. Throughout her articles documenting Hayashi's Marxist turn, Mizuno points out the frequently erroneous chronology of Hayashi's "Biographical Sketch." Moreover, both of Hayashi's postwar biographical works underscore Hayashi's desire to establish his nationalist credentials from an early age, as he refers to his flirtation with communism as based on fanaticism and illusion in his "Literary Reminiscences."[25] Mizuno, more than Shutō, utilizes Hayashi's literature produced while in middle school and as a higher school student to explore Hayashi's interest in Marxism and his participation in the radical student and cultural movements of the 1920s. The contrast is instructive if one begins with Hayashi's memory of his days as a middle school and higher school student, and then examines how he wanted others to interpret his Marxist turn in the 1960s.

23. The two main choices for those writing short biographies of Hayashi Fusao's early life have been Hayashi Fusao's "Bungakuteki kaisō" ("Literary reminiscences") in *Hayashi Fusao chosakushū*, vol. 2 (Tokyo: Tsubasa shoin, 1969), 222–410, first published by Shinchōsha in 1955, and the biographical sketch that Hayashi prepared for his *Selected Works*, Hayashi Fusao, "Fu: Hayashi Fusao nenpu," in *Hayashi Fusao chosakushū*, vol. 1 (Tokyo: Tsubasa shoin, 1968), 446–462. Our only prewar memoir is Hayashi Fusao's "Bungakuteki jijoden," in *Rōmanshugi no tame ni*, ed. Bungakukaisha shuppanbu (Tokyo: Bungakukaisha shuppanbu, 1936), 327–345. Hayashi's "Bungakuteki jijoden" ("Literary memoirs") first appeared in *Shinchō* 32, no. 11 (November 1935): 60–68, the same month he was released from Shizuoka prison, his third and final imprisonment for his Leftist political activities.

24. Shutō Motosumi, "Hayashi Fusao oboegaki," in *Kumamoto no bungaku*, vol. 3, ed. Kumamoto Kindai bungaku kenkyūkai (Tokyo: Banbisha, 1996), 136–148. See also Shutō Motosumi, "Gokō no bunjin tachi: Hayashi Fusao," in *Kumamoto no bungaku II*, ed. Kumamoto daigaku gakusei bu (Kumamoto: Kumamoto daigaku hōsō kōkai kōza, 1993), 133–148; and Shutō Motosumi, "Hayashi Fusao: kindai no yōkōro," in *Kindai bungaku to Kumamoto: suimyaku no hirogari* (Osaka: Izumi shoin, 2003), 94–109.

25. Hayashi Fusao, "Bungakuteki kaisō," 225.

Despite the hardships of his youth, his mother and others recognized Hayashi's intellectual abilities and nourished his love of learning. Hayashi finished elementary school in the local village, where he recalls the other students treated him as an outsider and just another mill girl's child.[26] His family had given up on sending him to middle school, but the teachers at the elementary school convinced Hayashi's parents to let him sit for the entrance exam to Ōita Kenritsu Ōita Middle School.[27] Hayashi placed second in the testing, and his mother resolved that she would work harder to put him through school. As the only youth in the village to enter middle school, Hayashi began his studies in 1916 at age thirteen. While a middle school student, Hayashi writes fondly of his mentor, Yamashita Tetsunosuke,[28] an art teacher who introduced him to many kinds of art, music, and literature, especially the literature of the Shirakaba (White birch) School.[29] Again, Hayashi remembers that his conduct at school was not always exemplary—the school administration even considered expelling him from school once, as a suspected ringleader of a school strike—but his grades remained excellent.[30] His love of reading continued, and he recollects that he quickly exhausted the collection at the middle school's small library and then visited the Ōita Prefectural Library for more read-

26. Hayashi Fusao, "Fu: Hayashi Fusao nenpu," 447.

27. Established in 1885, the Middle School is Ōita's oldest school. From 1951 the school was renamed the Ōita Kenritsu Ōita Uenogaoka Kōtōgakkō. Kurata Michifumi's article discusses the depictions of Ōita and the school in Hayashi's early literature with pictures of the school in his "'Mayu' 'Seinen' ni miru Hayashi Fusao no Genzō," *Viento: Ōita no kaze* 3 (March 2004): 14, accessed January 10, 2007.

http://www.pref.oita.jp/ 10400/viento/ vol03/p14_17.html.

28. Hayashi discusses at length the influence Yamashita had on him and many other students in Hayashi Fusao, "Yamashita Monka no Menmen," *Shūkan asahi*, August 14, 1960, 76.

29. The White Birch School formed around the journal *Shirakaba* (White Birch), which ran from 1910 to 1923. Elitist and aristocratic by birth and temperament, the writers who contributed to this journal stressed humanism (*jindō shugi*) and idealism (*risō shugi*) in opposition to the realism of the Naturalist writers. Moreover, they avoided the social and political issues of the day, preferring to focus on realizing their innate potential. Of this group, only Arishima Takeo attempted to deal with public issues. Both moralistic and hedonistic tendencies characterized the White Birch School of writers, but either way what the White Birch writers desired most was self-realization of the human potential. Donald Keene, "The Shirakaba School," in *Dawn to the West: Japanese Literature of the Modern Era, Fiction*, An Owl Book (New York: Henry Holt and Company, 1984), 441–505.

30. Hayashi, "Fu: Hayashi Fusao nenpu," 447.

ing materials. As his family grew even more impoverished, Hayashi recalls that his homeroom teacher arranged for him to work as a live-in private tutor.

This arrangement helped Hayashi pay for his schooling, and he met others who would become very dear to him while living with the Ono family, a banker's family in Ōita. The Ono family consisted of the husband and wife, the wife's younger sister, and several children whom Hayashi taught part-time. He became very close to the family. When he finished middle school and passed the difficult entrance exams to enter the elite "higher school" (*kōtō gakkō*) institution, the Ono family offered him financial assistance to attend the Fifth Higher School in Kumamoto. The Ministry of Education had developed the higher school institution as a means to prepare select students to enter the imperial university system; thus, a student's admission to an imperial university was guaranteed. However, entrance to the most prestigious of the imperial universities was competitive and entrance to the most distinguished departments within these universities even more so.[31] Hayashi writes that the Ono family agreed to send him twelve *yen* a month on the condition that he would sit for the exams to enter the Law Department of Tokyo Imperial University, which was the most distinguished department within the most prestigious Japanese university at that time. His mother and his aunt sent what they could to help him, he notes, but Hayashi relied on the money from the Ono family to pay for his room and board at the Fifth Higher School's dormitory. At age seventeen (1920) Hayashi headed off to Kumamoto carrying his love for literature and nurturing a secret crush on the sister-in-law living with the Ono family.[32]

Both of these loves would come to take a back seat to his political activities over the next four years, Hayashi records. Experiencing a sense of freedom and liberation long forgotten, he recollects that he continued to pursue his love for literature, art, and music by immersing himself in the hectic yet invigorating life of the higher school student. He joined an art

---

31. Henry Dewitt Smith, II, *Japan's First Student Radicals*, Harvard East Asian Series, no. 70 (Cambridge: Harvard University Press, 1972), 9.

32. Mizuno, "Hayashi Fusao kenkyū: yōshōnenki," 53. Hayashi in his "Biographical Sketch" writes that he entered the Fifth Higher School in 1919 (Hayashi, "Fu: Hayashi Fusao nenpu," 448), but Mizuno points out that the Fifth Higher School's official gazette (*kanpō*) records Hayashi's start as September 1, 1920.

and music group and sent in short essays and *tanka* poems to school magazines. With Hayashi's immersion in student life, his grades suffered, but what he remembers affecting him most during his time in Kumamoto was his intellectual encounter with various strands of socialist thought.

During the first year of his stay at the Fifth Higher School, Hayashi recalls that one of the self-proclaimed anarchist upperclassmen at the dormitory introduced him to the banned works of Kropotkin, Bakunin, Kōtoku Shūsui, and Marx. Exposure to these works piqued his interest, and he proceeded to read other socialist works by Japanese authors such as Yamakawa Hitoshi, Kawakami Hajime, and the writers in the socialist journal *Tanemaku hito* (The Sower). These writers' socialist themes appealed to him, so he and several other classmates organized a self-styled "communist" secret society called the R.F. Kai (literally, the Red Flag Society, the R.F. was an abbreviation for the German, *die rote Fahne*).[33]

After forming the secret group, Hayashi writes that he and the four or five other members sequestered themselves near the Shirakawa River for several days of training (*gasshuku*). During that time, he recalls that he decided to give up literature, music, and art. As a sign of his commitment, he states that he sold his musical instruments and painting utensils, quit his drinking, and cut his long hair. Finally, Hayashi recalls that he and another classmate from Ōita went down to the banks of the Shirakawa River and burned the bundles of love letters they had both written since arriving at school.[34] Hayashi's letters were to the younger sister of the Ono family, Hayashi Fusako. While he was in Kumamoto, Fusako had become the second wife in the Ono family following the premature death of her older sister. At that time, it was common practice for the younger sister to take the place of the elder sister if she passed away early in the marriage. Still, as a young man, Hayashi remembers it being a devastating blow that he hid behind a show of bravado and defiance, urinat-

---

33. Hayashi, "Fu: Hayashi Fusao nenpu," 448. See also Smith, *Japan's First Student Radicals*, 104. Here again Mizuno challenges the timing of the R.F. Kai and the H.S.L. in Hayashi's "Biographical Sketch," writing that other sources date the establishment of the R.F. Kai to 1922 and the founding of the H.S.L. to 1923, "Hayashi Fusao kenkyū: yōshōnenki," 54–55.

34. Hayashi Fusao, "Bungakuteki jijoden," in *Rōmanshugi no tame ni*, ed. Bungakukaisha shuppanbu (Tokyo: Bungakukaisha shuppanbu, 1936), 331. Hayashi's "Bungakuteki jijoden" ("Literary memoirs") first appeared in *Shinchō* 32, no. 11 (November 1935): 60–68, the same month he was released from Shizuoka prison.

ing with his friend on the burning love letters.[35] Hayashi writes that this experience marked a turning point in his life and found concrete expression when representatives of the Shinjinkai (New Man Society)[36] from Tokyo Imperial University visited the Fifth Higher School campus late in 1921.

Students from Tokyo Imperial University first established the New Man Society in 1918 to propagate Yoshino Sakuzō's theories about democracy. But by the early 1920s, the group had taken a decidedly Marxist turn and were looking for new ways of recruiting student activists. Likewise, members of the New Man Society were attempting secretly to organize a Kōtō Gakkō Renmei (Higher School League). Their goal was to establish ties with radical student groups in the higher schools and then have them acknowledge the leadership of the New Man Society.[37] In 1921, several New Man Society leaders went on a speaking tour through the higher schools of western Japan for this purpose; when they visited Kumamoto, they set up a chain of command with the R.F. Kai. Linking the activities of the R.F. Kai with those of the radical student groups from the other higher schools, the New Man Society created a vertical organization. This organization served the New Man Society in two ways: first, as noted above, they hoped to replenish their ranks every year by recruiting students from the higher schools—graduation was a serious obstacle to maintaining continuity in the New Man Society. Second, they attempted to establish relations with socialist movements in the provinces in order to provide some leadership for these provincial movements.[38]

On a more personal level, Hayashi recalls that the speeches of the New

---

35. Hayashi, "Bungakuteki jijoden," 332. Hayashi would later memorialize his love for Fusako by switching the last character, meaning "child" (房子), in her given name, to the character meaning "male" (房雄)—a move from a character commonly used to denote a feminine name in Japan to a character common in male names—to form the pen name by which he is most well known, Hayashi Fusao.

36. Here, I will follow Henry Smith's practice in referring to this group.

37. See Smith, *Japan's First Student Radicals*, 103–106, for the best discussion in English of the formation of the H.S.L. Smith notes that the Shinjinkai leaders made stops in Kyoto, Osaka, and Kagoshima as well as Kumamoto on their tour. In Kagoshima, they made contact with the newly formed radical student group called the Kakumeikai (Society of the Crane's Cry) at the Seventh Higher School. According to Smith, the leaders of this tour were Kuroda Hisao, Tomooka Hisao, Shiga Yoshio, Itō Kōdō, Sugino Tadao and Narazaki Akira, 105.

38. Smith, *Japan's First Student Radicals*, 106.

Man Society leaders deeply affected him and that he took his responsibility to spread communist propaganda to the students of the Fifth Higher School quite seriously. He writes in his memoirs that he had a "feeling of electricity" running through him after a meeting with New Man Society leaders.[39] A feeling of confidence ensued that on one occasion inspired the normally reticent Hayashi to overcome his stammering in one instance and deliver a long speech in a fluent speaking voice to his classmates. After a day or two, he reverted to his normal ineloquence, but he records that this was a type of religious experience for him, a miracle of sorts, originating from his association with an extremely "irreligious" group.[40] On the organizational side, under orders of the New Man Society, he remembers helping to put together a movement to raise funds to save the Russian farmers from famine, and organizing "cells" of socialist study groups. Later he helped put together a student protest movement that condemned the murders of Karl Liebknecht and Rosa Luxemburg, two leaders of the German Communist Party whom soldiers shot to death on January 15, 1919, in Berlin.[41]

Hayashi's involvement with the New Man Society and with leftist thought only intensified in the following years. He writes that he attended the first national meeting of the Higher School League in Tokyo during January of 1922. Acting as the representative of the Fifth Higher School group, he and twelve or thirteen other students representing groups from other higher schools spent their time learning Bolshevik organizing tactics. Their New Man Society hosts also introduced them to leaders of the secretly formed Japanese Communist Party such as Inomata Tsunao and Tokuda Kyūichi. At that time, Hayashi and the other students did not know about the formation of the Japanese Communist Party, nor did they realize the significance of the people they met at the Tokyo gathering.[42] Thus, despite passing the highly competitive entrance exams to enter the Law Department of Tokyo Imperial University in the spring of 1923,

39. See Hayashi's remarks in "Bungakuteki jijoden," 332.

40. Ibid., 332–333.

41. The police picked up Hayashi and brought him in for questioning about the student protest. It was his first run-in with the police, Hayashi remembers. Kawamori, "Hayashi Fusao den," 6.

42. Mizuno notes that the Japanese Communist Party did not formally organize until July 1922 so more likely this meeting took place in January of 1923, "Hayashi Fusao kenkyū: yōshōnenki," 54.

Hayashi notes that he perceived the admittance not as a step up in academic challenge, but as a deepening commitment to the socialist movement. Reflecting on his life as part of the Japanese literati during the interwar years, Hayashi would later write in his postwar memoirs that in fact he had "graduated not into college but *into the New Man Society.*"[43]

43. Hayashi Fusao, "Bungakuteki kaisō," in *Hayashi Fusao chosakushū*, vol. 2 (Tokyo: Tsubasa shoin, 1969), 222.

2

Humanism and Socialism

Hayashi Fusao's Marxist Turn in Literature

> I quickly turned over a small stone amongst the dayflowers and carefully slipped the nickel coin into the hole. As I replaced the stone, I can't say that the image of the old lady wearing glasses didn't pass before my eyes. But, once I pushed the stone down and covered the coin, I was overwhelmed by a huge sense of relief and joy.
>
> Inside our hut, there was my dad who'd returned from the factory, sitting alone and drinking his *saké* while some of the plaster from the wall rustled as it fell. I stood up and went inside. Then, without a word, I picked up the small folding table with dinner on it and brought it in under the light, where yet again I gazed at my dad's haggard face.
>
> —"Hakudōka"

In his "Literary Reminiscences" Hayashi writes that from 1955 on what literary efforts he made after his encounter with the New Man Society representatives took an increasingly political form. He comments that his teachers ordered him to join the school's Bungeibu Iin (Literature Club Committee) in 1922, but by that time, his interest had already turned to left-wing thought. He had already begun to think that literature and art were simply tools to spread Leftist propaganda.[1] Thus, as with his narrative of entering the radical student movement discussed in the previous chapter, Hayashi in the postwar period portrays his Marxist turn as a

Hayashi Fusao (Gotō Toshio), "Hakudōka," *Ryūnan* 184 (December 1922): 86–87.

1. Hayashi Fusao, "Bungakuteki kaisō," in *Hayashi Fusao chosakushū*, vol. 2 (Tokyo: Tsubasa shoin, 1969), 228. See also Hayashi's narrative of this shift from literature to politics in Hayashi Fusao, "Fu: Hayashi Fusao nenpu," in *Hayashi Fusao chosakushū*, vol. 1 (Tokyo: Tsubasa shoin, 1968), 448–449.

choice between literature and politics. However, it is evident, even in this brief passage above from one of his favorite short stories, which he wrote while a higher school student at Kumamoto, his turn to Marxism was not an either/or choice. Hayashi began to use his literature politically to explore the personal costs of industrial capitalism, as we see here with the narrator turning to petty theft and stealing the coin; thus, Hayashi's short story thus acts as a social critique of the modern historical development of Japan during the Meiji years. Still, the literary injection of the narrator's conscience pricking him, even as he buries the coin, the elaborate description of his father enjoying his *saké* in their shabby living conditions, and the narrator's delayed recognition of his father's exhausting labor at the factory reflect Hayashi's creative attempt to place this social critique within the bounds of literature.

Thus, in this chapter, we examine Hayashi's turn to Marxism through the short stories he wrote as a middle school and a higher school student. This comparison challenges Hayashi's postwar memory of choosing politics over literature, which he explained as a decision to enter the radical student movement while studying at the higher school in Kumamoto and attending Tokyo Imperial University. But a study of the humanist and increasingly socialist short stories he produced before entering the proletarian literature movement in 1925 as a full-time writer reveal Hayashi's dedication to literature, even as he participated in the radical student movement. Likewise, we glimpse both the uncertainty in Hayashi's turn to Marxism as well as his nascent political uses of literature to call on his fellow higher school students to join in the fight to resist the industrial capitalists' control of the economy and the state's authority over Japanese society. Hayashi's literature from middle school and higher school provides a useful corrective to his own memory of his Marxist turn and depicts a youth still quite committed to literature as a means to reflect on oneself and to examine state-society relations.

Although a complete collection of the Ōita Kenritsu Ōita Middle School's alumni journal *Ōita kōyūkai zasshi* (Ōita alumni journal) has not survived, the Ōita Prefectural Library does hold Volume 68 of the journal, which offers the earliest vantage point on Hayashi Fusao's development as a writer. Published in September of 1918, this volume includes two short stories and two *tanka* poems written by Hayashi. In these works, he uses the contrasting themes of light and dark, nature and humanity, life and death, ideal and reality, to consider the unfolding process of self-awareness and the self's relationship with society. He explores these themes through the protagonists' experiences while hiking, accidentally running across a snake in a field, cramming for an exam, and taking an idle walk on an early summer's day.

Hayashi's middle school literature reveals a typical youth in the midst of coming to grips with who he is, what it means to be a man, and the greater expectations of him as a middle school student. In this way, the White Birch School's emphasis on examining the human condition is predominant in Hayashi's initial short stories. His first and longest story, "Murasaki no tsuchi" ("Purple Earth"), begins with the main character exclaiming, "Why am I in such a hurry; I just don't get it," as he and his other friends head into the dark forest at the foot of a mountain.[2] As he makes his way up the mountain at different times and places the forest canopy recedes and the mist pulls back, allowing him to become "conscious of the light" and to become overwhelmed with joy at the abundance of the natural world surrounding him.[3] Our narrator interprets this beauty first in terms of colors but then dissolves the description into the Japanese cultural idiom of the mysterious and the primeval, musing that they were similar to those people portrayed in the paintings and the poetry of the ancients.[4] Mist envelopes the group again, swallowing up everything and leaving the narrator with a feeling of entering a hermit's hut.

This reoccurring motif of brightness and dimness elicits a cycle of different responses ranging from fear and trepidation to wonder and awe, depending on the occasion. At first, the narrator realizes that when they entered the clouds, he had felt unsure of himself and small, but then strangely he felt huge and wanted to show the world just how big he had become.[5] As they climb, the mist gives way as the group nears the summit, revealing large black boulders on the mountain. Their guide tells them of the Kannon rock close to the mountain's peak on the eastern side and the narrator seems happy, but once he reaches the eastern peak, he slips into self-introspection again. On the mountaintop, with the mist

---

2. Hayashi Fusao (Gotō Toshio), "Murasaki no tsuchi," *Ōita kōyūkai zasshi* 68 (September 1918): 44.

3. Ibid., 45.

4. Ibid., 46.

5. Ibid., 47.

enclosing the group, he did not feel big or happy anymore. A sense of vulnerability was only natural, he surmises, since they were not in their "little huts" any longer and they were confronting the coldness, the dampness, and the darkness. In essence, the narrator asks how a person can be happy when faced with reality.[6] At home, they were content and safe under the nurturing care of their families, but exposed to the natural world and out on their own as students on a field trip, he realizes how hard the real world can be. In this way, the narrator acknowledges the challenging transition from his and the other students' relatively sheltered family life into the greater social and intellectual world of the middle school.

Exhausted, the group seeks shelter from the cold, strong winds, and they build a fire to warm themselves before someone suggests returning home. Everyone agrees and, on the way down, the mist clears near the Kannon rock. The beautiful colors of the earth and clouds bring smiles to the group, but when one member proposes going back up the mountain, the rest chuckle knowingly and they continue down the mountain that is disappearing into the mist. With everyone lost in thoughts, the narrator observes breaks in the mist that hint at the unspeakable beauty it shrouds; however, he is the happiest when he escapes the wind and mist and reaches the foot of the mountain. He exclaims the virtues of having his feet planted firmly on the "purple earth" again. Hayashi, the author, intervenes with a final sentence stating that he based this story on a trip he took to Mount Yufu on August 7, 1917.[7]

While continuing his focus on the relationship between the natural and human worlds from "Purple Earth" in his second short story "Hebi" ("Snake"), Hayashi expands his subject to consider the roles of gender and experience on the physical boundaries between the self and the larger world around him.[8] Hayashi begins the story with the narrator enjoying the splendor of an early summer day. Walking through a field after the rain, the narrator observes the beauty of a wild rose bush, the steam rising from the earth, and the blue sky. Just then, he hears a sound that stops him in his tracks. As in the "Purple Earth," the narrator asks himself a similar

6. Ibid., 48.

7. Ibid., 49.

8. Hayashi Fusao (Gotō Toshio), "Hebi," *Ōita kōyūkai zasshi* 68 (September 1918): 51–53.

question, "Why did I start running away? I just don't get it."[9] He answers the question by acknowledging the fact that the mere sight of the small snake frightened him, awakening both a pleasant sensation of animal instinct and a vague darkness in his mind. Looking at the snake that had been startled by his footsteps, the narrator notices its scales shimmer like black pearls, and its eyes sparkle like those of a woman. He begins to shake uncontrollably, and then a cruel bestiality blocks his thought process as he stomps on the snake, severing it into two pieces. Nevertheless, the small snake's head still faces up at him, and its eyes glisten with pain, so he crushes its head with his other foot. Standing still, the narrator comments that he experienced calmness before the cruel reality of the snake's death overwhelmed him. As he slowly becomes conscious of what he has done, the narrator feels a "great remorse" welling up inside, and it moves him to tears. Suddenly, a silver fly lands on the dead snake's dark blood, and he runs away as fast as he can.[10]

In this story, the youth's encounter with the snake brings forth an examination of fear and its impact on the human condition. Mizuno Yukiko has argued that two intertwined aspects characterize the narrator's inquiry into the nature of fear in the story: the fear of death and the fear of and desire for the opposite sex.[11] When the narrator first comes across the small snake, he experiences danger and reacts with a childish pleasure, one born of animal instinct that both invigorates him physically, yet clouds his mind. It is fear that draws him closer to the snake as the narrator describes the "look" of the snake in feminine terms, which attracts but also repels the youth.

> Startled by his footsteps, the snake's mysterious body slipped deftly through the wild rose bushes and out onto the cattail-colored (*kabairo*) dirt where it extended itself to full length. Its small scales, each one resembling a black pearl, shimmered like the pupils of a woman's eyes. How its scales glistened and sparkled, a brilliant vermillion-shaded hue of yellow; what's more is if you listened closely, it was as if you could hear the pleasing sensation of the snake inhaling the warmth around it.

---

9. Hayashi, "Hebi," 52.
10. Ibid., 53.
11. Mizuno, "Hayashi Fusao kenkyū: yōshōnenki," 56.

> Seeing this figure, he became unsteady, as if he were drunk. Then suddenly, like a rain cloud moving in, an animal-like savagery closed his mind.[12]

Finally, instinct takes over, and the boy brutally kills the snake, revealing the petty cruelty of youth. Here the boy's actions are driven by his lack of experience with death and his lack of encounters with the opposite sex, which feeds both his curiosity and fear of the snake that represents these two parts of life for the author. Even with the snake mortally wounded, the youth remains fearful and uncertain of the snake staring at him, and he finally crushes its head, but then discovers that something about the "beauty" (*utsukushiku mieta*) of the snake's death somehow soothes and reassures him.

In the end, the fear and desire that fuel the narrator's attraction to and yet his repulsion of the snake reflect the youth's inner struggle between instinct and reason. Mizuno argues that the narrator's subsequent remorse and sadness at his cruel actions motivated by fear allow the author to explore the consequences of his actions based on the emotions of fear and desire, versus those actions derived from careful thought.[13] If the snake's death is the result of his initial actions predicated on fear, the youth is even more sickened by his response to the femininity he projected on the tiny snake, which in turn prompted the crushing of its head. These consequences, Mizuno suggests, are embodied in the boy's response to the silver fly's instinctual move to the dead snake's blood, in the end causing the youth to flee in disgust.[14] Ultimately, the silver fly represents the callous reality that confronts the youth: his cruel actions caused the snake's death, yet his life goes on while the snake's existence has ended. How can one not be perplexed by, on the one hand, the sudden brutality and the underlying thrill born of one's human fears and yearnings? And on the other hand, equally baffling for our narrator, is the sense of remorse and the despair that emerges from one's mind trying to cope with the results of one's actions.

From his background, this story further suggests that the fifteen-year-old Hayashi used literature as a way of exploring the conflict between his emotions and his duties. Considering that he was in the midst of dealing with his amorous feelings toward his first love, Hayashi Fusako, which

---

12. Hayashi, "Hebi," 52.
13. Mizuno, "Hayashi Fusao kenkyū: yōshōnenki," 56–57.
14. Ibid., 57.

was a forbidden love, it should not be unexpected that the White Birch School's focus on the human condition appealed to him. As with the "Purple Earth," reality is an experiential truth that leads to hardship and unhappiness in his second short story. However, the story in "Snake" differs from the narrative of "Purple Earth." In "Purple Earth," the beauty of the natural world dispels the youth's fears, and he comes to appreciate the entwined relationships between the natural and human worlds. In "Snake," the youth's experience with the natural world is unsettling, and his very human response to the snake's death leaves him confused as to whether instinct or intellect fuels the human condition. In the end, the pragmatic, yet cold reality of the natural world where the silver fly appears and feeds on the dead snake challenges the youth's idealistic understanding of the human condition and its complex relationship with the natural world. On a personal level then, "Snake" reads as a release of one youth's pent-up frustration at his impotence; the youth is anguished at being unable to restrain his desires from determining his actions. Moreover, the story acts as a commentary on the state of the human condition where the realities of life often overwhelm the mind's ability to respond reasonably to any situation, thus alienating one from the natural world.

Although there is no textual evidence of Hayashi commenting about possible influences on this short story, "Snake" seems to reflect a reading of Shiga Naoya's "Kinosaki nite" ("At Kinosaki") published just over a year earlier in the May 1917 issue of *Shirakaba* (White birch). Telling the reader that he is recuperating at Kinosaki hot springs after being hit by a train, the narrator in "At Kinosaki" views the deaths of three different animals he encounters there.[15] First, he views a dead bee that leads him to meditate on the loneliness of death and to imagine the repose in which the bee met that death.[16] Next, he watches a rat with a skewer through its neck and a group of boys throwing rocks at it as the rat struggles for its life and to keep from drowning under these impossible odds. Watching this scene unfold leads the narrator to consider all the steps he took to avoid death himself after the train hit him.[17] Finally, he sees a water lizard on the opposite bank of the river and throws a rock at it to get it to move. The nar-

15. Shiga Naoya, "Kinosaki nite," *Shirakaba* 8, no. 5 (May 1917): 132–140.
16. Ibid., 133.
17. Ibid., 135–136.

rator hits the water lizard with the rock and inadvertently causes its death, forcing him to confront the realization that life and death are in a way, accidental. He lived, but the water lizard did not.[18] By coincidence, he had survived being hit by the train, but a rock thrown in its general direction had killed the water lizard.

Shiga's meditations on these different confrontations with death may have provided an intellectual framework for Hayashi to cope, through the natural world in "Snake," with his own experience with death, although various factors changed the content of Hayashi's story. Unlike Shiga's "At Kinosaki," Hayashi comes across the snake in his path by chance and directly confronts some of those emotions associated with "death." With the small snake right in front of him, fear takes over, and the author tramples it. Still, the boy is alternately attracted to the "feminine" characteristics of the snake in the throes of death and repulsed by his instinctual fascination with it, leading him to further smash in the snake's head. Paralyzed by the conflict between what his senses tell him to do and what his mind tells him to do, the youth loses control of his emotions when he sees the silver fly coming to feast on the lifeless snake, and he escapes the scene as quickly as possible.

Where the narrator of "At Kinosake" calmly reflects on the coincidental nature of life and death, the narrator in "Snake" struggles with the consequences of his actions born out of fear and desire. He is momentarily able to regain his composure, but when the silver fly arrives, he loses that composure again, instead of being able to meditate calmly on his killing of the snake. While Hayashi does not tell us that the narrator is a youth in the story, it is difficult to think otherwise from the characterization of the narrator. Hayashi describes him as a sensitive person who had been moved to tears by the death of a crab, much less by the inadvertent death of the snake. Moreover, the narrator's feminization of the snake suggests a youth struggling to confront his initial experience with desire for the opposite sex.[19] In this way, the short story seems rife with the themes common to a young man's maturation process. This story uses the natural world as a substitute, focusing on a youth struggling to deal with a set of experiences

18. Ibid., 138–140.
19. Hayashi, "Hebi," 52–53.

that the author has not yet confronted directly in the human world, namely, watching someone die and confessing one's love for a woman.

Hayashi's final contributions to the journal, entitled "Oriori no uta" ("Occasional songs"), focus on the weak and their struggle for survival in a demanding world. Under this title, Hayashi includes two *tanka* poems: "Yowaki mono yo" ("To the faint-hearted") and "Shonatsu no hi" ("An early summer's day"). In the first poem, the author salutes all the other faint-hearted students who tire of, but cannot bring themselves to quit, the immediate task: their late night cramming for an exam. Is it in the name of glory that we with such heavy hearts continue our struggle to read all these textbooks, asks the author. In the poem's final line, the youth answers this question: "Oh faint-hearted! / 'Thy name is student' resounds through our minds."[20] Here the need for accomplishment and recognition motivates the youth's struggle to stay awake long enough to prepare for his exam. However, in the second poem, "An Early Summer's Day," a different emotion disturbs the youth's enjoyment of the beauty of an early summer's day: the injustice done to a discarded silkworm. Strolling down the path, he witnesses among the ashes on the roadside a weak, exhausted silkworm still clinging to the branch of a mulberry tree. In contrast to the lushness and the promise of the day, the youth is moved by the sight of the deserted silkworm awaiting death. He then reflects on what he has witnessed, as the icy wind blows that morning. Despite the signs of spring all around, there is always death in the midst of life.[21] What should have been an ode to the beauty of nature becomes a lament for the damage done to nature by humans in the name of silk production, the key export at the time for Meiji Japan's industrial capitalist future.

HAYASHI FUSAO'S TURN TO MARXISM AT KUMAMOTO

Once Hayashi became a higher school student in Kumamoto, he continued to explore increasingly negative themes in his literature, eventually writing the first socialist short stories that mark his turn to Marxism. Two scholars have previously studied these stories. Shutō Motosumi, a Japa-

20. Hayashi Fusao (Gotō Toshio), "Oriori no uta," *Ōita kōyūkai zasshi* 68 (September 1918): 70.

21. Ibid.

nese literature professor at Kumamoto University, first discovered the short stories that Hayashi submitted in the early 1920s to the Kōyūkai (the Fifth Higher School's alumni association) journal *Ryūnan*; and the scholar Mizuno Yukiko has prepared the most in-depth study of Hayashi's early life and literature.[22] The difficulty with Shutō's reading of Hayashi's higher school literature is that he accepts the publication dates of the stories at face value when Hayashi also adds a date written at the end of each story that reconfigures the production and interrelationships of these stories. Hayashi published the stories in the following order: "Unubore" ("Vanity"; volume 178, July 1921); "Mura" ("Village"; volume 182, July 1922); "Tomoshibi ni atsumaru mushi" ("Insects Gathering around the Light"; volume 183, October 1922); and "Hakudōka" ("The Coin"; volume 184, December 1922). But he actually *wrote* these works in this order: "Vanity" (volume 178, July 1921: *no written date given*); "The Coin" (volume 184, December 1922, *written August 19, 1921*); "Insects Gathering around the Light" (volume 183, October 1922, *written October 1921*); "Village" (volume 182, July 1922, *written May 24, 1922*).

While Shutō handles these stories as they were published, Mizuno argues that we should deal with the stories as they were written; although, curiously, she works from "The Coin" to "Village" and then lastly to "Insects Gathering around the Light." She does this to emphasize Hayashi's conflicted nature about Marxism before entering the proletarian literature movement, and because she deems "Insects Gathering around the Light" to be his best-written story of the group.[23] However, if taken in their written order, the stories follow a familiar narrative trope of beginning, middle, and end. First, the stories depict an awareness of oppression and poverty and how those experiences change a person. Next, the stories illustrate

22. Shutō's essay is a straightforward summary of these works that Mizuno develops into the first critical treatment of these stories. Here, I will refer to Mizuno's analysis in places, mainly to contrast my own reading of these stories with her perspective. For reference, here are the full citations of these two works: Shutō Motosumi, "Hayashi Fusao oboegaki," in *Kumamoto no bungaku*, vol. 3 ed. Kumamoto Kindai bungaku kenkyūkai (Tokyo: Banbisha, 1996), 136–148; and Mizuno Yukiko, "Hayashi Fusao kenkyū: yōshōnenki, saikentō," *Tsuru University Graduate School Review* 5 (2001): 50–64. At the end of her article, Mizuno thanks Shutō as well as two other people for their help in learning more about Hayashi's formative years in Ōita and in Kumamoto: Mizuno, "Hayashi Fusao kenkyū: yōshōnenki," 64.

23. Mizuno, "Hayashi Fusao kenkyū: yōshōnenki," 57–60.

the hesitation one endures before deciding to join the Socialist movement and accepting Marxist thought as the best available theoretical and organizational means to overcome poverty. Finally, through the story "Village," these stories reveal Hayashi's implementation of socialist theory in literature to affirm one's acceptance of Marxist theory and practice as the guiding premise of one's writing. This reading allows us to trace more readily Hayashi's uneasy shift to Socialist or Marxist-influenced literature over the course of his time at Kumamoto.

In addition to these published short stories, there is also evidence of an earlier work by Hayashi. In the March 1921 issue of *Ryūnan*, his story "Giga" ("Caricature") is listed as having received fourth place in a contest among the students for a literature prize. Unfortunately, the journal only reproduced the articles that received first, second, and third place in the journal, leaving Hayashi's contribution missing and forcing us as readers to rely upon the responses by each of judges to gain some semblance of the content and writing of his "Caricature."[24] Perhaps the most thorough is Akita Minoru who writes that the story is a rough sketch of someone drinking too much and then getting sick. Akita interprets the story as a diary of shame with an all too predictable ending, as loneliness envelops the drunk. Adding to Akita's appraisal, Kawase Kaichi observes that the story is broken up into four parts and that he particularly liked the symmetry of the first "caricature." There, Hayashi focuses on the worries of the main character in one corner of the hallway as he frets over being able to pass through it without waking up the drunk who reeks of alcohol and is sprawled out in the middle of the lighted hallway. The next two rough sketches are of the main character running around with his friends, and the fourth sketch is of the mountains. Kawase comments that he was fascinated by Hayashi's attempt to weave his real experiences into an imaginative description of the senses, though he was lukewarm to the self-questioning in the latter parts of the story.[25] Finally, Muka Yūkyōjin states that he believes this story to be a confession of the author's personal experiences, and then he goes on to argue that, instead of four separate sketches, the story reads like a short

24. "Kenshō bungeihyō," *Ryūnan* 177 (March 1921): 228.
25. Ibid., 234.

story under the naturalists' influence.[26] Since Kawase lists his review as being finished on December 25, 1920, we can surmise that Hayashi wrote "Caricature" before his other published works at Kumamoto.

In both of the reviewers' descriptions of "Caricature" and in his story "Vanity," we find Hayashi experimenting with themes that represent his transition to writing more politicized, socialist stories. At first, his short story "Vanity" reads as a continuation of his middle school literature. In "Vanity," the focus is on the relationship between two brothers, one a higher school student and the other a middle school student with the narrative centered on an exploration of these two youths' levels of self-awareness and self-awakening.[27] As the story begins, the middle school student and his younger sister are on the train platform to meet their older brother who is coming home from higher school for spring break. The younger sister and the middle school brother greet another older girl who has just gotten off the train, asking if she has seen their older brother. As they are talking together, the older brother gets off the train, but he is fidgety and out of sorts, seeing his younger brother speaking with the older girl. The older brother finally pulls his younger brother aside, scolding him for his lack of manners and for not introducing him to the older girl. At the time this befuddles the younger brother.[28] A couple of days later the older brother drops by his younger brother's room and begins to regale him with stories about how competitive life is in higher school and about his encounters with the opposite sex at school.[29] The story ends with the younger brother confronting his older brother about the absurdity of his stories, and claiming that the older brother's hesitancy on the train platform around the older girl betrayed his lack of experience with girls, meaning that all this bragging was just his "vanity."[30]

Considering this story within the context of Hayashi's memory of his encounters with Marxist thought while in his first year at Kumamoto, perhaps the self-questioning that is evident in the story is rooted in Hayashi's

26. Ibid., 240–241. An unusual name for a Japanese, the characters for Muka's full name are 無何有郷人.

27. Hayashi Fusao (Gotō Toshio), "Unubore," *Ryūnan* 178 (July 1921): 17–28.

28. Ibid., 17–19.

29. Ibid., 19–23.

30. Ibid., 23–28.

doubts about the individual's ability to affect change in the world. In this way, "Vanity" reads as a transitional piece and the beginning of his Marxist turn. Hayashi knew during his first year at Kumamoto that Hayashi Fusako had taken her sister's place in the Ono family and that traditional Japanese marriage practices had taken his first love from him, so it is no surprise that the futility of love is a key theme running through this piece. Moreover, we find the higher school student inventing an alternate reality in his stories where he is in control of his encounters with the three girls introduced in the story, only to have the middle school student emphatically point out the conceit of such a statement. When the younger brother reveals the truth about his older brother's fabrications, he ends with this line: "The ashes from the [older brother's] cigarette fell without a sound."[31] As he confronts his older brother, the younger brother's message is one of self-awakening, encouraging his older brother to acknowledge his limitations and the need to confront his weak points.

Nevertheless, as literature, the message is also public and suggests the depth of Hayashi's initial encounter with left-wing thought. Placed within the Marxist idiom, the younger brother plays the role of the proletariat chastising his "bourgeois" older brother for his feebleness, for becoming a victim, and for living in his fantasy world too long. As the older brother acknowledges that the ongoing fierce competition for knowledge among his fellow students in the dormitory has exhausted him, he reverts to his invented world for relief. But he also indicates that the producers of that knowledge, the teachers at the higher school, are arrogant, vain purveyors of that knowledge who control the classroom with their booming voices and strong presence. They do not physically harm us, says the older brother, as he backs down from his criticism of the higher school teachers. While he does admit to being intimidated at the higher school, he is too cowardly to fight that mistreatment. It is at this point that the younger brother calls his older brother a hypocrite and implores him to stand up for himself at school. Instead, the older brother changes the subject to the girls and reverts to his dream world.[32]

In this sense, we witness the author establishing a basic political message through the exchange between the brothers. Within the higher school

31. Hayashi, "Unubore," 28.
32. Ibid., 22.

setting, he advocates that those who have been mistreated by the official and unofficial authorities—namely the higher school teachers and his fellow students in this story—awaken from their pretend worlds where they have taken refuge and challenge those who have insulted them. From this viewpoint, a close reading of "Vanity" reveals that Hayashi's early exposure to Marxism did begin to shape his understanding of state-society relations. On the one hand, it contributed a larger desire for social justice to his emerging sense of self and his perception of personal aggrievement, and he began to associate oppression with the representatives of the state. On the other hand, it also added an acute consciousness of the need to enlighten and push others to rebel and confront those in power who control the commodity of knowledge. Thus, even though this story of two brothers explores human relationships and the process of self-awareness in the face of the older brother's weaknesses, the younger brother's chastisement of his older brother reads as a public rebuke against state repression of the individual and as a public call for action against such tyranny.

Hayashi's next written story, "The Coin," takes on a darker tone that builds on his previous character sketch of the drunken father and son in "Caricature." This story also initiates Hayashi's consideration of motives, through his literature, as to why one should turn to Socialism and Marxism as the means to confront authority. Here, the main theme is the awareness of poverty and the toll it takes on the narrator. From the opening introductory line, "This is from my dead friend's letter; he fell over like rust flaking off some ironware in K-city's shipbuilding factory," the tenor of Hayashi's literature changes. In "The Coin," he shifts thematically from human exchanges with each other to human relationships with the larger world around them and the social problems encountered in those interactions.[33]

"The Coin" relates the story of a thirteen-year-old boy whose mother had abandoned her family. The boy tells us that after his mother left, his father suddenly turned violent, even hitting him at times, and that he is deathly afraid of his father. They live in a small, run-down hovel with a dirt floor, and his one job after school is to come home and prepare the evening meal for his father. One night the boy is distracted while reading a book he borrowed from a friend, and he forgets to prepare dinner. When his

33. Hayashi Fusao (Gotō Toshio), "Hakudōka," *Ryūnan* 184 (December 1922): 80.

father returns from work, he curses the boy for not having the evening meal ready and bellows at him to get *saké* from the local store.[34] Taking the money, the boy goes to the store and buys the *saké*, but the old lady tending the store wants to gossip about his mother, and she gives him back too much in change. Noticing the extra coin on the way back home, the boy considers what to do with it. In school, he is lectured about morality every day, and he knows that returning the coin to the old lady is the right thing to do. Still, tonight the weight of the extra coin in his hand makes him feel overjoyed, and he turns toward home. Handing over the bottle of *saké* to his father, he also returns the expected amount of change and then heads back outside to find a place to hide the coin. As we read in the epigraph to this chapter, he drops the coin under a rock near the well. At first, he feels the sting of his conscience, but then a sense of relief and joy overwhelm him. Going back inside, he sets the table and has dinner with his father.[35]

Although the story was the last to be published, Mizuno Yukiko points out that "The Coin" marks Hayashi's first major attempt to articulate a decidedly Socialist point of view through his literature. We can tell from the date when it was written that Hayashi wrote "The Coin" first. The fact that he saved the work to publish as his last work at Kumamoto, Mizuno asserts that this story marks Hayashi's arrival as a self-conscious writer.[36] Moreover, she also notes that Hayashi thought enough of the piece to submit it to the school literature contest and had it republished in a 1927 collection of his stories.[37] When we read the story, we learn of a young man living in squalor, deprived of his mother, and enduring an overworked and alcoholic father. Mizuno argues that in this storyline we find the young Hayashi arming himself with Marxist theory for the first time. Here he employs Marxist social theory to emphasize the role of poverty in stripping us of our sense of morality.[38]

While Mizuno's analysis aptly captures the significance of this story in Hayashi's Marxist turn, she overlooks significant content in that turn. In

34. Hayashi, "Hakudōka," 80–83.

35. Ibid., 83–87.

36. Mizuno, "Hayashi Fusao kenkyū: yōshōnenki," 58–59.

37. See "Kenshō sōsaku saitenpyō," *Ryūnan* 178 (July 1921): 96–97, for Hayashi's submission of "Hakudōka" for the literary contest; and "Hakudōka" was republished in Hayashi's first collection of short stories entitled *Rōgoku no Gogatsusai: Hayashi Fusao Sōsakushū* (Tokyo: Shunyōdō, 1927), 257–270.

38. Ibid., 59.

this story, we can see that Hayashi delineates the types of "poverty" that drove the youth to petty theft. First, the loss of his mother, whom we find out later left the father for another man, leaves the boy with only one parent and a broken family.[39] Second, living in a rotting one-room shack with a mud floor and a blackened tatami mat to sit on indicates the lack of financial means.[40] Third, in describing the pale, haggard face of his father coming home in his blue factory clothes, Hayashi underscores the toll that factory work has taken on his father's physical and mental health, allowing little time or energy to devote to his son's education or care.[41] These are examples condemning the inequality of the industrial capitalist system and highlighting its negative impact on Japanese society in general. However, Hayashi is quite specific in this story in stressing the destructive influence of this economic system on the Japanese family even as he portrays the degradation of the Japanese working class in his short stories.

Although the author's attack on the industrialist capitalist system is apparent and the message that this poverty robs the youth of his morals is obvious, interestingly we find the youth throughout the story seeking edification through learning. We know he has just returned from school and that he is immersed in reading a traditional story of legend, lore, and love that he has borrowed from a friend; and that ultimately the reason he keeps the extra coin is to purchase a copy of the book. Likewise, the verbal abuse he took from the friend who taunted him for not being able to buy the book with his own money continues to haunt him.[42] Here, we find a fundamental conflict in the impact of Marxism on the author that will reverberate through much of his time in the Marxist literary movement. From his personal experience, Hayashi accepts and agrees with the Marxist stress on the evil nature of the industrialist capitalist economic system and its harmful impact on Japanese society. Nonetheless, as the means to challenge and overcome that system in his short stories, Hayashi often depicts education, not strikes or demonstrations or mass uprisings of the proletariat, as the preferred instrument to confront the inequities produced by the industrialist capitalist system. Even here, while Hayashi depicts a young man driven to such dishonest

39. Hayashi, "Hakudōka," 84.
40. Ibid., 80–81.
41. Ibid., 83.
42. Ibid., 81, 81–82, 82.

behavior because of his impoverished circumstances, he is sure to note that the youth knew the difference between right and wrong and was keeping the coin to help fund his studies. He is a victim of his circumstances, but it will be through his selfish desire for knowledge that the boy will overcome this crisis.

Perhaps, in "Insects Gathering around the Light," his second written short story at Kumamoto, we find Hayashi most directly dealing with his skepticism of Socialism as a way to fight the problems caused by the industrial capitalist system. The story is told from the viewpoint of a scion from the petty bourgeois, Sōichi, who finds out in the second part of the story that his father's business has gone bankrupt. Another student from the higher school, Sakai, learns of Sōichi's sudden financial difficulties and invites him to a worker's meeting. They meet up with a worker this time and are on their way to the meeting when they find out that the police have the meeting under surveillance. The group scatters, and Sakai leaves Sōichi with a woman activist to accompany him home. In their talk on the way, Sōichi realizes how different his outlook on life is from the activist's. After he returns to his room in the last part of the story, he reflects on their disagreements as he watches insects flying around the electric light in his room and around the candle on his desk. The story ends with Sōichi acknowledging that the circumstances of his life will surely change, but there is no clear resolution on his part as to how things will be different for him.

Since the story is told from Sōichi's point of view, it invites the reader to take his skeptical perspective on Socialism and the Socialist movement in general. Mizuno Yukiko certainly reads the story this way. For her, this is the story of a self-centered youth unaware of the larger world around him; however, through his father's bankruptcy, Mizuno explains, he is forced to confront society and its problems for the first time. What strikes her about this short story is the uncertainty and immaturity of the main character in his relationships with these various representatives of Socialism—the radical student Sakai, the factory worker Komegawa, and the woman activist whose words Sōichi finds deplorable. Mizuno asserts that what sets apart "Insects Gathering around the Light" from "Village" is the main character's skepticism toward the Socialist movement in general, and toward its ideology that divides the world between friend and foe, and sets people against each other. Here, we find the main character thinking rationally about the decision to associate oneself with the larger Socialist movement; as a result, he is not caught up in either the passion of the movement nor the reasoning of its ideology. As such, Mizuno argues that we have a glimpse in this story of Hayashi's ability to separate his identity from the larger Marxist movement, foreshadowing his future confrontations with members of the proletarian literature movement in the 1930s.[43]

The first problem with Mizuno's argument is its context. She reads this story as refreshingly different from the storyline in "Village," where we find the author offering an unquestioningly Marxist short story with the main character committed to the Socialist movement and Marxist ideology.[44] However, since Hayashi wrote "Village" after "Insects Gathering around the Light," Mizuno breaks the narrative relationship of these stories. In "Vanity" and "The Coin," we find the author portraying main characters who are increasingly aware of the oppression and poverty surrounding them, and who acknowledge the negative impact of those experiences on their choices in life.

With "Insects Gathering around the Light," Hayashi places a hopelessly naïve Sōichi at the center of this story and utilizes his inexperience and his awakening to pose some critical questions about the decision to enter the Socialist movement. In this way, Sōichi becomes Hayashi's alter ego, and one can read the story as a private and public questioning of the Socialist movement, and of Marxism as the proper theoretical avenue to tackle the social ills facing the country at this time. The final section where Sōichi watches the insects circling the candle light suggests that he has made his decision to become a member of the Socialist movement, but we find he is doing so for largely personal reasons. These reasons include his father's bankruptcy, a vague sense that the times are changing, and a concern that an individual will be left behind in these changing times unless he becomes part of a larger entity. Still, Sōichi has many doubts about an ideology that sets humans against each other instead of helping them to discover their inner beauty. Therefore, even though he has decided to participate in the Socialist movement itself, the reader also knows that the idealist Sōichi will carry these reservations and suspicions about the Marxist ideology with him. In this way, the story leaves one wondering if,

---

43. Mizuno, "Hayashi Fusao kenkyū: yōshōnenki," 60.
44. Ibid.

later on, Sōichi's reluctant mindset will have repercussions on his participation in the radical student movement.

Another problem with reading "Insects Gathering around the Light" strictly from Sōichi's perspective is that we miss the opportunity to consider the story's narrative from the perspective of the representatives of Socialism. First, we meet Sakai, a fellow higher school student, who comes across Sōichi while he wanders outside after receiving the telegram informing him of his father's bankruptcy. Sakai stops him and asks if anything is wrong. When Sōichi evades the question, Sakai tells him that he picked up the telegram that Sōichi had dropped and then he congratulates Sōichi on becoming poor. This is the best thing for you, Sakai tells Sōichi. Sakai then meets with another man in laborer's clothes, and he drags Sōichi along with them, flinging Sōichi's telegram into a nearby ditch.[45]

Next, Sōichi meets another worker by the name of Komegawa who lets him know that the police are watching the meeting, and they decided instead to go to Komegawa's place. As they walked on, Sōichi imagines that he will see a statue of Bakunin and a bundle of dynamite on the floor when he walks into the room. Instead, he finds that three of Sakai's friends are in the room; they are outraged about how news of the meeting leaked to the authorities and worried about how to return safely to their homes. To Sōichi's surprise, these "radicals" had very practical concerns about their organization. From Sakai's and Komegawa's point of view, it is Sōichi who is out of touch with reality and whose stereotyped and biased view of those in the Socialist movement is downright insulting.

Finally, in Part Five of the story, when Sōichi meets another member of Sakai's group, a woman activist, Hayashi underlines just how widely divergent the bourgeois intellectual's outlook on life is from that of a proletarian radical. Here, Sōichi begins to have some romantic inclinations toward her as he walks home with the young woman. He listens to her praise Komegawa for his expertise and up-to-date knowledge about the workers' struggles across the globe. She next goes into an extended discussion of the different workers' rebellions in South America and other places. That is when Sōichi breaks in with several questions: first, why should we worry about other people's problems and what is going on around the world; and

45. Hayashi Fusao (Gotō Toshio), "Tomoshibi ni atsumaru mushi," *Ryūnan* 183 (October 1922): 102–104.

second, shouldn't we try to find a more beautiful place in the world where we can live a quiet life by ourselves? "What the hell are you talking about!" the woman activist shrieks.[46] Still, in the company of this beautiful young woman, Sōichi wants to reveal his deepest thoughts.

> Instead of looking at a world of swords and bloodshed, fighting and revenge, betrayal and contempt, pain and regret, I want to gaze into a white pantheon. I want to look deeply into my soul. And, I want to find a way for others to carve out their own pantheons to house their beautiful souls. Some might call me a dreamer. ... In a loud voice, the woman yelled back, "Are you kidding me, anyone would call you a dreamer." ... She continued, "You son of a bitch, you're one of our enemies, aren't you? All this talk of humanity, generosity, passivity, one's soul, one's feelings—and then using these liberal ideas as a springboard for such an aerial performance. Well, maybe that kind of thinking was fine before humans discovered 'the larger human world around them' (*shakai*) and woke up from their lethargy, but not anymore."[47]

She goes on to enlighten Sōichi that all those things he learned at higher school, such as "self-reflection, meditation, religion, art, philosophy, and love," had nothing to do with today's world. Moreover, she asserts that his learning "had erected a rigid wall of pretense and insensitivity" between him and the world.[48] With this rejoinder, she walks off and leaves him, the enemy of the people, alone. With this young lady's socialist invective against Sōichi's idealistic humanism, Hayashi not only calls into question the usefulness of the bourgeois intellectual to the Socialist movement, but he also provides Sōichi as an example of the type of ignorance and stupor the leaders of the Socialist movement must overcome to change the world.

If this is the case, then in the concluding section of the story, we find Hayashi exploring the larger problem with intellectuals in the left-wing movement, how to motivate them to act. Part Six starts with Sōichi in his room contemplating what he learned from the young woman's words. Sitting at his desk, he observes an insect fly into the room, circle the electric light on his desk, and then suddenly fall on top of his desk. It gets up, starts

46. Ibid., 112.
47. Ibid., 113.
48. Ibid.

flying around the light, and then falls on top of the desk again. As the woman activist had said earlier, this was the epitome of an "aerial performance" (*kūchū geitō*), but the insect continues its performance nonetheless. On the other side of his desk, there is a lighted candle, and when Sōichi looks over at it, he notices the remains of a small insect that had flown too close to the candle's flame and died. Watching the other insect continue to circle the electric light, Sōichi reaches this conclusion: "Insects Gathering around the Light! Aren't they the pitiful symbols of humanity? One is dazzled by the light of a huge electric lamp, continuing its vain efforts repeatedly, while the firelight entrances the other one, and all at once it throws its body into the flames. Sōichi hung his head [in despair]."[49]

Sōichi then falls into a strange dream where his father is labeled "petty bourgeois" and a "time" monster (*"toki" no kaibutsu*) is devouring everything in its path. At that moment, a loud noise wakes him, and he sees the insect that had been flying around the electric light now stretched out dead on his desk. Such is the fate of us idealists, he muses, and he recalls the woman activist's words, that now is the time to distinguish between friend and foe, to think beyond one's individual wants and needs, and to make ourselves part of a larger movement. Times are changing, he ponders, and maybe his father's bankruptcy is one small sign of the changes to come. Reflecting back on the people he met that night, "Sōichi quietly turned his gaze to the candle on top of his desk. There he saw the body of the small, blue insect wrapped in a white shroud of wax, shining greenish gold in the light."[50] Hayashi ends the story with no clear statement of action by Sōichi, just a noncommittal rumination on the fate of those intellectuals who circle the light until mummified by their thoughts, unlike the radicals who fight for a cause and end their lives in a blaze of glory, flying into the flames. From this perspective, Hayashi's story reads more as a call to action, a plea for intellectuals like Sōichi to leave the shelter of their "white pantheons" and become more like Sakai who is involved in the radical student movement and the workers' movement. There is also a recognition that the leaders of the Socialist movement must prepare themselves to battle this kind of petty bourgeois apathy in the class struggle to come.

49. Hayashi, "Tomoshibi ni atsumaru mushi," 115.
50. Ibid., 116.

In "Village," Hayashi moves the setting of his last short story back to rural Japan; thus, Hayashi's "Village" reads as his first unabashedly Marxist literary work. Part One of "Village" introduces us to the factory girl Ohisa and her everyday struggles to make ends meet. Once we are introduced to her family and some of her friends and coworkers, Hayashi shifts the setting in the second part of the story to a wedding reception held in the factory owner's house. There, Ohisa and other villagers are working in the kitchen when Ohisa overhears the snobbish conversation between the bride's younger sister Tazuko and a friend. Tazuko tells her friend about Yoshimura Sōichi, the one villager who has risen above his birth and is attending the university. Later that evening, Ohisa inadvertently comes across Sōichi and Tazuko on a mountain path, and she overhears Sōichi telling Tazuko that he must end his relationship with her. Sōichi is determined to become more involved with the Socialist movement, which means that he must part with Tazuko to help the workers. In the story's final section, we learn that Ohisa's father has been hurt in a work-related accident and that she will have to begin work in the factory to help the family make ends meet. She meets Sōichi who encourages her to take care of herself in the factory, and he tells her that he is leaving the village to join the fight for others like her.

From the onset, "Village" is Hayashi's most definitive work of Socialist literature from his higher school days, both in theme and in spirit. Each of the main characters, Ohisa, Sōichi, and Tazuko, represent recognizable social classes in Marxism: the proletariat, the intelligentsia, and the bourgeoisie, respectively. In this way, Hayashi devotes this story to portraying the divide between these classes, with the intellectual Yoshimura Sōichi in due course choosing to bridge the gap between the educated and the working classes. Hayashi dutifully exposes the grinding poverty of the villagers and the harsh working conditions of the factory workers and other laborers. He also details the unfair working conditions that the villagers must endure, whether working a contract job or working for the Ishida family in their factory.[51] Thus, he uses the Marxist theoretical framework to under-

51. Mizuno asserts that one cannot ignore the sloppy nature of the piece: the attempt to combine what should have been two separate stories about Ohisa and then another focusing on Sōichi; the insertion of part of the narrative from "The Coin" in this story; and the sacrifice of individual character development for the sake of Marxist theory. Her interest in "Village" wanes quickly, as she crams her discussion of the story between her

score the larger social and economic problems facing the villagers, and their increasing awareness of the unequal relationships between themselves and the rich. Hayashi's objective privileging of the Marxist theory over the individual in "Village" makes it his first quintessentially Marxist short story.

Read in the order written then, Hayashi's "Village" also contributes to the narrative trope, marking his shift from humanist literature to Marxist politics at Kumamoto. Hayashi next wrote his first theoretical piece, "Puroretaria dokusai ni kansuru hito kōsatsu" ("Another Perspective on the Proletariat Dictatorship"), in December of 1922.[52] Published the same month in which he prepared it, Hayashi's writing of "Another Perspective on the Proletariat Dictatorship" suggests that he became more confident in his grasp of Marxist theory. Following his work on "Village," specifically, it appears he uses his literature as a catalyst for this first theoretical work. When examined in the order when they were written, from "Vanity" to "Another Perspective on the Proletariat Dictatorship," Hayashi's writings at Kumamoto form a narrative trope moving from his awareness of Marxism to his acceptance of Marxism as a means to confront the political and economic inequality he witnessed in his youth. Moreover, this transformation also supports his memories of his Marxist turn as a complete break from literature to politics with the final publication of "Another Perspective on the Proletariat Dictatorship."

However, the timing of his writing of "Village" forces us to consider a far more disorderly shift to politics than Hayashi's memory presents. Hayashi must have felt pressured to finish writing "Village" by the end of May, to meet the July issue's publication deadline. He had been working on "Village" since the late fall of 1921, and it is by far his longest written piece among the literature he published in Kumamoto. Perhaps the length of time it took to write "Village" reflects his increased involvement in the radical student movement, but it could also reflect his struggle with the Marxist ideology. Attempting to write a Marxist short story that was theoretical in form and content was perhaps more challenging than writing a story focused on the individual's maturation process. Also, the time that it

---

more productive analyses of "The Coin" and of "Insects Gathering around the Light." Mizuno, "Hayashi Fusao kenkyū: yōshōnenki," 59–60.

52. Hayashi Fusao (Gotō Toshio), "Puroretaria dokusai ni kansuru hito kōsatsu," *Ryūnan* 184 (December 1922): 11–31.

took him to complete a "Marxist" piece of literature, as he neared the end of his studies at the Kumamoto Fifth Higher School, hints at the tentative nature of Hayashi's decision to enter the Socialist movement. It points to a less than full break with the individual-focused humanism and idealism of the White Birch School's literature.

Another problem is the confusing narrative flow in "Village." Mizuno herself asks the question of why Hayashi inserted the outline of "The Coin" into the narrative of "Village." It was an unnatural break in the storyline, suggesting the rushed nature of Hayashi's preparation of "Village" as he set up what he considered the two stronger short stories. Moreover, Ohisa's reaction to the situation, once she realizes the boy's reasons for hiding the money, is noncommittal. Ohisa feels sad for the boy, and she empathizes with his plight, but she does not encourage him to hide the money, nor does she condemn the boy's alcoholic father. Instead, she takes the coin that the boy offers her and then walks him home.[53] Ohisa sympathizes with the boy from a third party viewpoint, laying the groundwork for the first person meditation of the boy's response to this situation in "The Coin," where he does take the coin and hide it for later use.[54]

Finally, the intertwining stories of Ohisa with Sōichi and Tazuko further muddies the narrative flow of "Village." Tazuko is the bourgeois pawn who, with her condescending views of the villagers and their dreadful existence, angers Ohisa but she never confronts him directly in the story. Ohisa overhears Tazuko's conversations, but it is Sōichi, the intellectual, who challenges Tazuko's views on life, and who finally puts an end to their relationship. One's class trumps one's feelings when it comes to Sōichi and Tazuko's love affair. Nevertheless, the story concludes with Ohisa deciding to enter the factory, partially based on her amorous feelings for Sōichi and on her admiration of his willingness to stand for her, a representative of the village and the working class. Not many proletarian short stories end with the main character reflecting on *the beauty of the smoke rising from the factory shining under the moonlight* (emphasis mine)! Although the framework of the story is distinctly Marxist, Ohisa's story, in particular, is a passive tale of one injustice after another happening to her, with Ohisa

53. Hayashi Fusao (Gotō Toshio), "Mura," *Ryūnan* 182 (July 1922): 1–6.

54. Ibid., 6.

frustrated but accepting of these wrongs for personal reasons, rather than fighting to change her socioeconomic situation. Ohisa knows the struggles of the villagers and the hardships she will face in the factory, but in the end, it is her secret love for the courageous and just Sōichi that convinces her to enter the factory. She resembles the boy in "The Coin" who puts the coin away for another day, hoping for a better life in the future. In this way, the narrative content of "Village" is a melding of Hayashi's previously written stories, containing the seeds of Hayashi's hopes, doubts, and fears.

Still, Sōichi's part in "Village" also expresses Hayashi's reasons for participating in the Socialist movement, and for tentatively accepting Marxism as the guiding principle of his literature as well as his politics. Here, Hayashi even uses the same name of the higher school student we met in "Insects Gathering around the Light," encouraging the reader to view this Sōichi's actions as a continuation of his intellectual maturation. Intriguingly, in "Village" we witness Sōichi making his decision to become part of the Socialist movement, with Hayashi giving him a family name here, perhaps representing Sōichi's growth to manhood in this story. At first, we learn in a conversation between Ohisa and a friend that Sōichi has stopped along the way in Kobe to observe a strike by a group of workers in the city, delaying his arrival in the village.[55] Next, as Tazuko is relating to her friend the story of Yoshimura Sōichi overcoming his poverty through his academic prowess, and gaining a scholarship from the province to attend college, Tazuko reveals that a detective has been shadowing Sōichi lately because he has gotten involved with some strange "ism."[56]

Toward the end of the story, Hayashi flips the narrative from "Insects Gathering around the Light" as Yamamura Sōichi takes on the persona of the young woman activist, and Tazuko repeats the previous Sōichi's bourgeois lines. Hayashi reveals this switch in the scene where Ohisa, on her way home from the wedding reception, stumbles across Sōichi explaining why he must break up with Tazuko. He starts with her love for the paternalistic way Jean-François Millet paints the farmers of the early nineteenth-century France, and he ends with her withering criticism of the conceited laborers that Emile Zola depicts in his novels: She is a daughter

55. Hayashi, "Mura," 6–10. In both stories, Sōichi's name is written as 「操一」.
56. Ibid., 16–18.

from a wealthy family, and his friends are all workers and laborers. How can she understand the troubles that the poor encounter, when she has never worried about the next day's meal? The world is divided into the rich and the poor, Sōichi declares, and our ways of understanding the world are different. Finally, those who think as you do are the enemies of those who think as I do. These are all reasons Sōichi gives, hoping to persuade Tazuko that they must stop seeing each other and go their separate ways. Tazuko, for her part, pleads with Sōichi that love is precious, and she wonders how he can let something like "class" tear them apart. Moreover, she is astonished that he would want to live among the poor and that he would want to work with the working classes again, particularly after having received an education and subsequently enjoying the privileges of the civilized world. Sōichi is determined, however, and Ohisa watches as they embrace and then part.[57]

Hayashi then confirms Sōichi's decision to join the Socialist movement in his last meeting with Ohisa. When she meets Soichi she was wandering along a mountain path one night after learning that her friend has died in a factory accident. He takes her hand and sympathizes with her worries, trying to assuage her fears of working in the factory. He even inquires how her father is recovering from his injury. Finally, Sōichi tells her that he is leaving the next day for Tokyo. There are so many young factory girls like her, and so many villages like this one, mired in poverty, that he can no longer stand by and do nothing, he says. After Sōichi leaves, Ohisa plops down on the ground, and she feels peace running through the night, enveloping her and the village.[58] The story ends here with Sōichi's expression of his need to fight for social justice, and his show of resolve to stand up for the rural poor in the villages and the working classes in the factories. Unequivocally, Sōichi's choice to enter the Socialist movement is based on his aspiration to defend those who cannot defend themselves. Running through Hayashi's last two written short stories at Kumamoto is a blatantly political call for action, grounded in an overtly Marxist understanding of class struggle. Still, the emphasis is on spurring others, like the young woman activist and Yoshimura Sōichi, to participate in the greater Socialist movement. In the end, it is Sōichi's very humanist yearning for

57. Ibid., 18–22.
58. Ibid., 22–26.

social justice that propels him into the Socialist movement, not his grasp of Marxist theory nor his appreciation for its sophisticated ideology.

Far from a total separation of literature and politics, Hayashi's short stories at Kumamoto tell of a youth who continues to use literature as a sounding board for his inner thoughts and reflections. At the same time, he has also decided to become a part of a larger movement and to subordinate his thoughts and actions to the will of that group. In this way, Hayashi's initial short stories position literature as a significant medium for his humanist inclinations and his eventual intellectual move to Socialism, and as a means to express those feelings at Kumamoto. Hayashi's final two short stories reveal a writer exploring the political uses of literature to draw others off the fence and into the fight, and to persuade others why this fight is necessary. Once he branches out into the political and theoretical worlds of the Socialist movement in Tokyo, the radical student movement begins to consume much of his time. However, until the outbreak of the second Sino-Japanese War in the late summer of 1937, he continues to turn to literature, particularly the mode of short stories, as his most potent means to express his viewpoint on a variety of issues.

3

To Inspire, Instruct, Entertain, and Reproach

Hayashi Fusao's Proletarian Children's Stories as Literature, Politics, and Reflection on His Time in the Radical Student Movement

One day, I'd left the hut and had started down to the coal mine. With my lantern swaying back and forth, I'd made it as far as the opening of the new mine shaft, when all of a sudden someone in the distance started screaming at me.

—Hey, asshole. Whatta ya think you're doing! There's dynamite ... !

(Oh, shit!) I thought, but it was too late. KABOOM! It was as if fireworks were being set off at a fair, and then like a ragdoll, up I went with the smoke, high into the air.

(Oh crap, I'm screwed!), then, (I'm a goner), I remember thinking. At that moment, I looked down—and it was a gift from above—below me was water. This is Hokkaidō, so the water was full of trout swimming about. I mean, how lucky could I get; that's right, there was a lake right next to the mine area.

(Thank god, I'm saved!), and relieved, I plunged into the water, where the frightened trout leaped all around me.

(Shivering!), I floated to the top and had a look around. The figures on the far bank were so small. Dammit! The blast had tossed me quite a way from the bank, so I had a long swim back.

—Ah, what luck, exclaimed the other miners who ran out to meet me at the lake's edge. But then, some strange guy came flying out of the office. He looked like an imported pig in a white vest. —The asshole, he was holding a huge gold watch in his right hand, and he was out of breath, his shoulders heaving.

Not a sight you often behold around these parts, it struck me. Then abruptly, he started yelling at me.

—Who the heck are you, I asked!

—I'm an executive from the company, he said!

—What the hell! I couldn't believe my eyes; I just couldn't. That's odder than a bull birthing a calf. You have to be shittin' me, an executive coming to the workplace! Well, that imported ... , no, no, that executive, whatta ya think he wanted with me? Well, he shouted,

"Hey! You were off company property without permission, two minutes in the air and twelve minutes in the water. — That's right. I saw it from the office window, with my own two eyes. So, I'm deducting fourteen minutes from your wages!"

—"Shin isoppu monogatari: gūwa saikō"

Once he moved to Tokyo in 1923, Hayashi's activities as a student radical and his work as a promising theorist for the socialist movement took much of his time, but he continued to write literature. He also dabbled in journalism, contributing articles to the Tokyo Imperial University newspaper. Many of the short stories he wrote from 1924 to 1926 were children's stories, in which he sought to entertain as well as to inspire and instruct the children of the working classes and the farmers, as he chronicled the social and economic inequalities in late Taishō Japan. As Mizuno Yukiko has noted, by the end of 1926 three characteristics had come to define Hayashi Fusao's writing technique: first, the injection of humor and passion in the main characters' relationships; second, the lyrical nature of his writing; and third, the search for a noble cause, an ideal for which one is willing to fight and sacrifice.[1] While all these traits are evident in his children's stories, Hayashi's emphasis on humor sets his children's stories apart from other proletarian children's literature of the day. Over time, Hayashi's desire to craft witty stories often overwhelmed the didactic nature of these children's stories.

Hayashi Fusao, "Shin isoppu monogatari: gūwa saikō," *Shinshōsetsu* 31, no. 10 (October 1926): 31–32.

1. Mizuno Yukiko, "Hayashi Fusao kenkyū: 'E no nai ehon' wo chūshin ni," *Shōwa bungaku kenkyū* 38 (March 1999): 8–10.

This tendency is evident in the first fable, "Jūyaku to dainamaito" ("Executives and dynamite"), partially quoted in the epigraph from Hayashi's October 1926 work entitled "Shin isoppu monogatari: gūwa saikō" ("New Aesop's Fables: Breathing new life into the allegory"). Here, Hayashi sets up a typical account of worker exploitation, with the narrator hearing this story from a teacher at a worker's school.[2] He has just finished lecturing to his students about wages and working hours. Then with everyone gathered around a warm stove, the teacher asks the students if they understood the lecture. One of the older students tells the group about his experience working for the Yūbari Coal Mine in Hokkaidō, and the lesson of exploitation is made clear with the executive docking the mine worker's pay. Even so, Hayashi's description of the worker's sharp tongue, his rough language, the laidback manner in which the student tells the story of being dynamited head-over-heels into the lake, and the satirical portrayal of the executive as an "imported pig in a white vest" huffing and puffing, overshadow the lesson being taught in the story. One wonders if not taking the lesson so seriously is the actual message in this story.

The rendering of the story invites a political reading of all of Hayashi's early children's stories. Considering that his collections of proletarian fairy tales and fables were some of his earliest short stories produced in Tokyo, we will first examine these stories within the history of proletarian children's literature and in terms of the defining elements of his writing style. Next, we will explore Hayashi's political use of fairy tales and fables in the context of his relationship with the radical student movement and the burgeoning Marxist literary movement of the mid-1920s.

Hayashi became interested in writing children's stories after translating some of the stories from the German socialist tradition of children's literature. As scholar Samuel Perry argues, this tradition was just as influential in Japan as the Soviet examples of children's stories. Perry notes that up to this point Japanese writers had traditionally portrayed childhood as a time of innocence, an idyllic period of life. Drawing on the work of proletarian theorist Makimoto Kusurō, Perry argues that during the first historical stage of proletarian children's literature, writers and

2. Hayashi Fusao, "Shin isoppu monogatari: gūwa saikō," *Shinshōsetsu* 31, no. 10 (October 1926): 30–32.

theorists focused on establishing a class analysis. Within this context, the writers could both depict the difficult lives of the working classes and explain why such a divide between the rich and poor existed. Perry marks the advent of proletarian children's literature in 1926 with the establishment of the first proletarian school set up in Kizaki village, located in Niigata prefecture. The need to develop appropriate teaching materials for the farmers' children prompted the Leftist newspaper *Musansha shinbun* to call for contributions to a new column entitled "Children's World" in the summer of 1926.[3] However, during the summer of 1924 Hayashi had already contributed translations of two fairy tales written by Hermynia Zur Mühlen to the journal *Shinjin* (New man), indicating at the end of the second translation that he intended to translate all six stories from Zur Mühlen's 1921 work *What Little Peter's Friends Tell*.[4] Zur Mühlen was an Austrian countess whose affinity for the poor led her into the socialist movement. Much of her early work focuses on fairy tales told from a Marxist viewpoint; she designed these stories to make workers' children aware of the injustice and inequality around them. In the original work, Zur Mühlen tells the story of "little Peter," who has broken his leg and who is laid up while his mother works all day at the factory. To keep him company in each of the tales, different objects (a piece of coal, a match, a glass bottle, the bed covering, an iron pot, and a snowdrop flower)

3. Samuel Perry, *Recasting Red Culture in Proletarian Japan: Childhood, Korea, and the Historical Avant-Garde* (Honolulu: University of Hawai'i Press, 2014), 16–24. As Perry explains, the *Musansha shinbun* was sponsored by the illegal Japanese Communist Party, but the newspaper itself was not banned from publication, *Recasting Red Culture*, 21.

4. Heruminiya Tsuuru Myuuren, "Sekitan no ohanashi: dōwa," translated by Gotō Toshio (Hayashi Fusao), *Shinjin* 29, no. 8 (August 1924): 49–53. Heruminiya Tsuuru Myuuren, "Macchi hako no ohanashi: dōwa," translated by Hayashi Fusao, *Shinjin* 29, no. 9 (September 1924): 60. Hayashi published the fourth and sixth stories in the December 1926 edition of *Bungei sensen*: Heruminiya Tsuuru Myuuren, "Chiisai Pētā," translated by Hayashi Fusao, *Bungei sensen* 3, no. 12 (December 1926): 90–98. These stories are taken from Hermynia Zur Mühlen, *Was Peterchens Freunde erzählen: Märchen* (Berlin: Malik-verlag, 1921). Incidentally, the table of contents list Gotō Toshio as translator, but the pen name Hayashi Fusao is used at the end of the piece, giving us perhaps Hayashi's first formal use of his pen name. In an earlier article contributed to the Tokyo Imperial University student newspaper, Hayashi still uses his real name: Gotō Toshio, "Marukusu no tanjō," *Teikoku daigaku shinbun*, vol. 73 (May 2, 1924): 6, so it appears that over the summer of 1924 Hayashi made the decision to use Hayashi Fusao in all his writing.

magically come to life, enlightening Peter about the situations that led them into his house.

In preparing these translations, Hayashi first discovered the fairy tale to be a form of literature with which he wanted to experiment. Moreover, it is clear that the humanist content and Zur Mühlen's sympathetic telling of these stories greatly appealed to his sense of social justice. From the beginning, the protagonist, Peter, is placed in a gloomy setting: in a small apartment with no heat, he waits all day in the dead of winter for his mother to come home. But, distraction soon finds Peter. He is captivated as he listens to the pieces of coal and the match tell their stories of adventure and humor. He empathizes with the plight of those harmed by the inequality of wealth, and he is angered with the injustice portrayed in each account. We even find the match captivated by the young fir tree's beautiful sacrifice as it extracts a measure of revenge, falling on the rich man who had the forest logged so that none of the poor villagers could go hunting in those woods. Hayashi's choice of translation is prescient in many ways, foreshadowing not only his autonomous inclinations toward literature, but also toward politics. As Lynda King writes, Hermynia Zur Mühlen would become famous for her children's stories in the 1920s, but as the communist party attempted to exert more influence over her and her writings, she left the party in the early 1930s. Stressing her independent stance from party doctrine, she eventually went to England, where she remained in exile during WWII to escape the Nazi takeover of her native Austria.[5] Although Hayashi does not mention Zur Mühlen in his memoirs and says little about these translations, in retrospect, both the stories and the author seem a fitting model for Hayashi's literature, as well as for the struggles he encountered with the organization and the ideology of the communist party in his own life.

Hayashi next moved from translating to preparing his own short stories, grounding these works in his reading of Western fairy tales and fables by Hermynia Zur Mühlen, Hans Christian Andersen, and others. Published in the June 1925 issue of *Shinjin*, Hayashi based the story "Dominiku

5. Lynda J. King, "Hermynia Zur Mühlen," *Dictionary of Literary Biography*, vol. 56, *German Fiction Writers, 1914–1945*, ed. James N. Hardin (Detroit: Gale Research, 1987), 320–322.

no byōki" ("Dominick's Illness") on his reading of a story from the March 1923 issue of *The Young Worker*, the official journal for the American Communist Party's Young Workers League.[6] The original story is narrated by a twelve-year-old about the troubles encountered by Dominick, the smartest kid in his class, because Dominick's family cannot afford enough for him to eat. The author tells the story with the idiom and phrasing of a worker's child from 1920s' America, but Hayashi smooths the language and reworks the story slightly. His goal is to have the reader identify with Dominick's plight, so he highlights the physical convulsions Dominick is having due to hunger pangs, discussing the problems his father has had in finding work, Dominick's growing pains, and, finally, the lack of food in his house. When the narrator in the story shares part of his lunch sandwich with Dominick, Dominick saves the remainder and eats it in class. For this transgression, he is scolded by the teacher who then calls in his immigrant mother to explain. In the original, the teacher cannot understand the mother. She utters in broken English that she will spank Dominick for being a bad boy, and the teacher tells Dominick to have his mother take him to a doctor to have him checked out. In Hayashi's story, the narrator emphasizes the mother's destitute nature: her shabby kimono, the small child she is holding, and that she endures the teacher's reproach in silence. As he ends with a poetic rhetoric that is much too polished for the original, the narrator laments:

> Answering my question, Dominick said that the doctor told him nothing was wrong with him, just that he hadn't had enough to eat.
>
> Once I asked him [why he wasn't getting enough to eat], he told me that his father only made six yen a week at work and that besides him there were four other mouths to feed at home. They were just able to give all the kids milk once a day and were in no position to give them milk three times a day.
>
> To make things worse, Dominick's father had been out of work the last two weeks. —I finally understood why, like dried meat, he was growing thinner day-by-day.
>
> His illness was called "poverty." Is there any doctor in the world who can cure this disease? (From *The Young Workers*[7])

6. Paul Paulowich, "Dominick's Sickness," *The Young Workers* 2, no. 3 (March 1923): 17–18, https://www.marxists.org/history/usa/pubs/youngworker/v2n3-mar-1923-yw.pdf.

7. Hayashi Fusao, "Dominikku no byōki," *Shinjin* 30, no. 6 (June 1925): 53.

This children's story is sentimental, tugging at one's proverbial heartstrings in its telling of poverty's toll on the working classes and on a sensitive and talented boy, in particular, much like the personality of the boy who narrates "The Coin" from Hayashi's higher school days.

FAIRY TALES TO INSPIRE AND TO INSTRUCT IN "A PICTURE BOOK WITHOUT PICTURES"

Building on "Dominick's Illness," Hayashi published several short vignettes in *Shinjin*, which he eventually collected for a larger short story he entitled, "E no nai ehon" ("A picture book without pictures"). In the first of these pieces that he published, "Kokusō" ("State funeral"), he specifically designates in the opening that this is a "children's story." He followed this with "Kokuminteki eiyō" ("The people's nutrition") and then "Koibito" ("Lover").[8] As Hayashi later acknowledges in his postwar memoirs, he drew liberally on Hans Christian Andersen's 1840 work *A Picture Book without Pictures* for these stories, even borrowing the book's title and the main motif of the moon addressing the narrator (in the case of Andersen's work, the narrartor was a painter).

These three would become stories from the first night, the second night, and the seventh night in "A Picture Book without Pictures." Mizuno Yukiko has also discovered that the fourth night's story, "Kimyōna moji Ein Märchen" ("Strange characters: A fairy tale"), was published in the November 1925 issue of *Kaihō* (Liberation). She also found the eighth night's story, "Porii no yūutsu" ("Polly's blues"), in the August 1925 issue of *Bungei Nippon* (Literary Japan).[9] In the same vein, Mizuno notes that for "New Aesop's Fables," his other work based on children's stories, Hayashi published several of the tales earlier in different journals as well.[10]

8. Hayashi Fusao, "Kokusō," *Shinjin* 30, no. 8 (August 1925): 31–32; Hayashi Fusao, "Kokuminteki eiyō: 'tsuki no monogatari,' sono ni," *Shinjin* 30, no. 9 (September 1925): 45; and Hayashi Fusao, "Koibito: 'tsuki no monogatari,' sono san," *Shinjin* 30, no. 10 (October 1925): 27–28.

9. Mizuno, "Hayashi Fusao kenkyū," 5.

10. Mizuno, "Hayashi Fusao kenkyū," 5. Mizuno gives the following two stories as examples, Hayashi Fusao's "Chinushi wo nite kuuta hanashi" in the December 21, 1925, issue of *Musansha shinbun*, and Hayashi Fusao's "Fune no kamisama" in the September 1925 issue of *Bungei sensen*.

Her point in separately listing these titles is to cast doubt on Hayashi's claims in his postwar memoirs that he left the journal *Marukusushugi* (Marxism) and stopped working as a Marxist theorist in 1925 simply because Fukumoto Kazuo, soon to become a leading theorist in the Japanese Communist Party, had criticized his work.[11] Mizuno argues instead that it was Hayashi's love of literature and his desire to focus on his creative writing in the proletarian literature movement that led him to shed his duties at *Marukusushugi*. In his "Bungakuteki jijōden" ("Literary memoirs") from 1935, Hayashi first asserts that it was a love affair gone wrong that led him out of the journal *Marukusushugi* and back into literature.[12] If one considers the discrepancies between his postwar and prewar memoirs on this episode in his life, perhaps Mizuno is justified in referring to Hayashi's rationalizations for leaving *Marukusushugi* as most likely "fictional."[13] Mizuno's larger point is to show that Hayashi continued to write fiction, even when he was taking part in the radical student movement as a member of the New Man Society or contributing theoretical pieces for *Marukusushugi*, the mouthpiece of the then defunct Japanese Communist Party.

Hayashi collected these short vignettes and then substantially revised parts of these pieces before publishing them in the journal *Shinshōsetsu* (New fiction) as "A Picture Book without Pictures" in May 1926, and as "New Aesop's Fables" in October 1926. Besides the night stories already mentioned in "A Picture Book without Pictures," Hayashi included several other stories that elucidated the struggles of the haves versus the have-nots around the world. For example, in the third night's story, New York City's fabulously wealthy gather for a charity ball and soldiers surround the gala event, mainly to keep the undesirables away. Moreover, the fifth night's story takes the opening piece from Andersen's *A Picture Book without Pictures* that tells the story of two separated lovers from India. Hayashi turns it into a colonial struggle between the native Hindus and the British. Here, the British capture the Hindu boy and put him in jail. He tries to escape,

11. Hayashi detailed description of this experience and Fukumoto's comments are found in Hayashi Fusao's "Bungakuteki kaisō," in *Hayashi Fusao chosakushū*, vol. 2 (Tokyo: Tsubasa shoin, 1969): 232–235.

12. For the most detailed description of the ill-fated love affair and Hayashi's reaction to it, see Hayashi Fusao, "Bungakuteki jijōden," in *Rōmanshugi no tame ni*, ed. Bungakukaisha shuppanbu (Tokyo: Bungakukaisha shuppanbu, 1936), 334–335.

13. Mizuno, "Hayashi Fusao kenkyū, 4.

but he is shot down by the British.[14] In the sixth night's story, we encounter the dreadful toll of modern warfare as the moon shines on an Italian cemetery. There, a man is speaking to the moon about the small graveyard he has created to honor the five thousand soldiers in his unit, all murdered by the manufacturers of modern science.[15]

Stories from the eighth and ninth nights focus on clashes between laborers and the police. The Irish peasant Polly is sightseeing in London when she encounters a struggle between the police and workers during a May Day march near the Piccadilly in Trafalgar Square. Next, the moon visits a Finnish youth who was manning the barricades as the police attacked a march by workers. The moon wants to see how the still defiant youth is doing, after spending more than ten years locked up in a Helsinki military prison.[16] Finally, the moon shows a humorous side, as he tells the story of a college student majoring in linguistics. This student ponders the origins of these "strange new characters,"—i.e., *fuseji*, elliptical marks usually consisting of Xs, Os, or dots inserted in the text to take the place of the original Japanese characters. Lastly, in the tenth night's story, the moon observes several children from Moscow's slums living in a mansion for the Russian landed gentry and the moon marvels at what change of events allowed the poor to rise to such heights.[17]

In her conclusion to *Being Modern in Japan*, Vera Mackie challenges us to consider the ways that "artistic works may at least have opened up a space for critique, and the possibility of imagining alternative futures and alternative modernities" during interwar Japan.[18] Through an examination of artistic productions of modern selves in the "bodies, practices, and spaces of urban Japan," Mackie suggests that these cultural artifacts may

14. Hayashi Fusao, "E no nai ehon," *Shinshōsetsu* 31, no. 5 (May 1926): 13–15, 18–19. In the original story, the girl puts a lighted lamp on the river and lets it go. If she can see the light until it passes from her sight, she believes her lover is still alive. In Andersen's rendition she sees the light all the way, but in Hayashi's version, the light sinks into the river with her lover's death. Then she too collapses on the sand and rolls into the Ganges River, which carries her body away.

15. Ibid., 19–21.

16. Ibid., 23–25, 25–26.

17. Ibid., 16–18, 26–28.

18. Vera Mackie, "Modern Selves and Modern Spaces: An Overview," in *Being Modern in Japan: Culture and Society from the 1910s to the 1930s*, ed. Elise K. Tipton and John Clark (Honolulu: University of Hawai'i Press, 2000), 196.

also imagine "resistance and excess" that the state was unable to contain entirely. Moreover, she asserts that scholars have not fully examined this possibility in studies of Japanese attempts at being modern during this period.[19] As a set of Socialist children's stories, Hayashi's "A Picture Book without Pictures" underlines the glaring disparities in an industrial capitalist society. He accomplishes this by contrasting the conflict between rich and poor, strong and weak, and dark and light.

These readily identifiable themes represent Hayashi's attempt to stake out the boundaries of this inequality through the urban, modern bodies, spaces, and practices he depicts in these stories. Beginning with the opening night's tale, he offers a fairy tale treatment of wealth, and the divisions as well as the partnerships it creates in modern societies. In that tale, the government gives the merchant's dog a royal burial; in another, the moon tells the reader about a lavish "charity" ball given in New York City; and the final night's story describes how the underprivileged were able to move into the opulent Russian mansions in the countryside. In the first story, we find the display of wealth defined physically, in the plush silk and extravagant incense used to wrap the dog's carcass, and in the beautifully appointed carriage that carries the dog. We also witness spatial divisions in the procession with five horse-drawn carriages and another three hundred people, including musicians playing a funeral dirge, following the carriages through the streets of Beijing at night.[20] Although the funeral is a traditional one in practice and place, Hayashi illustrates the modern alliance between capitalists and the state in several ways. First, the story identifies the main mourner as a merchant. Next, the merchant explains the cause of the dog's death, a heart attack, to a high government official sitting next to him in the carriage. In this way, Hayashi underscores the unfair collaboration of political power and economic wealth in the hands of the few and at the expense of the masses who could never dream of such extravagence in their lives.

In the third and tenth stories, the places, physical appearances, and the practices are perhaps the most representative of being modern for Hayashi. As the moon rises over New York City, the narrator refers to the city as one big "brewing factory," and the opening scene is a gaudy description

19. Mackie, "Modern Selves and Modern Spaces: An Overview," 186, 196.
20. Hayashi, "E no nai ehon," 11.

of the hotel ballroom, with its mauve curtains wrapped around chandeliers that present an auroralike glow for the guests.[21] A superb orchestra entertains the guests, and the group plays all the old waltzes to keep the audience dancing. We learn that this is a charity ball for New York City's wealthiest citizens who have arrived for a night of dancing, with an auction to follow. Philanthropy is necessary for a healthy society to develop, the director of the charity ball explains to the audience of gentlemen with glasses full of champagne in hand and to the ladies holding ivory-embossed folding fans. As the night ends with a dinner auction, the guests bid on rare dishes from faraway places. One lovely woman whispers into the ear of a gentleman beside her who is holding a glass of Chinese liquor that charity is nice.[22] He replies that she is right and that they should do more of this type of event to avoid the protests of others. Then, after the ladies and gentlemen eat their fill, the orchestra plays a foxtrot[23] and everyone returns to the dance floor. As noted earlier, the director's and this gentleman's worries concerned a group of undesirables, a group of local people who had earlier intruded upon the ballroom and called upon the guests to stop playing music from Europe. They had gone so far as to pull out sabers from the American Revolution and perform period war dances.[24] In this case, the narrator emphasizes the grievances of the local residents who take exception to the ostentatious display of privilege and affluence by Europeans who have moved to New York City, and who have become prosperous yet still live as if they were in Europe instead of America. Here the divisions are not only based on the distribution of wealth, but also on the subordinate existence of the local American residents who are dominated by the European elite.

In the final story, the narrator takes us to the Russian countryside where the moon realizes something is very wrong with the scenery. Previously, when he stopped by this country villa, it was owned by a wealthy gentleman from Moscow. That gentleman used to invite the nobility, landowners, and aristocrats from Moscow for all-night dance parties in the

21. Hayashi, "E no nai ehon," 13.

22. Ibid., 15.

23. In writing this passage, the young Hayashi obviously mistook the foxtrot dance to be a European dance form, though the foxtrot originated in the United States and is a distinctly American ballroom dance style.

24. Hayashi, "E no nai ehon," 14.

villa's beautiful salon; there, the gentleman's twelve servants would pamper his guests. He and his guests would play cards until morning, and then each carriage with twelve horses clamoring at silver bits would take the guests back to Moscow. Now, however, there are no more gentlemen covered in silk, no more ladies enveloped in clouds of perfume, no more anxious children nor miserable servants, observes the moon.[25] Here too, Hayashi represents the affluent lives of the modern elite: first, through the rich silks and heavy perfumes that cover their bodies; second, in his spatial description of the luxurious country villa with a card room and even a salon for dancing. Ultimately, he condemns the night of leisure that the urban elite enjoy in the countryside, contrasting their prosperity with the harsh toil of the servants. Moreover, the new faces of children from the Moscow slums who are now living in the villa underline the dividing lines in capitalist societies, and in this case, emphasize their eventual proletarian triumph over the economic inequity created by industrial capitalism.

These stories and others in "A Picture Book without Pictures" suggest the brutal lengths to which the rich, internationally, go to maintain their wealth and position in every cosmopolitan society. The rich merchant has connections with the Chinese ruling elite that allow him to give his favorite pet an official state funeral. The head of the charity ball in New York City hires soldiers to guard the event. He is afraid that the undesirable locals will make a scene, demanding that the fine men and ladies in the ballroom stop singing songs and performing dances from the old country. British colonialists use military force to put down an uprising of Hindu natives against their rule in India, with our hero shot twelve times trying to escape from captivity.[26] Finnish police use English warships, German weapons, and French soldiers to break up demonstrations by Finnish workers in support of their workers' union.[27] An Italian soldier survives the trench warfare of World War I only to lose his mind. He then creates a memorial to his lost unit, as an ode to the horrors of modern science: machine guns, poison gas, and tanks. Even innocent Polly witnesses the use of police force against a May Day rally in London.

Throughout these stories, modern governments and capitalists do not

25. Hayashi, "E no nai ehon," 27.
26. Ibid., 19.
27. Ibid., 26.

hesitate to turn to overwhelming military force and police oppression to keep the workers, colonial peoples, and locals in their place. Our narrator stresses governmental use of modern weaponry to protect capitalists and their interests, as we observe in the Finnish worker's story. He further chronicles the service that modern science provides to the state through these weapons, enabling it to protect national and private interests. As in the Italian soldier's story, we find the soldier memorializing the destructive nature of modern warfare as he prepares a cemetery with only fragmentary skeletal remains in it, an apt metaphor for the post-traumatic stress disorder ravaging the soldier after experiencing firsthand the brutality of modern combat.

Finally, this brute force is not limited to the battlefield but often takes place in the streets of urban areas like London. Police emerge from inside the memorial tower in Trafalgar Square that honors Admiral Nelson to meet the demonstrating workers. In New York City, a security chief positions soldiers behind a perimeter of a hundred cars stationed in front of the hotel's doorway and places fifty police officers around the hotel's rear entrance, just to prevent the locals from crashing the charity ball. In Helsinki, the young worker mans the barricade in the Finnish capital before he is captured, tried, and sent to serve his extended sentence in a military prison. In a lighter moment, our narrator also points out the government's use of censorship as a modern means to assert control over the populace. Here the college student learns that the government censorship office is responsible for the strange new characters he sees in the newspaper and journal articles. At the story's end, he wakes up to find that the notes on the napkin that he used to take down the information from his professor have turned into odd geometrically shaped characters. He exclaims, "Ah, these new characters the state created, they've already made their way into our everyday conversations!"[28]

Finally, as Mōri Toshio observes in his analysis of "A Picture Book without Pictures," this inequity is also expressed through the contrast of dark and light in these stories. Hayashi worked with this technique in his earlier humanist short story "Purple Earth" from his middle school days at Ōita. But in these stories, he does not romanticize this contrast of dark and light for self-introspection, nor use it to contemplate the weaknesses

28. Ibid., 18.

of man and the beauty of nature. Probably the best expression of Mōri's analysis is the second night's story, "The People's Nutrition."[29] Here the healthy, exceedingly perfumed gentlemen and ladies freely walk along the lighted streets of Berlin while the poor and starving keep to the shadows of those same streets as they move through the city. It is winter, and the loud noise of the city and the smell of gasoline are everywhere. Under the warped light of one gas lamp, a "small shadow" calls out the newspaper headlines for the evening edition of the *Berliner Daily*. The gloomy news that the people's nutrition is at an all-time low is eclipsed by the brilliance of the marriage announcement for a millionaire's daughter. Next, the narrator tells us that the "small shadow" is an old man who works as a newspaper vendor. Dressed in a gray coat, he is out on the streets trying to sell newspapers. He walks by a restaurant where steam clouds over a window, giving it a feeling of spring's warmth, but he shivers on through the cold night.

Even the final scene plays on this technique as a young gentleman, wrapped in a black cloak and dressed in a formal evening suit, walks out of another café on the other side of the road and heads for the streetlight. He asks for a newspaper, but the vendor does not reply. Instead of getting his newspaper, the young gentleman watches that "emaciated singular piece of flesh drop sideways onto the sidewalk without a sound."[30] Though it is clear that the well-dressed young gentleman intends to buy a newspaper, he walks toward the streetlight, not to the vendor in the story, and the story ends with the "small shadow" of the newspaper vendor wasting away and gently falling over sideways onto the sidewalk. Poverty engulfs the old man, and in due course takes his life as it threatened to do to Dominick in Hayashi's earlier tale "Dominick's Illness." In both stories, Hayashi treats poverty not just as a physical "illness" caused by a lack of nutrition, but also as a social illness. In the earlier story, the father's inability to find work in "Dominick's Illness" leads to the family's destitution. In "The People's Nutrition," it is the newspaper vendor's meager pay that does not allow him the money to afford a meal at the dreamlike restaurant. Moreover, the newspaper vendor is invisible to the young gentleman who

29. Mōri Toshio, "Hayashi Fusao no shōgai oyobi bungakuteki sōzō," *Tsurumi daigaku kiyō: dai'ichibu, kokugo kokubungaku hen* 31 (March 1994): 163.

30. Hayashi, "E no nai ehon," 13.

walked toward the street lamp to purchase a newspaper, and ultimately the vendor fades from sight into the darkness of the night. In both examples, the capitalist system not only fails the working class and impoverishes them but it also consigns them and their needs to the margins of society.

Poverty is also an issue in the seventh night's story, or "Lover," as Hayashi first entitled it. But unlike the stories above, in "Lover" we find a more concrete tale of destitution and its causes and effects. Here, the moon shines its light on a man walking along the Seine River in France and remarks that the man was as white as a clown's face, but that this effect was not simply due to the moon's light shining on him. The moon takes us into the man's home at the edge of town, where one young lady is sitting under a dingy lamp with her head in her hands. After the man, Jean, returns home and his face still looks ashen under that light, we discover the reason for his anxious face: A strike has been going on for almost four weeks, and his wife, Marie, is worried about how many more days their kids will have to go without bread to eat. She tells Jean that her father had been by that evening and will recommend that they end the strike at tomorrow's gathering. Marie pleads with Jean to end the strike, if not for those starved and exhausted men following him, then for her!

Here, more clearly than in the original text, Hayashi has revised the story so that Jean now runs dejectedly into Marie's arms and declares that he will end the strike. But instead of bolting from her arms, Jean "disappears" from the house with heavy steps.[31] He reappears on the banks of the Seine River, his face as pallid as a plasterer's as he stops to throw his hat onto the graveled road. This time the moon sees him determined, and with hope shining from his face. When he shakes his fist at the moon, he says, "Damn it, I'll do it. Only a couple more days—if we could only wait a couple more days, we'd triumph! ... Hey! Prometheus! I'm not weak, just an average Joe! Goodbye, Marie. Adieu, my love!"[32] As in the original story, we end with a cloud covering the moon's face so it cannot see in which direction the young French worker is headed.

More so than in the original text, Hayashi's revision employs the contrast of light and dark in this story to denote the emotions of the individ-

31. Ibid., 23.
32. Ibid.

ual characters and their actions. Here, the moon gives us the first names of both main characters, and we see them in a close, loving relationship being strained by an outside force: the drawn-out strike that is lasting much longer than previous work stoppages. As a result, Marie, from under the dim yellow light in their home, presses Jean to take some action to stop the strike and return to work so that they can properly feed their children. Up until he makes his decision, the moon describes Jean's face as pale from his worries, like a clown's painted face or that of a plasterer. However, when he makes up his mind, he is depicted as "starting to shine" (*kagayakidasu*) with "resolve" (*ketsui*) and "hope" (*kibō*), as he bids his wife goodbye and begins walking.[33] Does Jean do as Marie begs of him and return to the factory? Does he go back to work and negotiate an end to the strike, since he is one of the leaders? Does he leave Marie and join his fellow workers to see the strike through to the end? Does he leave the area and Marie and let the strike run its course? In this revised version, the insertion of Jean's wistful desire for only a couple more days so that the strike will succeed, plus the additional passage where Jean's face begins to shine with resolve and hope, noticeably tips the scales in favor of one of the two latter choices.

Hayashi's addition of "resolve and hope" at the end of the story separates it from "The People's Nutrition" and "Dominick's Illness," as well as from his earlier work "The Coin." There, the boy's hunger and impoverished home life lead him to resort to immoral behavior to acquire what he wants, a book to feed his desire to learn. Here, despite their desperate circumstances, and though we are not sure of the story's outcome, Jean's determination seems to find a way to "shine through" the darkness and the poverty. Perhaps, in the context of the overall work, Jean marks the transition from dark to light in the flow of the ten stories. Because soon after, we have the story of the Finnish youth who "believes in tomorrow" and "acts according to that belief,"[34] followed by the tenth night's story where the revolution has created a utopian welfare state allowing children from the Moscow slums to live in the villas of the Russian nobility.

Mōri Toshio has pointed out that through the emphasis in these stories on class struggle and poverty within a global context, Hayashi builds a

33. Hayashi, "E no nai ehon," 23.

34. Ibid., 25.

world socialist narrative juxtaposed with the Japanese case. First, people become aware of the social and economic inequalities around them; next, they recognize these discrepancies; and then the people form groups to take action to correct these disparities together. This eventually leads to the victory of revolution over government authority. While Mōri notes that Hayashi has nicely framed the content of this socialist narrative, he also asserts that it is Hayashi's innovative narrative structure that makes "A Picture Book without Pictures" so memorable. In particular, Mōri draws our attention to the way Hayashi strings together several stories that capture our attention because of the "lyrical" (*jojōsei*) and "romantic" (*rōmanteki*) telling of these children's stories. Thus, the contrast between the light and the dark takes on a social construct, since Hayashi focuses on the struggle for material resources between the wealthy elite and the impoverished masses. Ultimately, Mōri Toshio argues that Hayashi's poetic rendering of these stories complements the socialist message in the stories that compose "A Picture Book without Pictures."[35]

Thus, Hayashi's goal of inspiring children and instructing them on who and what has caused these social and economic inequalities is evident in "A Picture Book without Pictures." As Norma Field and Heather Bowen-Struyk note in their introduction to *For Dignity, Justice, and Revolution*, the proletarian literary movement was born in the context of an international "red decade" (1925–1935).[36] As a result, in Norma Field's introduction to the "Children" section of this anthology, she emphasizes that in *Shōnen senki* (Boys battle flag), the proletarian children's journal started in 1929, most of the heroes were international figures, such as Rosa Luxemburg (1870–1919) or Karl Liebknecht (1871–1919). She also notes that the editors filled its pages with descriptions of the "young pioneer" movements (the Soviet "pionīro") for proletarian youth all across the globe.[37] Accordingly, it is not surprising that Hayashi couched his first set of children's stories in the internationalist idiom. It was the language and the

35. Mōri, "Hayashi Fusao no shōgai oyobi bungakuteki sōzō," 163.

36. Norma Field and Heather Bowen-Struyk, *For Dignity, Justice, and Revolution: An Anthology of Japanese Proletarian Literature*, ed. Heather Bowen-Struyk and Norma Field (Chicago: University of Chicago Press, 2016), 3.

37. Norma Field, "Introduction," in *For Dignity, Justice, and Revolution: An Anthology of Japanese Proletarian Literature*, ed. Heather Bowen-Struyk and Norma Field (Chicago: University of Chicago Press, 2016), 190.

orientation of any young Socialist seeking to integrate their experiences within the larger flow of this movement and its organizations. Still, the emotive style and the humanist themes depicted in "A Picture Book without Pictures" reveal the influence of bourgeois literature on Hayashi. While it is clear that he wrote to instill hope in those who were a part of this revolutionary struggle and to encourage the youth to join and remain committed to the fight, these political themes do not overpower the essential appeal of the human element and the lyricism in the stories. In this way, the fairy tales in Hayashi's "A Picture Book without Pictures" share the youthful passion of his earliest literature produced in Ōita and Kumamoto. However, he did insert humor into these stories. That effort to entertain is most obvious in "State Funeral" and in "Strange Characters: A Fairy Tale." It is in Hayashi's next and last major children's story, published in the fall of 1926, where the desire to entertain becomes even more pronounced. In the end, this leads to a reflective piece on the nature of leadership.

ALLEGORIES OF LEADERSHIP IN "NEW AESOP'S FABLES"

From the opening of "New Aesop's Fables," Hayashi's narrative takes a turn to the fanciful, as an old elf appears out of the writer's tobacco smoke on a lazy Sunday afternoon and demands to know why more authors these days are not writing fables or "allegories." That is how the *furigana*—syllabic characters (*hiragana* and *katakana*) written next to the ideographic characters (*kanji*) to give the appropriate or desired reading of the ideographic characters—for *gūwa* renders that term. As we already noted at the start of this chapter, in the first story, "Executives and Dynamite," the narrator's satirical tale of worker exploitation sets the tone for this collection of fables. In it, the hilarity of the situation and the ridiculousness of the executive eclipses the lesson. Likewise, the second and seventh stories also target the elite for lessons in life and fun. In "Jinushi to dojō" ("Landlords and loaches"), the landlord portrayed in the story thinks that the tenant farmers are "going to boil us landowners and eat us."[38] He has spied on a peasant's meeting and has overheard a young peasant speaking about how a

38. Hayashi, "Shin isoppu monogatari: gūwa saikō," 33.

farmer's union is like a gigantic pot with fifteen or so loaches in it, and a big piece of white tofu in the middle. When you turn up the bright red flame on the pot, the loaches start to move around, and eventually they plunge into the pearly white tofu to escape the heat. That is why the peasants' and the workers' flag is always scarlet red, and the landowners' and capitalists' flag is always pearly white. Once the flame is hot enough, you boil the loaches, and then put a cover on the pot. Finishing his speech, he exclaims that nothing tastes better than boiled loach in tofu, which is why the perplexed landlord thought that the peasants were up to no good.

In his seventh story, "Fune no kamisama" ("The god of ships"), Hayashi continues his attack on the hypocrisy of capitalists, specifically focusing on one banker's experiences. In this case, the bank executive's investments have done so well that he has come to believe that religion is unnecessary and that economics scholars are the new "modern" gods of this world.[39] He goes so far as to have the exquisite household Buddhist altar—one that his father had built—removed from the house and destroyed when without warning, disaster strikes his business again and again. Following the financial crisis of 1920 and the Great Kanto Earthquake of 1923, the banker's businesses fail one after another. When his attempt to run a shipping company ends with several boats destroyed, the banker leaves for Shikoku Island to visit Konpira Shrine. There, he prays to the god of seafarers, having given his permission for carpenters to come and build a new Buddhist altar in his home.[40]

Unlike these three stories, where Hayashi used humor to disparage the leaders of industrial capitalism, the executives, and the landlords, the other stories focus on the rank and file in the Socialist movement. In the third story, "Onna to jamu" ("Women and jam"), the story revolves around the strange way that one youth expresses his resentment of women. Most likely, the narrator surmises, it is because the youth's girlfriend must have left him while he was in prison.[41] Continuing with this theme in the fourth story, "Tetsugakusha to koibito" ("Philosophers and lovers"), we find that in a triangular love relationship, the girl dumped one boy, and he is so angry that he would like to harm both the girl and the other man. His

39. Ibid., 43.
40. Ibid., 44–45.
41. Ibid., 34–35.

philosopher friend tells him that time is the best weapon; let forty or fifty years go by, and they will both be dead, the philosopher tells the dumbfounded lover.[42] Finally, in the fifth story, "Daigakusei to geisha" ("College students and geisha"), twenty students who have gone through the imperial university together gather for a party. They are nearing graduation and the talk soon turns to their job prospects after college, which are not good because of the competition for jobs. Eventually, they agree to pay a geisha for one night, but only for the four students who have not been with a geisha before. Everyone contributes ten *yen* apiece to pay for her services, and on the way back to the dorms, some students are quite happy, while others are not so happy with this arrangement.[43] While the main lesson in the first two stories seems to be: never trust a woman; in the last story, it seems that one should also not rely on one's friends, much less on one's college alumni. These fables emphasize the need for emotional maturation: first, to control one's feelings in dealing with others and, second, to manage one's life.

In the remaining two stories, Hayashi shifts his focus to the issues of mental and spiritual growth, respectively, the gaining of wisdom and perspective. In the sixth story, "Shinshi to bakuto" ("Gentlemen and gamblers"), the narrator is at an Izu hot springs recovering from an illness. His friend has come along, and to pass the time they want to play the card game *hanafuda* (flower cards), but they need a third player so they invite one of the cooks to join them. As it turns out, the cook was a professional *hanafuda* player. After he wins the game, he tells them his story about learning from his mentor, who was a crook in his own right, how to swindle the rich of their money. The eighth and final story, "Kanshu to shūjin" ("Guards and prisoners"), is set in a Japanese café as the narrator listens to an old man who is a foreigner from a Western country reflect on an unusual friendship between himself as a prisoner and two guards. The old man had wandered from country to country in the West but had somehow managed to land in the same prison twice. As the two talk over tea, the old man confides to the narrator that his interaction with these two prison guards while a prisoner stirred him to reexamine his life and rethink his belief in and support of the ideology for which he was imprisoned.

42. Ibid., 35–36.
43. Ibid., 36–39.

This is an interesting conclusion for a Marxist piece of literature that reflects the informal, passive, and ultimately reflective tone of "New Aesop's Fables." From its opening scene, in which the narrator has his discussion with a magical elf over the value of allegory, the mood of these stories is conversational. First, there is a closeness in the stories and that intimacy generates a sense of familiarity, welcoming the reader into the exchange. We find the main characters of the stories usually gathered around a stove, or at a table where tea, beer, or *saké* is served, or they are playing cards. At times the stories are told indirectly through a letter from a friend or by the narrator reflecting on his concern for the banker turned businessman. Consequently, Hayashi draws into the dialogue the reader, who is often disarmed by the entertaining tale of clueless, greedy, and suspicious elites and preposterous situations, as in "Executives and Dynamite," "Landlords and Loaches," and "The God of Ships." Sometimes it is the witty repartee between the youths as in "Women and Jam," in "Philosophers and Lovers," and in "College Students and Geisha," that interests the reader. In "Gentlemen and Gamblers" and "Guards and Prisoners," it is the sincere confessional stories of sinners that appeal to the reader. Second, unlike the stories in "A Picture Book without Pictures," these stories all take place in Japan. Resituating the locale to a more familiar place makes the readers feel as if the author is talking to them, and the stories become more personal when imagery allows the reader to envisage himself in one of these places or one of these situations. Third, the objective nature of the storytelling is less didactic than "A Picture Book without Pictures," where the lessons are couched in an overtly rhetorical style that highlights the social injustice created by industrial capitalism.

However, like the stories in "A Picture Book without Pictures," the narrator and the main characters are passive here, meaning that they observe the events and tell the stories but they do nothing directly to confront the wrongs witnessed in those stories. Hayashi structures these fables with a third person perspective, as a narrator observing the events as they unfold. Our only active character in "New Aesop's Fables," is the young farmer. He gives the fiery speech advocating the formation of the farmer's union to protect the tenant farmer's rights against the large landlords in the village. However, the teacher who tells us about the young man's oration asks others in the village what happened only after one of the landowners requests his help, and even then, although the teacher admires the youth's speech, we have no indication as to whether he too will join the fight. More than in "A Picture Book without Pictures," Hayashi defines the key determining factors in life as Providence and the gods, particularly in the two stories that conclude "New Aesop's Fables." As a result, readers feel that the narrator is inviting them into a conversation where they have been entertained, where they have learned some lessons, and where they have connected to the stories of shared experiences. Still, the passive narratives of the stories do not spur action, but instead lead to introspection.

The children's stories in Hayashi's "A Picture Book without Pictures" do command our attention as Hayashi fills in the picture book mostly with sad tales that cry out for social justice and pleading for redress. In "New Aesop's Fables," conversely, Hayashi seems to be painting portraits. Here, the main characters are a vindictive company executive, a suspicious landlord, a resentful prisoner, a spiteful lover, some discouraged university students, a cook seeking forgiveness, a skeptical yet vacillating bank executive, and a renegade wanting to explain his desertion. In this way, Hayashi's allegories in "New Aesop's Fables" seem to be much more than literature; these stories seem to imply, not so subtly in places, some problems with leadership in Japanese society in the mid-1920s, and also in the Socialist movement.

HAYASHI FUSAO IN THE STUDENT FEDERATION

Considering these allegories of leadership in the context of Hayashi's personal history reveals the multiple points of contention developing in his relationships within the radical student movement. Namely, the enthusiastic Hayashi experienced some less than satisfying interactions with the leaders of the movement. From the beginning, he wasted no time in immersing himself in the life of the university student radical. Soon after arriving in Tokyo, he borrowed a suit from a friend and participated in the 1923 May Day rally. Police officers detained him at the Kanda police station, but this detainment served to mark the first of his many run-ins with the police as a New Man Society activist.[44] The New Man Society was a leading organization in the Gakuren (Student Federation), a loose alliance

44. Hayashi Fusao, "Fu: Hayashi Fusao nenpu," 449.

of radical university student groups that formed in late 1922.[45] Their response to two broad political issues brought the Student Federation into prominence in the spring of 1923. Those issues were the institutionalization of military education in Japanese universities and the suppression of academic and political freedom on university campuses.[46]

Student Federation members confronted these issues on their own university campuses first. In early May, the leadership of the Bunka Dōmei (Culture League—a radical student group on the Waseda University campus and another leader of the Student Federation) found out that a student club had been reorganized as a right-wing group to advocate military education in the middle and higher schools. With the support of army officials, the Home Ministry, and other right-wing organizations, the Gunji Kenkyūkai (Military Study Group) held its founding ceremonies on May 10, 1923.[47] In protest, Student Federation leaders deployed several of its members to shout down speakers, from the Waseda faculty and administration and from the army, who spoke on behalf of the Military Study Group. Hayashi Fusao, his Teidai school cap safely hidden in his pocket, participated in the protest, helping drown out the speeches with his jeers.[48] Within a few days, retaliation ensued as members from the Military Study Group first used violence to break up a Student Federation rally on the Waseda campus, and then on May 15 passed a resolution calling for the dismissal of those professors thought to be leftists at Waseda University.[49]

Rioting followed each of these confrontations and university officials forced both the Culture League and the Military Study Group to disband.

---

45. Gakuren is an abbreviation for the Student Federation's formal name, Gakusei Rengōkai. Later in 1924 as Gakuren took on nationwide significance, the group changed its name to Gakusei Shakai Kenkyū Rengōkai (Student Federation of Social Science). For more information on the formation of Gakuren, see Henry Dewitt Smith II, *Japan's First Student Radicals*, 102, 113.

46. Smith, *Japan's First Student Radicals*, 110, 116.

47. Information on the date of the founding ceremonies and the support of the army for the Gunji Kenkyūkai comes from Smith, *Japan's First Student Radicals*, 108, and information on the support of the Home Ministry and right-wing organizations for the Gunji Kenkyūkai comes from George M. Beckmann and Okubo Genji, *The Japanese Communist Party 1922–1945* (Stanford: Stanford University Press, 1969), 67.

48. Kawamori Yoshizō, "Hayashi Fusao den," 6. Teidai is an abbreviation for Tokyo Teikoku Daigaku (Tokyo Imperial University).

49. Beckmann, *The Japanese Communist Party 1922–1945*, 67.

Despite this setback, the Student Federation fight against military education continued. In the wake of the May 1923 antimilitary-education protest on the Waseda campus, the Student Federation leadership sent Hayashi to Hokkaidō. There his mission was to instruct the students at Otaru Commercial Higher School on how to organize and protest the introduction of military education courses into their curriculum. Formal Student Federation efforts to oppose the militarization of the Japanese educational system lasted for another couple of years. However, in April of 1925, the Council on Educational Policy approved a plan to make military education compulsory in the public school system, and to make it voluntary in private schools and at the university level. Leaders of the radical student movement continued to oppose military education when and where they could, but with military education formalized as Ministry of Education policy, Student Federation leadership began to shift their focus to the issues of academic and political freedom. Emphasizing these issues was a necessary step because, from late 1925, government officials began a crackdown on student radicalism in the universities that forced the New Man Society underground in 1928.[50] Both the New Man Society and the Student Federation voluntarily dissolved into the Japanese Communist Youth League in late 1929.

During these years, Hayashi came to play a larger role in the journalistic and literary endeavors of the New Man Society. In the summer of 1923, he returned to Kyūshū where he tried to organize the students, as many members of the New Man Society did when they returned to their hometowns during summer vacation.[51] Having had little luck in his summer activities, Hayashi returned to Tokyo that fall and became a reporter for the university's student newspaper. He became a reporter ostensibly to promote the New Man Society's leftist viewpoint in the newspaper, but he relished his new position.[52] He also wrote leftist pamphlets and manifestos

50. Smith, *Japan's First Student Radicals*, 118–119.

51. Ibid., 182.

52. Some examples of his reporting are: Hayashi Fusao (Gotō Toshio), "Marukusu no tanjō" *Teikoku daigaku shinbun*, vol. 73 (May 2, 1924): 6; Hayashi Fusao, "Futatsu no kao: Torurā hihan oboegaki," *Teikoku daigaku shinbun*, vol. 122 (June 15, 1925): 4; Hayashi Fusao, "Mitsu no kaikyū tōsōgeki," *Teikoku daigaku shinbun* vol. 130 (September 14, 1925): 4. Hayashi Fusao, "Puroretaria geijutsu no riron: runacharusukī no 'shingeiju-

(*gekibun*) for the Student Federation, including one based on his experiences as a student supporter in the Osaka Metropolitan Streetcar Strike of July 1924.[53]

His writing skills caught the attention of his colleagues at the New Man Society. With Sano Manabu in exile overseas, Hayashi along with others assisted in the translation of *Lenin's Complete Works* in Sano's place.[54] His ability to read English and German gained him other translating work, enough so that he could pay for his living expenses. Shiga Yoshio, one year his senior in the New Man Society, invited him to become a contributing editor to *Marukusushugi*, a legal journal that was the theoretical mouthpiece for the outlawed Japanese Communist Party in late 1924. Hayashi contributed his first article to the journal in November 1924. The managing editor, Nishi Masao, approved the article and published it in the March 1925 issue of *Marukusushugi*.[55] From 1925 into 1926, Hayashi went on to contribute several articles to the journal on the theme of opportunism (*hiyorimishugi*), but during that same time, he writes that he also started to move away from political theory and into literary activities.

The impetus for this move, he tells us, came from a love affair gone wrong during the late spring of 1925. Hayashi had fallen for a young woman from the Japan Women's College; but she, in turn, fell in love with Hayashi's close friend, Shiga Yoshio. Shiga and the young woman married and Hayashi, unable to stand the sight of them together, asked Shiga to release him from his formal duties at *Marukusushugi*. He also requested that Shiga allow him to work in a different part of the student movement.

---

tsuron' wo yomu," *Teikoku daigaku shinbun* vol. 157 (March 1, 1926): 4; and Hayashi Fusao, "Atarashiki Fujimorishi: 'ōkami he!' yonde," *Teikoku daigaku shinbun* vol. 184 (October 15, 1926): 8.

53. See Hayashi, "Hayashi Fusao nenpu," 450, and Hayashi Fusao, "Bungakuteki kaisō," 231–232, for Hayashi referring to his participation in the strike and the *gekibun* he wrote for the Student Federation. See Kikukawa Tadao, *Gakusei shakai undōshi* (Tokyo: Chūō kōronsha, 1931; reprint, Kaiguchi shoten, 1947), 230–245 (page citations are to the reprint edition), for information on the Student Federation's participation in the strike.

54. Sano Manabu was a former member of the New Man Society, a former lecturer at Waseda University, and a member of the Japanese Communist Party's central committee.

55. Hayashi Fusao, "Waga kuni ni okeru hokyū seikatsusha undō," *Marukusushugi* (March 1925): 45–58.

Shiga consented and asked Hayashi to lead a new study group that the New Man Society was forming to spread Marxism among students interested in literature.[56] The leaders of the New Man Society created the Shakai Bungei Kenkyūkai (Socialist Literature Study Group) in the spring of 1925, but the group did not become active until that fall. Originally, the New Man Society leaders had designed the study group as a means to attract more students from departments outside their strongholds of law and economics into the socialist movement.[57] However, under Hayashi's guidance, the members of the group who were truly interested in literature began to study literature in earnest.

By February of 1926, Hayashi and the group had come under increasing criticism from the New Man Society leaders for their literary activities. Hayashi and certain members of the group reacted to this criticism by forming the Marukusushugi Geijutsu Kenkyūkai (Marxist Arts Study Group; better known by its abbreviation, Marugei) as a separate organization within the Socialist Literature Study Group. Members of the Marxist Arts Study Group invited writers outside the New Man Society into Marugei in order to distinguish their group from the Socialist Literature Study Group sponsored by the New Man Society.[58] Marugei concentrated on applying Marxist thought to their literary endeavors, eventually advocating for the politicization of the proletarian literature movement.[59] The Marxist Arts Study Group and its members would fulfill their goal, but Hayashi was still a member of

56. For the most detailed description of the ill-fated love affair and Hayashi's reaction to it, see Hayashi Fusao, "Bungakuteki jijōden," 334–335. Hayashi does not mention Shiga by name in the piece; but in Hayashi, "Hayashi Fusao nenpu," 451, he makes it clear that the "other man" was Shiga Yoshio.

57. The New Man Society planned not only a study group for Marxist literature, but also a group to attract medical students. For more information on their plan, see Smith, *Japan's First Student Radicals*, 146–149.

58. Original members of the Shakai Bungei Kenkyūkai included Nakano Shigeharu, Tani Hajime, Kaji Wataru, Sano Seki, Hisaita Eijirō, Kawaguchi Hiroshi, Ōtsuka Haruo and later Kamei Katsuichirō, Kubokawa Tsurujirō, Nishizawa Ryūji, and Miyaki Kikuo. When the group became independent and formed the Marxist Arts Study Group, the following writers joined it: Yamada Seizaburō, Sasaki Takamaru, Senda Koreya, Yanase Masamu, Hayama Yoshiki, and Ogawa Shin'ichi. I have taken this information from Kawamori, "Hayashi Fusao den," 8–9, and Hayashi, "Hayashi Fusao nenpu," 451.

59. Hirano Ken et al., eds., "Narupu kaisan zengo to '*tenkō*' no mondai," in *Tōron: Nihon puroretaria bungaku undōshi* (San'ichi shobō, 1955), 56. This discussion was originally published in April 1954 issue of *Kindai Bungaku*.

the New Man Society, and he took part in its political activities, despite objections to his leadership of the literary study group.

Hayashi participated in the Student Federation's "Second Congress" (Gakuren Dainikai Zenkoku Taikai) as a representative of the New Man Society. Hosted by members of the Kansai section of the Student Federation on the Kyoto Imperial University campus, the Student Federation convened its Second Congress on July 16, 1925, with eighty representatives from fifty-nine schools gathering on the campus.[60] Buoyed by the passage of the Universal Manhood Suffrage Act on May 5, 1925, and the passage of other social legislation under the Katō Takaaki cabinet, the radical student movement flourished. By mid-1925, the Student Federation had established a highly organized left-wing student movement with official ties to the radical wing of the Japanese labor movement and unofficial ties by some of its members to the clandestine Japanese Communist Party. As its activities increasingly spread beyond university campuses, police officials grew concerned and began to monitor closely the involvement of Student Federation members with these off-campus radical groups, particularly with the party.

Activity in the Kyoto area by members of the Student Federation made the police suspect that the students might be attempting to help revive the Japanese Communist Party. Following a May 1923 police search of the offices of Sano Manabu and Inomata Tsunao, who were lecturers and party members on the Waseda campus, police conducted a major roundup of party members in June. This roundup contributed to the decision by the Communist Party to dissolve officially in March 1924, yet the police remained alert for any signs that party members might be ready to reconstitute it. Therefore, when the Kyoto police found antimilitary-education posters placed on the campus of Dōshisha University in November 1925, the head of the Kyoto Thought Police believed he saw the work of the party behind Student Federation protests against military education, and he received permission to carry out arrests of its members.[61] Known as the Kyoto Student Federation Incident of 1925–1926, Kyoto police carried out a mass arrest of the Kansai Student Federation members on December 1, 1925. The police entered the university without authorization and searched

60. Matsuo Hiroya, "Kyoto Gakuren jiken: hatsudō sareta chian iji hō," in *Nihon seiji saiban shiroku: Shōwazen*, ed. Wagatsuma Sakae (Tokyo: Dai'ichi hōki shuppan, 1970), 70.

61. Richard H. Mitchell, *Thought Control in Prewar Japan*, 72.

the campus dormitory where the members lived. They hoped to find evidence to indicate that the students were forming a secret society or were in possession of seditious materials.[62]

Although the police found no evidence of any secret society and had to release the students soon after their arrests, they did find enough evidence to rearrest and indict the Student Federation members for violation of the Peace Preservation Law (*chian iji hō*). Newly enacted in April 1925, the Peace Preservation Law defined illegal groups and movements in ideological terms. It went beyond the Peace Police Law (*chian keisatsu hō*) of 1900 that stressed the secrecy of the group or movement, and an intent to incite rebellion. Under the Peace Preservation Law, the police could now prosecute anyone whom they could link to a prohibited ideology. In Article One, Paragraph One of the Peace Preservation Law, illegal ideology is defined in two ways: first, as an ideology espousing ideas that the state interprets as threatening the *kokutai* (national polity) or Japan's political system; and second, as an ideology that condemned the private ownership of land.[63] Using the left-wing texts and other materials they obtained during their first search, Kyoto police began indicting Student Federation members again on January 15, 1926.

This time the police extended the scope of their arrests to Student Federation members outside the Kansai area. In reality, they were indicting the Student Federation and the radical student movement itself; thus, this time the police included in the indictments four leaders of the New Man Society who had participated in the Second Congress. Police charged Hayashi, who had just taken over from Shiga Yoshio as the secret chairperson (*himitsu iinchō*) of the Student Federation in December 1925, for violating both the Peace Preservation Law and the Publication Law (*shuppan hō*) in the incident.[64] In late March 1926, police came to the headquarters of the New Man Society in Ueno's Sakuragichō and arrested Hayashi in his school uniform. Then, they took him to Kyoto where he spent the

62. See Smith, *Japan's First Student Radicals*, 189–194, and Mitchell, *Thought Control in Prewar Japan*, 70–77, for the best English language sources on the incident. Smith's account is largely a summary of Kikukawa's discussion of the incident in his *Gakusei shakai undōshi*, 352–386.

63. For a translation of the first three articles of the Peace Preservation Law, see Mitchell, *Thought Control in Prewar Japan*, 63.

64. See Kawamori, "Hayashi Fusao den," 9, for Hayashi succeeding Shiga; and see Kikukawa, *Gakusei shakai undōshi*, 360, for a listing of the charges against Hayashi.

next five months in detainment.[65] After his preliminary hearing that September, the police released him on bail. However, by then, university officials had suspended him indefinitely from the university, and he became a full-time writer in the left-wing literary movement.[66]

Questioning the Support of Left-Wing Thought

In "New Aesop's Fables," published at the end of his first stint in a Kyoto jail cell from March to September of 1926, Hayashi calls into question the leaders and the leadership of the Student Federation. From 1923 to 1926, he experienced firsthand many of the stereotypes of vindictive, suspicious, and vacillating leaders within the movement itself. His allegories may depict the executives and bankers, but the emphasis is on the undesirable qualities and the inappropriate actions of Student Federation leaders. In much the same way, the middle set of fables present students, a group that Hayashi knew best, in an unfavorable light that highlights their spiteful, resentful, and unhappy temperaments. Finally, two of the allegories in the second half of "New Aesop's Fables," almost certainly written at the end of his detainment, present disillusioned characters seeking forgiveness and justification for their actions, for instance, the cook who just wants to play a round of cards without resorting to parlor tricks to win the hand.[67] Still, the most pertinent fable is the last one "Guards and Prisoners," because the story revolves around a subject foremost in Hayashi's mind.

Introducing "Guards and Prisoners," the narrator notes that he heard this story while having tea with an old man from the West who said that he had been in prison twice, once for six months when he was twenty-two, and again for one year when he was forty-three. While there was nothing new about going to prison, the old man had drifted from town to town and country to country during his youth, so it was strange that somehow he found himself in the same prison twice.

> ... —in this country, you would call it "fate," I imagine, says the old man.
> There is an old scripture in my country that tells us that "it is harder for a camel to pass through the eye of a needle than it is for a rich man to enter

65. Hayashi describes his arrest in Hayashi, "Bungakuteki jijōden," 310.

66. Smith, *Japan's First Student Radicals*, 193.

67. Hayashi, "Shin isoppu monogatari: gūwa saikō," 40.

> the gates of a prison." Still, when I arrived at the gate, I checked, and it seemed like a camel, a rich person, or any other lesser beast, could fit through the gate, if it so desired, [he jokingly informs the narrator].[68]

Admitting to feeling lonely and helpless the first time he was in prison, the old man explains to the narrator what it was like to be in a prison cell, and how he passed the time by waiting for the prison guards so that he could learn something about what was happening outside the prison gates. From the start, the senior of the two guards was more talkative, and he learned the results of the general election from him. When he asked if there was anything of note in the elections, the younger guard angrily replied that there was nothing, but when pressed by the prisoner, the younger guard revealed that the head of the conservative political party had been in their holding cell. Was he there in place of a wealthy executive, asked the prisoner? That is how it always works, he told the guard. No, said the guard, a bit startled, but as a favor to him, each day we had to cough up fifteen dollars to pay for his lunch. That was like several weeks' worth of my salary, complained the young guard.[69] From that point on, the prisoner developed a close relationship with the guards. When he complained about the shortness of their exercise period, the old guard countered that he was tired from walking up and down steps all day, so he should feel glad not to have to walk that much. When he asserted that at least "you have a home to go back to," the young guard remarked that "home sweet home" is just some old poet's dream. His roof leaked and his kids were hungry and whining all the time. What's more, his wife always nagged him to do something about them, as they ran around the house out of control.[70] Thanks to the friendship he developed with the guards, the six months passed by quickly, he reveals to the narrator.

When fate brings him back to the same prison—we never learn what crimes he committed—he is surprised to find the younger guard still there, though the guard has aged considerably after twenty years. He asks about the older guard and learns that he has just passed away while working at the prison.[71] Waking up at night, the old man hears the guards'

68. Hayashi, "Shin isoppu monogatari: gūwa saikō," 45–46.
69. Ibid., 47.
70. Ibid.
71. Ibid., 47–48.

footsteps as they make their rounds, and he sees how much older the guard on the iron deck appears now, standing there as if he is half-asleep. The light above the guard casts his shadow against the wall, and in the silhouette, his face looks like a skeleton from some impressionist painting. It sets the prisoner to thinking: will this guard also die in prison; who is the prisoner here, the man incarcerated for a year, or the guards who spend their whole lives in prison?[72] After taking a break from his story and resting, the old man returns to this question:

> ... Who was the prisoner there? No, I'm not going to tell you some nonsense—such as, he was the real prisoner while I wasn't.
>
> Both of us, yes, both of us were prisoners. I, the bad person, as well as the guard, the good person, was a prisoner. —The only difference was that the court had set my stay in prison, while his time there was indefinite.
>
> Still, I wrestled with this question daily. Who knows, maybe that is why I ended up in prison again? Now that I think of it, like the camel and the rich man, perhaps the safest way to pass through life is not to think of anything at all, not to adhere to any form of thought (*shisō*) after all.[73]

With this declaration, the old man finishes his story.

In stark contrast to his later short stories on prison life, here Hayashi makes a sharp delineation between the coldness of the prison facility itself and the warmth of the two guards in the story, both seeming quite human. While the guards choose to stay there for the work and the pay, it is "fate" that leads the old man through the prison gates twice. Ultimately, the old man concludes that both are prisoners: the prison guards because of their own choice to go into this line of work and the old man because of his intellectual decision to follow some "ism." Financial necessity shapes these prison guards' lives. They complain about having to pay so much for the head of the conservative political party's lunches. They grumble about the physical toll on their bodies of walking up and down stairs all day, and they gripe about how they can barely afford a house that does not leak when it rains. As the old man observes at the end of the story, the prison guards are prisoners too, but of the capitalist system that trades their work and, in due course, their bodies, for just enough salary to raise a family in a run-down shack. If economics defines the guards' "imprisonment," then

72. Ibid., 48.
73. Ibid.

it seems that ideology circumscribes the old man's life. He speaks of "fate" and quotes from scripture (*keiten*)—though never acknowledging that these are biblical quotes—and, desiring knowledge most of all, he asks the guards for information regarding the elections and who won them. He speculates that maybe his continual struggling with this problem of who here the real prisoner is has led him back to prison in some way. Lastly, he ends with the dual assertions that not only should he stop thinking too much, but also that one should not accept any formal system of thought. He should be more like the camel or the rich man, like those who do not fit through the eye of the needle of prison because they do not waste their time worrying and thinking about the problems of the world. We never learn outright what he has done for the court to sentence him to prison, much less to which proscribed ideology he belongs. However, it appears that his belief in this ideology lands him in prison twice, forcing him to reconsider not only his involvement with the group that espouses this ideology, but also his belief in this system of thought. In this way, "Guards and Prisoners" exhibits some of the ambivalence we found in Hayashi's earlier story "Insects Gathering around the Light." Perhaps the old man's sense of doubt reflects Hayashi's uncertainty regarding both the socialist political movement and socialist thought in general after his detainment. But in "Guards and Prisoners," the narrator never specifies the movement or the prohibited "ism" for which he is imprisoned.

Even more than this, what stands out in Hayashi's "New Aesop's Fables" is his political use of literature to convey his displeasure with the political movement, its ideology, and its leaders. This pattern persists long after he enters the proletarian literature movement in 1926. Based on this reading of "New Aesop's Fables," neither Hayashi's insistence that his move from politics to literature was a decisive one, nor Mizuno Yukiko's assertion that Hayashi was always a writer first and an activist second rings true. From what we have examined thus far, it is clear that Hayashi both enjoyed writing literature and continued to take part in politics. Therefore, in "A Picture Book without Pictures," we find evidence of the key traits that defined his fiction: the humorous, yet intensely lyrical depictions of social and economic inequity in late Taishō literature, as well as the search for a noble cause that will continue to animate his proletarian short stories. Nevertheless, in "New Aesop's Fables" as in his higher school works "Insects Gathering around the Light" and "Village," we also find what is becoming a recognizable pattern for him: the use of literature to deliver a political message. This time, instead of pushing the intellectuals to get off the fence and take action, Hayashi's allegorical tales attempt to identify problems with how the leaders and members of the Socialist movement conduct themselves. These are themes, both creative and political, that Hayashi will further develop in his proletarian short stories concerning the lives of factory girls, student radicals, and labor organizers during the late 1920s.

4

Politics and Literature

Romanticizing Factory Workers, Student Radicals, and Labor Organizers in Hayashi Fusao's Proletarian Literature

> —With a thud, Moriyama stood bolt upright. He grabbed the back of the chair with his left hand and thrust out his right hand in front of him. "The hell with it, I'll do it! I'll show you I can do it, so listen up!"
>
> What a booming voice! It resounded through the room. He started his speech. The one he'd been practicing to give the day of the meeting. He enthusiastically waved both hands through the air [as he spoke]. They [the police officers] gathered around the table and stared blankly, their mouths agape. ...
>
> I guess it was at that moment, that I became so fond of that word, [fool]. Yes, I vowed with all my heart, to show everyone that I could become one of those fools with [Moriyama] too.
>
> —"Baka"

Before his first police detention from the spring to the summer of 1926, Hayashi Fusao produced some of his most memorable works of proletarian fiction. He expanded on the political theme of encouraging others to join in the fight for social justice found in "Insects Gathering around the Light" and "Village." But then, drawing on his personal experiences, he tightened his focus to create several striking, individual proletarian heroes to emulate. Our first example in these works is the factory worker Moriyama in Hayashi's short story "Baka" ("Fool"). In the epigraph, we find

Hayashi Fusao, "Baka," *Shinjin* 30, no. 12 (December 1925): 9.

Moriyama confronting the police directly in an effort to establish a union at his workplace. His passionate speech not only leaves the policemen witnessing the spectacle dumbstruck, it obviously inspires the narrator to strive for that same level of dedication to the cause. From a political perspective, Hayashi is delineating the type of leader needed to push the movement forward: Moriyama is willing to learn and to mentor others about the cause, and when the time for action arises, he meets the opposition with courage and determination. Moriyama's audacity and warmth win the day, in considerable contrast to any of the leadership figures we observed in "New Aesop's Fables" from October 1926.

In this way, Hayashi's first encounter with the police seems to have had quite a negative impact on his assessment of the Socialist movement and on how he depicted its leaders in his writing. Thus, here, we will examine his romantic depictions of leaders in his proletarian short stories written and published before his detention and through his release from police custody in September of 1926. These stories have much more in common with the poignant cries for justice found in his children's story "A Picture Book without Pictures," which he also wrote before his time in police custody. As such, here we will focus on the romantic tone of his first works of proletarian fiction; then in Chapter 5, we trace the influence of his initial detainment on his increasingly cynical portrayal of the Socialist movement, which, as we have noted, appears in his writing of "New Aesop's Fables." Finally, these two chapters set the background for our study of Hayashi's *tenkō* in Chapters 6, 7, and 8, where his time in prison and his antagonistic relationships within the proletarian literature movement led him to turn his time in the movement into a memory. He then reworks that memory and ultimately, attempts to displace it from his past altogether.

From a more historically interpretative perspective on these chapters, however, Hayashi's short stories revolve around three major proletarian progtagonists: the factory worker, the student radical, and the labor activists. These three stock characters figure prominently in Hayashi's proletarian fiction from the mid-1920s through the 1930s, where he often explores the difficult lives of factory workers and the efforts of student radicals and labor activists to organize those workers into unions. These were subjects that he had already incorporated into his creative writing while at Kumamoto, specifically in his last two stories, "Insects Gathering around the Light" and "Village." In these stories, we find factory girls in "Village" and student radicals and labor organizers in both works as the main characters who are attempting to deal with the socioeconomic challenges that confront them in the workplace, on the streets, and at home. As we observed previously, Hayashi had personally witnessed life in the factory, observing his mother's work in the rural silk mill near their village outside of Ōita, and had participated in the radical student movement while at Kumamoto Fifth Higher School and as part of the New Man Society in Tokyo. He also drew from a variety of outside sources, in addition to his own experience, for the material in his fiction. Thus, over the next three chapters we examine in chronological order several of Hayashi's proletarian short stories that both depict life in the factory setting through the global experiences of women and men, as well as the work of student radicals and labor organizers. He returns time and again to these themes and characters in his creative writing, albeit in different forms. He does so first to highlight the exploitation workers encountered, and second, to point out both positive and negative examples of how student radicals and labor activists attempted to organize workers so they could protest their mistreatment. Finally, he utilized his proletarian short stories to chronicle for posterity the lives of these activists and laborers in the movement for posterity.

WHY WE FIGHT!

In his short story "Fool," published in the December 1925 issue of *Shinjin*, Hayashi gives us a dynamic portrayal of a worker engaged in an actual struggle to form a worker's union. Our narrator sets the stage, reminiscing that it was five or six years ago in a certain town in northern Kyūshū when he learned to like the sound of the word "fool."[1] He was a young worker at a printing factory when he met a labor activist called Moriyama who was about ten years older than he was. Whenever there was time, Moriyama would pull a book out of his pocket and start reading, to the point that the book's cover had turned black from the ink on his hands. Unfortunately, at this workplace, the older workers often bullied the

1. Hayashi Fusao, "Baka," *Shinjin* 30, no. 12 (December 1925): 5.

younger ones, like himself, into buying snacks and other goods for them. Our narrator refused to play this game but these bullies trapped him in one of their schemes, and he was taking a beating when Moriyama came to his rescue.[2] From then on, they became friends and he began to visit Moriyama's house, where he learned more about the teachings in this book. Moriyama told him that instead of fighting each other, workers should join forces in a labor union. Our narrator took the message to heart and helped Moriyama in spreading his message to other printing factories in town.

Once they gained enough support from other workers, they decided that it was time to hold a rally where they would give speeches and try to gather more backing for a labor union. They rented out the courtyard of a temple and decided on the date of January fifteenth for the rally, posting handmade flyers around the town. The police, learning of the rally, summoned the narrator to the police station at the appointed time.[3] Once he arrived, the narrator was escorted to a room by one of the officers. There he joined the rest of the workers. As we observed in the opening epigraph, he described the confrontation between the police chief, a little man sitting arrogantly in a big chair, and Moriyama. While the other members sat on their rickety chairs and cowered before the police chief, Moriyama was defiant and answered the chief's questions with confidence and in a resounding voice.

Next, the chief interrogated Moriyama about the group's intentions, and Moriyama told him that they planned to hold a rally where the union members would give speeches. So the chief asked if the purpose of the speeches was propaganda. When Moriyama confirmed that they were, the chief in a condescending voice inquired if Moriyama even knew what the word "propaganda" meant, and he disparaged their efforts saying, "Who'd give a shit about what you punk workers have to say anyway[?] What fools!"[4] The chief went on with his tirade, trying to force Moriyama to back down. Suddenly, Moriyama got up, turned his chair around, stood on the chair, and began his speech in a booming voice that silenced the chief. Seeing their leader take such bold action, the rest of the group stood up on their chairs and gave the speeches

2. Ibid., 6.
3. Ibid., 7.
4. Ibid., 8.

they had been practicing. Moriyama ended by turning to the group in the room and quietly telling them, "You all heard what he said. Every one of us is a fool. So at the very least let's train hard to become fools!"[5] From that point on the narrator swears that he would show everyone the fool he has become, and thus concludes the story.

Hayashi develops one of his favorite motifs in this short story: an active depiction of a labor organizer viewed through the eyes of a third-person narrator. Here the narrator is a young laborer who has just started his job in a printing factory. We do not learn much more about him but instead move immediately to his relationship with Moriyama, the hero of the story. Moriyama is a taciturn fellow, and the narrator does not know much about him other than that he is always seen pulling out an ink-stained book to read during his free time. That is, until the narrator has a run-in with the older factory workers and Moriyama aids him in his struggle against them. What impresses the narrator during the tussle is Moriyama's insistence that they are all comrades and that they should not be fighting among themselves.

As Hayashi comes under Moriyama's influence, he finally grasps what Moriyama means by these words. He then learns about this organization called a worker's union and joins in Moriyama's efforts to reach out to the workers within his factory and to those in other printing factories to create a united workers' union for printers. The attempt to advocate for the right to organize ultimately leads to the confrontation with the police chief, who seeks to denigrate the workers' efforts to form a union through verbal abuse. Moriyama, however, responds to the police chief's harsh words with a formal retaliation, giving the speech he had prepared for the upcoming rally. In this way, Moriyama elevates himself, and thus their cause, above the police (i.e., representatives of the state) in multiple ways. His thundering voice drowns out the police chief and the officers' jeers, but he also literally places himself above the opposition by standing on his chair to deliver his speech, and his actions inspire the other workers, including the narrator, to stand up and give their speeches as well. The police chief stares in disbelief at the workers' conduct and the narrator, emboldened by Moriyama's words and deeds, tells the reader that he is still playing the "fool" some five or six years after this incident.

5. Hayashi, "Baka," 9.

The narrative in "Fool" reads as a precursor to Hayashi's two most well-known short stories, "Ringo" ("Apples") and "Mayu" ("Cocoons"). Leaders of the Teidai branch of the Student Federation dispatched Hayashi to Hokkaidō in the late fall of 1925.[6] There, his mission was to help the students of the Otaru Commercial Higher School organize a student-led protest movement against the military education classes that school officials forced them to take as part of the school curriculum. As background material for "Apples," which Hayashi published in the February 1926 issue of *Bungei sensen* (Literary Front), he drew on a story that a Hokkaidō newspaper played up while he was in Otaru.[7] The narrator in "Apples" opens by describing, in a letter to a friend, the pristine winter setting of Hokkaidō. He continues by mentioning a man from the union he had been waiting to meet the day before. He began first by relating to his friend the story of how they first met at a local tavern, but he then pauses the letter and reflected on his meeting with the man from the union from the day before. He continues the letter to his friend and tells him the strange story that the man told about how one "catches salmon with apples" (*ringo de sake o tsuru*): Winter means unemployment for many in Hokkaidō since the farming industry comes to a halt and there are not enough factory jobs to employ the excess labor force. As a result, the fisheries entice these workers onto boats to fish for salmon in the rough winter waters of the Sea of Okhotsk. In lieu of an

6. Hayashi dates his trip to Hokkaidō as the spring of 1923 in his "Biographical sketch" [Hayashi Fusao, "Fu: Hayashi Fusao nenpu," in *Hayashi Fusao chosakushū*, vol. I (Tokyo: Tsubasa shoin, 1968), 450.]; however, the Otaru Higher Commercial School Incident did not take place until October 1925, so it is more likely that Hayashi was sent to Hokkaidō following the incident, and then wrote the story over the winter, publishing it in the February 1926 issue of *Bungei sensen*. For more information on the Otaru Commercial Higher School Incident, see Kikukawa Tadao's *Gakusei shakai undō shi* (Tokyo: Chūō kōronsha, 1931), 273–275, 336–345; reprint, Kaiguchi shoten, 1947. It is Kamei Hideo in his review of "Apples" who points out in part two of that review, that it was the Tokyo Imperial University branch of the Student Federation which dispatched Hayashi to Otaru after the disturbance became known all over the country: Kamei Hideo, "Kamei Hideo no hatsugen: bungaku no naka no ringo," http://homepage2.nifty.com/k-sekirei/otaru/apple_06.html. (accessed November 8, 2011).

7. In response to a joint review of his work the previous month, Hayashi confirms that the trading of apples for salmon was an actual news story that he read while in Hokkaidō the previous year. Hayashi Fusao, "Hihyō ni tsuite," *Bungei sensen* 3, no. 12 (December 1926): 28. The citation for the joint review is as follows: Yamada Seizaburō and others, "Hayashi Fusaoron: sayoku bundan shinsakkaron, ni," *Bungei sensen* 3, no. 11 (November 1926): 74–77.

hourly wage, they offer the seasonal laborers thirty-plus salmon apiece from the total catch to take back with them to Otaru. That way the laborers can sell the salmon in town and provide for their families during the lean winter months.

However, once the boat catches all the salmon it can hold and begins to sail back to Otaru, a strange negotiation begins as the supply of vegetables run out and the workers start to suffer from scurvy, a disease that threatens their lives. Out of thin air, the captain of the ship produces a barrel of apples. He then offers to exchange the apples for the salmon that the owner had promised the workers as payment. If the workers could trade just one salmon for one apple, the humiliation would have been less but the ship's captain demands that the workers trade three salmon for an apple. In the end, the workers return to Otaru with nothing to show for their exhausting work except their lives, and the fisheries owner has a shipload of salmon that cost him next to nothing in labor costs.

Having told his story, the man then says that the fisheries are recruiting workers again to fish for salmon, but this time, he and his fellow seasonal laborers will join forces and take the apples from the captain and his crew. Abruptly, the man became suspicious and began to question the narrator as to whether he could trust him narrator with his plan. In the next moment, he brusquely pushes aside the narrator's coat collar, revealing the Nihon Rōdō Kumiai (Japan Congress of Labor Unions) union badge on the narrator's undershirt. At the same time, the man pulls open his own coat and uncovers the red ID badge of the Japan Sailors' and Stokers' Union on his t-shirt. At this, they both share a hearty laugh and shake hands. In this letter, the narrator informs his friend that they have succeeded in organizing more than 300 of the 1,200 dockworkers into a united labor union and hope to get more to join before the winter season of unemployment starts again.[8]

In "Apples," Hayashi underscores the actual exploitation of the workers, illustrating how the man was lured into the fishery owner's trap and explaining why the workers on the fishing boat submitted to such humiliation. As in "Fool," we have a third-person narrator, in this case, a student radical acting as a labor activist, writing to his friend about the story of a heroic worker. Unlike the young worker in "Fool," however, the narrator in

8. Fusao Hayashi, "Apples," in *For Dignity, Justice, and Revolution: An Anthology of Japanese Proletarian Literature*, ed. Heather Bowen-Struyk and Norma Field, trans. Jeff E. Long (Chicago: University of Chicago Press, 2016), 68–75.

"Apples" is already actively engaged in labor organization and does not need to be inspired to join the movement. He belongs to the Japan Congress of Labor Unions, as the end of the story reveals. Still, it is also obvious that the narrator admires the worker's decision to return to the fishing boat and fight the capitalists' manipulation of the workers. In "Apples," with the emphasis on the worker's tale of abuse, Hayashi gives us a more compelling account of why one should become part of a workers' union or enter the socialist movement. Since the young worker in "Fool" is looking back and giving us Moriyama's example that inspired him to join the radicals, the focus in the young man's account is on how Moriyama stood up to the bullies at work and met the police chief's challenge head on. Hayashi also highlights how Moriyama went about gaining support for a united printers union through study groups and preparing a rally to spread the word to other laborers. We learn little of what it was like to work in the printing factory itself. But in "Apples," we get a better look at the physical hardships the workers face on the fishing boat. Likewise, the narrator details the ship captain's manipulation of the situation surrounding the lack of fresh vegetables on board to take back the workers' "wages," as one by one the effects of scurvy ravage the seasonal workers.

Unlike in "Fool," where the narrator is more serious and nostalgic as he recalls his start in the socialist movement, the narrator in "Apples" conveys the experience to his friend through a letter, which suggests the desire to make the man's story accessible to others. The injection of humor into what could have been a rather gloomy story of worker exploitation makes the tale entertaining not only for the friend reading the letter, but also for the audience of the short story as well. As we noted in Chapter 3, this becomes one of the key characteristics of Hayashi's appeal to the readers. Rather than apply a strict "realist" approach to writing a story in which the author simply recounts the brutal mistreatment of the workers scene for scene, the narrator establishes the closeness of the human relationship between the student labor organizer and the dockworker before moving into the tale of abuse onboard the ship.

However, in their review of "Apples," Hayashi's fellow proletarian writers were less sanguine regarding his desire to entertain. On a theoretical level, the infusion of passion and humor into the story of "Apples" reflected Hayashi's method of using literature as a means to convey Marxist theory to his readers. His description of the social injustices involved in the

Hokkaidō salmon fisheries echoed previous literary efforts, as in "A Picture Book without Pictures," for example, to invite the audience to identify with hardships confronting the proletariat. Nevertheless, there is a problem with this technique, as noted by Nakano Shigeharu and other members of the joint review group in their review of "Apples" in the November 1926 issue of *Bungei sensen*. The problem is that the emotional appeal of the story about apples overshadows the desired result of informing the readers about the need to organize into labor unions and challenge the bourgeois management.[9] While Nakano and others wanted Hayashi to stress the intellectual appeal of Marxist theory as a universal and rational way to cope with the social problems facing imperial Japan in the 1920s, Hayashi wanted to captivate readers with the gallant struggle of the workers against tyrannical oppression.[10] He wanted his stories to inspire others to act and to follow the lead of the workers, uniting with them to confront the inequities propagated by the Meiji state and the industrial capitalists in modern Japanese society. Thus, as Mizuno Yukiko observes, Hayashi's socialist literature often brought both its main characters and its readers to Marxism by drawing attention to the social injustices the working classes experienced in Taishō Japan.

Hayashi would build on this technique in his short story "Kōen no aibiki" ("Rendezvous in the park") published in the April 1926 issue of *Bungei sensen*.[11] Here the main character, Ueno Juntarō, becomes a policeman and he learns that the park on his regular beat has had a high number of public indecency incidents because it is a popular place for midnight rendezvous between lovers. The rest of the story revolves around Juntarō's repeated attempts to apprehend a pair of lovers in the act. In each case, he comes up with different plans to arrest a couple in the park, but every time he pounces on the suspects, he discovers they are either a group of recently laid-off workers or seasonal employees with no place to stay, who cannot afford regular lodgings on their pay, and instead sleep in the park. Hayashi's comical descriptions of Juntarō's machinations and the farcical outcomes of his efforts complement his work in "Apples." His use of wit in

9. Yamada Seizaburō and others, "Hayashi Fusaoron: sayoku bundan shinsakkaron, ni," *Bungei sensen* 3, no. 11 (November 1926): 75.

10. Mizuno Yukiko, "Hayashi Fusao kenkyū: 'E no nai ehon' o chūshin ni," *Shōwa bungaku kenkyū* 38 (March 1999): 10.

11. Hayashi Fusao, "Kōen no aibiki," *Bungei sensen* 3, no. 4 (April 1926): 48–54.

"Rendezvous in the Park" and "Apples" led established writer Kaneko Yōbun, in his survey of up-and-coming young writers, to call Hayashi an "intellectual humorist" (*chitekina yūmorusuto de aru*) of his day.[12]

Still, both "Apples" and "Rendezvous in the Park" underscore the serious theme of management's exploitation of seasonal laborers. While Hayashi uses humor, he does so to highlight the differences between perception and reality in certain relationships. For example, in "Rendezvous in the Park," the mocking depiction of policeman Ueno's efforts to seize a pair of lovers in the act reveals the policeman's lack of awareness of the real troubles that seasonal workers face in their efforts to provide for their families. As such, this short story underscores the state's attempts to modernize the economy without considering the dislocation and irreparable damage the move to industrial capitalism has caused the social unit of the family.

In "Apples," Hayashi employs irony to cast doubt on the relationship between the student radical and the seasonal laborer. He draws attention to the mutual suspicions that existed between the working classes and the educated student radicals as they worked together in the Socialist movement. He ultimately resolves the tensions between the student and the seasonal worker in the story, but the sections in the narrative detailing how they met and the worker's doubts about the student also set forth some precarious faultlines in this relationship. The worker's direct experiences of exploitation and physical hardship give him a different motivation to be involved in the movement, as opposed to the student radical's intellectual understanding of socialism and the ethically conscious need to organize labor to fight management's mistreatment of its workers. In "Apples," Hayashi highlights the slippage between theory and practice, a point that most likely spurred Nakano's critique of the short story: if what brings worker and student radical together in "Apples" is the desire to fight the injustice of this economic relationship, why not consider mutual agreement on the teachings of Marx or other left-wing theorists?

Hayashi's next major short story, "Cocoons," published in the July 1926 issue of *Kaihō*, would build on his mother's firsthand experiences in the silk mill. In this way, it works to gain the main character's (as well as

---

12. Kaneko Yōbun, "Dōnin zasshi ni miru shokubō subeki shinsakka," *Shinchō* 23, no. 10 (October 1926): 7.

the reader's) empathy for the dangerous working conditions and many hardships that the silk mill girls confronted at the factory. While combining elements of plot and style from "Fool" and "Apples," the narrative in "Cocoons" is perhaps the most lyrical of all Hayashi's proletarian fiction, contrasting the sentimental feelings of the narrator with the main character's sense of desperation to evoke an emotional response from the reader. As in "Fool," the story starts with a third person narrator, but instead of immediately setting the stage for the main character, the narrator waxes sentimental about the city person he has become. To introduce the story, he tells us that "Whenever I see cocoons[,] I am reminded of Yasuo Sakai."[13] In the text, a page break sets off this opening paragraph, and then our narrator recalls the story of his best friend Sakai from middle school. We learn that Sakai is uncommonly intelligent but poor, and that the narrator regularly helps him by paying Sakai's school fees with his own money. Next, the narrator reflects on his memories of Sakai, framing each recollection with an experience longer and more complex than the previous, with each section set apart from the other by page breaks.

The story progresses from metaphor to realism to romanticism and propaganda. With each memory, the story underlines the destructive influence of industrial capitalism on Sakai's family. Then it describes Sakai's attempts to confront the social and economic inequality arising from this economic system. In his first memory of Sakai, the narrator recounts their experiences playing up in the hills overlooking the school. Here, through the metaphor of a snake devouring a frog, Hayashi develops the political theme of the state's victimization of Japanese society. In the first scene, which hearkens back to Hayashi's penning of "Snake" while a middle

13. Fusao Hayashi, "Cocoons," in *The Cannery Boat and Other Japanese Short Stories* (New York: International Publishers, 1933; reprint, AMS Press, 1970), 255 (page citations are to the reprint edition). This work is now available online thru the HathiTrust Digital Library: http://babel.hathitrust.org/cgi/pt?id=mdp.39015011421032. While the translator of "Cocoons," or of any of the other short stories in the book for that matter, has not been listed, we now know that William Maxwell Bickerton who taught English in Japan at the time translated these works; see Norma Field's explanation in *For Dignity, Justice, and Revolution: An Anthology of Japanese Proletarian Literature*, ed. Heather Bowen-Struyk and Norma Field (Chicago: University of Chicago Press, 2016), 104. For more information on Bickerton's role in the Japanese proletarian literature movement, see Fujio Kano and Maurice Ward, "Socialism Is a Mission: Max Bickerton's Involvement with the Japanese Communist Party and Translation of Japanese Proletarian Literature in the 1930s," *New Zealand Journal of Asian Studies* 16, no. 2 (December 2014): 99–120.

school student, the narrator describes a snake swallowing a frog it has caught, and then Sakai killing the snake and releasing the dead frog from its grasp.[14] Next, the narrator tells the story of Sakai's fight against Ōkawa, the scion of the town's silk mill owner. The narrator sets the scene in the same place Sakai ran across the snake killing the frog, immediately connecting the two scenes. Then, in pitting Ōkawa the school bully and two cronies against Sakai for not showing enough respect to his school seniors, the narrator makes clear who the snake is and who the frog is. However, Sakai fights back and even pulls out a penknife and stabs Ōkawa to stop the gang's attack on his person.[15] In this metaphor, the narrator views Sakai as a proletarian hero ready to struggle against inequality in both the natural and the human worlds. Even so, Sakai does not take pleasure in the battle, and the narrator finds him dejected after the confrontation. He also wonders out loud why Sakai keeps a silkworm inside his school desk.[16]

In the next section, metaphor turns to reality as Sakai invites the narrator to go into town with him. Sakai takes the narrator to a silk mill to meet his mother; she wants to thank the narrator for all he has done to help her son at school. On their way back to the dormitory, Sakai tells the narrator about his early life. He explains how he and his mother were reduced to poverty once his father died, and how his mother, much older than the other mill girls, took the job in the silk mill to pay his middle school fees so that he could continue his education. Although he was uncomfortable staying in school knowing that his mother was suffering, Sakai reveals that she was counting on him to finish his education and make something of himself to restore the family fortunes.[17] In this way, the narrator establishes the events that led to the economic exploitation of Sakai's family and his mother's sacrifice so that he could pursue his education.

Sakai then informs the narrator of his other reason for taking him to the mill. He wanted to explain to his friend why he acted the way he did after the showdown with Ōkawa. He reveals to the narrator that he had been miserable because he was disappointed in himself for having attacked Ōkawa over "a personal grievance."[18] Ōkawa always makes fun of

14. Hayashi, "Cocoons," 256.
15. Ibid., 257.
16. Ibid., 258.
17. Ibid., 260.
18. Ibid., 261.

him since his mother worked for Ōkawa's father, so he should have ignored the bullying. He also realizes that he possibly has made work for his mother more difficult by harming Ōkawa, the son of the mill owner. With the narrator's help, Sakai comes to recognize that his mother's work keeps him in school where he can study in order to achieve his mother's goal, which is to improve the family's status through his education. In wounding the son of a capitalist, he may have endangered his mother and obstructed her dreams for him, thus pointing out the immense difficulty for the poor to improve their place in society and the great cost it takes to succeed in this society.

Again, Hayashi implicates the role of industrial capitalism in destroying the traditional Japanese family system. Sakai becomes a flawed hero in Hayashi's "Cocoons," hoping to use his mental capabilities to restore the family fortunes and confront the social inequality facing him, yet eventually resorting to violence to drive away Ōkawa and his goons. In this memory, the narrator exposes the contradictions that force Sakai to overcome his birth into poverty by attending middle school and making use of his intellect. Still, Ōkawa's verbal slights also drive Sakai to attack the very leaders of this social system that allows his mother to work, that might potentially allow Sakai to improve his place as well as his family's standing in society.

In the narrator's final memory of Sakai, he wraps the call to action in a sentimental and reflective conclusion to the story. Occurring a couple of years after the narrator's second memory, they are together in high school when Sakai's worst fears come true. They are up in the hills talking about their lives when Sakai tells the narrator that he still has his white cocoon, and the narrator asks if his mother is still working in the mill. Sakai answers that she will not leave until he finishes school. Sakai further reveals his changing perspective on life, driven by his misgivings about the harsh reality of factory life for the mill girls. He has personally witnessed the mill girls withering away like boiled cocoons, as the factory owner gets richer and richer. What's more, he knows that his mother will not leave the mill until Sakai has restored the family name and fortune. But as long as his mother is in the mill, Sakai worries that her life is in danger, just like the other mill girls. The narrator relates that Sakai's premonition of his mother's demise finally becomes a reality just as they are about to graduate high school. The narrator lends Sakai money for the train fare home and sees him off at the train station. He then shares the contents of a letter Sakai sends him a week later.

In the letter, Sakai tells the narrator about his mother's funeral. A few of the mill girls had braved the threats by the mill foreman and skipped work to say a final farewell to his mother, but many others were too afraid to show up. Here, having set forth an emotionally laden background, the narrator at the end of the story finally makes his argument for others to join the fight against capitalism as Sakai divulges that he will not return to school to graduate. During the funeral, he realized that his mother's death was not just a local problem, but also a result of greater historical forces at work: "Sitting before this urn, my thoughts turn to *the system,* which silently, with subtle force, destroyed my mother's life. The cocoons get thinner, the reels fatter—the dead black body of the grub" (italics mine).[19] Moreover, Sakai declares to the narrator that he has discovered another path for his life, one that, unlike his cowardly attack on Ōkawa over a private matter, is an honorable fight: "There was not only one cocoon. My mother was not the only sufferer. In this land of ours alone, how many millions, no, tens of millions of human beings, like the cocoons in the boiling water, were having their lifeblood sucked away from them? It may sound funny to you to say it abruptly like this. But I know the enemy I have to fight."[20]

Our narrator ends with a Marxist rationale for confronting and struggling with those who perpetuate the industrial capitalist system: the Meiji state and those capitalists who reap the benefits from this economic system. With a final word, Sakai ends the letter by telling the narrator to take the white cocoon from his desk and keep it as a memento of his mother.[21] After a page break, the narrator notes that it must have been ten years ago that he received this letter from Sakai. Even though he now lives in the city, whenever he does see cocoons it still takes him back to that time. He then asserts somewhat altruistically that "there is no need of cocoons to remind me of Sakai now. I, too, have joined the ranks of those he calls "Comrades!"[22]

In essence, much like the plot in "Fool," we have the origin story of a young "comrade." The narrator has joined the socialist movement largely

19. Hayashi, "Cocoons," 265.
20. Ibid.
21. Ibid., 266.
22. Ibid.

due to the influence of another, but the similarities end there. Unlike Moriyama who is a mentor figure, Yasuo Sakai is a friend, one the narrator respects, and their relationship is a parallel one with its gives and takes. While the narrator is better off financially than Sakai and regularly aids him when he needs money, he acknowledges that Sakai is much better at schoolwork. Likewise, Sakai's difficult circumstances lead him down the path to socialism more readily than the narrator. Even where it is depicted that city life has distanced the narrator from the changing of the seasons and the natural world of his rural upbringing, he seems much less motivated to join the cause and more animated by sentimentalism throughout the story. Additionally, the narrator seems more in control of his emotions, while Sakai fluctuates between anguish and anger, lashing out at the bully Ōkawa, yet repeatedly despairing over his mother's sacrifice in the silk mill. We do not learn as much about Moriyama in "Fool" as we do in about the life of Yasuo Sakai in "Cocoons." Sakai is referred to by his full name in the opening paragraph, and the narrator is drawn to Sakai because of his classmate's temperament and personal history, both of which are fleshed out in more detail than Moriyama's character in "Fool." From what we read in this account, at least, the narrator comes to socialism based on his observations of Sakai's tormented life. He also witnesses the terrible toll that the industrial capitalist system takes on Sakai's mother while she worked in the silk mill, rather than from any formal actions Sakai took as a socialist. At the end of the tale it is clear that the narrator has had little contact with Sakai over the last ten years so it is Sakai's personal life, not his political example, that has inspired the narrator to join in another equivalent relationship with Sakai. This time instead of being his school friend, the narrator has become Sakai's "comrade" in the left-wing movement.

The story in "Cocoons" shares much with the organization of "Apples," particularly in emphasizing why one should join the socialist movement. However, there are significant differences between the two stories. Much of the lyrical appeal in "Cocoons" derives from both Hayashi's detailed description of the silk mill and his investment in the characters of Sakai and his mother. Nowhere in "Apples," or "Fool" for that matter, do we have an account of the factory floor as elaborate as the one in "Cocoons." In the scene where Sakai introduces the narrator to his mother, he describes what happens to the cocoons once they enter the modern silk mill, an outcome that foreshadows the fate of the mill girls handling the cocoons:

> Inside the mill, murky with steam and dark like the inside of a kitchen on a rainy day, the old-fashioned spindles turned noisily. The foul smell of dead grubs and the heavy humid air almost suffocated you. Before each girl stood two pots full of boiling water, one big and one small; in the small pot white cocoons kept bobbing up and down. One or two boiled cocoons would be transferred by the girl's hand into the bigger pot and, as they danced round in the hot water, they gradually became thinner. At the same time an almost invisible thread passed from them, above the girls' heads, and was wound round the droning spindles behind. With the revolutions of the belt the reels of silk became fatter and the cocoons thinner. When one cocoon had been completely unwound, the little black grub would appear floating dead on the surface.[23]

Sakai eventually comes to view the cocoons' fate as a metaphor for the future of the young women who work in the mill, a point he makes to the narrator later in the story:

> "Lately I've begun to have doubts about life," he said. "For instance, take that mill: now there are about three hundred girls working there. They're mostly from fifteen to twenty-four years of age, all farmers' daughters from the neighboring villages. When they arrive they're young, country girls with good strong bodies, but after a year or two they begin bandaging up their throats and coughing suspiciously; their eyes become red and swollen, and their fingers whitish and rotten, and then they return home. Some of them wither and die while in the mill, and you hear sometimes of girls getting their hair caught in the machines.
>
> The humid air; the long hours from morning right on into the night; insufficient food—when I see those girls under such conditions, wearing out their young bodies before my very eyes, I think of the kettles and of the cocoons which the girls reel.
>
> Each one, boiled in the hot water, becoming thinner and thinner; its life drained from it by that single invisible thread, until finally the black grub—now a useless dead thing—is cast up on the surface of the water.
>
> But on the other hand—and this is what you've got to notice, isn't [it] ... —exactly corresponding to the reels winding and winding above the girls['] heads [are] a group of men who grow continually fatter and fatter![24]

23. Hayashi, "Cocoons," 259.
24. Ibid., 262–263.

Finally, the fate of the cocoons and the mill girls becomes personal when Sakai finds that his mother has passed away, leaving him with neither the means nor the will to finish higher school or to attend university as she had wished. He joins the socialist movement to get back at the industrial capitalist system that took his mother's life and to protect the other mill girls who have very little say in their lives, much less about the factory conditions under which they work.[25] The narrator, through his personal experiences with Sakai that included meeting his mother and owing to Sakai's firsthand portrayal of life in the silk mill, is convinced to join the left-wing movement. He becomes one of Sakai's "comrades," just as Hayashi hopes that readers would get caught up in the wave of emotion running through "Cocoons," commiserate with the silk mill workers' plight; and perhaps, much as he had, contribute to the noble cause of the socialist movement. What sets the narrative in "Cocoons" apart from the seasonal worker's tale of abuse in "Apples" is, first, the personal nature of the relationships depicted between Sakai and his mother as well as the friendship between the narrator and Sakai. Moreover, Hayashi's intimate knowledge of the silk mill and the method of manufacturing silk separates these two stories. He leaves us with a tale of brutal exploitation, which he romanticizes in the narrator's memory. There it becomes a pivotal, yet sentimental period of maturation, much different from the unpredictable and often hilarious relationship portrayed in "Apples" between the narrator and the seasonal laborer.

While acknowledging these differences, what links these stories is Hayashi's emphasis on purity. Throughout the story in "Fool," the narrator portrays Moriyama as a dedicated leader of this cause. Still, more important to the narrator, whom he protects, mentors, and guides, it seems that Moriyama has a pure heart, and Hayashi depicts him as an ideal leader for the Socialist movement. In "Apples," the emphasis is on the pristine setting of Hokkaidō, the honest work, the straightforward hearts of the seasonal workers, and the nutritional value of these perfect apples. In the end, it is the chicanery of the ship owners and the brazen onboard negotiation of the captain and his officers with the workers that compromise and threaten the purity of the apples and the seasonal workers. Thus, in "Fool," Hayashi condemns the police for their role in repressing workers,

25. Hayashi, "Cocoons," 265.

a theme he continues in "Rendezvous in the Park." In "Apples" and "Cocoons," respectively, he changes his focus to the role of capitalists and their accomplices in spoiling those perfect Hokkaidō apples, and in turning the white silkworms into dead, black grubs. Moreover, the capitalists manipulate and exploit the labor of those long-suffering seasonal workers in both "Apples" and in "Rendezvous in the Park," and the factory owner harms and contributes to the death of Sakai's mother in "Cocoons." She is someone with pure intentions, sacrificing herself in the silk mill so that her son can gain an education and restore the family name. From a political perspective, Hayashi's proletarian short stories from this period reflect the main character types of Marxist works. However, they are also grounded in an emotional call for public action to cease the sullying of those pure hearts of the workers, and to end the marring of those pure natural products that industrial capitalists' harvest, manufacture, and then sell for a profit after taking advantage of the workers' hard labor. Read from the viewpoint of leadership, these stories construct romantic factory-worker, student-radical, and labor-activist heroes who strive to overcome their circumstances and to fight for social and economic justice.

HAYASHI FUSAO'S TIME IN PRISON

Hayashi's depiction of leadership figures changed considerably in his proletarian short stories after his release from detention in Kyoto. This shift to a romantic portrayal of proletarian heroes is different from Hayashi's satire of leadership in "New Aesop's Fables," which he published just after his release from detention. Hayashi wrote "Cocoons" while sitting in a Kyoto detention cell. Thinking that his mother must be having a hard time because he was in jail, Hayashi writes in his "Literary Memoirs" that he wrote "Cocoons" at a feverish pace, whether he was in his cell or some office, and even when guards were standing watch over him.[26] Hayashi entrusted "Cocoons," along with "A Picture Book without Pictures," to Fujimori Seikichi who came down from the New Man Society's Tokyo headquarters in Ueno's Sakuragichō to receive the manuscripts.[27] Fujimori

26. Hayashi, "Bungakuteki jijōden," 340.

27. Hayashi, "Fu: Hayashi Fusao nenpu," 452. Hayashi had actually written "A Picture Book without Pictures" before "Apples" and "Cocoons," but the editors of *Bungei sensen*

had "Cocoons" published in the July 1926 issue of *Kaihō* and "A Picture Book without Pictures" published in the earlier May issue of *Shinshōsetsu*. Hayashi received seventy *yen* for "A Picture Book without Pictures" and thirty *yen* for "Cocoons."[28] Fujimori made sure the money went to Hayashi's mother to help with her living expenses. At the time, she was living in Tokyo acting as housemother of the New Man Society dormitory. Hayashi had moved his mother from Ōita to Tokyo to live with him in the dormitory when his father passed away in 1924. She knew nothing about communism or Marxism, but her presence added a touch of warmth to the otherwise cold and austere setting of the dormitory.[29]

One reason for the change may have been Hayashi's interaction with the police and the courts, which did not end in 1926. In May 1927 the Kyoto District Court convicted Hayashi and the other students of violating the Peace Preservation Law. Evidence brought against Hayashi included his participation in the deliberation on and the drafting of the Student Federation platform that the Second Congress adopted during its July 1925 meeting.[30] Judges at Kyoto's district court determined the platform to be subversive in its ideological origins and its intent; they ruled that Hayashi's role in creating the platform was a violation of the law. Lawyers for the students appealed the decision, and the case against Hayashi and a few others arrested in the affair became a long, drawn-out matter. Upon his conviction, however, the administration at Tokyo Imperial University took steps to expel Hayashi officially from the Law Department, and the three other New Man Society members arrested with him, Kore'eda Kyōji, Murao Satsuo, and Matsumoto Tokuichi, from the Humanities Department.[31]

---

published "Apples" earlier, making it his first published short story. Fujimori Seikichi would go on to become a well-known writer in the proletarian literature movement after graduating from Tokyo Imperial University.

28. Hayashi, "Fu: Hayashi Fusao nenpu," 452. Hayashi writes in his "Literary Memoirs" from 1935 that he received no money for "Cocoons"; but in "Biographical Sketch" published in 1968, Hayashi recalls that he did receive thirty *yen* for publishing "Cocoons."

29. Kawamori, "Hayashi Fusao den," 7. An image of Hayashi's mother working as the house mother of the New Man Society dormitory appears in Nakano Shigeharu's autobiographical work, *Muragimo* (*Gut Feelings*), published in 1954.

30. Mitchell, *Thought Control in Prewar Japan*, 76.

31. Ishidō Kiyotomo and Tateyama Toshitada, eds., *Tokyo Teidai Shinjinkai no kiroku* (Tokyo: Keizai ōraisha, 1976), 390.

The Osaka Court of Appeals upheld Hayashi's conviction in December of 1929 and sentenced him to a two-year prison term. He received a much lighter sentence than former students who had joined the outlawed Japanese Communist Party in the meantime and whom the police had rearrested in the March 1928 and April 1929 roundups of party members. Nine of the former students appealed the case to the Japanese Supreme Court, which on May 27, 1930, upheld the conviction and ordered them to begin serving their sentences.[32] From July 1930 to April 1932, Hayashi served one year and nine months of his sentence for violating the Peace Preservation Law. During that time the authorities moved him from Ichigaya to Chiba and finally to Toyotama prison. While awaiting the Supreme Court's decision, police rearrested Hayashi in the spring of 1930 on charges of illegally providing financial support to the communist party. This incident is known as the *Kyōsantō Shinpa Jiken* (Japanese Communist Party Sympathizers' Incident). Government officials designed the Peace Preservation Law to isolate the party and, as Yasuhiro Okudaira has pointed out, one means of accomplishing this goal was for the government to punish those who attempted to aid the party.[33] Consequently, in May of 1930, the police arrested several members of the proletarian literature movement, including Hayashi, Kobayashi Takiji, and Nakano Shigeharu for donating money to the party. During that same time, they also arrested several university professors, including Miki Kiyoshi (Hōsei University), Hirano Yoshitarō (Tokyo Imperial University, Law Department), and Yamada Moritarō (Tokyo Imperial University, Economics Department), for aiding the party.[34] Because of Hayashi's previous arrest, the court eventually sentenced him to a one-year prison sentence in 1934.[35] Hayashi served this sentence from November 1934 to November 1935 in Shizuoka prison.

Indisputably, Hayashi's experiences in prison affected his decision to distance himself from the Marxist literature movement after 1926. His nonstop internal struggles with the proletarian literature movement's leadership also had a considerable impact on his subsequent departure

32. Komori Kei, ed., *Shōwa shisō tōseishi shiryō: bekkan (jō) shisō tōseishi kenkyū hikkei* (Tokyo: Seikatsusha, 1981), 689.

33. Yasuhiro Okudaira, "Some Preparatory Notes for the Study of the Peace Preservation Law in Pre-War Japan," *Annals of the Institute of Social Science*, no. 14 (1973): 68.

34. *Tokyo Asahi shinbun*, 20 May 1931, *gōgai* (special edition), p. 1. The government placed a one-year moratorium on the release of this information about the Japanese Communist Party Sympathizers' Incident to the public.

35. Mōri Toshio, "Hayashi Fusao no shōgai oyobi bungakuteki sōzō," 138, 140.

from the movement. Through the various permutations of the movement and changes to its leadership group, Hayashi began to use his proletarian short stories to critique the left-wing cultural movement's leaders and its members. In his works of literary criticism from these years, he writes that he refused to subordinate his creative writing style to the political demands of the proletarian literary movement's leaders. He believed proletarian literature needed protecting from those political forces—this time from the authority of the Japanese Communist Party and Stalinism—that sought to subsume and to subordinate its distinctive characteristics under Stalin and the Comintern's greater political goals. From this perspective, the satire of leadership in "New Aesop's Fables" marked a distinct shift in Hayashi's proletarian short stories from the autumn of 1926 into 1929.

5

Literature as Political Staging Ground

Defining Factory Workers, Student Radicals, and Labor Organizers in Hayashi Fusao's Proletarian Literature

> Prologue
>
> There seems to be no way around it. —In the textile mill, there's lint. In the paper mill, there's scrap paper. Among humans, there's human trash. So in the socialist movement, there must also be socialist trash. —We can't get away from human trash, scrap paper, and lint. ...
>
> Epilogue
>
> Scrap paper goes into the trash can. Lint goes into the trash can. There is no other place for human trash except for the wastebasket of history. You damned fools! Get the hell out of the socialist movement. Scram!
>
> —"Kuzu"

From September 1926 on, Hayashi became a full-time writer in the proletarian literature movement, but two professional experiences greatly transformed his writing from romanticizing to defining the appropriate behavior and actions of the worker, student radical, and labor organizer in his short stories. First, his early encounters with the supporters of theorist Fukumoto Kazuo's ideas, in and out of the proletarian literature movement, proved hostile, marginalizing him in both the movement's political

---

Hayashi Fusao, "Kuzu," *Bungei shijō* 3, no. 2 (February 1927): 63, 69.

and cultural realms during the mid-1920s. Likewise, he struggled with the communist leadership of the proletarian cultural movement over the much-debated issue of the relationship of politics to literature during the later 1920s, which eventually led him out of the proletarian literature movement altogether by the 1930s. In the short stories we examined in Chapter 4, we found Hayashi identifying the ideal factory worker, student radical, and labor organizer as open, honest, hardworking, often naïve, and loyal to friends and the movement. These traits characterized his formative experiences with the political and cultural organizations of the left-wing movement; thus, he came to cherish, admire, and want to preserve them in his own short stories, if not in the organization of the Leftist movement.

However, as we find in the epigraph taken from his short story "Kuzu" ("Trash"), Hayashi began to use his literature as a political weapon. Written in the months after his detention in Kyoto, in this story he began to attack and attempt to force out the writers with whom he had disagreements, as if he had been charged with taking the trash out to the garbage can. As distasteful as this metaphorical assault is, the theme and tenor of his proletarian short stories shifted dramatically when he was a full-time member of the proletarian cultural movement. During these years, he vehemently denounced writers associated with the Japanese Communist Party who ultimately gained control of shaping policy within the movement. In this chapter, we examine first the issues that fueled Hayashi's political fight against the communist leadership of the proletarian literature movement. Second, we trace how he wrote his proletarian short stories to define who he thought should be part of the movement and then to highlight how those members as representatives should conduct themselves within and outside the movement.

ON THE BATTLEGROUND OF POLITICS AND LITERATURE

Hayashi and members of the Japanese Communist Party interacted frequently, but Hayashi never became a party member. As noted in Chapter 3, he argued that because Fukumoto Kazuo criticized his theoretical writings in 1926, he chose literature over politics. Fortunately, for Hayashi, the proletarian literature movement was on the upswing with the revival of the journal *Bungei sensen* in June 1925. Historically, the proletarian literature movement originated in February 1921 when Komaki Ōmi, who had just returned from a period of study in Paris, founded and published the first volume of the journal *Tanemaku hito* from his home in Akita prefecture. Once Komaki relocated the journal to Tokyo, he expanded the size of the editorial staff as the journal's readership grew. Influenced by the socialist and anarchist thought of Kōtoku Shūsui and Ōsugi Sakae at home, and Kropotkin and Bukharin abroad, the journal's writers contributed articles on the social problems facing Japan, and on theoretical problems facing the acceptance of proletarian literature in Japan.[1] Any momentum gained by the movement, however, ended with the "radical" scare that followed the Great Kantō Earthquake on September 1, 1923. At that time, mobs attacked socialists and Koreans who were alleged to be plotting against the Japanese people. *Tanemaku hito* folded in that same month, but its former leaders revived the journal in the spring of 1924. Despite changing the name to *Bungei sensen*, the journal published issues until January 1925 when the members could no longer draw enough readers to keep the journal afloat financially.

When *Bungei sensen* resurfaced in June of 1925, the leadership of the journal aimed to reenergize the socialist cultural movement by expanding the scope of literary contributors to the journal. As part of this change in policy, the editors began seeking articles from sources outside their normal circle of writers. One place they searched for promising talent was the radical student movement on university campuses. Hayashi's first contributions were pieces of literary criticism on the new generation of proletarian writers and on Akutagawa Ryūnosuke's "Shuju no kotoba" ("A Foolish Man's Words").[2] Hayashi kept writing articles for *Bungei sensen* almost every month even after his release, becoming a regular contributor to the journal.[3]

With its new start, members of *Bungei sensen* pointed out two chal-

1. G.T. Shea, *Leftwing Literature in Japan: A Brief History of the Proletarian Literary Movement* (Tokyo: The Hōsei University Press, 1964), 86–87.

2. Hayashi Fusao, "Shinjidai tenbō," *Bungei sensen* 2, no. 3 (July 1925): 2–3, and Hayashi Fusao, "Shuju no kotoba," *Bungei sensen* 2, no. 4 (August 1925): 6–7. The title of Hayashi's second article was a pun on the title of Akutagawa's story and meant literally "sundry words."

3. Kawamori Yoshizō, "Hayashi Fusao den," in *Hayashi Fusao, Shimaki Kensaku*, vol. 28, Gendai Nihon bungakukan, ed. Kobayashi Hideo (Tokyo: Bungei shunjū, 1969), 8.

lenges that would dominate the time and energies of the movement from 1925 until its end in 1934. First, they needed to establish and maintain an organization where proletarian writers could meet and debate the burning issues of the day; second, they needed to clarify the relationship between politics and literature.[4] Several writers made proposals to establish a proletarian writer's league in the fall of 1925, but perhaps the strongest stimulus to organize came from outside Japan. At the Fifth General Meeting of the Comintern in July 1924, proletarian writers from the Soviet Union made an international appeal for proletarian writers around the world to organize and unite. Their appeal and the plans of the *Bungei sensen* writers came to fruition when on December 6, 1925, over one hundred people met to establish the Nihon Puroretaria Bungei Renmei (Japan Proletarian Literary Arts League), known informally among its members as Puroren (Proletarian League).

In the inaugural meeting that December, Hayashi records that the members of Proletarian League elected him to the central committee of the group.[5] His acceptance into the upper echelons of the *Bungei sensen* group facilitated the development of a close relationship between a literary group he had helped to start at Tokyo Imperial University, the Marxist Arts Study Group, and the writers at *Bungei sensen*.[6] The editor-in-chief of *Bungei sensen*, Yamada Seizaburō, and writers such as Sasaki Takamaru (also elected the chairperson of the Proletarian League's central committee) and Hayama Yoshiki from the journal, joined the Marxist Arts Study Group when it formed in early 1926. The close ties between the two groups paved the way for other students in the Marxist Arts Study Group, like Nakano Shigeharu, to have their works published in the journal. More significantly, it allowed members of the Marxist Arts Study Group to play a major role in the organizational and theoretical development of the left-wing literature group.

By establishing a broad alliance among writers whose main political frame of reference was anticapitalism, the leaders of the Proletarian League had sacrificed organizational and theoretical direction for inclusiveness. Members of the League aired their differences of political view-

---

4. Shea, *Leftwing Literature in Japan*, 132.

5. Hayashi, "Hayashi Fusao nenpu," 451. For a list of those elected to the Proletarian League's first central committee, see Shea, *Leftwing Literature in Japan*, 135.

6. Shea, *Leftwing Literature in Japan*, 132–133.

points in the pages of *Bungei sensen* throughout 1926, to the extent that the journal, supposedly devoted to "cultural" affairs, became a battleground for political theory.[7] Disagreements among the members reached a climax at the Second General Meeting in November 1926, when members of the Marxist Arts Study Group joined the proceedings in force and helped to form a separate faction among the writers. This faction advocated that Marxism become the guiding theory of the Proletarian League, and several of its members, including Nakano Shigeharu, Hisaita Eijirō, and Yanase Masamu, were elected to serve on the League's new central committee.[8] Combined with Hayashi, Sasaki, and Yamada (elected to be the chairperson of the central committee), they succeeded in gaining control of the meeting and pushing those writers who believed in anarchist, syndicalist, and other forms of socialism out of the group. To symbolize its new beginning, the members of the Proletarian League voted to change its name from Nihon Puroretaria Bungei Renmei to Nihon Puroretaria Geijutsu Renmei (Japan Proletarian Arts League). They called the new group Purogei (Proletarian Arts) for short and retained *Bungei sensen* as Proletarian Arts' official journal.

Fukumoto Kazuo's Cadre in the Proletarian Literature Movement

Infighting on the issue of political viewpoint within the proletarian literature movement meant constant change and reorganization among proletarian writers. The next major breakup began in March 1927 over the introduction of Fukumoto Kazuo's political theory into the movement. Until then, Yamakawa Hitoshi's ideas largely guided the Japanese Communist Party.[9] A member of the first Japanese Communist Party from

---

7. Yoshio Iwamoto, "Aspects of the Proletarian Literary Movement in Japan," in *Japan in Crisis: Essays on Taishō Democracy*, ed. Bernard S. Silberman and H.D. Harootunian (Princeton: Princeton University Press, 1974), 162. Most scholars trace the initial theoretical effort to make the proletarian literature movement a Marxist movement back to literary critic Aono Suekichi's essay in the September 1926 edition of *Bungei sensen*, "Shizen seichō to mokuteki ishiki." See Shea, *Leftwing Literature in Japan*, 137–140.

8. See Odagiri Susumu, ed. *Gendai Nihon bungei sōran: uemaki* (Tokyo: Meiji bunken, 1969), 719, for a list of the new central committee members and those whom the leadership of Proletarian Arts purged from the league.

9. The debate between the Marxist ideas of Yamakawa and Fukumoto, which has been raised to the status of "isms" in Japanese: Yamakawaism versus Fukumotoism is covered widely even in the English-language press. For the best summary of the debate and its

1922 to 1924, Yamakawa incorporated the empirical conditions of Japan into his understanding of Marxism and argued in broad terms that Japan had already undergone its bourgeois revolution during the Meiji Restoration. Therefore, it needed to prepare for a one-step proletarian revolution against the bourgeoisie and Japan's capitalist government. Structurally, he argued, the best way to prepare for this revolution was for party members to mix with and become part of the proletariat and expand the struggle to include the peasants and the intelligentsia. From its inception, the inclusive and pragmatic nature of Yamakawa's call for a proletarian party, one that was part of the masses, resonated with the membership of the Proletarian League and its attacks on capitalism from all socialist fronts.

Fukumoto, on the other hand, argued that the development of a proper class-consciousness among the proletariat in Japan must be the priority. Throughout 1925 and 1926, Fukumoto called for a restructuring of the Japanese Communist Party so that it could become the elite, vanguard group to carry on the theoretical struggle for ideological purity and to develop a "correct" understanding of Marxism. First, the party members must separate the false Marxists from the others before they attempted to guide the masses. Only then could the Japanese Communist Party lead the two-step revolution, guiding the proletariat and helping them to build a true bourgeois democracy in Japan. At that point, the party could help the masses carry out the proletarian revolution, Fukumoto argued.

When Fukumoto and others met to reconstitute the Japanese Communist Party formally in December 1926, the other members recognized him as the party's theoretical leader. What he brought to the Japanese Marxist movement was a Leninist perspective on the role of the communist party in the proletarian revolution. While radical students and members of the party had translated and read Lenin's works to some extent, Fukumoto was the first Japanese scholar to succeed in applying Lenin's interpretation of Marxism and theory of political action to the Japanese situation. He also was the first to popularize Marxism-Leninism on a large scale in Japan. Starting in December 1924, Fukumoto spread his

---

significance within the Japan Communist Party, see George M. Beckmann and Okubo Genji, *The Japanese Communist Party 1922–1945* (Stanford: Stanford University Press, 1969), 107–137. For its significance in the left-wing student movement, see Smith, *Japan's First Student Radicals*, 162–185, and within the proletarian literature movement, see Shea, *Leftwing Literature in Japan*, 137–152.

ideas through the articles he published in *Marukusushugi*. In these articles, he criticized Kawakami Hajime's writings on Marxist economics, explained dialectical materialism to left-wing students, and questioned Yamakawa's theory concerning the Japanese Communist Party's organizational strategy.[10]

Within the socialist literary group, the students in the Marxist Arts Study Group were the first to come under the influence of Fukumoto's ideas on political party organization, and to apply them when they established a vanguard faction to take over the league of proletarian writers in November 1926. By this time, Nakano Shigeharu and Kaji Wataru had become the leaders of the Marxist Arts Study Group, which disbanded officially when its members took control of Proletarian Arts. Subsequently, they began to concentrate their energies on guiding the proletarian literature movement.[11] Under Fukumoto's influence, Nakano and Kaji believed that literature should reflect the political views of the communist party and serve as a propaganda machine to instigate a revolution in the Japanese literary world. Nakano interpreted this to mean that the writer was a warrior who used words as his weapon to carry revolution into the world of print. Thus, the writing of literature was a political act done with revolutionary intent. It aimed to create an image of a proletarian world that would displace the images of the capitalist world sold by the mass media.[12]

Once Fukumoto's cadre gained control of the Marxist cultural movement, they began a sustained attack on those writers who resisted the application of Fukumoto's political theory to literature. Hayashi drew their attention for several reasons. First, those belonging to Fukumoto's cadre labeled him an advocate of Yamakawa's vision of the Japanese left-wing movement, a vision that viewed the communist party "as an intellectual vanguard for spreading the truths of Marxism-Leninism, but not as an active political agent."[13] Although Hayashi denied being a follower

10. Smith, *Japan's First Student Radicals*, 166–168.

11. Hayashi states that from his standpoint Nakano had taken the lead of the Marxist Arts Study Group by the time that Proletarian Arts came into being in "Narupu kaisan zengo to '*tenkō*' no mondai," 56. Tomone Matsumoto asserts that the Marxist Arts Study Group dissolved into Proletarian Arts in her dissertation, "From Marxism to Japanism: A Study of Kamei Katsuichirō (1907–1967)" (Ph.D. diss., University of Arizona, 1979), 66.

12. Miriam Silverberg, *Changing Song*, 79–80.

13. Beckmann, *The Japanese Communist Party 1922–1945*, 54.

of Yamakawa, many within the radical student movement considered him to be under Yamakawa's influence. Japanese intellectual historian Tsurumi Shunsuke points to Hayashi's early literary activity in the Marxist Arts Study Group, in the Proletarian League, and the Proletarian Arts group, and in his early works published in *Bungei sensen*—Yamakawa had influenced these groups initially—to explain why leaders of the communist party linked his writing with Yamakawa's views.[14]

Besides Hayashi's early works and his involvement with these groups, Tsurumi also points to Fukumoto's criticism of Hayashi's theoretical works in *Marukusushugi*. For several of Hayashi's fellow New Man Society members who had since joined the Japanese Communist Party and had come under Fukumoto's influence, Fukumoto's criticism of Hayashi was a verdict, censuring Hayashi for compromising his Marxist views.[15] Thus, fellow New Man Society members such as Shiga Yoshio, Kore'eda Kyōji, Murao Satsuo, Kadoya Hiroshi, and Asano Akira, who became members of the Japanese Communist Party between 1925 and 1926 never invited him into the party.[16] Despite Hayashi being a leader of both the radical student movement and the left-wing literary group, Fukumoto's criticism of Hayashi and the perception of him being a supporter of Yamakawa discredited him in the eyes of the Fukumotoists.

In addition to branding him a Yamakawa-ist, Kore'eda and the others rebuked Hayashi for his contributions to the bourgeois media. Hayashi had met Kawabata Yasunari for the first time in March of 1926. Kawabata encouraged Hayashi to write something for the journal to which he belonged, *Bungei jidai* (Literary Age), and in December 1926, Hayashi contributed an essay written in the neo-impressionistic Shinkankaku (New Perceptionalist School) style.[17] Moreover, while in Kyoto for his trial during the spring of 1927, he published another New Perceptionalist School-style short story in *Kaizō* (Reconstruction), one of the three most popular mainstream periodicals of the day.[18] He was determined to provide for his

14. Tsurumi Shunsuke, "Kōki Shinjinkai'in," 119–120.

15. Ibid., 119.

16. Ibid., 123.

17. Matsumoto Keiko, *Higanbana*, 125. The essay Hayashi contributed was "Rōgoku no gogatsusai," *Bungei jidai* 3, no. 12 (December 1926): 22–42, a story based on his feelings experiencing May Day while the Kyoto police detained him in jail.

18. Hayashi Fusao, "Shuhai," *Kaizō* 9, no. 5 (May 1927): 70–83. Gregory J. Kasza has listed *Kaizō* along with the *Chūō kōron*, another monthly periodical, and the *Asahi shin-*

mother as best he could before entering prison. Thus, he contributed articles and essays to a wide variety of journals and newspapers, no matter their political orientation, to build up his savings.[19] The response from the left wing was predictable. Writers from the socialist literary movement cautioned him about publishing his works in the non–leftist media and communist party members criticized him harshly for what they called his "right-wing tendencies."[20]

Another reason pro-Fukumoto writers focused on Hayashi was that he defended the special nature of literature within the political movement. He argued that the proletarian literature movement should be Marxist in theoretical orientation, so he supported the removal of non-Marxist writers in the Proletarian League's First General Meeting. However, he also states that he did not believe that one should sacrifice literary style solely for the sake of a political agenda. In the end, he asserts that even though he did not consider himself an advocate of Yamakawa's political theory, he did believe that a literary piece could be both artistic and express a Marxist point of view.[21] In his editorial piece for the February 1927 issue of *Bungei sensen*, Hayashi made this claim, insisting that an artistically well-written piece of literature would only make the political perspective presented in the piece more powerful and popular among the masses.[22]

Coinciding with the publication of Hayashi's editorial was the communist party's attempt to establish its hegemony over proletarian cultural movements. The Japanese Communist Party began its foray into the cultural movement by creating a "literature and arts" column in its official newspaper, *Musansha shinbun*. Sano Manabu, now the managing editor

---

bun, a nationally published newspaper, as the three major publications in early Shōwa Japan. See Kasza's *The State and the Mass Media in Japan 1918–1945* (Berkeley: University of California Press, 1988), 44.

19. Matsumoto, *Higanbana*, 125.

20. Kawamori, "Hayashi Fusao den," 10.

21. Hayashi, "Bungakuteki kaisō," 243.

22. Shea, *Leftwing Literature in Japan*, 146. The original article to which Shea refers is Hayashi Fusao, "Shakaishugi bungei undō: shasetsu (shizen seichō to mokuteki ishikisei, shakaishugi bungaku to geijutsu kachi)," *Bungei sensen* 4, no. 2 (February 1927): 6–9. Since the article is an editorial, it is left unsigned in the journal; but in a footnote to the original table of contents, Odagiri Susumu confirms that Hayashi penned the article, *Gendai Nihon bungei sōran*, 151.

of the newspaper, invited Hayashi to be a reporter for this column at the start of 1927.[23] Initially, as Kaji Wataru explains it, the main purpose of the "literature and arts" column was to help the communist party raise funds by advertising the performances of proletarian artists. However, once the leadership "of the party realized how popular the column was among its readers, they changed their policy to take political advantage of that popularity.[24]

After Hayashi's editorial came out that February, Kore'eda Kyōji approached Kaji about writing a rebuttal to the editorial in the *Musansha shinbun*. The essence of the rebuttal was that at all costs literature and the arts must conform in practice to the political guidance of the party. Kaji met with Kore'eda several times about the article before Kaji published it in the February 5, 1927, edition of the newspaper.[25] Surprised and angered, Hayashi responded heatedly to Kaji's criticism in the March issue of *Bungei sensen*. However, Kaji's criticism still came from the official mouthpiece of the Japanese Communist Party, a source outside the left-wing literary group. It was Nakano Shigeharu, Hayashi's underclassman at Tokyo Imperial University, who brought Kaji's Fukumotoist attack directly into the proletarian literature movement. Preparing a response to Hayashi's February editorial, Nakano attacked Hayashi for insisting on the independent nature of literature within socialist literature. He did this in an essay published next to Hayashi's response to Kaji in the March issue of Proletarian Arts' official journal, *Bungei sensen*.[26] Thus began the communist party's first major attempt to establish its hegemony over the proletarian literature movement, using its literature and arts column as a launching pad for political censure of the group's members and organizations.

---

23. Hayashi, "Hayashi Fusao nenpu," 452.

24. Kaji Wataru, "Kantan na okotae: nigatsugo, yongatsugo no zadankai wo yonde," in *Tōron: Nihon puroretaria bungaku undōshi*, ed. Hirano Ken et al. (San'ichi shobō, 1955), 82.

25. Kaji Wataru, "Iwayuru shakaishugi bungei wo kokufuku seyo," *Musansha shinbun*, February 5, 1927.

26. Hayashi Fusao, "Tēze ni kansuru gokai ni tsuite: Kajikun ni kotaeru," *Bungei sensen* 4, no. 3 (March 1927): 149–155, and Nakano Shigeharu, "Keshō shitsutsuaru shōshiminsei," *Bungei sensen* 4, no. 3 (March 1927): 120–122. For Nakano bringing Kaji's attack on Hayashi into the Leftist literary movement, see Asukai Masamichi, "Bunka undō ni okeru kyōsanshugi: senkyūhyaku nijūnana, hachinen wo chūshin ni," in *Nihon shakaishugi undōshiron*, ed. Watanabe Tōru and Asukai Masamichi (Tokyo: San'ichi shobō, 1973), 293.

Nakano's and Kaji's attacks on Hayashi and other socialist writers such as Aono Suekichi, who specifically endorsed the application of Yamakawa's political theory to literature, split the Proletarian Arts group into pro-Yamakawa, anti-Fukumoto, and pro-Fukumoto factions. During the Special General Meeting held in late March 1927, the pro-Fukumoto faction gained control of the leadership of the Proletarian Arts group. That June, at a meeting of the Proletarian Arts Central Committee, Hayashi and fifteen other writers withdrew from the league and several days later founded a separate league of proletarian writers called Rōnō Geijutsuka Renmei (Worker-Peasant Artists League) or Rōgei (Worker's Arts), taking with them the journal *Bungei sensen,* which became the league's official journal. Thus began another round of realignment and political discord that lasted until the Japanese government began to clamp down on the communist party in March of 1928, giving the proletarian writers a common cause around which to rally.

Communism and the Proletarian Literature Movement

The writers in the Worker's Arts group were from the pro-Yamakawa and the anti-Fukumoto factions and had united in their opposition to Fukumoto's undue influence over the Proletarian Arts writers. They had their own falling-out in November 1927, following the announcement of the Comintern's 1927 Thesis from that previous July. In the Thesis, the Comintern criticized both Yamakawa's and Fukumoto's political views. Still, the Thesis did not become widely known in Japan until Kurahara Korehito, a literary critic who had studied in the Soviet Union for two years before joining the movement in March 1927, translated and published excerpts of it in the October 1927 issue of *Bungei sensen.*[27] Soon after Kurahara had published the partial translation of the Thesis, Yamakawa submitted an article to *Bungei sensen,* where he attacked Fukumoto's influence over the *Musansha shinbun* and its writers.[28]

A debate ensued among the members of the Worker's Arts group over whether they should publish the Yamakawa article. The pro-Yamakawa supporters within the Worker's Arts attempted to take advantage of this

27. Yamada Seizaburō, *Puroretaria bungakushi: fūsetsu no jidai,* vol. 2 (Tokyo: Rironsha, 1954), 142.

28. Ibid., 144–145.

debate to reestablish the primacy of Yamakawa's political theory within the proletarian literature movement. Kurahara, Hayashi, and Yamada, who were part of the editorial staff, were the first to object to Yamakawa's article. They did so because, while the Comintern had criticized both Yamakawa and Fukumoto, Yamakawa had not acknowledged the criticism of himself—only that of Fukumoto in the article.[29] As the debate grew heated, Kurahara led the group of writers opposing the publication of Yamakawa's article out of the Worker's Arts group. On November 11, Kurahara and the others established a new proletarian writers league called Zenei Geijutsuka Dōmei (Vanguard Artists League), known as Zengei (Vanguard Arts) among its members.[30]

Hardly had the Vanguard Arts group begun to publish its new journal, *Zenei* (Vanguard) in January 1928, when its leaders met with the leaders of the Proletarian Arts group to discuss reconciliation between the two groups. Thus, the split between the remaining members of the Worker's Arts and Vanguard Arts groups, as George Shea notes, was a political one.[31] Those who supported Yamakawa's socialist political solutions for Japan—he was no longer a member of the Japanese Communist Party in 1926—gathered around his theoretical journal, *Rōnō* (Laborer-Farmer). Yamakawa and others had established the journal in December 1927. Members of the Worker's Arts group who favored Yamakawa's ideas incorporated them into the Worker's Arts organization and *Bungei sensen*. Under different guises, this group continued publishing until 1932, but it became increasingly isolated from the main flow of the proletarian literature movement.

On the other hand, the members of the Vanguard Arts group who did support many of Fukumoto's Leninist political views also supported the Japanese Communist Party's *Musansha shinbun*. However, they were against the haphazard introduction of Fukumoto's political theories into the production of proletarian culture. Thus, the artistic argument between the members of Vanguard Arts and Proletarian Arts concerned how to interpret and incorporate the party's official political views within the arts, which ultimately made reconciliation much easier because, in gen-

29. Yamada Seizaburō, *Puroretaria bungakushi*, 145.

30. Arima Tatsuo, *The Failure of Freedom: A Portrait of Modern Japanese Intellectuals*, Harvard East Asian Series, no. 39 (Cambridge: Harvard University Press, 1969), 194.

31. Shea, *Leftwing Literature in Japan*, 151.

eral, they agreed on the content of the party's political views.[32] The disagreement between the members of the Vanguard Arts and the members of Proletarian Arts groups involved how to express these views within the proletarian cultural movement. In the spring of 1928, police carried out mass arrests of suspected communist party members, spurring the merger of these two groups into the Zen Nihon Musansha Geijutsu Renmei (All Japan Federation of Proletarian Arts).

The founding of NAPF (pronounced "Nappu" in Japanese, its name is taken from Esperanto is Nippona Artista Proleta Federacio) coincided with the rise of Stalinism in the Soviet Union and renewed government efforts to suppress domestic radicalism at home. What this meant for the movement over the next few years was the intense politicization of the proletarian cultural group's organizations and artistic production. For those like Hayashi who had fought to have the special qualities of literature acknowledged within socialist literature, this meant that they would revisit the frustration and disappointment of the late Proletarian Arts days, a time when proletarian writers clashed fiercely over Fukumoto's brand of Marxism-Leninism. Hayashi recalls that the late Proletarian Arts days were a time when "in every field, the old warriors were criticized. These attacks infuriated me, and I started acting like a stubborn old man. There were those who made amends and returned to the [left-wing] camp, but there were also those who did not return. Within the proletarian literature movement, Hayama [Yoshiki] and his group were the first to tire [of the communists and leave]. Over time I too became disgusted and bolted from the left-wing movement in the end."[33]

WHO SHOULD LEAD! WHO SHOULD FIGHT!

Unquestionably, the internal strife he experienced in the movement colored much of Hayashi's fiction from 1927 to 1929. During these years, he strove to define what he considered the ideal type of labor organizer, student radical, and factory worker as someone committed to their work, the

32. Ibid., 152.

33. Hirano, "Narupu no kaisan zengo to '*tenkō*' no mondai," 60. See Shea, *Leftwing Literature in Japan*, 164, for the fate of Hayama, who left Tokyo in 1934 and never returned to the left-wing movement.

movement, and the goal of social justice, hearkening back at times to the children's story format and to the use of humor to enliven these tales. His goal was to sketch out the desired traits of the worker and the organizer, as well as to denounce the harmful practices of those whom he believed tainted their honorable work. Particularly in his stories from 1927, we find Hayashi writing his proletarian short stories to stress the qualities of loyalty and morality, virtues that he obviously thought those who had sided with Fukumoto and the Communist Party's leadership had forgotten.

In "Trash," published in the February 1927 edition of *Bungei shijō* (Literary Marketplace), Hayashi gives us twelve different fables, each one highlighting a different type of corrupt behavior that gives the socialist movement a bad name. The first two tales are the longest, with the other eight stories following in rapid succession. In the opening tale, a young worker gains the sympathy of the union secretary, a Mr. Nagamura, whom he then fleeces for money, even accepting Nagamura's new shirt right off his back.[34] In the second tale, we learn that the movement has finally found a worker in the tobacco factory who is willing to help them organize the thirty laborers there into a union, but he will only do so if the movement will fund his work. Of course, the worker takes the money and they never hear from him again.[35]

These two fables are cautionary tales. The other fables recount the exploits of several half-hearted comrades who stain the socialist movement's reputation with their inexplicably bad conduct, boastful talk, and outright cowardice. In essence, Hayashi uses these tales in "Trash" to demarcate the boundaries between acceptable and unacceptable behavior within the socialist movement, identifying many unscrupulous and shameful deeds in which these pieces of "human trash" engage. As we saw in the epigraph, Hayashi concludes this short story with a declaration insisting that this kind of human trash remove themselves from the socialist movement.[36] This short story is an angry work, oozing frustration with his comrades and taking them to task metaphorically for the upheaval in the movement. Most likely, the members of the movement would have recognized themselves in the story, and Hayashi's writing here is pointed and designed to

34. Hayashi Fusao, "Kuzu," *Bungei shijō* 3, no. 2 (February 1927): 63–64.
35. Ibid., 64–66.
36. Ibid., 66–69.

inflict pain. The two tales in Hayashi's "Kindaiteki jōsei: ichimyō 'tōsei musume kishitsu'" (Modern Ladies, or by Another Name, "The Temperaments of Young Ladies Who are up on the Latest Trends") are in the same vein.

Published in the February 1927 issue of *Shinshōsetsu,* one short story contrasts the inappropriate conduct of the *moga* or "modern girl" with the proper spirit of a young lady bus conductor to discover how the modern age has transformed Japanese women.[37] The first tale is set on the streets of Ginza as two men from a newspaper company, one who acts as the story's narrator and his friend "S," visit the Tsukiji Little Theater to take in a play. Unbeknown to "S," one actress in the play is one whom he considers the epitome of a "modern girl," described as the precocious daughter of a bureaucrat working in the Foreign Ministry. Living the bohemian lifestyle, she invites herself over to their table that evening. She smokes and drinks, she thinks her Italian boyfriend would look better with blue eyes, and she even launches into a diatribe against the American social activist Margaret Sanger. Sanger supposedly had said that it was okay for a man to visit the red-light district, but not a woman. The girl wants to visit the red-light district and begs "S" to take her there so she could lose her "rose petals." The tale ends with "S" encountering the girl later that evening and her chastising "S" for running away from her at the theater—after all, she had announced to everyone that he was her new boyfriend—leaving "S" disgusted with the *moga* actress and her unseemly behavior.[38]

If the first story depicts a young woman who represents everything that is wrong with Japan's "modern girls," the second tale praises the working girl as the antidote for society's ills. The general narrator begins the second tale with a poem by Nakano Shigeharu that concerns the sufferings women conductors on the Tokyo city buses face every day at work. He follows this with a newspaper article on the inequity of the Tokyo city bus company's policy: the company provides overcoats for their male employees but require female employees to bring their own winter coats to wear while they work. The narrator is a newspaper reporter, and he is sent to interview a woman conductor at the Tokyo city bus company's main office. In that interview, the woman introduces herself as a member of the union women's division and is modest in appearance and bashful at first, but soon opens up as she

37. Hayashi Fusao, "Kindaiteki jōsei: ichimyō 'tōsei musume kishitsu,'" *Shinshōsetsu* 33, no. 2 (February 1927): 250.

38. Ibid., 251–257.

discusses the different problems the women face at work. Her boss, listening to the conversation from his office, pulls her aside and tells her to stop disparaging the company when she is on company property. But the woman refuses to back down, saying that she is a part of the union now. She asks the reporter if he would like to take a ride on her bus since they will pass by Tokyo station. Consequently, the narrator gains an admiration for the woman as she calls out the names of the bus stops, punches passengers' tickets, and sticks her bare hand out the window to signal turns as the bus round the curves.[39]

In the epilogue that follows, the general narrator returns to his opening question about the impact of the modern-age on Japan's young women.[40] However, this ending is misleading in a sense because it is obvious from the way the men in the stories respond to each woman's actions as to which woman the general narrator admires. For example, as soon as "S" realizes that the "modern girl" is in the play, he forces the narrator to get up and leave the theater immediately, hoping to avoid encountering her in person. When he tells the narrator at the teahouse about their first date and all the crazy things she said, "S" explains that he became dizzy just listening to the young woman's request. "The more she talked, the more [his] head was overwhelmed like the show window of a glass shop during an earthquake ... ," he told me.[41] Likewise, the narrator sympathizes with "S" in putting up with such shameful behavior, and relates at the end of the tale "S"'s disgust with the girl's announcement that "S" is her new boyfriend. As he leaps off the bus at Tokyo station, the reporter describes himself as humbled and feeling small after being in the presence of the female bus conductor. Her work skills on the bus amazed him and her resolve in the confrontation with her boss impressed him. The tale itself is a heroic ode to her example, replete with a poem and a newspaper article singing the praises of the women conductors before we even get to meet the woman at the center of the story.

Since Nakano Shigeharu supported the Fukumotoists in the political

---

39. Hayashi, "Kindaiteki jōsei," 263. To learn more about the difficult working conditions for the so-called bus girls (*basu gāru*), see Alisa Freedman's chapter on their place in Tokyo life in *Tokyo in Transit: Japanese Culture on the Rails and Road* (Stanford: Stanford University Press, 2011), 173–224.

40. Ibid., 264.

41. Ibid., 256.

debate, Hayashi's inclusion of Nakano's poem here is meant to embarrass him. It is a reminder to Nakano that at one time he stood with the working classes. Hayashi wraps himself in the cloak of proletarian heroism here, and his fictional story seems meant to place Fukumoto's call for vanguard intellectual elites to form and to lead the left-wing cultural movement within the framework of bourgeois elitism symbolized by our *moga* in this story. In his mind, Hayashi and those who backed the Marxist struggle for social justice in the Proletarian League stand with the female bus conductor. Furthermore, through this short story, Hayashi places a symbolic medal around the necks of the Proletarian League members for remaining true to the working classes.

If these two fables scrutinize appropriate behavior in the workplace, two other stories by Hayashi that year focus on lessons of love. Published in the May 1927 edition of *Kaizō*, "Shuhai" ("Parting cup") focuses on a love triangle between friends who were members in a socialist youth group—Kawamura Yasuo and Suzuki Shuichi—and a girl named Kondō Keiko.[42] Of the two youths, Suzuki is the more committed student radical and it is through his influence that Kawamura is led into the socialist movement. We learn that Keiko was previously Suzuki's girlfriend before he became a socialist. A rivalry develops between the two boys until Suzuki wins back Keiko's love. Kawamura vows revenge. After stealing a pistol from a friend's house, he confronts Suzuki with it but then turns the pistol on himself instead.

In this story Hayashi leaves us with a portrait of infidelity by Suzuki both to his friend Kawamura and to the socialist movement in general. In the second chapter of the story, Suzuki warns Kawamura that love is an act

42. In the opening and conclusion of "Parting Cup," Hayashi not so surreptitiously indicates that he based this story on his friend Kawabata Yasunari's life. Hayashi met Kawabata in the spring of 1926 after Kawabata wrote a favorable review of "Apples" and reached out to Hayashi to complement him directly on the story. Hayashi discusses Kawabata's influence on "Apples" in "Kawabata Yasunari no utsukushisa," *Bungaku jidai* 1, no. 4 (August 1929): 128–129. Kawabata had reviewed "Apples" publicly and liked the story well enough to write Hayashi personally and suggest that he work on making the narrative more "poetic," what Hayashi interpreted to mean as working on the accuracy, density, and preciseness of his phrasing in his revisions to "Apples." Hayashi's revised version, which has become the standard edition of this short story, came out in a collection of his short stories, *Bungei shinjin sōsho daisanpen: Ei no nai Eihon* (Tokyo: Shunyōdō, 1926), 84–97. Hayashi published the revised version in December 1926, which includes many grammatical changes to the narrative and some additions to the text, enhancing the readability and the flow of the story following Kawabata Yasunari's recommendations.

of the petty bourgeois.[43] Suzuki argues that such sentiments represent a step back in his commitment to the socialist movement, since being in love would hinder his ability to devote his energies to their work. Likewise, Suzuki repeatedly assures Kawamura that he is no longer in love with Keiko and that he will "give" her to Kawamura, insisting that he is beyond such personal commitments now.[44] When Kawamura challenges Suzuki to see who can win Keiko's love, Suzuki casually restarts his relationship with her and just as offhandedly informs Kawamura that she is his girlfriend again.[45] Hayashi presents Suzuki as the backslider here. By pursuing this love affair, he betrays not only his friend who eventually commits suicide but also the movement and its ideals.

The hero in our next story, while not a member of the socialist movement, depicts the selflessness and love that Suzuki should have shown. "Koi to yūrei" ("Love and Ghosts"),[46] published in the July 1927 issue of *Bungei kōron* (Literary Review), tells the story of Atsushi, a young man who after being discharged from the military, returns home and finds work in the local silk mill. There, he is in charge of keeping the machinery on the factory floor running smoothly. Although he is part of the factory's management group, Atsushi falls in love with one of the mill girls, and when she is hurt, he saves her, helps nurse her back to health, and attempts to protect her from the factory owner. He is unsuccessful in his efforts and sentenced to prison for his trouble. In the end, weakened by working in the factory and from his time in prison, he succumbs to illness shortly after his release, becoming somewhat of a martyr to the cause.

Despite being a bit of a clown and unwanted by his father who tells him not to return home when his military service is over, Atsushi is put forth as a model of fidelity here. There is no happy ending for our hero, but unlike Suzuki from "Parting Cup," Atsushi is a true friend of the factory girls. He is a proletarian hero who follows his heart, not his mind or his whims as does Suzuki. Moreover, even though he starts out as a member of the management, Atsushi's experiences lead him to empathize with the

43. Hayashi Fusao, "Shuhai," *Kaizō* 9, no. 5 (May 1927): 74.

44. Ibid., 76.

45. Ibid., 78.

46. Although Hayashi originally entitled this story "Koi to yūrei, he renamed it "Kōjō no yūrei" ("Factory ghosts") in later collections of short stories that included this work. See Hayashi Fusao, "Kojo no yurei," in *Kusari* (Tokyo: Shunyōdō, 1928), 45–60.

plight of the mill girls and, in due course, support them over the factory owner and the other foremen. While the story in "Love and Ghosts" is more of an elegy to Atsushi and his brave sacrifice in the fight against the rich, he does remain loyal to the working classes.

In "Parting Cup," Suzuki betrays Kawamura for love. Read within the ongoing struggle between the ideas of Fukumoto and Yamakawa in the proletarian literature movement, Hayashi again seems to be identifying the Fukumoto group as disloyal compatriots to the movement and to their fellow proletarian writers. In this story, he condemns them for misleading the members of the movement, and then leaving them abandoned and isolated, just as the management does to the injured mill girl in the factory's bleak infirmary. Both Kawamura and Atsushi meet tragic ends, as did many proletarian writers who decided to leave the movement and find other ways to convey their support for the working classes in Japanese society. In this way, even with the injection of humor in "Love and Ghosts," these two proletarian short stories also read as scathing attacks on the damage done to the movement by what Hayashi viewed as the capricious manner in which the party attempted to assert its political control over its creative writers.

Hayashi waited to publish his next proletarian short story until well after the nationwide arrests of Japanese communists on March 15, 1928. Its somber tone alone attests to the real threat facing Leftists at the time, merely being a part of the socialist movement did not necessarily make one a "true friend" of the proletariat. From reading Hayashi's September 1928 work "Mittei" ("Spies") published in *Senki* (Battle Flag), loyalty was a serious and even a fatal flaw within the movement itself. In "Spies" Hayashi turned to a historical example of political treachery to symbolize the impact of the March 15, 1928, roundup of the movement. He writes of the unsuccessful peasant uprisings in 1884 and through the narrative in "Spies" examines the failings of the local Jōmō Jiyū (Liberal) Party following the Gunma Incident of May 1884.[47] The story is straightforward: A hunter discovers a brutalized corpse off the side of a road, and police begin their investigation of the crime. Meanwhile, the narrator reveals the corpse's identity to the reader and traces the man's death back to his role as a police spy working within the Liberal Party. From here, we learn more

47. Hayashi Fusao, "Mittei," *Senki* 1, no. 5 (September 1928): 9.

about how the other members were able to catch the spy in the act, and how they went about determining the spy's fate, in due course carrying out his execution and attempting to hide his identity by stripping the flesh from his face.[48] The story concludes with the police discovering the identity of the spy and tracking down the leadership of the Liberal Party as the members flee Gunma prefecture. The police catch them all and they go to prison.

Hayashi uses this tale of deception as a means to explore the history of Meiji peasant uprisings against the state during the 1870s and 1880s. But he also spends much time describing the different means by which spies infiltrate the political organization from without or how the police recruit them from within. In addition, Hayashi details the party members' decision to execute the spy and the killing itself as complex matters. They took time to reach a consensus, which they handle sloppily as the spy almost escapes his death.[49] In "Spies," we find not only a reminder that police infiltration of dissident organizations has in fact happened in reality but the story poses a warning to the remaining members of the socialist movement to be on guard against such spies. It is possible that Hayashi even exacts a measure of fictional retribution on those police informants who aided the authorities during the police arrests on March 15, 1928.

From the harsh portrayal of a political organization under attack, Hayashi moves to portraits of student radicals aiding others. In his January 1929 story "Ori no naka no yonnin" ("Four Caged People") published in *Senki*, Hayashi tells the story of a student radical detained in a police lockup near Ueno station and the different people he meets as a result of his time in jail. It is a tale of reconciliation and marks the beginning of several short stories where Hayashi emphasizes cooperation in the wake of the state's attack on the Leftist movement. The story is broken up into four tales, and it starts with a young boy who worked for a laundry shop that had recently gone out of business, forcing the boy to sleep in Ueno Park. A police officer finds him there and brings him to the jail to sleep for the night. When the boy asks the policeman to let him urinate before he goes to sleep, he is told to hold it until the next day. That is when the student

48. Hayashi, "Mittei," 23–24.
49. Ibid., 11–22.

radical intervenes, leading the other detainees in a protest against the jailer for not allowing the boy to use the restroom. Eventually, their loud voices wake up the lieutenant who then tells the jailer to let the boy go to the lavatory.[50]

The second tale is about a newspaper delivery man who was out searching for new customers in his district when he came across burglars robbing a house. There was already a tense standoff between the police and the burglars at the house, and while the two men and a woman made their escape, a man with a pistol covered their getaway, gunning down two of the policemen.[51] Next, we have the tale of a thief who is taken in by the police for questioning in connection with the burglary that was witnessed by a newspaper delivery man. The suspect assures everyone that he was not the one who shot the policeman. In the final tale, the police release the student radical from jail, and he comes across another prowler hiding in Asakusa Park. After talking with him, the student decides to help the prowler, and together the two evade the police. When they part, the student radical tells the other man that if he meets one of his comrades to let them know that he is still alive.[52] Thus Hayashi portrays the student radical as a strong figure, as someone who leads, and as a trustworthy person whom others can look to for help, just as we saw in the first and last tales of this collection of stories.

We see much of the same spirit with more enthusiasm for the student radicals depicted in Hayashi's March 1929 work "*Shinbirusukugō* jiken" ("*Simbirsk* Incident") published in *Kaizō*. The story begins with a photo sent by a Chinese student who was a university friend of the narrator.[53] Intrigued by the worker's flag in the photo, the narrator takes it to several of his friends, but none can identify it. In the meantime, the narrator reveals that he is having his own troubles with the law and that he was in Osaka for another court hearing when he unexpectedly learned the story behind this flag.[54] There, he receives a visitor, Kitajima Kōzō, an older member of the socialist movement, whom the police have allowed to check

50. Hayashi Fusao, "Ori no naka no yonnin," *Senki* 2, no. 1 (January 1929): 38–41.

51. Ibid., 43.

52. Ibid., 46–47.

53. Hayashi Fusao, "*Shinbirusukugō* jiken," *Kaizō* 11, no. 3 (March 1929): 41.

54. Ibid., 43.

on the narrator and the other two students with him in the holding cell.[55] Kitajima sympathizes with their difficulties, and he tells them a story from his time in the movement, the 1917 attempt to welcome a Russian steamer called the *Simbirsk* into the Soviet fold.[56] Of course, the flag in the photograph sent by the Chinese student was the flag that Kitajima had quickly made before trying to contact the captain of the *Simbirsk*. It read, "Welcome, our Comrade! / Long Live Sovéet Republic!! / Nippon-Rōdōsōdōmei (Japan General Federation of Labor) / Kobe-Shibu (Kobe-branch office)."[57] Everyone felt cheered up after Kitajima's story, but the police moved the narrator and his friends to separate cells after that night. The narrator concludes the story by noting that on the third day, the police led him before the head of the High Court, but that he still wonders whatever happened to his Chinese friend.[58]

Though heavily censored, the passion in Kitajima's story shines through in the "*Simbirsk* Incident." Here the desire to extend a hand to the Russian captain and welcome him, his crew, and the steamer *Simbirsk* into the socialist movement under the Soviet flag is foremost in the hearts and minds of Kitajima and his comrades. Kitajima regales the narrator with a tale of initiative, daring, and friendship from an old comrade. It is a story that matches the zeal that the narrator's Chinese university friend Lee Yangon shows in 1923 as he leaves his studies in Tokyo to participate in the burgeoning Chinese revolution. The only check on this excitement seems to be the narrator himself. His complaints temper the youthful zest that colors much of the story since he returns periodically to his problems: his untimely arrest, his lengthy detainment in jail, the discomfort of his holding cell, and the court hearing being closed to the public. However, Kitajima's story mostly recalls the times and places in the socialist movement when the revolutionary spirit reigned supreme, and the willingness to reach out to others defined the movement and its members. We are also reminded that the socialist movement is international through the inclusion of the Russian ship, the *Simbirsk*, and its crew flying the Soviet flag; the narrator's Chinese friend from the university; and his friend's decision

55. Hayashi, "*Shinbirusukugō* jiken," 45.

56. Ibid., 46–48.

57. As recorded in an uncensored reprint of "*Shinbirusukugō* jiken" in Hayashi Fusao, *Tokai Sōkyokusen* (Tokyo: Senshinsha, 1930), 161.

58. Hayashi, "Shinbirusukugō jiken," 52.

to return to China to participate in the developing communist movement there in the 1920s.

Pointedly, Hayashi returns to a humorous approach in his April 1929 work "Tōshaban no kiseki" ("The Mimeograph's Miracle") published in *Senki*. "The Mimeograph's Miracle" closes out this set of short stories, which highlight the idealistic, passionate, yet unpretentious nature of the student radicals and labor activists who should be leading the socialist movement. Starting in a fairy-tale fashion, the narrator purports to tell the story of the mimeograph's miracle. Almost immediately, he subverts the significance of the "miracle" by comparing the mimeograph to a bashful boy embarrassed at having his story exaggerated by the use of a term like "miracle" for his accomplishments. He does observe, however, that the mimeograph is a compact but nimble tool, not unlike the brave but adorable young drummer boys with their paper garrison caps that play for the proletarian Young Pioneer's League. Then, the narrator introduces the character of the "elves." He notes that elves often play a key role in Western fairy tales and that they are full of a "proletarian"-like spirit. For example, in the story of the poor shoemaker who is bullied by a rich landowner, the elves sew up a pair of boots while the shoemaker slumbers, exhausted from the day's work. In much the same way as the boyish mimeograph, the elves are the ones who do not mind working tirelessly in a filthy office.[59] Yet, there are also differences, the narrator tells us. Where the elves work in place of the shoemaker and act in an imaginary world, we are the ones who stay up all night, making use of the mimeograph in our very real fight against an imperialist, reactionary government always at our heels. That being said, the narrator notes that we have grown fond of the mimeograph, not only for its usefulness in carrying out our union's struggle against imperialism and anti-communist groups like the Kenkokukai (National Foundation Society) but also in its humble mechanics that allow anyone to become skilled in its rhythmic use within a week.[60]

59. Hayashi Fusao, "Tōshaban no kiseki," *Senki* 2, no. 4 (April 1929): 112–113. Hayashi refers to the elves from the Brothers Grimm story, "The Elves and the Shoemaker," here described as "pygmies" in hiragana in the story. He does not explain this word choice, but perhaps it is to underscore the lack of appreciation for the elves, and thus, the narrator's work, or perhaps Hayashi is attempting to place the elves in an imperialist context by employing a derogatory term sometimes reserved for colonized people.

60. Hayashi Fusao, "Tōshaban no kiseki," *Senki* 2, no. 4 (April 1929): 113. Formed in 1926 the *Kenkokukai* was a prewar ultranationalist group whose guiding spirit was the

Here, Hayashi pays tribute to the work of the "grunts" or the "elves" in the socialist movement, essentially arguing that their work endures, while that of the leaders does not. In returning to the same allegorical style in "New Aesop's Fables," the reader anticipates a rebuke of the communist leadership, and Hayashi does not disappoint in this fanciful tale, laden with sentimentality and nostalgia. Next, the narrator moves from his discussion of the mimeograph's appeal to describing the incident in which the labor activists are involved, affirming that the mimeograph's story is akin to a miracle.[61] In this part of the story, we learn that Satō and Kawamura were clerks for a now-defunct Workers-Farmers Federation in provincial Japan. They are preparing to form a new provincial workers' party and have been working nonstop at the mimeograph for a week. Satō is exhausted and arrives at the station late for the meeting. As he passes through the ticket gate below the station, he notices officer Sunada of the Tokkō (Special Higher Police) sitting on a bench in the waiting area and thinks that the meeting has been broken up and that he is about to be arrested. Instead, Sunada waves Satō over and, in a whisper, warns him to get out while he can. The police have arrested over twenty of his comrades thus far, Sunada explains. Looking over Sunada's shoulder, Satō realizes that Sunada is telling the truth and he bolts from the station, escaping arrest.[62]

In hiding, Satō and Kawamura struggle to come up with an explanation for Sunada's actions. Kawamura speculates that Sunada must have had a falling out with his department head, and his hunch seems to be confirmed when a few days later the rumor that Sunada has resigned from the Special Higher Police spreads. Satō wonders if Sunada has undergone a *kaishin*, "a change of heart to amend one's past mistakes," about working for the Special Higher Police and, if so, what caused his "change of heart"?[63] Another man rescued that day was Ōtani, the head

---

anarchist and virulent anti-communist Akao Bin while major nationalist figures like Hiranuma Kiichirō and Tōyama Mitsuru played advisory roles in the group. For more information, see Richard Storry's *The Double Patriots: A Study of Japanese Nationalism* (Chatto & Windus, Ltd., 1957; reprint, Westport, CT: Greenwood Press, 1976), 35–37 (page citations are to the reprint edition), and Ivan Morris, *Nationalism and the Right Wing in Japan: A Study of Post-War Trends* (New York: Oxford University Press, 1960), 67–68.

61. Hayashi, "Tōshaban no kiseki," 114.

62. Ibid., 115.

63. Ibid., 116–117.

of the preparatory committee, and he takes Satō with him on a trip to canvass the countryside for help in starting a new workers-farmers party. While stopped at a railway station in the mountains, they encounter Sunada who is now a silk merchant stepping into their train. They greet each other, then Sunada smiles as they talk about the changes in their lives. Finally, Ōtani brings up the subject of Sunada's warning at the railway station, and Sunada tells Satō and Ōtani the story of how the Special Higher Police chief reduced his salary. When Ōtani observes that this explains his personal hostility toward his boss and his job and why he resigned from the Special Higher Police, but that it does not explain why Sunada showed them such goodwill at the railway station, Sunada reveals the mimeograph's miracle.[64]

Here the narrator breaks into the story to explain that what follows is the story Sunada told the two men on the train, but that he has taken the liberty of reworking the story to make it read more like a novel. In his story, Sunada recalls the morning when he was in charge of surveillance on a certain office where the police suspected young radicals were producing revolutionary propaganda. As dawn started to break, there was snow on rooftops and a bone-chilling wind blew. He observed a group of young men working in the second-floor office that had broken shutters. His superior had ordered Sunada to break up the group and arrest them and Sunada certainly heard the sounds of a mimeograph at work. Although faint, the simple gradation of the worn-out mimeograph was unmistakable. Sunada found the transparency of the sound soothing and a bit otherworldly.[65] It took him back to another time and place set in his childhood, while he stood there at watch in the alley. These youths were willing to stake their lives on this work with no recompense for their efforts. Running through Sunada's mind was the thought that no matter how clichéd a set of ideas became at the level of language, the idea itself still had the enduring potential to reach others' hearts anew. With this in mind, Sunada slipped his hands into his pockets, dropped his head, and quietly departed the alleyway.[66]

In an interesting digression from Hayashi's previous short stories, here the heroes of "The Mimeograph's Miracle" are the rickety mimeograph

64. Ibid., 117–118.
65. Ibid., 119–120.
66. Ibid., 120.

and the fallen Special Higher Police officer. Thematically, this short story certainly revolves around the lives of young labor organizers and an incident involving a run-in with the Special Higher Police, but the "intellectual humorist" side of Hayashi asserts itself in the meandering narrative of this story. That noted, the digression also seems purposeful in defining which particular characteristics of Satō and Kawamura, the labor organizers, as expressed through their work on the mimeograph persuaded Sunada to walk away from their arrest and to warn them of the police trap at the railway station. In line with Hayashi's previous stories, the qualities of enthusiasm, idealism, youth, a willingness to sacrifice, and working long hours with little reward and no expectations of individual recognition are the traits that move Sunada. Identifying with Satō's and Kawamura's youthful commitment to their cause, Sunada decides to protect them from the certain harm that will befall them at the police station.

What is different here is the way the narrator links these traits to the world of fantasy and imagination. From the opening of the story, Hayashi intentionally treats the mimeograph anthropomorphically, as a modest boyish figure that, along with the "elves" from the Western fairy tales, not only helps the downtrodden but can also work unexpected changes in the humans who operate it and in those who hear it. The mimeograph's miracle lies in the simple progression of sounds that emanate from the human manipulation of the machine, unlike the elves who can do the work in place of humans.

Thus, the mimeograph's minor miracle is in its nostalgic appeal to Sunada's heart. The sound transports Sunada back to memories of his youth in an idyllic countryside, and the youth's capacity to follow his ideals no matter the cost moves Sunada. Even so, the fact that the narrator breaks into the story and divulges that he has taken Sunada's explanation on the train and fictionalized it for the reader is merely our final reminder that he invented this story. Although from the onset Hayashi places the story in the realm of whimsical children's stories from Western literature, the narrator tells the story with such gusto and sincerity, that the reader momentarily forgets that rickety mimeographs and fallen Special Higher Police officers can be heroes only in the readers' imaginations.

In reality, "The Mimeograph's Miracle" was published in the April

1929 issue of *Senki*, the same month that the Special Higher Police carried out their follow-up raid on April 16, 1929, rounding up remaining Leftist student radicals and labor organizers not captured during the nationwide police raid of March 15, 1928. Consequently, Hayashi's latest proletarian fairy tale reads as a desperate last call for those with a passionate desire for social justice to guide the socialist movement in its time of need.

Setting the story in the realm of the fanciful also suggests that Hayashi thought that such idealists existed only in one's imagination now. Thus, the story also seems to reflect his acknowledgment that the politicians were taking over the leadership of the proletarian cultural movement as a whole and that political expediency was quickly becoming the guiding spirit of the movement's creative arts. With the movement's idealists either in prison or pushed to the margins of socialist cultural organizations, Hayashi places the existence of proletarian literature movement within the domain of fantasy along with the worn-out mimeograph's "miracle" and Sunada's sentimental act of deliverance at the railway station. In this way, "The Mimeograph's Miracle" reads as a combination of the plea, evident in his earlier children's story "A Picture Book without Pictures," for those who desire social justice to join the movement with the denunciation of leadership figures found in "New Aesop's Fables."

Intriguingly, in "The Mimeograph's Miracle," Hayashi insists that the idea of socialism still has the potential to move others to action if the leaders can transcend their intellectual disputes over the language in which the idea is expressed. From his perspective, that meant leaving alone the movement's creative artists to write Marxist-influenced fiction that would appeal to the hearts of the masses and bring them to a Marxist understanding of society, not ordering the writers to produce propaganda pieces that explained the workings of Marxist and Communist thought for the workers.

In his paper comparing Hayashi and Nakano Shigeharu's rejection of "ready-made words" (*dekiai no kotoba*) to express a literary "truth" (*makoto*), Japanese scholar Naitō Yoshitada asserts that Nakano pushed writers to stick to the truth of every word used in their fiction, because "literature reflects the changing times" in which we live.[67] Conversely, Naitō

67. Naitō Yoshitada, "Bungaku-teki 'shinjitsu' no mondai: Nakano Shigeharu to Hayashi

argues that Hayashi also rejected the use of these "ready-made words" in his essay, "The Spirit of Service to the Emperor" ("Kinnō no kokoro"), which he contributed to the Overcoming Modernity Symposium of 1942. He did so, however, because these words were historically derived from Western usage, and thus carried a different meaning not applicable to the "truth" of the Japanese living under the rule of the Emperor. Therefore, Naitō observes, from Hayashi's perspective, these words were based on a subjective "truth" and should be considered false.[68]

Here, in "The Mimeograph's Miracle," we find Hayashi making a similar proposal to the communist leaders of NAPF: put aside the ready-made language of Marxism since it does not give meaning to the working classes' participation in the movement. Instead, Hayashi underscores the role of the idea upon which socialism originates as the key motivating factor that will draw others to the movement. In practice, Hayashi defines that idea as the youthful spirit of service driving the comrades Satō and Kawamura's work in "The Mimeograph's Miracle," and it is their honest labor and the mimeograph's simple operation that prompts the Special Higher Police officer Sunada to look the other way. To put it in Naitō's terms, Hayashi asserts that the "truth," which will bring others to a Marxist understanding of Japanese society, is in the ability of those reading proletarian literature to identify their interests and concerns within the idea of socialism. Furthermore, they should want to engage in the sincere work of spreading this revolutionary ideal of social justice and equality. Although Nakano and others would not politically agree, Hayashi's message is very clear in "The Mimeograph's Miracle": stop the divisive intellectual debate and political struggle to define the socialist movement, or risk losing more members.

Hayashi made his final entreaty to the remaining leaders of NAPF to allow him and other proletarian writers to use their creative faculties, with an extremely intimate yet emotional story of Korean and Japanese laborers in "Chijō" ("Lust"), published in the June 1929 issue of *Shinchō* (New Currents). Here our main character is Saitō Hyōkichi, a young Japanese man who is a skilled worker at a printing factory. To aid a Korean worker

---

Fusao no tenkō" (paper and handout presented at *Tenkō* in Trans-war Japan: Culture, Politics, History: An International Workshop, Hinsley Hall, Leeds, UK, July 1, 2017): 4.

68. Naitō, "Bungaku-teki 'shinjitsu' no mondai," 5.

and his family, Saitō has signed a lease in May on a row house in his name so that Kim Ch'oegŭn, his wife Cholyŏn, and their six-year-old son Hagsu can have a place to stay.

From this point on, things go astray for all parties. A labor dispute at the factory puts both of them out of work. Saitō finds a job as an unskilled laborer in another printing factory, but Kim enters the ranks of the unemployed. He runs an *oden* (a Japanese-style hot pot dish) stand for a while and finds temporary work from time to time, but he is not able to find permanent employment. Thus, Saitō must pay the rent for himself and the Kim family.

Adding to this strain in their relationship is Saitō's unexpected tryst with Kim's wife one June night. The next morning, Kim tells Saitō that he is indebted to him for his help, and he blames himself and his wife for the encounter and their pitiful circumstances. Saitō then moves out of the apartment temporarily, but Kim sends his wife and son to Saitō. He asks Saitō to return and live in the apartment and take care of his family while he searches for another job in a different part of Japan. Eventually, Saitō relents, moves back to the apartment, and for all intents and purposes, becomes the man of the house. One September evening after visiting a local festival with the son, Saitō returns to the apartment to find that Kim has returned, murdered his wife, and attempted suicide. A police detective interrogates Saitō, confirming that he was having an affair with Kim's wife and blaming the whole situation on "lust." In the last scene, Kim calls for Saitō and with his final breath, he asks Saitō to take care of his son Hagsu.

Saitō and Kim begin as coworkers in the printing factory and cohabitants in the tenement, but poverty and society's expectations separate them and drive them apart in this story. Saitō evinces the spirit of service that defines the socialist movement and its members in Hayashi's previous two tales, as he willingly sacrifices his comfort and his wages to assist a fellow worker and his family. Then things take a turn for the worse, which Saitō attributes first to the mass firing from the printing factory and then to Kim's inability to secure another steady job. Unlike Saitō who finds employment, though not a job that matches his skills, Kim's bout of illness and his marginalization in Japanese society keep him from finding a full-time position.

Throughout the story, we have markers of Kim's ancestral origins in colonial Korea: from the introduction of the Korean language and Korean songs in the text to Kim relating his family history to Saitō. We learn that Kim and his wife come from a little village outside of Seoul and that the Japanese colonial police took several family members off the land into forced labor. To avoid the colonial police, Kim and his family flee their village and depart from Pusan to Japan where he worked many different factory jobs as they made their way up the Japanese islands to Tokyo.[69] We also discover that Kim will not serve liquor at his *oden* stand because several drunken Japanese customers have turned over his cart and threatened him with violence to get out of paying their bill.[70] In addition, early on in the tale, Saitō himself witnesses the unfair treatment of a Korean worker who was pushed aside by the conductor as he tries to buy a ticket to get on a tram.[71]

Discrimination compounds the misery and injustice of poverty illustrated in the immigrant life of Kim's family. Even the landlord observes that Koreans will be unable to secure a lease for an apartment unless a Japanese person vouches for them.[72] As in the "*Simbirsk* Incident," Hayashi reminds us that the social ills facing the proletariat are global in scope, and here he links those social problems and the Japanese socialist movement not only with the fight against industrial capitalism but with the struggle against imperialism and colonialism. Hayashi touched on this subject in the story of the Hindu girl and her lover crushed under British imperialism in "A Picture Book without Pictures."[73] Then, he expounded on the military aspect of this struggle in his January 1928 piece "Daishingun" ("The Great Advance") in *Bungei kōron*, where he depicted the fierce but ultimately futile resistance of Australian aborigines against the advance of a massive British army.[74]

Still, Saitō argues that the bourgeois' expectations of behavior and lifestyle that they thrust upon a proletariat with little ability to live up to those expectations are, in the end, what mostly separate Kim and him-

69. For the Korean language and songs, see Hayashi, "Chijō," 56, 60–61, and for the background of the family, see page 68.

70. Hayashi, "Chijō," 62–63.

71. Ibid., 58–59.

72. Ibid., 57.

73. Hayashi Fusao, "E no nai ehon," *Shinshōsetsu* 31, no. 5 (May 1926): 18–19.

74. Hayashi Fusao, "Daishingun," *Bungei kōron* 2, no. 1 (January 1928): 155–159.

self. Part of the crucial night when Saitō gives into his lust and shares Cholyŏn's affections for him are hidden because of censorship, but enough is left for the reader to recognize that the affection is mutual and to witness Saitō's sense of guilt emerge when he realizes what he has done. This night complicates Saitō's relationship with the Kim family, and he eventually departs the row house and moves into a separate apartment. Moreover, this pivotal scene in the narrative serves to highlight the mental constraints that the ruling class places on the working class to frustrate them and keep them apart.

After Kim's sudden departure jolts Saitō, he must confront the guilt he feels about his immoral behavior in conjunction with his worker's sense of pride in responding to Kim's description of him as his *onjin*, his "benefactor." First, he faces his sense of guilt and recognizes that all these terms used to define the conditions of living (husband and wife, chastity, an affair, jealousy, relationships, morality, emotions) are derived from the ruling class's conception of how life should be lived. Why should these meaningless terms developed by the wealthy to describe their lives circumscribe the happiness of Kim and his wife? Saitō concludes that he should find contentment in everyday life and not dwell on such bourgeois concept as jealousy.[75] Next, following Hagsu's pleas for him to move back in with them, Saitō tackles his conscience. With Kim gone and Saitō sharing living arrangements with Cholyŏn, they become "a couple," and he has had to work through the painful anguish that his conscience caused him over the night that he spent with Cholyŏn. It is only in fairy tales that a young couple living together can avoid physical relationships, no matter the circumstances. Only those who cannot imagine such situations can come up with such concepts as "morality" and "principles," and once these ideas emerge, they stifle one to the point of robbing one of life, Saitō reasons.[76]

Lastly, when he is with the police, and they are interrogating him about his relationship with Kim, Saitō finally overcomes his sense of pride and recognizes what Kim meant in appointing Saitō as his benefactor. Much too easily, the detective tries to blame Kim's suicide and his wife's murder

75. Hayashi, "Chijō," 71.
76. Ibid., 72.

on a secret love affair. "Why in the hell would someone die over jealousy when he was barely eking out a living[?]" Saitō muses, "It wasn't because of my and Cholyŏn's relationship that Kim killed himself." However, in this case, he thought it was worthless trying to explain that to the chief justice. "They'll label it as 'extreme lust' and move on, and not just these policemen but no one in this world wants to take the time [to know why Kim murdered his wife and killed himself]," Saitō concludes.[77]

Saitō realizes that the detective's goals are pragmatic. He does not want to mull over the poverty, the unemployment, the underemployment, and the outright discrimination that this "inferior ethnic people" has encountered as a colonized people on the Korean peninsula. Nor does the detective care that what Kim and his extended family have experienced firsthand as migrants in Japan proper were extenuating factors for Kim's murder of his wife and his suicide. The detective simply wants to establish the illicit relationship between Saitō and Cholyŏn; that way, he can conclude the investigation as quickly as possible.[78] As such, the detective can assure the bourgeois world in which they reside that "lust" was the reason for Kim's actions, certainly not the act of a foreign laborer desperate for work so that he could provide for his family.

Though Saitō says that he understood Kim's feelings about that night when he starts working through his feelings of guilt, he only overcomes his pride when he acknowledges how Kim appreciated his help as a fellow worker in caring for his family. Through Saitō's relationship with the Kim family, Hayashi elucidates the pitfalls into which the working class stumbles in trying to live up to the "normative" behavior established by bourgeois society. We also follow Saitō in his attempt to surmount these barriers that "modern" society places between workers in maintaining human relationships. Even though Saitō seems able to work through those obstacles, the story's conclusion confirms that it will not be an easy task for Saitō to help Hagsu overcome bourgeois society's expectations of him. The police have left Hagsu with a newspaper article describing his parents' deaths, and in the article, it states that "a Korean by the name of Kim Ch'oegŭn whose wife was taken from him by Saitō, murdered his wife and

77. Hayashi, "Chijō," 75.

78. Ibid.; the reference to the Kim husband and wife as a *rettō na minzoku* appears on page 63.

took his own life due to extreme lust."[79] Despite Saitō's encouragement to Hagsu that he will understand in time why his parents died and that he should grow up to be a strong worker, this artifact of "modern" society, the newspaper article, also ensures that Hagsu will also have a bourgeois understanding of what and who ended his parents' lives. A burdensome challenge remains for Saitō: how to raise Hagsu as a worker's child and live up to the expectations of a worker's family instead of falling for modern bourgeois society's definitions of morality and lifestyle.

In characterizing the worker through Saitō's example, Hayashi exposes the bourgeois means of social control over workers' actions and behaviors, and the difficult path a laborer must tread to see through the illusion that an industrial capitalist society purposely perpetuates as universal. At the same time, in carefully defining that path for other workers through Saitō's example, Hayashi also provides a specific model for members of the working class to emulate in their struggles to make sense of their own proletarian lives in early Shōwa Japan. Instead of accepting bourgeois society's definitions of morality, this story suggests that the proletariat must be like Saitō and carve out their own paths. "Lust" is an apt ending message in Hayashi's late proletarian short stories that attempt to define the proper conduct of those associated with the socialist movement, and it would coincide with Hayashi's departure from the proletarian cultural movement.

By the late 1920s, Hayashi began to forge a separate path within proletarian literature, distancing himself from the orthodoxy of the communist leaders' vision for the relationship of politics and literature. Rather than trying to live up to party expectations of literary works meant as propaganda and to agitate against the state, he argued that there was a need to develop a worker's literature for those nurtured under the wing of NAPF, particularly for those who were dissatisfied with its control and found its direction of their work stifling. Ultimately, he conceded the difficulty of starting anew while NAPF existed and party members were still leading the movement. Still, while he continued writing proletarian short stories in the Marxist vein, he was determined not only to pursue his own way but also to stand with others who desired to build their bridges out of NAPF. Again, with these short stories we have more evidence of Hayashi's

79. Ibid., 77.

continued use of his literature as a staging ground to put forth his political positions. As a result, reading “Lust” from this standpoint leads one to view this short story as Hayashi’s declaration of independence from NAPF’s leadership as well as from its attempts to define the proletarian writer’s creative work, and from its political philosophy. No longer would he follow the dictates of the Japanese Communist Party over the proletarian literature movement, and in his subsequent proletarian short stories, Hayashi wrote to eulogize the movement, in essence, figuratively consigning it to history’s trash bin.

6

Departing the Movement and Enabling *Tenkō*

Remembering Factory Workers, Student Radicals, and Labor Organizers in Hayashi Fusao's Proletarian Literature

> Clang! That's the sound of rock striking a hollow bronze piece. Amazingly, the rock danced off the head of the bronze statue and rolled across the grass in the yard. Both the sound of the rock striking the statue and the fact that it hit its target gave great pleasure. ...
>
> And so, after placing our seals on the petition [requesting Mr. Mayone's release], we felt something akin to despair. At that time, we didn't want to put our seals [on the petition]. We did it because of *outside pressure*. But then, it wasn't our own actions that put the company president in handcuffs and a shackled waist-belt. That was also due to *outside pressure*. (Emphasis in the original)
>
> —"Mayone Yonekichi-shi no dōzō"

Hayashi's disillusionment with the proletarian literature movement and its leadership only grew more acute between 1928 and the time when the movement officially disbanded in 1934. As is evident in the quote above from "Mayone Yonekichi-shi no dōzō" ("Mr. Mayone Yonekichi's Bronze Statue"), he increasingly found himself caught between two distressing choices as a proletarian writer: Either give in to the unwanted dictates of

---

Hayashi Fusao, "Mayone Yonekichi-shi no dōzō," *Kaizō* 12, no. 1 (January 1930): 127, 136.

the communist leadership guiding the proletarian literature movement and write left-wing propaganda pieces or surrender to the Japanese state's intensified determination to remove all left-wing voices from the political stage and force novelists to write nationalist propaganda works. In the same way that the management in Mr. Mayone's factory forced its workers to write in support of Mr. Mayone's release, the leaders of the underground communist party further extended their hegemony over the socialist literature organizations. In the story, the workers had nothing to do with Mr. Mayone's arrest, which was due to political considerations. The authorities charged Mayone with a crime, and then the police arrested and imprisoned him. While the workers did not like Mayone, theirs was a hollow victory, much like the bronze statue. About all the workers could do to express their displeasure with him and the factory's management was to cast stones at the statue in their free time and play subtle tricks mocking him. The factory workers were not in control of their fates, and they could not affect any real change in the running of the factory, much less in the governing of Japanese society. Hayashi's sense of being stifled by a higher authority is palpable in this short story, as depicted in the workers' frustration that the police have the power to imprison the factory owner at will, but the workers, as a group, have little influence over the workplace.

Published at the beginning of 1930 before Hayashi served his first prison sentence, "Mr. Mayone Yonekichi's Bronze Statue" captures well his sense that this was the beginning of the end for the proletarian literature movement, an end Hayashi would blame on both the communist leadership of the movement and on the government. Since the organizations of the proletarian cultural movement were still legal during the late 1920s, communist party leaders attempted to transform these proletarian cultural groups into mouthpieces for their prohibited views, particularly after police decimated the ranks of the clandestine Japanese Communist Party with nationwide roundups of communist party members and sympathizers on March 15, 1928, and April 16, 1929. Moreover, Prime Minister Tanaka Giichi led the government in taking several proactive steps against radicalism in Japan. First, in 1928 he banned several organizations in the radical labor and youth movements known to have ties to the Japanese Communist Party, including the New Man Society. Then, he used an imperial decree to amend the Peace Preservation Law to allow for the death penalty. Finally, he pushed the Home Ministry to devote more of its resources in a drive to combat the spread of radicalism all across Japan. In the wake of these measures, the communist party showed incredible resilience. Whenever the government banned one of its affiliated organizations, communist party members attempted to reorganize it under a different name. After two more mass arrests of suspected communists in February 1930 and October 1932, the Japanese Communist Party eventually lost its organizational coherence as a national political organization and lapsed into small, isolated groups that police could easily disperse.[1]

As legal outlets for communist propaganda and activities began to diminish, party members within the proletarian cultural movement were successful in reorganizing NAPF into a political movement to assist the communist party. Under the leadership of party member Kurahara Korehito, the members of NAPF voted to dissolve the league on November 12, 1931, and replace it with a more highly centralized and stratified league.[2] On November 27, they announced the formation of the Nihon Puroretaria Bunka Renmei (Japan Proletarian Culture Federation) more commonly known as KOPF ("Koppu" in Japanese, from its Esperanto title, Federacia de Proletaj Kultur Organizoj Japanaj). KOPF consisted of a central council; a secretariat; four councils for women, children, youths, and peasants; a Publishing Section; the Editorial Staff for *Puroretaria bunka* (Proletarian Culture—KOPF's official journal); and an Honorary Central Council Members' Section.[3] The Nihon Puroretaria Sakka Dōmei (Japan Proletarian Writers' League) and other independent proletarian cultural leagues remained as separate organizations and sent representatives to KOPF's Central Council to participate in general policymaking meetings for the league. As in NAPF, the proletarian writers in the Writers' League provided the main leadership for KOPF. As a result, when the Writers' League folded in March 1934 under the strain of internal and external pressures, KOPF too lost its guiding force and disintegrated. The breakup of the Writers' League left the other proletarian cultural leagues to follow their separate paths and marked the official end of the socialist literature movement in Japan, although the proletarian writers, both individually and as

1. Beckmann, *The Japanese Communist Party 1922–1945*, 238.
2. Shea, *Leftwing Literature in Japan*, 208.
3. Ibid., 209.

members of other literary groups, continued to influence Japanese literature into the wartime years.

Hayashi was in prison from July 1930 to April 1932 and missed the reorganization of the proletarian cultural movement as KOPF. After the authorities released him from prison and he returned to the Writers' League, he noticed that the leaders and the theoretical direction of the group had changed to such an extent that, to him, the Writers' League and KOPF had become little more than a communist party political organization hiding behind the facade of a cultural movement.[4] Even while Hayashi was involved in NAPF, the editorial staff of *Senki*, the official journal of NAPF, began to allocate more space in the journal to members of the outlawed radical labor and peasant's movements so that they could carry out their agitation-propaganda work legally. Late in 1930, the Japanese Communist Party took over *Senki* from NAPF altogether, transferring management of the journal to the agitation-propaganda section of the underground communist party in what scholars call the "Senkisha Incident."[5] NAPF carried on its work either in the Writers' League journal *Puroretaria bungaku* (Proletarian Literature) or in its new official journal *Nappu* (NAPF) created in September 1930.

When the members of NAPF voted to reorganize into KOPF, not only did the organization of KOPF come to resemble that of the Japanese Communist Party, but party members within KOPF argued that all proletarian writers should join the party formally. In a 1954 roundtable discussion concerning the proletarian literature movement, Kurahara Korehito acknowledged that one of his goals as a party member in the 1930s was to turn the central committee of NAPF into a "branch office" (*shutten*) for the Japanese Communist Party so as to popularize the party's political agenda and produce communist writers.[6] With the transformation of the proletarian cultural movement into KOPF, Kurahara moved a long way

4. Present-day scholars concur with Hayashi's assessment that party members within the proletarian cultural movement turned it into a political movement under control of the clandestine Japanese Communist Party. For more information, see Asukai Masamichi's *Nihon puroretaria bungaku shiron* (Tokyo: Aoki shoten, 1982), 60, and Rin Shukumi, "Puroretaria bungaku no kaitai," in *Jidai betsu Nihon bungakushi jiten: gendaihen*, ed. Jidai betsu Nihon bungakushi jiten henshū iinkai (Tokyo: Tokyo tōshuppan, 1997), 94.

5. Asukai, *Nihon puroretaria bungaku shiron*, 118, 120.

6. Hirano Ken et al., eds., "Nihon puroretaria bungaku undō no saikentō," in *Tōron: Nihon puroretaria bungaku undōshi* (San'ichi shobō, 1955), 30. The editors from the jour-

toward achieving his goal. In the early 1930s, several of KOPF's most well-known writers and literary critics joined the party. These included Nakano Shigeharu (1931), Kaji Wataru (1932), Kobayashi Takiji (1931), Miyamoto Kenji (1931), and Miyamoto Yuriko (1931).[7] To show that the proletarian cultural movement was not just a localized phenomenon, KOPF encouraged its affiliated leagues to join with international communist organizations. In February 1932, the Writers' League merged with the Kokusai Kakumei Sakka Dōmei (International Union of Revolutionary Writers) to become the Kokusai Kakumei Sakka Dōmei Nihon Shibu (Japan Branch of the International Union of Revolutionary Writers). Among its members, they still referred to the proletarian writers' league as the Sakka Dōmei (Writers' League) or NALPF ("Narupu" in Japanese, from its Esperanto acronym, Nippona Alianco Literaturistoj Proletaj).[8] In time, many members of KOPF became political agents for the communist party, which inevitably brought unwanted attention from the police and further alienated the proletarian cultural movement from the public.[9]

Following the Manchurian Incident in September 1931, the founding of Manchukuo in February 1932, and the wave of popular nationalism that swept over Japan in the meantime, police targeted the KOPF leadership in a series of arrests between March and April 1932. They succeeded in capturing many of its leaders and forcing many others underground. Police suppression of its meetings and censorship of its publications severely curtailed the political activities of KOPF. This external suppression notwithstanding, internal dissension among its members, once again over the relationship between politics and literature, contributed greatly to the eventual dissolution of the Writers' League in March 1934.[10]

---

nal *Kindai bungaku* (Modern literature) organized this roundtable discussion in 1954 and published the discussion later that year in their journal.

7. Information on when these writers entered the Japanese Communist Party can be found in Shiota Shōbē et al., eds., *Nihon shakai undō jinmei jiten* (Tokyo: Aoki shoten, 1979), 414, 157, 247, 550, and 552.

8. Kubota Masafumi, "Sakuhin kaisetsu," in *Nihon gendai bungaku zenshū: puroretaria bungakushū*, vol. 69, ed. Itō Sei (Tokyo: Kōdansha, 1969), 399.

9. Beckmann, *The Japanese Communist Party 1922–1945*, 214.

10. Shea, *Leftwing Literature in Japan*, 229–232. See also Germaine Hoston's extended discussion of this problem for Sano Manabu, in her chapter "*Ikkoku Shakai-shugi*: Sano Manabu and the Limits of Marxism as Cultural Criticism," in *Culture and Identity: Japanese Intellectuals during the Interwar Years*, ed. J. Thomas Rimer (Princeton: Princeton University Press, 1990), 168–190.

Immediately after Hayashi's release from prison in the spring of 1932, he became involved in this debate over politics and literature, playing his most active role in the movement since 1925 and 1926. In a series of theoretical and then literary works he published in a variety of journals and newspapers in the summer and fall of 1932, he challenged the Stalinist direction that party members had introduced into the proletarian literature movement. In contrast, his response to Japanese imperialism on the Asian continent was muted. Published in the May 1933 edition of the *Yomiuri shinbun*, his comments to Mr. Kawabe, a reporter from the newspaper, were primarily personal reflections on his life and studies in prison.[11] When asked to consider the changes in Japan after spending two years in prison, Hayashi noted the continuing internal decay of Japanese society, but he seemed to be more preoccupied with the changes in the Writers' League than with Japan's external relations and its involvement in the Manchurian Incident.[12]

Stalinism and Artistic Values

Not only had the political and cultural organizations of the Japanese left-wing radical movement in general shifted considerably by 1932, but after almost two years in prison so had Hayashi Fusao's position, particularly regarding the debate over politics and literature. As Shea and others have suggested, the attempt by party members within the proletarian literature movement to apply the political theory they had just learned from the Comintern directly to the proletarian cultural movement harkens back to a recurring problem in Japan, that of uncritically accepting and implementing ideas and systems from the West.[13] Even recent studies, such as Mats Karlsson's article on Kurahara Korehito's guidance of the socialist literature movement, admit that organizational mistakes made by the leadership contributed to the demise of the movement. Even so, Karlsson argues that Kurahara's critical perspective on the weaknesses of the literature produced by the movement's writers was in line with the literary method

11. Hayashi, "Gokuchūki," 87–145.

12. Hayashi, "Shutsugokuki," in *Hayashi Fusao chosakushū*, vol. 3 (Tokyo: Tsubasa shoin, 1969), 146–152.

13. Shea, *Leftwing Literature in Japan*, 234. See also Moriyama Shigeo's *Nihon Marukusushugi bungaku: bungaku toshite no kakumei to tenkō* (Tokyo: San'ichi shobō, 1977), 199.

of proletarian realism advocated by a contemporary group of moderate Soviet writers.[14]

By the spring of 1932, Kurahara Korehito was in jail. In his absence, police had forced KOPF's two main leaders, Kobayashi Takiji and Miyamoto Kenji, underground. Kobayashi and Miyamoto used pen names to hide their identities, but in their articles they supported the communist party's theoretical interpretation that the cultural movement must catch up with the political movement in turning out working revolutionaries, and they pushed proletarian writers who were still active to become party members. They also became increasingly harsh in their criticism of proletarian literary movement members. For example, if a writer insinuated that the party was overpoliticizing KOPF or disagreed with any decision made by the party, Kobayashi and Miyamoto would censure that writer for being "opportunistic" or for having "right-wing tendencies." Both expressions were the buzzwords of Stalinism and a sign that Stalin's extreme paranoia and his "purge" mentality had made its way into the socialist literary groups via those with ties to the communist party.

Hayashi was the first to balk at Kobayashi's and Miyamoto's insistence that the proletarian writer be required to join the communist party and become a revolutionary agent for the party. He did so in a series of articles published in 1932. While in prison, he concluded that a writer must separate politics from literature because a writer had a different insight into the world than a politician or a scientist. He made this argument in his essay "Sakka no tame: sakka no shikaku to ninmu to kenri to" ("For the writer: the qualifications, responsibilities, and rights of a writer"), which he serialized as an article in the May 19, 20, and 21 editions of the *Tokyo Asahi shinbun*.

In this article, Hayashi first attacked the use of political resolutions (*ketsugi*) and theses (*tēze*) by the Writers' League to guide literature, claiming it produced writers and readers who could not think critically. He stressed that these inexperienced writers and readers, along with commercial publishers, were the main reason that proletarian literature was at the point of collapse in Japan. He then asserted that the responsibilities and qualifications of a politician and a writer were different. Thus, although

14. Mats Karlsson, "Kurahara Korehito's Road to Proletarian Realism," *Japan Review* 20 (2008): 260–262, doi: 148.137.160.22.

Stalin, who had labeled proletarian literature as nothing more than a vulgar expression of Marxism, may be the greatest of politicians, he did not have the training to be a writer.[15] Finally, he argued that the writer not only had the responsibility but also the right to use his qualifications as a writer to produce "a historical novel," not "a vulgar explanation of history."[16] In other words, a historian should prepare a work based on historical facts, while a writer should write a literary piece set in a historical timeframe. Here, Hayashi endeavored to establish the right of the author to draw upon a country's rich literary tradition and the great writers of the past to write literature. His attack on the leadership of the Writers' League blamed them for following Stalin's political leadership instead of their literary instincts, to the detriment of the proletarian cultural movement as a whole.

Hayashi continued to criticize the KOPF leadership's political policies in his "Bungaku no tame ni" ("For literature"), published in the July 1932 issue of *Kaizō*. In this essay, he made a pointed attack on proletarian literature by showing what the Writers' League could learn from both literary tradition and the great writers of the past and present about writing poetry, about improving their prose, and about producing better proletarian fiction. First, he studied the poetry of Takasugi Shinsaku, a Chōshū samurai who participated in the Meiji Restoration, and then Heinrich Heine, a German romantic poet. Hayashi was interested in how Takasugi, while under house arrest, and Heine, while facing death, openly expressed their feelings of self-doubt and hesitation. His conclusion, that exposing one's imperfections and wavering openly in a poem only makes the poem more human, was an affront to the party leadership.[17] By 1932, government suppression had pushed the Japanese Communist Party as a political organization into such an extreme position that it could no longer tolerate any talk of deviation from the official party line, nor could it stand any open questioning of the party's political policies, particularly by a strong and seasoned voice such as Hayashi's.

Hayashi continued his attack by putting forth Shimazaki Tōson, a re-

15. Hayashi Fusao, "Sakka no tame ni: chū, sakka no shikaku to ninmu to kenri to," *Tokyo Asahi shinbun*, 20 May 1932, p. 9.

16. Ibid.

17. Hayashi Fusao, "Bungaku no tame ni," *Kaizō* 14, no. 7 (July 1932): 108.

nowned writer from the naturalist school in Japanese literature, as a model for proletarian writers. He praised Tōson for only using punctuation marks native to Japanese prose in the writing of his historical novel *Yoake mae* (Before the Dawn).[18] To contrast, Hayashi then explained how Kawakami Hajime and others invented new punctuation marks in Japanese to express the colon and semicolon from Western literature. However, the problem with this new set of punctuation marks (including the exclamation and question marks) was that no Japanese author had yet made them feel natural or made them feel "Japanese," while writing fiction.[19] Thus, adapting this foreign punctuation was a task for the proletarian writer, Hayashi noted, but it was a task that would have gone unnoticed if, while serializing *Before the Dawn*, Tōson had not commented on the unnaturalness of these punctuation marks in the first place.

Hayashi's praise for Tōson and his *Before the Dawn* extended into the realm of content. In addition to being surprised at the lack of "foreign" punctuation marks in *Before the Dawn*, he also commented that Tōson had captured the essence of viewing history from the bottom up with his *kusamura* ("from the underbrush") approach to writing about the Restorationist movement in late Tokugawa Japan.[20] Hayashi then boldly asserted that *Before the Dawn* illustrated how proletarian writers should approach the writing of history because Tōson's literary genius transcended the narrow understanding of current writers, much as Marx's intellectual genius transcended that of the current generation.[21] Thus, for the proletarian literature movement to develop further, Hayashi argued, proletarian writers must be willing to learn from the literary conventions of the past to overcome the extreme obstacles that face them in the present. By attacking the narrowness of the movement's current literary views and its writers' understanding of history, Hayashi drove home his main point that the proletarian writer needed to explore views outside the party's interpretation of history and literature. Establishing this new standpoint, he hoped, would enable the proletarian writer to overcome suppression by

18. Shimazaki Tōson, *Before the Dawn*, trans. William E. Naff (Honolulu: University of Hawai'i Press, 1987).

19. Hayashi Fusao, "Bungaku no tame ni," 110–111.

20. Ibid., 114.

21. Ibid., 115.

the police and the alienation from the masses that the socialist literature movement was experiencing in Japan.

Finally, Hayashi declared in "Sakka toshite" ("As a writer"), the last of the series of essays published in the September 1932 issue of *Shinchō*, that literary expression meant more to him than political allegiances. From the opening lines of the essay where he states, "I have made up my mind. I'll wager my life on literature," Hayashi set the tone for his decisive and defiant polemic.[22] First, he conveyed the wavering he had experienced over the question of whether literature should be subservient to political demands or separated from politics outright. He surmised that within the Writers' League, political demands most often had come before literary expression and that, likewise, he had sacrificed literary quality to meet the political needs of the party in his own writing. Initially, he believed that the cause for his wavering on this issue was either the stressful times he lived in, or his struggle with his moral principles as a member of the intelligentsia.[23] However, he concluded that the real reason he had wavered so much was that "he did not correctly understand what literature was."[24]

Hayashi then noted how a Soviet literary critic's comments concerning his work helped him to understand better what literature was. The literary critic, who was living in Japan at the time, separated Hayashi's works into two categories: those of a reporter and those of a writer. Hayashi did not understand the distinction the critic was making, but, in hindsight, he interpreted the difference between making a report and writing literature this way: reporters simply give the facts, while writers use their creative imagination to make penetrating observations about society and the world around them. Illustrating this difference with numerous examples, he described how in serializing his historical novel *Seinen* (Youth), he was trying to build on Shimazaki Tōson's example in *Before the Dawn*. Compared to Mori Ōgai's historical novels that were too straightforward, and to Kikuchi Kan's and Akutagawa Ryūnosuke's works of historical fiction that were too allegorical, Tōson's work came close to striking a balance between history and fiction, and Hayashi praised Tōson for his attempt.[25] Nevertheless, he criticized *Before the*

22. Hayashi Fusao, "Sakka toshite," *Shinchō* 29, no. 9 (September 1932): 57.
23. Ibid., 57.
24. Ibid., 58.
25. Ibid., 62–63.

Dawn as still too historically oriented and finally settled on Tolstoy's *War and Peace* as the best model from which to draw inspiration in writing his historical novel *Youth.*[26]

Ending his essay in a flourish, Hayashi argued that now was the time for "a proletarian renaissance" in Japanese literature. During the Meiji period, the naturalist writers succeeded in developing a literary movement based on bourgeois realism, but instead of bringing their middle-class outlook to bear on society and state, the writers in this group chose to turn inward and study the individual. In so doing, they lost the chance to address the social ills of Meiji society directly. Members of the White Birch School wrote from the perspective of the aristocracy who had lost their position within the middle-class, capitalist society that had emerged in Taishō Japan. While they succeeded in condemning the middle class for the depraved nature of capitalism, writers of the White Birch School were unable to overcome their elite consciousness and connect with the working classes. Thus, Hayashi asserted that the only intellectuals who could overcome their elite consciousness and who could create a new culture grounded in a working-class understanding of a capitalist society were truly proletarian writers in the Writers' League.[27] They would lead the proletarian renaissance and turn it into reality, Hayashi hoped.

Hayashi's critical assault on the leadership of KOPF in these essays was perhaps more of a warning at this point, because he was still a proletarian writer and supported the Writers' League.[28] Still, he made two key points. First, he claimed that in pressuring writers and intellectuals to become full-time revolutionaries, the communist party was asking them to perform tasks for which they were unsuited. Second, he noted that the pressure to fulfill political duties before writing literature was tearing apart the Writers' League and threatening its very existence, both as a legal organization and as a viable literary group. Hayashi did not confine his rebuke to just these theoretical essays but integrated his censure of the communist party and its leaders into the writing of his short stories. This criticism is systematically evident first in his shift from pointing out the behavioral flaws as well as the strengths of student radicals, labor organizers, and fac-

26. Ibid., 63.
27. Ibid., 65.
28. Moriyama, *Nihon Marukusushugi bungaku*, 201.

tory workers in his proletarian short stories; then in recounting elements of their struggle; and finally by honoring and memorializing the activists and workers' sacrifices for the cause. In this way, Hayashi moved from an active, committed struggle to improve the composition of the movement as a living, growing organization to a reflective act of remembering what from his perspective had become a stymied struggle for social justice.

CHRONICLING THE HUMAN COSTS OF THE STRUGGLE

Published soon after "Lust," in the September 1929 issue of *Shinchō*, Hayashi's "*Robin Fuddo* jiken" ("The *Robin Hood* Incident") marks this political adjustment in his writing from defining the desired traits of workers and organizers to paying tribute to their suffering and toil. From the opening of the tale, Hayashi explains that this is a "true story," that he will change the names of the people in the narrative as is customary and leave it up to the readers to tell who is who in the story. The narrator begins with an introduction to the Yanagishima Settlement sponsored by Tokyo Imperial University, which he describes as the "university's colony" planted in a workers' town to bring the knowledge of the university to the workers and the experience of living with the workers to the university.[29] Then he explains that some of the money to sponsor that settlement came from a group called the Student Federation for the Kantō Disaster Educational Recovery (Kantō shinsai kyōiku fukkō gakusei renmei), which is the main subject of this story. With most of his fellow activists incarcerated either in Ichigaya prison or Toyotama prison, the narrator also notes that he wants to put this episode down on paper just as he remembered it, since it was such a remarkable incident. The story starts with the Great Kantō Earthquake of September 1, 1923, and the narrator saying that he was at home in Ōita that summer doing socialist enlightenment work for the New Man Society when he read about the devastating earthquake and the attack on socialists in the local newspapers.[30]

Although he wanted to return to Tokyo, one of his friends, Nakano

29. Hayashi Fusao, "*Robin Fuddo* jiken," *Shinchō* 26, no. 9 (September 1929): 2.
30. Hayashi, "*Robin Fuddo* jiken," 4.

Satsuo, from the New Man Society visited his home with a resolution from the Society's main office in Tokyo. It stated that members in the provinces were to remain where they were and work on building a recovery fund for the organization. They instructed members to approach Tokyo Imperial University alumni residing in their regions and to request financial help for a cultural restoration project.[31] Contacting alumni for donations worked well but his friend Nakano had a more daring plan. He argued for renting the popular 1922 film *Robin Hood* starring Douglas Fairbanks from the United Artists office in Kobe and then using local connections in Kyūshū to set up showings of the film to students and to the public so that they could take in a larger amount of contributions. After gaining approval for the funding project under the name Student Federation for the Kantō Disaster Educational Recovery, the narrator describes how they would use the local university alumni associations to gain support from the local governments as well as the schools. They would have one showing at an elementary school in the morning, a noon performance at a girls' middle school, and then a final viewing at night open to the public. Asking for donations to help with the recovery in Tokyo with each performance, the activists did very well in their tour of Kyūshū, but they succeeded particularly well in the town of Ōmuta, an industrial town dominated by a Mitsui mining operation. There, the main office put them in touch with a couple of alumni who worked for Mitsui. These alumni then aided the student activists in every way possible, treating them as honored guests and arranging for multiple performances in several of the schools.[32] They received by far the largest amount of donations in Ōmuta, enabling them to clear well over 4,000 *yen* for the entire tour to send back to the New Man Society office in Tokyo. Hoping that half of the money would go to socialist movement activities, the student activists were disappointed to find that the main office poured all of it into funding the startup of the Yanagishima Settlement Project.[33] Our narrator ends the story by describing Nakano's attempt to infiltrate the Mitsui mining operation in Ōmuta several years later. This time, the alumni who had helped them

31. Ibid., 8–9.
32. Ibid., 11–14.
33. Hayashi, "*Robin Fuddo* jiken," 15.

earlier were waiting at the train station with police to pick him up as a spy, but he dressed so shabbily that they could not recognize him and he was able to return safely to Tokyo. For the narrator, this final memory fits in with Nakano's first visit to his home that fall of 1923 when his scruffy appearance so shocked his mother that she was afraid to let him into the house. Only after Nakano left the house and took a bath, washed his clothes, and shaved did his mother welcome him into the house, the narrator tells us.[34]

While drawing our attention to the innovative spirit of these student radicals, the focus in "The *Robin Hood* Incident" clearly is on memorializing their boldness and daring. From the start, the narrator tells the story in retrospect, as a noteworthy memory from his past. In many ways, "The *Robin Hood* Incident" also reminds one of the idealized tales of exploitation and loss like "Apples" and "Cocoons," particularly since Hayashi portrays the New Man Society activists as heroic figures in his account. Nevertheless, instead of the narrator joining the socialist movement or calling for others to take up the struggle against social injustice, the narrator concludes with an add-on story that details Nakano's disheveled appearance and recalls another place and time in their personal history together. Throughout the piece, the narrator notes that the other student radicals who took part in this incident are now incarcerated. Thus, in writing this story, he is acting as a scribe to chronicle their audacious plan to help restore the finances of the socialist movement after the earthquake. We learn that there are consequences for their actions. For example, we learn at the end of the story that the alumni from the Mitsui mining company who helped them some years before were angry enough to wait for Nakano at the train station in Ōmuta, just to turn him in as a spy. We also discover after all their hard work, the main office did not distribute the funds the student radicals raised as they had hoped.

Hence, this is not a romantic tale to inspire others to join the noble cause of socialism, nor is it attempting to underline the positive and negative aspects of the students' behavior and actions as representatives of the socialist movement. Instead, the narrator is keen to highlight the names, places, and dates of this incident, almost as a chronicler taking down the facts of an event to preserve it for posterity. Moreover, the narrator em-

34. Ibid., 15–16.

ploys the use of fiction as a means to capture the emotions that he and the other student radicals expressed and experienced as they carried out their plan. In addition to the facts of the incident, the narrator also records the feelings of the New Man Society activists. He relates the shock at hearing news of the Great Kantō Earthquake, the students' pride in developing such a brash plan, and the disappointment they experienced in witnessing the funds they had raised in Kyūshū being allocated for another purpose by the Society's main office in Tokyo.

This story represents an interesting change in the tasking of Hayashi's fiction, presumably because it follows the second major round of police arrests of Leftists on April 16, 1929. As a consequence, it also points to the beginning of Hayashi's more cynical interpretation of the proletarian literature movement, and his changing place in that movement from participant and activist to observer and scribe. Here in this story, Hayashi records what happened and how factory workers, student radicals, and labor organizers experienced that past. In essence, he preserves those memories for others to witness the heyday of the fading socialist movement. Still, as we have already observed, Hayashi often used his literature as a means for politically driven commentary on the movement and its leadership, and that tendency is evident here as well. In this case, the students are raising money to help with the recovery of the New Man Society itself, but when they turn in the money collected, the main office uses the money to sponsor the Yanagishima Settlement Project. Hayashi's narrator records the displeasure of the students with this choice, indirectly suggesting the NALPF writers' discontent with other decisions made by the main office of KOPF and with the fallout from those choices. Thus, even though Hayashi shifts his short stories' objective to remembering the movement, he does so to underline the human costs of the KOPF leadership's determination to force its writers to become politicians and agents of the party.

Hayashi's "Kinema no gaidoku" ("The Evils of Cinema"), published in the October 1929 issue of *Bungaku jidai* (Age of Literature), highlights the real dangers that young socialists faced. At the same time, this short story concentrates mainly on personal relationships, drawing attention to the consequences of the labor activist's involvement in the socialist movement when it came to those relationships. At the center of this story is the mother-daughter relationship between Eiko and her widowed mother,

Okome. Eiko works at a government office and the salary she draws allows them to live comfortably. However, Okome begins to worry about her daughter when Eiko has her hair bobbed in the "modern girl" style and begins to stay out at night. Okome shows her daughter a newspaper article about police arresting delinquent girls caught out late at night, but Eiko explains that she is simply out enjoying the cinema with her friends.[35] Then, the police show up at Okome's door and ask to search Eiko's room. They also tell Okome that they are holding her daughter for questioning, and Eiko finally returns home five days later. The next day she hands her mother her severance pay from the government office.[36] Eiko meets with a friend from the socialist movement early the following morning and tells her friend that she can only work for the union a couple of times a week. When the friend asks if her mother knows about her involvement with the movement, Eiko firmly declares that she does not want her mother to find out about her union work. Her mother is aging and will pass away soon. Then, with a smile, she says that she will always tell her mother that she is going out to the cinema instead.[37]

While the story places Eiko in the socialist movement working for a union, the emphasis is on her transformation into a "modern girl" and, more pointedly, how that change profoundly affects her relationship with her mother. We do learn that she is a clever labor activist when she tells her friend that she has hidden the documents related to her work with the union in her father's Buddhist memorial tablet; that way, the police will not discover them during their search.[38] Likewise, we also know that she is dedicated to her work and that she is determined to continue helping the union whenever she can, but all of this information comes on the last page of the story. Perhaps we could give it more weight if it led to her start in the socialist movement, but we are never given a hint as to why Eiko joined the movement. Even more, we never learn why she, an employee in the Insurance Section for the Secretary of the Ministry of Communications (*Teishinshō*), is working for the movement.[39]

We observe the changes in her appearance and in her living habits that

35. Hayashi Fusao, "Kinema no gaidoku," *Bungaku jidai* 1, no. 6 (October 1929): 223.
36. Ibid., 225–226.
37. Ibid., 226.
38. Ibid.
39. Hayashi, "Kinema no gaidoku," 222.

lead her to become a "modern girl," but Eiko does not disclose any motivation for her involvement in the socialist movement. Instead, she describes herself as her mother's "cane and pillar."[40] Okome depends on Eiko, but she reacts with dismay as she witnesses Eiko's external transformation. Eiko also never confronts her mother or confides in her about why the police came to their home to search her room, or why the police pushed to get her fired from her work.[41] She is content to allow her mother to think that she has turned into an irresponsible daughter rather than tell her the truth: that she is a socialist and working for a union.

In the end, Eiko tells her friend that her mother will not last much longer, and from the description of Okome's reaction to Eiko losing her job, we view firsthand the consequences of participating in the socialist movement. In the beginning, Okome is quiet but displays a vibrant personality. However, her demeanor changes by the story's end. She stares vacantly into space when her daughter tries to hand her the severance pay envelope. Then, after sitting for a long time, she asks her daughter in a whispery, withered voice what will become of her without a job.[42] While Eiko's transformation is dramatic, Okome's deterioration is tragic, leading Eiko to keep the truth from her mother forever. In this story's acts of reflection, sympathy, and remembrance for the sacrifices made by family members, the labor activist Eiko acknowledges the destructive impact of the socialist movement on her relationship with her mother. Considering that, up till now, Hayashi had blamed the government for destroying family relationships in Japanese society, it must have been galling for the KOPF leaders to read him now accusing them of doing the very same thing, and publishing that criticism in a bourgeois journal. In terms of Hayashi's evolving sense of victimization, in "The Evils of Cinema" we find him aligning the communist leadership of KOPF with the Japanese state as fellow conspirators.

Hayashi's 1930 short story "Mr. Mayone Yonekichi's Bronze Statue," published in the January issue of *Kaizō*, expands this condemnation to the organizational level. This story of factory life centers not on the grim lives of the workers in his factory, but on the factory owner Mayone and his

40. Ibid., 221.
41. Ibid., 224–225.
42. Ibid., 221, 225.

scheming to use his economic fortune to gain political power. Mayone operates a factory that makes ceramic goods, and we learn that the bronze statue is the result of the company employees' and the artisans' "volunteering" to have a portion of their check withheld each month to pay for the statue, as Mayone believes in the "we-are-all-one-big-family" method of running his factory.[43] During the weeks after the ceremony, the workers turn to throwing rocks at the bronze statue to express their unhappiness at their lost wages. While Mayone is embarrassed, he is angrier at having failed to have his statue built in the city's central park, where he wanted it to be the center of public attention.[44] We learn that the municipal government refuses to honor Mayone because he has never donated any money to its public works projects. Mayone works on obliging the city assembly members to recognize him and his company's success, and in time, they give him a medal for his efforts.

However, in the general election, there is a changeover in leadership and the police discover that Mayone has used his influence and money to pay off the members of the trade association to sponsor him for the medal. The police arrest him but company management compels all five hundred workers to sign a petition in support of their employer's innocence.[45] In reality, the workers are gathered around the bronze statue for a grand party and a work stoppage. They celebrate by placing ceramic handcuffs and a ceramic waist-belt around Mayone's statue, but the guards destroy them. Still, there is also sadness among some workers in their realization that it was an outside power that put the real handcuffs and waist-belt on Mayone. In the end, another worker creates a ceramic medal and places it on the chest of the Mayone statue for all the workers to enjoy.[46]

Here, we have a portrait of worker discontent. But even in the course of the story, it is obvious that outside forces rather than their efforts led to the arrest of Mayone. The workers are willing to take some risks to express their unhappiness over having their wages withheld to build the bronze statue, but never do the five hundred artisans and workers rise as one to stop the deduction to their wages in having the statue built. Instead, the

43. Hayashi Fusao, "Mayone Yonekichi-shi no dōzō," *Kaizō* 12, no. 1 (January 1930): 127–128.

44. Ibid., 132.

45. Ibid., 135.

46. Ibid., 135–136.

focus of this short story is first on the humorous and indirect nature of the workers' protests, and second, on Mayone's vain manipulation of the city assembly to force its members to acknowledge him as a key contributor to the local economy. Mayone is never depicted as a malevolent boss. He treats the two workers caught throwing stones at the statue leniently, and we learn that this is due more to Mayone's distress over his political ineptness.

Ultimately, it is worker vulnerability, rather than worker triumph or worker initiative, that defines this story. Only the city assembly and the police can end Mayone's schemes to have his greatness recognized. As for the workers, they can only express their frustration by throwing stones at the bronze statue. Mayone, however, is not satisfied with docking the workers' pay to erect a bronze statue to himself. He needs affirmation from both the city and the prefectural officials that he is an important person. His pride and ego take him down as the authorities arrest him for his crimes, leaving the workers to celebrate his downfall. Unlike the previous stories that highlighted the good and bad traits of workers, this story underscores the factory owner's character flaws, and there are no noble causes for which to give one's life here. Hayashi leaves us with a story by an author trying to show his prowess as an "intellectual humorist," rather than a story of proletarian literature, it would seem.

Here, the struggle between management and workers is a farce, and the story is more melodrama than a victory for the workers. Thus, the emphasis on Mayone's actions precludes any real heroics from the workers. Perhaps, with the defeat of a greedy capitalist factory owner while the workers endure his venal attempts at self-promotion, the story signifies the downfall of industrial capitalism. Instead of learning more about worker exploitation, the workers' struggle to overcome that exploitation, or how workers should conduct themselves, what remains is a story that emphasizes the owner's vanity and deceit. Even though the mistreatment of the workers is evident, they are unable to extricate themselves from the situation through any organized expression of disobedience. Through the entertaining scenes of workers' throwing rocks at the bronze statue and the artisans snickering at the ceremony, the narrative employs indirect demonstrations of disrespect for Mayone, rather than acts of defiance. The narrator describes the workers as complying with everything the factory's managerial group wants, from the degrading act of tossing of flower bouquets at the feet of the bronze statue to the coerced and shameful signing of the petition to support Mayone.

Much more than the other short stories chronicling workers fighting the good fight, this story draws attention to the factory workers' impotence, records their feeble bluster in the face of this oppression, and exposes just how little they can do to change their circumstances. Obscured in the humorous overtones of the story is the tragic and wretched end of the workers' movement as seen through the narrator's eyes. Written in the wake of the major blow administered to the socialist movement as a whole by the previous March 1928 and April 1929 police arrests, Hayashi's attempts to confront state authority had also failed. As we noted earlier, the Osaka Court of Appeals officially denied his appeal in 1929 and the court ordered him to serve a two-year sentence from the spring of 1930 for violating the Peace Preservation Law in 1926. Thus, Hayashi was enduring both humiliation and suffering in the wake of his own futile confrontation with the state. Preparing for his imprisonment, he found himself caught between the ineffectual leadership of KOPF and the overwhelming power of the police as he surrendered to the authorities to start his prison sentence that summer of 1930.

VENERATING THE FIGHT! ENABLING HAYASHI'S *TENKŌ* IDEOLOGY!

Hayashi returned to the subject of the labor organizer and factory worker after his release from prison in 1932, once again overtly celebrating their youthful idealism and enthusiasm in his writing. As such, he set the course for his *tenkō* by first revisiting the socialist movement's past, and then eulogizing what he wanted to remember about that time. He established his rhetoric of *tenkō*, an ideology of fictional, lived experience through which he began to write into existence a remolded boyhood, enabling his *tenkō* ideology for a different self, and for an alternative perspective from which to criticize the state's oppression of Japanese society. Published in the January 1933 issue of *Kaizō*, Hayashi's "Sodateru" ("Childhood") represents the first step in this shifting path as he focuses on the mental life of Takeuchi, a labor organizer reflecting on his education as a socialist activist for the workers.

"Childhood" starts with Takeuchi playing a game of *kendama* with seven-year-old Toshio. Takeuchi is renting the room above a secondhand tools shop and Toshio is the shopowner's child. Told in hindsight by a third-person narrator, the first chapter highlights Takeuchi's affable side as viewed from Toshio's perspective.[47] In the second chapter, we learn more of Takeuchi's secret life as a labor activist. In chapter 3 of the story we follow him as he surreptitiously makes his way to a meeting with other members of the group he is leading. Next, we learn of their intended target, the Hinode Fertilizer plant. One member of Takeuchi's group is Fujita, who is undergoing his first experience working for the labor union movement. He is unfamiliar with this region, and while staking out the plant in a wet field, he comes down with a fever. Fujita is barely able to make his report to Takeuchi, but he is moved by his young comrade's dedication and spirit.[48]

Takeuchi then takes on the work of scouting the plant in chapter 4 of the story, which in turn leads him to ponder his path to this point. We discover that Takeuchi left home when he was seventeen and worked for ten years in various factories before joining the labor movement.[49] When the leadership sent him to his current region two years earlier, Takeuchi's mentor in the movement taught him everything he knew. Takeuchi recalls the first time he handed out flyers for a group demonstration among workers, and he now wants to pass on what he has learned from his mentor to Fujita.[50] In the final chapter of "Childhood," Takeuchi and his group watch the demonstration they have been planning take place. Since it does not happen the way he expected, Takeuchi uses the confusion of the scene to search the crowd for a worker they can approach.[51] In a short postscript, the narrator asserts that this is the first third of a planned three-part work. However, since he put all his heart into every paragraph here, it is fine if the reader takes this piece as an independent work that stands alone.[52]

Takeuchi's story reads much like a character sketch that turns into a labor activist's diary, since we first learn about our main character's personality and then on how he spends much of his time reflecting on his

47. Hayashi Fusao, "Sodateru," *Kaizō* 15, no. 1 (January 1933): 204.
48. Ibid., 210–213.
49. Ibid., 215.
50. Ibid., 216–221.
51. Ibid., 224–228.
52. Ibid., 228.

formative years in the movement. Throughout the story, Hayashi gives a series of personages or events that act as catalysts to jog Takeuchi's memory or to provide background information about Takeuchi's character, which is the case in the first chapter. Here, we learn from Toshio that Takeuchi is a caring and a kind person. Takeuchi is also a careful person. He makes sure it is Toshio at the door before sharing his books, and even Toshio notices the difference between the relaxed Takeuchi at ease in playing *kendama* with him and the vigilant Takeuchi who is anxious and on edge at times. Toshio's perceptive observations about Takeuchi's personality set the stage for other chapters. We learn that Takeuchi is an experienced member of the labor movement and we follow him as he models his leadership skills with Fujita. We also learn of Takeuchi's distrust of the intellectual class, as he contrasts the worker's sincere heart with the deceit of the intellectual put in the same situation as Fujita. In the final chapters, we find Takeuchi reminiscing about his training in the movement.

Not only does the introspective nature of this journal-like story set it apart, so too does the open hostility directed toward the intelligentsia. This is much more than a memoir that records the work of labor organizers who sacrificed their lives working in the field. It also acknowledges which types of student radicals contributed to the movement, as well as those who did not. Takeuchi, several times during the narrative, mentions his wariness of intellectuals because they could not be trusted to take responsibility for their mistakes and failures in carrying out the orders of the labor movement. Takeuchi admires only his mentor, "*Megane*" (Glasses) the intellectual, who reads German books in his free time. Takeuchi's respect derives from his belief that "Glasses" is committed to his work both heart and soul, unlike most other college graduates Takeuchi has met in the movement. They tend to use their intellectual aptitude to make excuses; they lack perseverance and they dislike the drudgery of carrying out the less glamorous tasks assigned to them by the movement.[53] By placing Takeuchi, who has an impeccable worker background, at the center of this account, Hayashi defines him as the ideal type of labor organizer. Moreover, in stressing Takeuchi's desire to pass on what he has

53. Hayashi, "Sodateru," 211–213, 221.

learned to the newcomer Fujita, Hayashi signals his intention to chronicle Takeuchi's work for others to admire later.

"Childhood" is one of the most censored short stories of Hayashi's career, with large parts of chapter 3 replete with *fuseji*, and the text in chapter 4 obscured, not just by *fuseji* but also with several sections of up to thirty to forty characters cut from the narrative. These are the two sections where Takeuchi is deep in retrospect about his time in the movement, and where he compares and contrasts the student radicals' and the workers' involvements in the labor movement. Consequently, "Childhood" reads as a memorial to subsequent labor organizers like Takeuchi and "Glasses," underscoring their contributions as being worthy of praise. Their heartfelt devotion and sacrifice to serve the working class drew them to the labor movement, in distinct contrast to those student radicals who sought glamor and adventure in this line of work, and who, consequently, should be dismissed and forgotten.

However, the emphasis in the title is on the training or the upbringing of Takeuchi and his group. Thus, we learn much about Takeuchi's education in the movement and much about his mentor's role in nurturing Takeuchi's love for his work as a labor activist. In addition, the narrative also highlights the movement's lessons in trying to organize the workers. The demonstration that Takeuchi and his group instigated starts with several male workers riding bicycles on a dirt bridge over a lake that connects the town with the Yasendai Iron Foundry and the Hinode Fertilizer plant. They ride over the bridge into town at closing time for the factory, and the women workers join them, riding bicycles and wearing different-colored gloves and shawls that drape down to their legs. Takeuchi notices something strange about the colorful procession, however. The young workers, both girls and boys, had dressed up in their finest clothes. The women had put on makeup and the men were wearing suits as they rode through town. Instead of scowling workers expressing their discontent with current working conditions, they look like young ladies and young gentlemen out on a date, and the festival-like scene prompts Takeuchi to smile bitterly at the "modern" turn of the demonstration.[54] In the end, Takeuchi has to find another worker from whom to solicit help so that the labor organizers can have a direct presence and voice in the factory. It becomes a

54. Ibid., 222–223.

learning experience for the labor movement as well, showing its immaturity with hilarious results.

In this fashion, Takeuchi not only honors the work of young labor activists like Fujita, but he also turns back the clock on the socialist movement and its membership. What Takeuchi describes is a golden age in his mind, a time when its members were sincere in their motivations. Likewise, their attempts to organize were earnest, even if they did not always succeed. As we are reminded in the narrative, this was a time before the devious and lazy intellectuals became overly involved in the movement, and in the heavily censored text of the story we have a graphic account of the state's excessive intervention in the proletarian writer's work at present. While Takeuchi's disapproval of intellectuals as a group is evident, what stands out more in "Childhood" is his attempt to remember his beginnings in the movement and further, to separate and isolate certain memories as a starting point for others, as well as for himself—to begin all over again. Hayashi expands on this narrative of temporal displacement in his July 1933 tribute to the factory workers in "Shōnen" ("Boyhood"), also published in *Kaizō*.

In "Boyhood" Hayashi builds upon the memoirs of Aso Hiroshi, a young factory worker who would eventually become a writer of proletarian literature himself, to underscore the hardships that young factory apprentices encountered in the printing industry. Using the memoir form as the basis for his fictional story, Hayashi explores familiar ground in "Boyhood" as sixteen-year-old Yanagita Yasuji keeps a journal of his experiences working in the Fukuda Printing Company. Building on the character sketch and diarist style in "Childhood," Hayashi transforms the narrative into an actual journal based on the writings of a factory worker. Even so, in documenting Yasuji's interactions with representatives from a variety of left-wing viewpoints and his increasingly confused responses to these characters, Hayashi also attempts to redefine and then remake his own Marxist past.

From the beginning of the journal dated September 20 to its final entry on October 30, Hayashi treats the reader to an in-depth look at the life of the apprentice worker, from the workplace to the cafeteria and even into the factory's sleeping and bathing quarters. Yasuji suffers as he struggles to adjust to the long hours standing on the factory floor, the poor food in the cafeteria, and the bedbugs that congregate in the dirty futons in the boarders' sleeping area.[55] Soon Yasuji complains of the exhaustion that leaves him unable to sleep soundly, and he writes of others' objections to the stinginess of the cafeteria staff in doling out their food and on the hierarchical relationship between the adult workers and the young apprentices.[56] At one point in the narrative, Yasuji tells how the boss called him and several other workers off the factory floor and moved them into a hallway deep inside the factory where they were kept for over twenty minutes. Only later does he discover that the printing factory was being inspected and that the boss wanted to keep out of sight all workers who were under the legal age of eighteen.[57] As this section ends, we find Yasuji increasingly chafing at the formal and informal economic and social hierarchies that frame the lives of apprentices.[58] Thus, Hayashi sets the stage as he illustrates the difficulties of factory life, honoring those like Yasuji who work under these distressing conditions.

Next, the narrative examines the growing rift between the socialist and the humanist, using the distinction developed in "Childhood" between the worker and the intellectual as a bridge to that discussion. Starting with the section where he explains how he remembered the differences between the Chinese characters (*kanji*) so that he could set the type for these characters, Yasuji also notes that he had similar problems in mastering the different *katakana* for foreign loanwords like *interu* (interline) and *interi* (intelligentsia). Fortunately, as Yasuji mentions, *interi* is a word that Sugiyama, another worker in the factory, uses frequently. Yasuji then recounts that Sugiyama always praises him by saying that he will become a good proletariat.[59]

Eventually, Sugiyama recruits Yasuji to join the socialist movement. When they meet in one of the used bookstores in the Kanda district, Yasuji describes Sugiyama as acting like a white-collar employee for a company in speech and physical features, despite growing up in the Yotsuya district of Tokyo and being a true *Edokko* ("child of Edo"). However, like the description of "Glasses" in "Childhood," Yasuji then notes that Sugiyama was a fearless member of the socialist movement, though nobody

55. Hayashi, "Shōnen," 5–11.
56. Ibid., 13–14.
57. Ibid., 16–17.
58. Ibid., 34.
59. Ibid., 15–16.

would guess this from his relatively privileged upbringing.[60] In essence, Hayashi depicts Sugiyama as an intellectual whom Yasuji trusts and who acts as his mentor.[61] The more immediate comparison is with Takeuchi's mentor in "Childhood," but Sugiyama's and Yasuji's relationship also reminds one of Moriyama's bond with the narrator in Hayashi's 1925 short story "Fool." The difference here is that Sugiyama does not embrace his lower-class upbringing like Moriyama does, nor do we observe him planning and leading a demonstration as Takeuchi does and as Moriyama attempts to do in "Fool."

Sugiyama's work here is political and ideological, turning the young worker Yasuji into a bourgeoning socialist under his guidance. Yasuji does not organize his fellow workers or participate in any demonstrations or strikes against management here. Instead, he tries out new socialist ideas in his discussions with an older worker, Yoshida, whom Yasuji discovers is a humanist intellectual and a writer who admires the poet Ishikawa Takuboku's work.[62] Yoshida is also part of a coterie literature journal called *Faust*, and Yasuji obtains a copy of the journal from his friend and reads it. It does not take long before Yasuji tires of reading Yoshida's poems about love, angst, the seasons, and loneliness. In the next entry of the journal, Yasuji writes down the lyrics of a revolutionary song that he sings at work, and he declares that it is more elegant than any of Yoshida's poetry.[63]

Subsequently, the October 15 journal entry begins with Yasuji writing about how disconcerting his initial intellectual confrontation with Yoshida had been. Yoshida declared that Takuboku was a genius and Yasuji countered that Takuboku's writing was sentimental. Then, in an aside, Ya-

---

60. Hayashi, "Shōnen," 27–28.

61. Ibid. Much of the section where we learn of Sugiyama's role as Yasuji's mentor in the socialist movement has been reduced through censorship with sections of 112, 18, and 23 characters deleted from the October 13 entry of the journal as well as other parts of the narrative replaced with *fuseji*.

62. Donald Keene observes that "Takuboku is undoubtedly the most popular and beloved tanka poet of modern times, not only because of the great individuality of his poetry but because his life captured the imagination of the Japanese," in his *Dawn to the West: Japanese Literature in the Modern Era, Poetry, Drama, Criticism*, An Owl Book (New York: Henry Holt and Company, 1984), 41–42; see pages 41–48 for Keene's discussion of Takuboku's poetry.

63. Hayashi, "Shōnen," 20–21. The lyrics are to an Italian revolutionary song that has been translated into Japanese.

suji makes clear that he did not know that much about Takuboku's work, just that he hated the maudlin way in which Yoshida always sang Takuboku's songs. Yoshida retorts that humans are emotional beings and that it is not a crime to express those sentiments honestly. Yasuji admits that inside he feels the same way, but he tells Yoshida that, unless we as human beings can put aside our emotions, the weak will remain oppressed. Instead of a sappy expression of feelings, we need to be resolute and stand up for ourselves, he asserts, to which Yoshida calls him "presumptuous." Admitting that he is simply parroting the arguments that Sugiyama has taught him, he confesses that Sugiyama's words are of course correct, but that what Yoshida said does not seem wrong either. Confused, Yasuji reverts to a childish rejoinder to hide his bewilderment, which only enrages Yoshida more and he walks away from their conversation, leaving Yasuji feeling small and unhappy that Yoshida's first impression of him was that of an impudent boy.[64] Yasuji and Yoshida's skirmish of ideas is reminiscent of Nakano Shigeharu's criticism of Hayashi's 1926 short story "Apples" for his use of emotion to capture the hearts of readers instead of employing Marxist theory to entreat the readers to think more about the exploitative relationships defined in "Apples."

Yasuji's next clash with Yoshida is noted in his October 20 journal entry and this time focuses on the controversial subject of religion. The entry starts with a paraphrase from Yoshida, asserting that no one can deny the need for religion and that the priests and monks who convey Christ's message to others are the cause of the problems with Christianity, not Christ himself. In their hearts, all people seek some higher power to comfort themselves and the entity that gives them that reassurance is God. "I am against this notion of yours that Marx's teachings can explain all the workings of the world," Yoshida insists. In response, Yasuji asks Yoshida if he is willing to turn the other cheek if someone slaps him, and he maintains that religion is nothing but a convenient tool. Flustered, Yoshida tells Yasuji to take some time to truly read the Bible. Though he is not a Christian, Yoshida affirms that all humans search for something that will warm their hearts and soothe their souls. "This is what you do not seem to understand yet." Yoshida's voice trails off, and Yasuji realizes that Yoshida is trying to

64. Ibid., 22–23.

placate him by acknowledging his youthfulness. Instead, this only inflames Yasuji who retorts that the Bible is a book of lies.[65]

Yoshida responds to Yasuji's outburst by telling him that he misunderstood his main point. He explains that Christ is a human who lived and died as a man whom the priests and monks had turned into a god. It is the human Christ's words and actions that give us such solace, Yoshida emphasizes. Taken aback by this argument emphasizing the humanity of Christ, Yasuji in an aside concedes that he is simply regurgitating what Sugiyama has taught him about religion's role in human society, but that he just cannot bring himself to believe in religion. Maybe this is because of his personality, or maybe it is because he is a worker, he muses. Weary of Yasuji's petulance, Yoshida accuses him of being a quarrelsome boy, one who likes to provoke others because he cannot grasp why people need a godlike figure in their lives. Their conversation ends with Yasuji answering that he is just fine with Yoshida labeling him belligerent. Later, Yasuji walks up to the third-floor area where the clothes are being dried and he reflects on his discussion with Yoshida. He confesses again that he has little confidence in what he said and that he was just bluffing his way through their conversation, yet he does feel better now and whistles the revolutionary song noted earlier in the journal.[66]

Yoshida's denunciation of Christian leaders for creating a "false god" out of Christ and his teachings is blatant in this section. It is interesting that we have the humanist intellectual Yoshida making this accusation here, while the socialist Yasuji stews in his boyish ignorance. Still, Yoshida's insistence that all humans search for a higher power to give meaning to their lives and to comfort them reads as an ode to the power of humanism. This admission in "Boyhood" is remarkable, as is Yasuji's flailing attempts to counter Yoshida's arguments. It is also an acknowledgment that emotion is a meaningful part of people's lives, and that people do look to a higher power for solace by placing that search for meaning within a religious context.

The next journal entry highlights Yasuji's desire to improve his knowledge of socialism. Yasuji writes that he visited Sugiyama and borrowed a book entitled *Musansha seiji kyōtei, daigobu, rōdō undōshi* (A study of

65. Hayashi, "Shōnen," 29.
66. Ibid., 29–30.

proletarian politics: Volume 5, History of the workers movement). We learn that he was at Sugiyama's place because Sugiyama lectures on socialism every Thursday evening but Yasuji has trouble reading this dense book. He finally asks a friend to explain the relationship between the owner's desire to turn a profit and his exploitation of the workers. After an hour of attempting to teach Yasuji, his friend gives up. Exasperated, his friend ends his explanation with the same childish retort Yasuji gave Yoshida in their earlier meeting.[67]

In the lengthy exchange between Yasuji and Yoshida, the emphasis is on the impotence of the socialist movement and the convoluted, perplexing nature of socialism for Yasuji. In the initial section of this story, Yasuji is depicted as the typical enthusiastic youth of Hayashi's proletarian short stories; but here, the intellectual leader Sugiyama leads Yasuji astray and down a path he does not truly comprehend. Sugiyama is described as a member of the elite and as an ideologue who fills Yasuji's mind with revolutionary songs and socialist teachings. While Yasuji can reproduce these teachings in his dialogue with Yoshida, he does not grasp the meaning of the words, nor the nuances in the theoretical arguments he is mimicking, and each meeting ends in further frustration and confusion for him.

Much like our female activist from Hayashi's "Insects Gathering around the Light" who responds to Sōichi's humanism with rank sarcasm, here it is the humanist Yoshida who at first encourages Yasuji to think beyond the socialist teachings he has learned. In their next meeting, Yoshida, though tiring of Yasuji's peevish rejoinders, attempts to push Yasuji intellectually to move past the Socialist mantras he recites from Sugiyama's lectures. In their final talk, Yoshida accuses Yasuji of being an agitator, altogether stopping the dialogue between them. Throughout, Yasuji regresses in his understanding of Socialism and fails in the movement's goals to persuade others of the rationale of Marx's vision for social change. In the end, it is the humanist intellectual Yoshida who is revealed to be the warm, kind, and thoughtful mentor figure whom Yasuji should have followed. Sugiyama is simply duping Yasuji with a doctrine that he cannot

67. Ibid., 30. This work is a Japanese translation of Alexander Emel's 1930 book, *Lehrbücher des proletarischen Klassenkämpfes, Band I, Leitfaden zur Geschichte der Arbeiterbewegung.*

grasp by himself, that he cannot explain to others, and that his fellow workers cannot even help him understand.

As such, the character Yasuji seemingly acts as a stand-in for Hayashi's youthful encounter with Marxism, allowing Hayashi to build and project a different narrative of his years as a student radical and labor activist to his readers. This time he portrays his time in the socialist movement as largely wasted, as Yasuji echoes the youthful idealism of Hayashi when he joined the movement. However, in this case, Hayashi's enthusiasm ultimately is exploited by the communist leaders of KOPF—represented by Sugiyama here—for political purposes he cannot fathom, and whose zeal for writing socialist literature he loses in the protracted wrangling of the politics versus literature debate within the proletarian literature movement. Thus, Hayashi's reinterpretation of these years as a squandered boyhood, one that would continue through his postwar writings, began to take form in his proletarian revisionist fiction first. Through writing Yasuji's experiences in "Boyhood," Hayashi began extricating his past experiences from the political Left, even as he suggests how KOPF's political agenda has tainted his idealism and passion. Furthermore, in writing "Boyhood," which reminds one of characters and themes in his first proletarian short stories that romanticized the movement, he attempts to reclaim these works of literature from the proletarian literature movement's canon. The first step in Hayashi's *tenkō* ideology, was to admit that he had been deceived so that he could retrieve those experiences to use as a base upon which to set a new course and to find a new meaning for his professional life.

The narrative in "Boyhood" concludes with Yasuji searching for a proper proletarian model to emulate. He discusses the characteristics of several workers in the factory, but none of them act or look like "workers," leaving Yasuji confused because he is sure that factory workers should not depart so widely from the expected dress and lifestyle of workers. He gives one more example of a worker who is a thief, stealing the salary envelopes of those who accidentally drop them on the ground, rather than returning the envelopes to their rightful owners. If we were more like *workers*, Yasuji reasons, we would not have these problems (emphasis mine).[68] Thus, Yasuji asserts that the proletarian worker would provide a proper ethical model

68. Hayashi, "Shōnen," 32.

for his fellow factory workers. At this factory, the workers are either lost in the anachronistic working traditions of the Tokugawa era or drowning in the self-indulgent modern lifestyle of the present. Hence, Yasuji suggests that there are no proletarian workers in his factory deserving of his respect, so he must look elsewhere for help.

Accordingly, this conclusion in "Boyhood" ends with a statement enabling Hayashi's *tenkō* ideology. Yasuji's continuing search for an ethical model reflects Hayashi's desire to create another intellectual world in his fiction, one where he can recover his sense of idealism and youthful fervor to correct the wrongs of Japanese society. This mission was one that Hayashi had already started in the writing of his historical novel *Seinen* in 1932. Furthermore, in that novel's ensuing installments, *Sōnen* (Adulthood) and *Rōnen* (Old Age), he indicated a desire to continue.[69] In this way, his proletarian short stories "Childhood" and "Boyhood" imitate his work already in progress with his writing of *Youth* but they are written within the stylistic contours of proletarian literature. Thus, Hayashi would terminate his time in the socialist movement with the writing of his 1938 novella *Sun and Roses*, a semiautobiographical fictional retelling of his childhood and boyhood experiences that is reminiscent of his work in "Cocoons." This time, his political goals were first to displace his time as a student radical and proletarian writer and then to replace the left-wing radicalism of his middle school and higher school days with the memories of a cultural nationalist youth in the making.

69. Hayashi writes of his plans for this trilogy in his memoirs from his time imprisoned in the 1930s: Hayashi Fusao, "Gokuchūki," in *Hayashi Fusao chosakushū*, vol. 3 (Tokyo: Tsubasa shoin, 1969), 46–47. While he would complete his writing of *Youth* and *Adulthood* during the prewar years, Hayashi did not finish the trilogy in the postwar years.

7

Crossing the Threshold

Hayashi Fusao's Tenkō *Ideology and the Marxist Legacy of Dissent*

Dad shut the front doors of his business and then drove out the remaining customers and guests. Mom had had enough and was trying to stop him when he struck her with his fist. At long last, he pulled out the *katana*. Mom grabbed me, and we hid in the annex. She was feverish.

"A devil, yes, that's what he is. No human being would put a child through this." In between sobs, she stroked my hair.

I thought she was spot on in using the word devil. There he was, his eyes bloodshot, with sallow, high cheekbones, if that wasn't a devil's face, what was? The devil had drawn the pale sword and was hacking at the poles in the *tokonoma*. Once he's finished with 'em, then he'll come for us! Realizing this, I burst out crying.

From down the hallway, we heard the sound of small, frightened footsteps coming toward us.

Ma'am, run away! It was our maid Kiyo who was bent down on her knees at the doorway.

Down the hallway, we heard thunderous footsteps running toward us, then the sound of the *shoji* being broken. Mom took me under her arms, and barefooted she stumbled (*koronda*) through an open space between the shutters into the garden.

Outside, a moonlit night—like something out of hell! To the touch, the air felt like glass, like the sound of glass shattering to pieces! ...

... Kiyo placed me next to my Dad. She told him, "Here is your beloved son, sir. Please, give him a hug." Dad looked over at me with what he in-

> tended as a smile. Still, it seemed more as if he was crying. As for me, I turned away, unwilling to face him.
>
> —"Umi to Tobiuo no ko to"

To create a new mental world in his fiction, Hayashi Fusao turned to the *shishōsetsu* ("I-novel") form as a means to establish the authenticity of his experiences. Nonetheless, in as much as the hero of these stories was his mother, a factory worker in a silk mill, these were Hayashi's final proletarian short stories. Japanese literature critic Honda Shūgo asserts that turning to the *shishōsetsu* style was the norm for most of the former proletarian writers who started writing *tenkō* literature in the 1930s, especially those who sought to maintain some sense of subjectivity during the war years.[1] It was a natural move since the *shishōsetsu* form was meant for self-discovery, Honda explains, and it allowed these writers to re-create a new mental state for themselves, shedding the concerns of the larger world around them and the shackles of theory. In this way, Honda continues, it was a return to a pure, natural state and the *shishōsetsu* novel was a means for these writers to revitalize their sense of self and to restore their desire to write.[2]

In the emotional scene above, excerpted from his 1930 autobiographical short story "Umi to Tobiuo no ko to" ("With the sea and the offspring of the flying fish"), Hayashi takes us back to a crisis point in his childhood. This memory is a deliberate starting point for him, and in recounting his father's alcohol-infused rampage and his mother's heroics, we find him confessing as to why he took up the pen in the first place. Likewise, in the scene of his attempted reconciliation with his father, Hayashi captures the mortification and the anger that still fuels his rage at an economic and social system that drove his family to such extremes. Hayashi wrote this work before his first imprisonment, and here we find him engaged in a work of remembrance that fits with the proletarian

---

Hayashi Fusao, "Umi to Tobiuo no ko to," *Kaizō* 12, no. 8 (August 1930): 7–8, 9, and *Taiyō to Bara: kakioroshi chōhen shōsetsu* (Tokyo: Toryō shoin, 1947), 13–14.

1. Honda lists Tokunaga Sunao, Sata Ineko, Tsuboi Shigeru, and Moriyama Kei as examples of former proletarian writers who have turned to the *shishōsetsu* form in his *Tenkō bungakuron*, 3d. ed. (Tokyo: Miraisha, 1985), 179.
2. Honda, *Tenkō bungakuron*, 180–181.

short stories we examined in Chapter 6. Still, it is also an attempt, by the adult Hayashi, to reclaim his past and reproduce the self through a different lens. In this way, his narrative in "With the Sea and the Offspring of the Flying Fish" fits into Honda's explanation of why so many *tenkō* writers chose the *shishōsetsu* style after leaving the proletarian literature movement.

Moreover, the genre also moves Hayashi's *tenkō* ideology to the next step of establishing the sincerity and the "truth" of his turn from the left-wing literary movement. As we will study in this chapter, Hayashi utilized the *shishōsetsu* form subsequently in these proletarian short stories to verify his change of direction toward a cultural nationalist critique of the Japanese state. Accordingly, the *shishōsetsu* style of writing was appropriate for this endeavor, because as Edward Fowler argues, the claims of sincerity in the *shishōsetsu* are "a strategy of discourse." Building on this key point in his examination of the *shishōsetsu*, Fowler writes, "For once we grasp sincerity as an ideology rather than as a vague, ultimately inaccessible emotion, we can understand how it controls the mode of literary production. Candor becomes a commodity that writers have no choice but to produce and critics no choice but to appraise."[3] Hayashi's "rhetoric of confession," as Fowler labels it, obliges others to respond to his writings in "With the Sea and the Offspring of the Flying Fish," in "Arubamu" ("Album," published October 1936), and in "Mukashi no ehon" ("A Picture Book of Days Gone By," published March 1937) as outward confirmation of Hayashi's belief in this new intellectual path.

In this manner, Hayashi imposed the *shishōsetsu* writing form rather systematically in these three stories to authenticate his *tenkō* to cultural nationalism. These short stories would eventually become the first three chapters of his 1938 novella *Sun and Roses*. Therefore, a study of these three stories reveals, on the one hand, the legacy of dissent that he assumed from his days as a proletarian writer into his work with the "Bungakukai" (Literary World) group during the war years. Still, in writing the final seven chapters of *Sun and Roses*, Hayashi sought to forget his student radical boyhood symbolically. In its place, then, Hayashi substituted a different set of memories—less hostile toward the Japanese elite, and more in tune with a government-supported display of nationalism centered on the

---

3. Edward Fowler, *The Rhetoric of Confession: Shishōsetsu in Early Twentieth-Century Japanese Fiction* (Berkeley: University of California Press, 1988), 69.

Japanese people and the Japanese land—that he refashioned out of his past to finalize his *tenkō* ideology. Alan Tansman has shown in his work on authors from this same era how their literary endeavors to evoke a time of peace and fullness separate from the chaotic progression of modern life skirted the boundaries of fascism, even if the authors did not intend such an interpretation of their work.[4] Thus, Hayashi's completion of his *Sun and Roses* in August of 1938, conversely, represents the end of his initial efforts to manipulate the *shishōsetsu* form to write a cultural nationalist criticism of the Meiji state. Hereafter, Hayashi strives to actualize the *tenkō* ideology that he continued to develop throughout the wartime years. Hence, in this chapter, we examine his autobiographical proletarian short stories to trace the final steps in his move from a "politics of literature" ideology—one that he developed in his higher school literature at Kumamoto—to a "*tenkō* ideology" built on this "myth of sincerity."[5] While freeing himself of the directives from the communist party leadership of KOPF, Hayashi's *tenkō* to a cultural nationalist stance carried its own set of tensions and compromises that he ultimately anticipates in these short stories as well.

REMEMBERING WHY I FIGHT! TRANSFORMATIVE MEMORIES

Published in the left-wing journal *Kaizō* and finished just before Hayashi entered prison in July 1930, the first story "With the Sea and the Offspring of the Flying Fish" is written in the first person and gives us three memorable scenes from the author's childhood in the port town of Ōita. Reliving through his writing some of the personal hardships that he and his mother

4. Alan Tansman, "Images of Repose and Violence in Three Japanese Writers," *Journal of Japanese Studies* 28, no. 1 (Winter 2002): 114. Tansman has expanded considerably on this argument in two works reconsidering what he refers to as "fascist moments" in Japanese culture of the interwar and wartime years. He argues that the ideology of fascism found its ultimate expression in Japanese aesthetic and literary sensibilities. See his "Introduction" in *The Aesthetics of Japanese Fascism* (Berkeley: University of California Press, 2009), 1–33; and his "Introduction" in his edited volume, Alan Tansman, ed., *The Culture of Japanese Fascism* (Durham: Duke University Press, 2009), 1–28, where he places his interpretation of Japanese cultural fascism in the larger historical context of the 1930s.

5. See Chapter 3 in Fowler's *The Rhetoric of Confession*, 43–70, where he explicates this myth.

experienced in witnessing his father's turn to alcoholism and domestic violence, Hayashi, on the professional level, seeks to establish his proletarian credentials before heading to prison. Even so, the story also venerates certain memories from his childhood, particularly his mother's heroic efforts to protect and to provide for Hayashi. In privileging these memories from his youth, Hayashi fictionalizes his childhood and begins the creation of a fresh canvas upon which to inscribe a new way of life for himself as a writer.

Hayashi entitles each section of this piece separately and, in the first section, which bears the same title as the short story, the narrator sets the geographic and social scene of his Ōita. First, he describes the sea and the beach around the port area where he grew up, and then he moves to a class-based analysis of his friends. The narrator observes that they came from the three main occupational backgrounds that dominated this port town: the fishing industry, the merchants, and the entertainers who worked at the inns. Being from a merchant family, he intermingled with all these groups, and in general, it was a pleasant childhood, growing up as part of the petit bourgeois (*shōshimin no kōfuku*).[6]

Next, in the section titled: "Tsukiyo to Amadera" ("The moonlit night and the Buddhist nunnery"), the narrator turns to the misery his father caused the family during his youth and how those difficulties ultimately forced them to leave the city. Here, we learn of the incident detailed in the epigraph, but our narrator also prefaces and supplements the incident with detailed background information from his mother about his father's pitiful life, explaining how his father's attempts to expand his business came to naught, driving him into bankruptcy.[7] In his third story, "Neko to Kusa no Mi" ("The cat and the fruit of the wild grasses), the narrator describes his trip to the small village of Kita Taiheiji on a late summer day. Next, he turns to his unhappiness at having to carry the family cat and the circumstances that led to the trip. Finally, he ends with his first impressions of the village and its people. The story ends with the narrator declaring that he will write the sequel to this story after two years' time has passed.[8]

6. Hayashi, "Umi to Tobiuo no ko to," 3–6.

7. Ibid., 6–8.

8. This chapter has been influenced by a reading of cultural theorist M.M. Bakhtin's discussion of the "chronotope," a term he uses to refer to the coexistence of time and space

Placed in the analytical context of our previous chapters, Hayashi's story of his youth and the crisis that shaped his life read like a personal reminder of what motivated him to become interested in and join the socialist movement in the first place. Instead of writing about workers and activists he encountered in the movement who are worthy of our tribute, here Hayashi turns to his own past. Similarly, he does not highlight others' actions and responses to key events in their lives that make their sacrifices so praiseworthy, but turns instead to the crisis event in his youth. The narrator notes that on this terrible night his childhood ended. However, for Hayashi, this experience also defined his rationale for becoming a student radical in the New Man Society, and then a writer for the proletarian literature movement. Standing outside that narrative, as the author writing in the summer of 1930 about an event that happened seventeen years before, Hayashi reveals at the end of the story that he is about to encounter another crisis event in his life, an absence of two years' time. We, as the readers, recognize this statement as Hayashi reporting to Ichigaya prison, where he served a two-year sentence for violating the Peace Preservation law and the Publication law.[9]

His study of what happened in his boyhood, before entering prison, becomes an opportunity for Hayashi, as the author, to reconsider and recast his first act of disobedience toward authority, in this case against the familial authority figure of his father. Following his father's passing, the narrator's mother explains to him the difficulties his father encountered in marrying into her Samurai family and his lack of education and ambition. She also describes how the modern businessmen from out of town moved into the port town and transformed it so that the native, old-style merchants like his father had little chance of surviving. Listening to her, the narrator admits that, for the first time, he gained a new appreciation for the misfortune that plagued his parents' lives.

---

in the narrative form, particularly his explanations of the chronotopes of biographical time, encounter, the road, and threshold, in his work *The Dialogic Imagination: Four Essays*, trans. Caryl Emerson and Michael Holquist, ed. Michael Holquist (Austin: University of Texas Press, 1981), 224–258. An extended dialogue with this concept has been omitted, however, in order to keep the focus on the development of Hayashi's *tenkō* ideology.

9. See Kikukawa Tadao, *Gakusei shakai undōshi* (Tokyo: Chūō kōronsha, 1931; reprint, Kaiguchi shoten, 1947), 360 (page citations are to the reprint edition), for a listing of the charges against Hayashi.

Likewise, he also has the chance to rethink the urban versus rural, traditional versus modern encounters of his youth. In the first part of the story, we see the children of merchants, entertainers, and fishermen interacting through play and the narrator affirms that he was a merchant's child who could bridge the gap between the other social classes.[10] As such, the narrator establishes his social origins in the petty bourgeois, not with the working class. These were good times, he concedes, before the mother and son, looking like refugees, wind their way out of the port town to a small village. Here too, the narrator begins to notice the coarseness of the working class as people from different backgrounds meet. The "urban" narrator, for example, is surprised by the peasants screaming at him to step out of the area where they traditionally separate the rice grains from chaff. What he thought was an athletic field actually had both functional value for and traditional significance in the life of the peasants. Our narrator juxtaposes the "modern" with the "traditional" again as he comments on how the new silk textile mill's bright red gate contrasts with the tattered thatched roofs of the peasants' dwellings in the village.[11]

In this way, the narrator halts the flow of time in the first scene, and then meanders through the timeless and quotidian setting of his rural Japanese childhood in the two final scenes. The narrator's description of this scenery allows him to soften his memories of the one horrific night that shattered his boyhood growing up in Ōita, although his loathing of his father remains clear. That sense of anger at the authority figure is brought to a climax midway through the story and then pushed to the margins, permitting the narrator to romanticize the role of his mother in her extraordinary efforts to save the narrator from his father's wrath and provide for his well-being. Decentering the event that defined much of his childhood tribulations, the narrator then begins a new life in the village of Kita Taiheiji. Thus, even when his father arrives in the village to live with the narrator and his mother, the narrator plays a secondary and subordinate role to his mother. She works in the silk mill and provides for the family's needs, which raises her to the level of hero in this very personal story. The narrator tells us he will return to this narrative later, but essen-

10. Hayashi, "Umi to Tobiuo no ko to," 3–4.
11. Ibid., 15.

tially, he sets the stage for an alternate story of his life, one detailing his mother's many sacrifices for him and his family.

From this perspective, the narrative in "With the Sea and the Offspring of the Flying Fish" works on multiple levels. For the audience in prewar era Japan, Hayashi's publication of this story in the left-wing journal *Kaizō*, just before he enters prison, reaffirms his commitment to the socialist movement. His representation of his major crisis in the story reflects his fears as a youth and his dislike of authority, while his authorship of this text in 1930 represents his private concerns with his upcoming prison stay. In this way, his fictional account of his mother's strength and his own defiance suggests his political use of this short story to shield others from his own misgivings about his imminent separation from his family and from the movement itself.

At the same time, this story was also an act of regeneration as the narrator shifts the subject of the story away from his father's failure to highlight and then idealize his mother's positive role in his life. There is a new story to tell here, one that has now been sketched out spatially, temporally, and even populated with its own set of characters. Hannah Arendt in her introduction to a set of Walter Benjamin's works of literary criticism argues that Benjamin saw himself as a collector stocking the shelves of his library with precious remnants of the past that were meaningful to him. Arendt asserts that, in Benjamin's mind, history and its authority as tradition had already been destroyed by the early twentieth century. Thus, for Benjamin, she notes, "The collector not only withdraws from the public into the privacy of his four walls but takes along with him all kinds of treasures that once were public property to decorate them."[12] Arendt observes that from Benjamin's perspective this gesture of picking up fragments of the past and removing them from public view was not to increase their value or enhance the collector's social status. Ultimately, for Benjamin, she writes, it was a means of putting his past in order, an expression of "genuineness" because these objects held a unique and personal value only for him.[13] Much like Benjamin's collector, the writer Hayashi Fusao

12. Hannah Arendt, "Introduction, Walter Benjamin: 1892–1940," in *Illuminations*, trans. Harry Zohn, ed. Hannah Arendt (New York: Schocken Books, 2007), 43.

13. Ibid., 43–44.

begins to build the four walls of his private library in 1930 with this story. The first wall exhibits episodes from his childhood within the writing of "With the Sea and the Offspring of the Flying Fish," where he inventories his memories of those days. He then adorns that section of his library with glimpses of his mother's heroism in the face of personal hardship and social stigma. Six years later, when he faces another crisis event in his life, this time his public *tenkō*, he returns to this story once again to further expand his library of fragmented remnants of the past.

Hayashi Fusao's Separation from KOPF

Hayashi's departure from KOPF started with his move from Tokyo to Kamakura. Upon his release from prison in April 1932, he and his family moved to a temporary residence in Yanakahatsune-chō. Yanakahatsune-chō is located in Tokyo's Taitō-ku between the Ueno and Nippori railway stations and is known for its large cemetery, the Yanaka Reien (Yanaka Cemetery). While renting a place near the cemetery, he spent the next several months working on the first part of his historical novel *Youth*. Fatigued from his time in prison and overwork, he became sick with pleurisy in September 1932. He writes that when Kamimori Shitetsu, an acquaintance, visited him and saw how ill he had become, Kamimori summoned Hayashi to his house in the Nagoe valley of Kamakura for rest and recuperation.[14] Kamimori was best known as a leader in the Nihon Rōdō Kumiai Hyōgikai (Japan Council of Labor Unions) during the late 1920s before leaving the left-wing movement and becoming active in the Japanese publishing industry.[15] Hayashi notes that he met Kamimori during the 1927 split between the members of the Workers Arts and Vanguard Arts groups in 1927. Kamimori took an interest in Hayashi and Murayama Tomoyoshi, a playwright, actor, and writer in the proletarian literature movement, and became something of a "patron" to them.[16] Another reason Hayashi left Tokyo was that his clashes with the KOPF's leadership had become even more intense, and the differences between them even

14. See Hayashi Fusao, "Fu: Hayashi Fusao nenpu," 455, for the timing of the move to Kamimori's house; and Hayashi Fusao, "Bungakuteki kaisō," 334 for Hayashi's description of how Kamimori insisted on his moving to Kamakura.

15. Matsumoto Keiko, *Higanbana*, 130.

16. Hayashi, "Bungakuteki kaisō," 335.

more pronounced. As he put it, "I couldn't endure seeing their [the NALPF writers'] 'class-warrior faces' (*kaikyūteki tōshigao*) ever again."[17] Once he recovered from his illness, he found a place to rent next to Kamimori's home and in the summer of 1933 moved his wife and mother from Tokyo to live with him.[18] He became a permanent resident of Kamakura and never returned to live in Tokyo.

The move to Kamakura was significant in two ways. First, it placed geographic distance between himself and Tokyo, the hotbed of left-wing activity in Japan. Tokyo was the center of the left-wing movement and the home of the *mabo* (short for *Marukusu bōi*) and the *ega* (short for *Engerusu gāru*), the Marx boy and the Engels girl. Known to hang out in the Shinjuku area of Tokyo, the "Marxist youths" represented one aspect of generational change in 1920s Japan along with the more well-known *mobo* (modern boy) and *moga* (modern girl).[19] Novelist Dazai Osamu hints at how much the Marxist youths were a part of the Tokyo experience when one of his characters relates, "A secret Communist meeting [was] ... just one more of the sights of Tokyo."[20] Dazai also suggests the seriousness with which the Marxist youths took themselves and their Marxist studies: "I found it uproariously amusing to see my 'comrades,' their faces tense as though they were discussing matters of life and death, absorbed in the study of theories so elementary they were on the order of 'one and one

17. Hayashi, "Bungakuteki kaisō," 362.

18. Kagoshima Tatsuo, *Gendai Kamakura bunshi: yukari no shōsetsuka tachi*, Kamakura sōsho, vol. 30, ed. Nuki Tatsuto (Kamakura: Kamakura shunjūsha, 1984), 198.

19. Edward Seidensticker remarks that in addition to Shinjuku, the Marx boys also gathered at many of the National Railways' Chūō line stations. Edward Seidensticker, *Tokyo Rising: The City since the Great Earthquake* (New York: Alfred A. Knopf, Inc., 1990), 51. Albert M. Craig argues that the images of the *mabo* and *ega* and the *mobo* and *moga* in the 1920s' media have unduly influenced scholars' images of generational change in Japan. Craig's point is that our image of generational change in Japan relies too heavily on university youths who represented the minority of youths in the 1920s. Nonetheless, he also recognizes that the *mabo* and *ega* did present powerful images of the youth for the Japanese public. Albert M. Craig, "Introduction: Perspectives on Personality in Japanese History," in *Personality in Japanese History*, ed. Albert M. Craig and Donald H. Shively (Berkeley: University of California Press, 1970; reprint, Michigan Classics in Japanese Studies, no. 13, Ann Arbor: Center for Japanese Studies at The University of Michigan, 1995), 14 (page citations are to the reprint edition).

20. Osamu Dazai, *No Longer Human*, trans. Donald Keene (New York: New Directions Publishing Corporation, 1958; reprint, Tokyo: Charles E. Tuttle Co. Publishers, 1984), 65 (page citations are to the reprint edition).

makes two.'"[21] The *mabo* and the *ega* considered themselves the antithesis of the bourgeois *mobo* and *moga*; thus, it is not surprising to find Kobayashi Takiji, in his critique of Hayashi's works, making references to the "modern boy's" lifestyle—the *mobo* frequented the dance halls and cafes in Tokyo—to accuse Hayashi of acting like a member of the bourgeois literati rather than a proletarian writer.[22] Neither, then, was it surprising to find Hayashi retreating to Kamakura to avoid the polemics of the *mabo* and *ega* in Tokyo.

Second, the move to Kamakura put Hayashi in touch with a large group of writers, literary critics, and artists already residing there. Scholars have referred to this group informally as the Kamakura *bunshi* (literati) or the Kamakura *gumi* (group). Kamakura was the ancient capital of the Japanese warrior government from 1185 to 1333 and still has a reputation in contemporary Japan as a "historic town" (*rekishi no machi*). It attracted numerous literati because of its ties to Japanese history as well as its reputation for a slower pace of life, but it was still within easy commuting distance of Tokyo. Well-known writers such as Izumi Kyōka, Shimazaki Tōson, Natsume Sōseki, Akutagawa Ryūnosuke, and Osaragi Jirō spent part of their lives in Kamakura during the Meiji and Taishō periods. Following the Great Kantō Earthquake in 1923, many more Japanese literati made their way to Kamakura where they shared friendships, often despite their intellectual differences.[23] From Hayashi's perspective, Kamimori obviously played the main role in getting him to settle in Kamakura, but the friendship that developed between himself and influential literary critic Kobayashi Hideo, who had moved to Kamakura a year earlier than Hayashi in 1931, affected his literary career most profoundly in the coming years. Hayashi remembers Kobayashi as the writer who introduced him to the world of the Kamakura literati.[24]

Although coming from different literary worlds, Hayashi had read some of Kobayashi's works while in prison and had come to admire them.

21. Dazai, *No Longer Human*, 66.

22. Kobayashi Takiji, "Uyokuteki henkō no shomondai," *Puroretaria bungaku: fukuseiban* 1, no. 12 (December 1932): 29.

23. Nakano Kōji, ed., *Kanagawa bungaku sanpoten: Kamakura, bungaku no Arukadeia* (Yokohama: Kenritsu Kanagawa kindai bungakukan, Zaidan hōjin Kanagawa bungaku shinkōkai, 1995), 27.

24. Hayashi, "Bungakuteki kaisō," 342.

Once he moved to Kamakura and recovered from his illness, he visited Kobayashi's home, close to his own, and developed a cordial relationship with him. Kobayashi Hideo was a constant critic of Marxism and the proletarian writers. However, he and Hayashi got along well, and when Takeda Rintarō—a fellow proletarian writer who, like Hayashi, was looking for an organizational alternative to KOPF—talked to Hayashi about forming a new journal in the spring of 1933, Hayashi spoke to Kobayashi about joining the group. Kobayashi responded favorably, and he, Takeda, and Hayashi went to see Kawabata Yasunari—another old acquaintance of Hayashi—who also liked the idea. Kawabata then invited three other writers, Hirotsu Kazuo, Uno Kōji, and Toyoshima Yoshio,[25] to join the new journal. Later, Fukada Kyūya, also from Kamakura, joined the Literary World group to form the original eight *dōnin* (coterie) for their journal, *Bungakukai* (Literary World).

While all the members of the coterie worked hard on the journal over the summer of 1933, the friendship between Hayashi and Kobayashi and their literary viewpoints greatly shaped the direction of *Bungakukai*. For Hayashi, his participation in the Literary World group gave him the organizational alternative to KOPF that he desired. His inclusive vision of writers coming together around literary rather than political themes was evident in the composition of the original coterie. Hayashi and Takeda were proletarian writers. Kobayashi and Kawabata were writers from the *geijutsuha* ("artistic school") who stressed art for art's sake. Hirotsu, Uno, and Toyoshima were established writers who focused more on the self and one's mental state, writing *shishōsetsu* ("I-novels") and *shinkyō shōsetsu* ("mental state novels"). Fukada was more of a *hanbunkashugi* ("anticulturalist") writer who sang the praises of nature and wrote about mountains and mountain climbing in his works. Throughout its run during the early Shōwa years (*Bungakukai* was published from October 1933 to April 1944) the Literary World coterie remained open to a wide variety of writers. This included *tenkō* writers such as Shimaki Kensaku and Murayama Tomoyoshi, writers from the Japan Romantic School such as Kamei

---

25. Toyoshima's name does not appear among the list of *dōnin* until the December 1933 issue of *Bungakukai*. See editor's note to Hayashi Fusao's introductory essay, "'Bungakukai' sōkan no koro," published in *Bungakukai: fukkokuban* 1, no. 1 (October 1933; reprint, Tokyo: Nihon kindai bungakukan, 1975), 1 (page citations are to the reprint edition).

Katsuichirō, and other well-known writers, critics, and intellectuals such as Yokomitsu Riichi, Nakamura Mitsuo, Miki Kiyoshi, and Kawakami Tetsutarō. Kobayashi even extended an invitation to Nakano Shigeharu to join the group, but he refused.[26]

In joining the Literary World group, Hayashi was also able to act on his rhetoric of protecting literature from politics. He wrote that the Literary World members turned the journal toward a more *junbungaku* ("pure literature") direction than Tanaka Naoki, the publisher from Bunka Kōronsha who first managed the journal, had envisioned originally.[27] Hayashi and Takeda both sought to free literature from the "political constraints" that the KOPF leaders had imposed upon the writers and their works of proletarian literature. Still, the journal also played an important role during the 1930s of reasserting artistic qualities obscured with the rising acceptance and profusion of *taishū bungaku* ("popular literature" for the masses) in Japan.[28] Hayashi wrote that what he and the other members of the Literary World group could agree on was that literature had a particular path and that the best means for discerning the *hondō* ("right way") for literature was through one's own *kan* ("subjective instincts").[29]

Essentially, the Literary World group decided to insist on the primacy of literature within the journal, a move that Hayashi supported publicly by calling for a *bungei fukkō* ("cultural renaissance") during the fall of 1933. In his literary review column for the *Tokyo nichinichi shinbun*, he commented that several new journals with a cultural emphasis appeared on the Japanese literary scene in 1933, making him believe that "literature was making a comeback" within the Japanese literary world.[30] Writers and scholars have credited Hayashi for coining the phrase "cultural renaissance" and the Literary World group for initiating the *bungei fukkōki* ("cultural renaissance period") that lasted roughly from the middle of 1933 to 1937 and the outbreak of the Sino-Japanese War.[31] One of the main

26. Tōgō Katsumi, "Bungei fukkō no mosaku," in *Jidai betsu Nihon bungakushi jiten: gendaihen*, ed. Jidai betsu Nihon bungakushi jiten henshū iinkai (Tokyo: Tōshuppan, 1997), 102.

27. Hayashi, "Bungakuteki kaisō," 316.

28. Nakano, *Kanagawa bungaku sanpoten*, 30.

29. Hayashi, "Bungakuteki kaisō," 328.

30. Hayashi Fusao, "Bungaku wa fukkō suru: bungaku zasshi zokushutsu no igi," *Tokyo nichinichi shinbun*, 28 October 1933, sec. F, p. 14.

31. For an example of a writer from the period referring to Hayashi as the herald of the

goals of this "renaissance" was to protect Japanese literature and culture from the militarism and right-wing political ideologies that flourished in 1930s Japan.[32] Besides the right wing, Hayashi also wanted to protect Japanese literature from left-wing Stalinist ideologues. Thus, removed from the confines of Tokyo and the KOPF leaders as he was, his Literary World group and this feeling that Japan was on the brink of a "cultural renaissance" gave him the confidence to call for the end of KOPF more strongly, and the freedom to declare his *tenkō*.

Hayashi Fusao's *Tenkō* Declaration

In the spring of 1936, Hayashi ultimately did declare his *tenkō* following two hostile encounters with former proletarian writers. After his release from Shizuoka prison in November 1935, he set about establishing the Dokuritsu Sakka Kurabu (Independent Writers' Club) in the January 1936 issue of *Bungaku hyōron* (Review of Literature). Boasting an initial membership of eighty-three, the officers of the club were Eguchi Kiyoshi, Aono Suekichi, Hayashi Fusao, Hirabayashi Taiko, and Matsuda Tokiko.[33] No sooner had the club held its inaugural meeting in late January than a section of its membership led by Nakano Shigeharu began to call for the club to allow writers from progressive liberal backgrounds to join it. Nakano made his argument in two articles that he published in the April issues of *Bungaku hyōron* and *Kaizō*.[34]

Nakano's arguments struck an odd note for many, as literary critic Hirano Ken has noted.[35] Hirano points out that, initially, Kubokawa Tsurujirō

---

bungei fukkō movement, see Wada Heisuke's column, "Katatsumuri no shikaku: 'fukkō' to 'fukkatsu,'" *Tokyo nichinichi shinbun*, 20 December 1933, p. 15. For the timing of the *bungei fukkōki*, see Noguchi Fujio's *Kanshokuteki Shōwa bundanshi* (Tokyo: Bungei shunjū, 1986), 98.

32. Odagiri Susumu, "Kaisetsu," in *Bungakukai: fukkokuban* 1, no. 1 (October 1933; reprint, Tokyo: Nihon kindai bungakukan, 1975), 28 (page citations are to the reprint edition).

33. Senkin Kanji, "'Dokuritsu Sakka Kurabu' setsuritsu shuisho: bijutsu undō no hōkō to, shakaishugi riarizumu ni kan shite," *Bungaku hyōron* 3, no. 1 (January 1936): 132–133; quoted in Hirano Ken, *Bungaku: Shōwa jūnen zengo* (Tokyo: Bungei shunjū, 1972), 158.

34. Nakano Shigeharu, "Kurabu e no kibō," *Bungaku hyōron* 3, no. 4 (April 1936): 102–105; and Nakano Shigeharu, "Dokuritsu Sakka Kurabu ni tsuite," *Kaizō* 18, no. 4 (April 1936): 131–139.

35. Hirano, *Bungaku*, 161.

had argued against starting such a writers' club. Kubokawa had questioned to what degree such a writers' club could separate itself from its former literary movement and literary theories, and Hirano asserts that Kubokawa's argument made much more sense than Nakano's position on this issue in light of the extreme socio-political and cultural battles being fought in Tokyo.[36] The only way Hirano can account for Nakano's line of reasoning was to contend that Nakano may have been attempting to introduce the *jinmin senzen senjutsu* ("popular front strategy": the idea of combining the socialists and liberals, members of the political left and center, to counter the militarism of the extreme right wing) into Japanese literature.[37] Considering that Tokyo had been held hostage that February by a contingent of young military officers calling for a "Shōwa Restoration" and that militarism was growing increasingly more virulent in early 1936, Hirano makes a good case for considering Nakano's argument within this context.

That same April, Hayama Yoshiki, Hayashi's friend from early on in the proletarian literature movement, published three open letters to Hayashi in the *Tokyo nichinichi shinbun*, questioning whether Hayashi could truly call himself a proletarian writer anymore. Written on the fifth, the seventh, and the eighth of April, Hayama first denounces Hayashi's historical novel *Sōnen* (*Adulthood*). Hayama openly queried how anyone writing such a piece could call himself a proletarian writer.[38] Hayashi wrote *Adulthood* as a continuation of the story in *Youth*, and it was being serialized in *Bungakukai* at that time. In his next column, Hayama argued that Hayashi had lost his proletarian viewpoint and that what he was writing now (referring to *Adulthood*) was not proletarian literature but something Hayashi felt "obligated" to call proletarian literature.[39] Finally, Hayama condemns Hayashi's participation in the Literary World group by calling attention to the hypocrisy of his participating in a group com-

36. Hirano, *Bungaku*, 160–161; Kubokawa made his argument in "Sakka kurabu ni tsuite no kansō," *Bungaku hyōron* 2, no. 12 (November 1935): 146–149.

37. Hirano, *Bungaku*, 162.

38. Hayama Yoshiki, "Soko ni shizumu: Hayashi Fusao ni tou, ichi," *Tokyo nichinichi shinbun* 5 April 1936, sec. G, p. 11.

39. Hayama Yoshiki, "Soko ni shizumu: Hayashi Fusao ni tou, ni," *Tokyo nichinichi shinbun* 7 April 1936, sec. A, p. 9.

prised of both proletarian and bourgeois writers, while calling for a proletarian-writers-only group in the Independent Writers' Club.[40]

Hayashi's response to the criticism was immediate and decisive. Writing on the eighth of April in *Miyako shinbun*, he announced his *tenkō* publicly. He wrote that he realized that there was almost nothing proletarian about him anymore, and that because of this realization, he would give up any pretense of being a proletarian writer starting from that day.[41] Acknowledging that such a declaration made him ineligible to participate in the Independent Writers' Club, Hayashi asked Tokunaga Sunao and Nakano Shigeharu to find someone to take his place within the club's leadership.[42] Hayashi repeated this declaration in the three articles responding to Hayama's criticisms of him, which he published in the April 16, 17, and 18 editions of the *Tokyo nichinichi shinbun*.

In these articles, Hayashi gave his *tenkō* a more definitive tone than before. He wrote, "I give up being a proletarian writer. Just as Nakano, you [Hayama], and Mamiya Mosuke have indicated, there is nothing proletarian about me anymore. Of late, I have come to understand this clearly."[43] Hayashi tells Hayama that he has been thinking about making this decision for a long time, so Hayama is not directly responsible for his *tenkō*. However, he does tell Hayama that his criticism did allow him to make this decision more easily, giving him a sense of closure and "a feeling of being finished" (*todome o sasareta ki ga suru*) with the writers of the movement.[44] Hayashi next turned to the topic of what he would do after spending some ten years writing proletarian literature. He wrote that most likely he would pursue his present path with the Literary World coterie and in writing *Adulthood*. He dismissed outright the idea that he might turn to writing nationalist (*Nihonshugi*) literature, but he also acknowledged that it was inconceivable for him ever to call himself a proletarian writer again.[45]

40. Hayama Yoshiki, "Soko ni shizumu: Hayashi Fusao ni tou, san," *Tokyo nichinichi shinbun* 8 April 1936, sec. A, p. 9.

41. Hayashi Fusao, "Haishi o sengensu: puro sakka no jishō," *Miyako shinbun* 8 April 1936, p. 1.

42. Hayashi, "Haishi o sengensu," p. 1.

43. Hayashi Fusao, "Hayama Yoshiki ni kotau, ichi," *Tokyo nichinichi shinbun* 16 April 1936, sec. G, p. 9.

44. Hayashi, "Hayama Yoshiki ni kotau, ichi," p. 9.

45. Hayashi Fusao, "Hayama Yoshiki ni kotau, ni," *Tokyo nichinichi shinbun* 17 April 1936, sec. A, p. 9.

Lastly, Hayashi agreed with Hayama that he did feel a sense of "obligation" (*giri*) toward proletarian literature.[46] Therefore, he would continue helping with the administrative affairs of the Independent Writers' Club until other members could find someone to take his place. He also related that although many fellow proletarian writers tried to talk him out of quitting the movement, his mind was made up. He was finished with the proletarian literature movement. He concluded by reminding the other proletarian writers that, although he was no longer a proletarian writer, he would continue to behave the same as he always had toward them, calling out to them when he sees them on the streets and praising them when he likes what they had written.[47] With this as his final pronouncement, Hayashi left the organized Marxist movement permanently.

RELOCATING THE STRUGGLE AND REDEFINING THE TERMS OF THE FIGHT

In "Album," published in October 1936 soon after his *tenkō* announcement, Hayashi shifts to a third-person narrative. He compares and contrasts the disparate, yet interconnected lives and desires of two young men, Ōtomo Katsuji and Hayami Takeo, who are growing up in a rural village during the late Meiji years. The story opens with Takeo describing the fall of one of the village's established families, the Ōtomo family.[48] Then he recounts his own family's disgraceful retreat to this small village where they rent a mud-walled storehouse from the Ōtomo family. From that point, the focus is on the trials and tribulations that confront him and Katsuji, difficulties that end in Katsuji's arrest and imprisonment. Takeo, in contrast, adapts to life in the rural school system and much of his story focuses on the inequalities, as Takeo views them, of Meiji society, mainly through its educational, family, and social systems.[49]

---

46. Hayashi Fusao, "Hayama Yoshiki ni kotau, san," *Tokyo nichinichi shinbun* 18 April 1936, sec. A, p. 11.

47. Hayashi, "Hayama Yoshiki ni kotau, san," p. 11.

48. Hayashi Fusao, "Arubamu," *Kaizō* 18, no. 10 (October 1936): 67.

49. This section condenses and summarizes much of the extended analysis of "Album" from my earlier article, Jeff E. Long, "Songs That Cannot Be Sung: Hayashi Fusao's 'Album' and the Political Uses of Literature during the Early Showa Years," *Japan Forum* 19, no. 1 (March 2007): 69–88.

In "With the Sea and the Offspring of the Flying Fish," Hayashi revisited the scenes from his childhood that motivated his search for social justice. Six years later, he made some interesting changes in how he continues this story. First, he shuns the strict *shishōsetsu* style from "With the Sea and the Offspring of the Flying Fish" and reverts to the third person short story format in "Album" to resume the story. His mother is still the hero figure of this narrative, and she will play a pivotal role in the storyline, but the focus now turns to Takeo and his struggle to succeed. Moving the story from autobiography to the realm of semi-autobiography, this adjustment to narrate his "true story" recalls Hayashi's work in "The *Robin Hood* Incident" from 1929. Thus, it should not surprise us that in "Album," Hayashi returned to the short story style to remember and memorialize scenes from his life, as he had done to comment on the proletarian literature movement. However, this shift signals Hayashi's desire in writing about his personal history to move from modifying his past to creating a different set of memories of his childhood. No longer will he expect the reader to treat the narrative as his unmediated thoughts and actions. As such, the story of Takeo and Katsuji's lives is meant to push forward a new narrative of Hayashi's youth, and his first step was to establish that there were both Marxist and cultural nationalist elements in the experiences from his early years.

Hayashi, thus, writes about not only the discrimination evident in Takeo and Katsuji's childhood, but he also includes sections reflecting on the natural beauty of the land in "Album." As a result, we have many scenes in this story where Hayami Takeo, the son of a former samurai family, is treated unequally by the eldest daughter of the silk mill's owner in the village. We also find that once Takeo passes the middle school exams and starts school, the students from wealthy families look down on him. In particular, the rich industrialist's son Ōsaki Sōichi, who is the Ōsaki Ironworks owner's son, regards Takeo with disdain.[50] Furthermore, Katsuji's story is also tragic, as a judge sentences him to six years in prison for the accidental death of a higher school student with whom he had an altercation. Hayashi makes clear that Meiji society now prioritizes the will of the industrial capitalists over the work of the common people, and that the Japanese state is dedicated to protecting the wealthy and

50. Hayashi, "Arubamu," 74–79.

enabling their success in society. In this way, he gives ample evidence of the social injustice that fueled his Marxist perspective on his childhood. Nevertheless, Hayashi also depicts Takeo striving to improve his life through the Meiji educational system and thus attempting to raise the Hayami family out of ruin to meet Meiji social expectations. Takeo works hard, employing his artistic skills to make enough money to sit for the middle school exam. On the exam, he writes an essay stating that he hopes to become a naval officer one day.[51] Thus, along with Hayashi's Marxist interpretation of Japanese society, there is also a cultural nationalist vision of traditional Japan, particularly in Takeo's storyline.

Once he constructs a fictional place for both the Marxist and cultural nationalist experiences in his youth to coexist, Hayashi's narrative in "Album" concludes with a startling admission, one that anticipates the next step in his *tenkō* ideology. Returning home from visiting Katsuji in prison, Takeo realizes that no one was singing in prison, and he attempts to sing aloud himself. At first, the wind silences his song and then when he tries to whistle instead, the abrasive sound of his own voice stops him. As Takeo notes, unlike the prisoners who could not sing inside the prison walls, those on the outside had many songs to sing, but did that mean they were truly free to do as they pleased? Were they free to sing whichever song they chose?[52] Here, Hayashi acknowledges the multiplicity of voices and views that continued to exist independent of the Japanese state's drive for homefront unity in early Shōwa Japan in "Album." What was needed then was the creation of a place in literature for those songs that could no longer be sung. In this fashion, Hayashi relocates his struggle for social justice within the bounds of literature, and he redefines the terms of this fight into the cultural nationalist expression of protecting the Japanese land and the Japanese people.

This admission constructs the second wall of Hayashi's private library of his youth. As a collector, Hayashi selects those memories—and in this case those voices being silenced in the mid-1930s by the authorities—to place on the shelves. Hannah Arendt in her discussion of Walter Benjamin notes that Benjamin knew "that there is no more effective way to break the spell of tradition than to cut out the 'rich and strange,' the coral and pearls,

51. Hayashi, "Arubamu," 72.
52. Ibid., 83.

from what had been handed down in one solid piece."[53] Thus, in the midst of the push for orthodoxy in Japan, and the building of a new national tradition, we find Hayashi picking up those pieces of his youth associated with his fight against social injustice and with his desire to pursue his education during the Meiji years. Separating these memories from the greater context of his youth and then lovingly placing them in an honored place alongside his mother's heroism, Hayashi celebrates his heritage of rebellion and his desire to rise above his social station in that library. Nevertheless, for him, the act of commemoration is also the next step in breaking with tradition and starting a new story.

Crossing the Threshold: Uneasy Alliances and the Marxist Legacy of Dissent

Hayashi's last autobiographical short story, "A Picture Book of Days Gone By," published in the early spring of 1937, portrays the difficult decision made by the main character to accept financial help from the owner of the silk mill in which his mother works so that he can afford to continue his middle school education. Focused almost exclusively on Takeo—the character embodying cultural nationalism in "Album"—the story in "A Picture Book of Days Gone By" highlights the author's decision to work within the Meiji social structure for change. However, the narrative locates the setting at the end of the summer vacation where we learn that Takeo confronts another crisis moment in his life. Takeo decides to take up his sketchbook and watercolors to visit the school one last time; but first, he must slip past his father, Tomitarō, who is making rope out of straw in the shed. Tomitarō sees him and reminds Takeo that he is supposed to help him take the straw rope to town that day. Takeo says that he will return by then and escapes up the road to school as fast as he can.[54] Thus, the opening scene establishes the unresolved tension between son and father as Takeo shirks his duties and flees up the hillside to the middle school.

The second part of this scene focuses on another defining moment in Takeo's life: will he or will he not be able to attend his second year of middle school? Once he reaches the school, Takeo laments that its main

---

53. Hannah Arendt, "Introduction," 42.
54. Hayashi, "Mukashi no Ehon," 1.

gate is closed to him. Circling around the school, he pushes open one of the classroom doors and enters the school grounds where he wistfully makes his way through the schoolyard to the athletic grounds, stopping to paint a picture of the school auditorium's chapel-like tower. After finishing the watercolor of his school, he entitles it, "Goodbye, My Middle School!" and drops the painting on the ground. Just then from behind him, his Japanese language teacher—who is given the nickname "Mr. Moon" for his round face—calls out to him. Takeo is startled, and the teacher who has always favored him for his excellent written work picks up the painting. After praising Takeo's painting skills, the teacher asks him to explain the meaning of the title. Takeo retrieves the picture from his teacher and explains that he is quitting school to become a factory worker. Before his teacher could object, Takeo says his farewell and bolts from the school grounds.[55]

In Takeo's road of life, he has reached another junction that will bring several people from various social classes together to resolve this crisis and put him back on the road to success. As already noted above, for Takeo formally to cross through the school's main gate, it will take the efforts of both his mother Oteru from the silk mill and his friend Ishii Mihoko, the silk mill owner's oldest daughter,[56] to find a solution that will allow Takeo to continue his studies. Oteru must first calm her drunk husband. He is fuming, since Takeo did not return to help him deliver the straw rope, and he further berates his son for pursuing his studies rather than work in the factory and help the family make a living. Then Oteru must summon the courage to approach her manager at the silk mill for help with this personal matter. At the same time, Mihoko writes to Takeo and convinces him to wait before quitting school. She also intervenes with her father, the mill owner, and recommends Takeo as a good candidate to tutor her younger brother Ichirō for the upcoming middle school entrance exam. From opposite ends of the Meiji social scale, Oteru, the mill girl, and Mihoko, the spoiled rich girl, work for the common goal of returning Takeo to the classroom.[57]

Once in school, Takeo faces a less dire dilemma. He is forced to wear

55. Hayashi, "Mukashi no Ehon," 2.

56. This is "Horiguchi Sahoko" from "Album," but Hayashi has renamed her in this piece, though he does not explain the reason for the change in name here.

57. Hayashi, "Mukashi no Ehon," 4–8.

his *gētoru* ("leggings") that have mildewed in the heat and humidity of the summer. His old nemesis, Ōsaki Sōichi, son of the owner of the ironwork, tracks down Takeo after an embarrassing day at school and further disparages him. They get into a scuffle and "Mr. Moon," the Japanese language teacher, happening upon the scene, steps in, separates them, and then sends Ōsaki and his friend on their way. Next, the teacher lectures Takeo on being so concerned about external appearances. It is what is inside that matters, he says. Ōsaki is an inferior student, the teacher continues to tell Takeo, so ignore his attempts at provocation and stop fighting him. In the end, it would take the teacher's mediation to keep Takeo headed down the right path at school and away from the traps set by Ōsaki, son of the rich industrialist.[58]

Approaching the threshold, the narrative completes two more relationships, each one suggesting that Takeo is coming to terms with authority. First, Takeo takes a detour from his story to tell the reader briefly about their landlord Ōtomo Okume's visit with her son, Katsuji, who was in prison. Okume notes that Katsuji has lost weight. However, he looks healthier and more muscular than before and he is still excited about his plans for the future. Okume reports that he is happy to hear that Takeo is back at school and that Katsuji is saving money to pay for his own vocational training to become a printing press operator. Returning to his own life story, Takeo remarks that life has been good of late. Things are going well with his studies, and when he finishes at school, he tutors Ichirō at the Ishii home for two hours. Then he heads to the night duty room at the silk mill where he eats dinner with the mill's stoker, Sanpei, and reads books that Mihoko has loaned him until his mother is finished with work in the evening. As for the village folk, they have become more accepting of the Hayami family. Takeo observes that villagers have always viewed education negatively, mainly because they perceived those students who attended middle school or higher school as parasites living off their parents' hard labor. However, with Takeo working to help pay for his school expenses, the villagers have begun to change their minds about education. Furthermore, they have started to boast about having a middle school student in their

58. Ibid., 8–11.

midst, and those mill girls' kids who used to harass him in elementary school now sometimes come to talk with him as friends.[59]

Second, Takeo also explains that even his father, Tomitarō, has started to come around and to view his son's desire for education in a different light. Takeo comments that his father has started drinking noticeably less and that one evening his father had a surprise for him. Drunker than he had been in a long time, his father presents Takeo with a new set of leggings. This is a turning point for the Hayami family, as Oteru joins Tomitarō for a drink to celebrate their son's success at middle school, and the scene ends with the whole family laughing and enjoying their family time together.[60]

Thus, Hayashi brings Takeo's unease and rebellion against the authority figure of his father to a conclusion here. Similarly, he also shows Katsuji accepting the state's authority over him in prison, with Okume reporting that Katsuji is growing stronger as he trains and studies for a job in the printing industry. Along the way, we find Takeo also readily assenting to the Ishii family's financial assistance and to his Japanese language teacher's advice to keep focused on his studies and develop his mind. In a sense, we find Hayashi attempting to define the boundaries in which Takeo will recognize the influence of others to guide him. As long as authority figures like his teacher, Mr. Ishii, and his father allow him to pursue his education or, at minimum, acknowledge the value of that quest, Takeo is willing to follow their advice and to accept their support for him. Even in Katsuji's case, we find him acceding to state power in prison because it promises a better and brighter future for himself and his mother. Yet, even as we find Hayashi's symbolic point of denouement in his formal struggle with state power, we also discover a new point of departure in the second half of the story that discloses the potential consequences of this compliance.

At this point, Hayashi introduces the narrative of his July 1927 story "Love and Ghosts," integrating Takeo into that story and using it as a means to clarify Takeo's relationship with Mihoko and her family. From the beginning, we learn that the stoker, Sanpei, with whom Takeo shares his meals in the night duty room, was in the same army unit as Katsuji,

59. Ibid., 11–12.

60. Hayashi, "Mukashi no Ehon," 12.

and that he was with Katsuji the night when Katsuji confronted the higher school students. Hayashi next establishes Takeo's sympathy for Sanpei, and he details the harsh conditions on the factory floor where Sanpei and the mill girls work. Takeo wanders through the factory wishing that he could visit Mihoko's room, but he is very much aware that the Ishii family is wary of his presence in their home. Mihoko said that they would be able to meet every day, Takeo muses, but in reality, a considerable distance has grown between them since he has become Ichirō's tutor.[61] From here, Hayashi retells the story of Sanpei's relationship with the mill girl Okun, ending with Sanpei incarcerated in the same prison that currently holds Katsuji. In the course of the story, Takeo helps Sanpei separate Okun's body from the silk-reeling machine that entangled her hair, and Takeo is subjected to Mr. Ishii's cold, disapproving stare as he orders everyone back to work, when he realized that Okun did not perish from her injuries.[62]

After finishing Sanpei's and Okun's sad story, Takeo reveals that his relationship with the Ishii family has slowly changed for the worse. He discusses how different members of the Ishii family, sometimes purposely, and at times unwittingly, proceeded to ignore him, belittle him, and in Mihoko's case, even patronize him and his mother. The more time he spends with the Ishii family, the larger the gap grows between himself and Mihoko. Takeo recognizes that a *nakatagai* ("falling out") with Mihoko looms on the horizon, and with this realization, he also discerns the limits of his relationship with the wealthy elite. Even though he has accepted the Ishii family's financial support to continue his education, this is an uneasy alliance, and he is unwilling to consummate that relationship, as his exaggerated reaction to Naohira's teasing exposes later in the story.[63]

Ultimately, Hayashi concludes "A Picture Book of Days Gone By" with a new point of departure for his semi-autobiography. Takeo is chafing under the constraints of working for the provincial elite to finance his dream of studying, and the reader is left with the question of whether he will accept these restrictions. Are these simply the sacrifices to be made to

61. Ibid., 12–13.
62. Ibid., 16–17.
63. Ibid., 19–21.

pursue his dream or will he find a way to express his dissatisfaction with this situation? How will he confront the emerging tension between his yearning to rise from the bottom of the Meiji social scale for his mother's sake and the realization that those in positions of economic power supporting his studies show such open contempt for the peasants and for the other villagers with whom he resides?

In the end, "A Picture Book of Days Gone By" also acts as a reminder of the distance that separates Japan's ruling elite from the masses, and of the intellectual's tenuous position as an intermediary between these groups. Takeo's recognition of the tensions that will characterize the new road he has chosen in his life plays out as he moves from tutoring in the Ishii house to his conversation with the new stoker, Naohira, in the night duty room. Moreover, the encounter with Naohira is a metaphor for the different challenges he will face with this new direction in his life. Unlike Sanpei, to whom Takeo felt close and with whom he was willing to take a stand against the horrid treatment of the mill girls, his encounter with Naohira is less pleasant. Takeo describes him as *niya niya* ("grinning") as he revels in the discomfort he has caused Takeo. Takeo's uncomfortable interaction with the new stoker adds to the social anxiety that he is already experiencing in his relationship with Mihoko and her family. While he has accepted the support of the Ishii family, his tutoring of Ishii Ichirō does not necessarily mean that he mentally identifies himself with the elite, nor that the Ishii family members are fully comfortable with him in their presence.

Instead, the story closes with Takeo's consciousness of the ambiguous social position he now occupies, caught between the provincial elite for whom he works in order to study at an elite institution and the rural poverty of the poor peasants and workers with whom he dwells. His shift in the final scene from the Ishii manor tutoring Ichirō to the silk mill's night duty room where he feels more at home, neatly represents his movement between these two social worlds. Naohira's teasing, however, unsettles Takeo, leaving him with an even greater sense of ambivalence as to his place in society. He has crossed the threshold and he is firmly on the path to success in the modern industrial capitalist world. Still, even though he feels more at ease in the company of laborers and peasants, Naohira's playful banter suggests that perhaps they do not view him as fully belonging to their group either.

This unresolved tension at the end of "A Picture Book of Days Gone By" stands as a metaphor for the uncomfortable duality Hayashi experienced after his final separation from the proletarian literary movement and its writers in 1936. There is a strong sense of dislocation that runs through the narrative, almost as if the author Hayashi is considering the ramifications of his *tenkō*, contemplating what he has sacrificed, and realizing that he can no longer return to his home in socialist literature. We find this in the incorporation of his earlier proletarian short story "Love and Ghosts" and the scene directly out of "Cocoons" where Takeo confronts Ōsaki Sōichi and his goons in this short story. This time, Hayashi is not content simply to retrieve these stories; he inserts them brazenly in "A Picture Book of Days Gone By" as if he is altering his proletarian fiction in this narrative to infuse it with new meaning so that he can stake out a new direction in his life.

Here, we find Hayashi fleshing out the third wall of his private library of treasures from his youth. As Hannah Arendt observes in her discussion of Walter Benjamin as a collector, in Benjamin's sense of history "the collector destroys the context in which his object once was only part of a greater, living entity ..."[64] as a means of inscribing the object with a new meaning for the present. In this section of the library, Hayashi privileges key scenes from his previous proletarian short stories, breaking the context in which he wrote these stories and inserting them into a very different framework. "For Benjamin to quote is to name, and naming rather than speaking, the word rather than the sentence, brings truth to light,"[65] Arendt asserts. In this way, Hayashi fills the third wall of his library with badges of honor from his youth. These are his cherished examples of the "truth" of his struggles with authority in the past, now placed in the present narrative to support a different path to confront the problems of the day.

Hence, the text in "A Picture Book of Days Gone By" is filled with purpose. Takeo is willing to work with those in authority, as long as they support his desire to educate himself. As such, he seems to indicate a readiness to take whatever steps necessary to return to middle school and complete his education. In this way, the represented world in the text

64. Hannah Arendt, "Introduction," 45.

65. Ibid., 49.

highlights his encounters along the road leading to a decision made, followed by his unceasing support for the oppressed workers in the silk mill. Thus, the represented world in the text depicts the obstacles that a determined youth from the working class overcame to stay in school. As the narrative ends with Takeo's apprehension at what he recognizes is an inevitable confrontation with Mihoko, he also finally accepts that his struggle to return to middle school has set in motion a new set of challenges that he must face sometime in the future.

To the general audience, the created world in "A Picture Book of Days Gone By" reads as nostalgia for the defining moments in one's childhood to which anyone can relate. There are always significant trials and tribulations that shape our future life choices and force us to confront how we choose to achieve our goals. The reader can identify with the difficulties that Takeo faces in the story but also root for him to overcome those challenges and continue to pursue his goal to study. Thus, "A Picture Book of Days Gone By" is a typical "underdog" story of someone who has not forgotten his roots. In the last section of the story, we discover that Takeo's spirit and his empathy for the downtrodden in Japanese society remain undiminished. However, in the story's last sentence, we find Takeo, at last, grasping some of the consequences of his life choices and the ambiguous situation between the haves and have-nots into which his pursuit of education has placed him. We also wonder whether that realization will change him in the future.

Most likely, writers and intellectuals reading the journal *Kaizō* in 1937 would have read Hayashi's story within a different context. Those who cared to read his story would be thinking of his official political *tenkō* in 1932 and his public statement of *tenkō* in literature from the previous spring. They remembered the formalized literary aestheticism (*bungaku shugi*) he espoused in his work with the Literary World group and the way he pushed the *bundan* (Japan's informal establishment of writers, critics, publishers, and readers) for a "cultural renaissance" in literature through the 1930s. They also noted his inclusion in one of the best-known cultural and ethnic nationalist literary groups of the day, the Japan Romantic School from August of 1936. In the story, Hayashi may be considering what he lost by agreeing to work with the state, but this March 1937 text is a clear statement that the choice to work with state authority was the right decision to make. It is doubtful, then, that the conclusion of the story, where Takeo concedes that an "estrangement" with Mihoko is imminent, resonated strongly with his fellow writers. In reality, a few months after the publication of "A Picture Book of Days Gone By," Hayashi joined the state-sponsored Shin Nihon Bunka no Kai (Society for a New Japanese Culture) in July 1937, confirming that he was indeed working with representatives of the Japanese state.[66]

From the author's viewpoint, however, the narrative in "A Picture Book of Days Gone By" does reflect his ongoing mental attempts to reconcile his spring 1936 decision to separate himself from the proletarian literature movement, even as he acknowledges having made the appropriate decision to leave left-wing politics. Hayashi may have capitulated to state power and abandoned the politics and the analytical framework of Marxism, but he also recognized that the Marxist legacy of dissent and opposition to authority remained in his sense of rebelliousness. Thus, his use of literature as a means to reflect on and think through his conflicting emotions while standing at another crossroads in his life reminds one of his first Marxist stories at Kumamoto, and of his use of literature to mull over his decision to commit himself to the socialist movement in 1922. Instead of the conscientious shift from a humanist to a socialist viewpoint, this narrative from 1937 is in one sense a deliberation on Hayashi's choice to prioritize the cultural nationalist elements in his ideology of literature.

---

66. For more information on the Shin Nihon Bunka no Kai's origins, see Mikiko Hirayama's article, "From Art without Borders to Art for the Nation: Japanist Painting by Dokuritsu Bijutsu Kyōkai during the 1930s," *Monumenta Nipponica* 65, no. 2 (2010), 375–376. At this point, Hayashi's choices stand in stark contrast to those of someone like the former proletarian writer, Takeda Rintarō, also a member of the Literary World group, who argued that his fellow writers needed to fight the encroaching fascism in Japan of the mid-1930s. For more on Takeda's stance, see Richard Torrance, "*The People's Library*: The Spirit of Prose Literature versus Fascism," in *The Culture of Japanese Fascism*, ed. Alan Tansman (Durham: Duke University Press, 2009), 56–79; and Ethan Mark's article, "The Perils of Co-Prosperity: Takeda Rintarō, Occupied Southeast Asia, and the Seductions of Postcolonial Empire," *American Historical Review* 119, no. 4 (October 2014): 1184–1206, for an assessment of the limits to Takeda's critical analysis of Japanese imperialism in Java during the Asia-Pacific War, particularly pages 1196–1206. Much like Hayashi's turn to a cultural nationalist means to criticize the government, Mark observes that Takeda's indirect condemnation of Japanese imperialism in Indonesia was read differently in the context of wartime Japan, muting its influence.

At the same time, in this story Hayashi also pays homage to the influence of Marxism in shaping his understanding of state-society relations and on his writing. In this way, he highlights the Marxist legacy of dissent and his desire to oppose the Meiji state and the wealthy elite that support the state. It is a tradition that continued to inspire Hayashi in his steadfast need to fight for the integrity of the Japanese people and the Japanese national land. From Hayashi's perspective, this cultural loyalty would endure in his use of the cultural nationalist analytical framework to assess the development of the Meiji political and economic systems during the wartime years and beyond. Nonetheless, placed in the context of his evolving *tenkō* ideology, this proletarian short story places Hayashi on a new path, working for the industrial capitalists and writing literature within the bounds of acceptable discourse as defined by the Japanese state. Crossing that organizational threshold from KOPF into the Literary World group, becoming part of the Japan Romantic School, and subsequently accepting the government's invitation to help with the Society for a New Japanese Culture brought the *tenkō* ideology that he had conceived in his literature to fulfillment in his professional life.

8

Evoking the Idyllic Childhood

Sun and Roses *and Hayashi Fusao's Turn to Ultranationalism*

Biting my lip, I glared hard at the teacher from behind, but eventually, I turned over and wandered up the mountain behind the middle school, where much like a rampaging wild boar I stomped up the red dirt path.

On the mountain, the flowers of the paulownia tree were blooming. The pure wind was filled with the sun-drenched fragrance of the tree's resin. At my feet, a beetle spread its prismatic wings and flew easily down the path, as if it were guiding me along.

While the natural world abounds with such beauty, why is the human world so deluged, so darkened by the unreasonable acts of men, wondered Takeo?

—*Taiyo to Bara**

... Every passion borders on the chaotic, but the collector's passion borders on the chaos of memories. More than that: the chance, the fate, that suffuse the past before my eyes are conspicuously present in the accustomed confusion of these books. For what else is this collection but a disorder to which habit has accommodated itself to such an extent that it can appear as order?

—"Unpacking My Library: A Talk about Book Collection"†

Hayashi wrote the last seven chapters of *Sun and Roses* from the spring of 1937 through the summer of 1938 and then published the novel in August

---

*Hayashi Fusao, *Taiyō to Bara: kakioroshi chōhen shōsetsu* (Tokyo: Toryō shoin, 1947), 87–88.

†Walter Benjamin, "Unpacking My Library: A Talk about Book Collection," in *Illuminations*, trans. Harry Zohn, ed. Hannah Arendt, 59–67 (New York: Schocken Books, 2007), 60.

1938 with Kawade Shobō, a publishing house best known for its journal *Bungei* (Literary Arts), which celebrated the arts.[1] In these chapters, Hayashi largely collapses together the tension between the intellectual and the state, and the tension between the intellectual and the wealthy elite leading Japanese society. He shifts the narrative from the social nexus of the factory worker's family to the network of relationships among Takeo and the representatives of state authority and his interaction with the children of rich industrial capitalists in town. He also moves more of the geographical context from the village to the middle school and the town than in previous chapters. While the Marxist legacy of dissent is evident in the main character's initial rebellious behavior, soon Takeo is punished for his defiance, and he throws himself wholeheartedly into his studies for the remainder of the novel. His capitulation is summarized in the epigraph that begins the chapter. Humiliated in his attempt to defend himself, he can do little more than glare at the middle school teacher who physically assaulted him. Leaving the scene indignantly, he retreats to the natural world where he seeks solace by ruminating on the "unreasonable acts of men." This transition captures Takeo's last act of dissent in the novel. As the narrative progresses, his feelings for the silk mill owner's eldest daughter also change. He becomes more sympathetic toward her as she experiences the hardships of her father running the factory into bankruptcy and losing the mill to a local banker. In due course, the novel concludes with the main character confessing his love for the eldest daughter and with the hope that the two of them will come together at some point in the future.

More significantly, in writing these chapters, we find Hayashi encapsulating his *tenkō* ideology and bringing it to life in his fiction. The first step was to remold his time in the socialist movement. Thus, he reworks the image of a serious student radical and revolutionary writer that he and the other youths in the movement tried to project outwardly into the persona of a group of gifted scoundrels, engaged in a mischievous resistance to the powers-that-be. From Chapter 4 of the novel we immediately find Takeo at a literal crossroads where he meets the new math teacher Kadoma who dresses, walks, and conducts himself as if he were a naval officer or a military man. Kadoma teaches Takeo the brutal price of defying the authority

1. Hayashi Fusao, *Taiyō to Bara: kakioroshi chōhen shōsetsu* (Tokyo: Kawade Shobō, 1938).

of the imperial state, in this case talking back to his teacher. Kadoma further informs Takeo that the beating he receives is also a warning to remember his place in the school hierarchy. Although he is a superior student in the classroom, he must learn to always show respect and bow to those in power. Out of anger and humiliation, Takeo skips school that day and heads up the mountainside where he runs into the members of the "pirate club." They are also protesting Kadoma's viciousness and the complicity of the principal who ignores Kadoma's harsh treatment of students. Their opposition takes the form of impish noncompliance: playing hooky from class and sitting by the mountain stream, smoking, eating snacks, dangling their feet in the water while one of them plays a tune on his harmonica. In Chapter 5, Takeo becomes fast friends with the members of the pirate club. Their carefree, yet rebellious spirit infects him with a renewed hunger to struggle against Kadoma and those like the Horiguchi family who take advantage of peasants and workers to enrich themselves.[2] However, by the end of the chapter, Kadoma catches all of them in the midst of scheming against him and brings them before the principal for punishment. At that juncture, they decide to stop any overt demonstrations against Kadoma and the principal, and we hear nothing about Kadoma in the remaining five chapters.

In the two chapters, Hayashi symbolically rehashes the failure of his attempts and those of the Marxist cultural movement to oppose the government's treatment of the farmers and laboring classes in Japanese society. Hayashi portrays the imperial state's representatives in stark terms. Kadoma is a violent, cruel instructor who believes in a military style of discipline within and outside the classroom. The pirate club members refer to the principal by the nickname *tanuki* ("raccoon dog") because he is a hypocrite: he is rumored to engage in all sorts of debauchery at night, but during his classes gives long lectures on public and personal morality.[3] At the same time, the members of the pirate club are depicted as bourgeois intellectuals, acting more like juvenile delinquents than serious revolutionaries. Subsequently, it is their lengthy debate at school about how to

2. Hayashi has shifted the name of the Ishii family back to the original Horiguchi family in the remaining chapters of *Sun and Roses*. Again, there is no explanation from the author suggesting why he made this change.

3. Hayashi Fusao, *Taiyō to Bara: kakioroshi chōhen shōsetsu* (Tokyo: Toryō shoin, 1947), 109.

get even with Kadoma, not an actual strike or demonstration, which allows Kadoma to capture the members so easily. Finally, after being punished, they decide that, rather than fighting back, just the knowledge alone of the pirate club's existence will be enough to annoy Kadoma and the principal. Settling on this resolution brings a nervous chuckle of relief to Takeo and the other members of the pirate club.[4]

Neither the imperial state representatives nor the revolutionaries of the proletarian literature movement are rendered in the best light here. Kadoma and the principal are callous and duplicitous keepers of orthodoxy. Likewise, Hayashi exposes the "*rasu*" or "rascals"—as they prefer to call themselves, rather than *furyō* (delinquents)—as lacking in competence and commitment, with a false air of intellectual superiority that allows them to dismiss their defeat with ease. In this fashion, Hayashi recasts the leaders of the movement as pompous elitists whose show of support for the common people has its limits and who care mostly about their own well-being. At the same time, he also implicates the state representatives in viciously forcing the intellectual community back into its place under the thumb of government authority. Ultimately, we find Hayashi, the collector, building the last wall of his private library in these chapters. He stocks the shelves of this wall with his boyhood memories and then turns both sides—Kadoma and the principal as well as the "rascals" from the pirate club—into caricatures to hang on the wall. They are laughable reminders of his youth and his Marxist past to be forgotten and dismissed in the present context of 1938 and the beginning of the war in China.

Hayashi's next task in *Sun and Roses,* after reshaping the narrative of his time in the socialist movement, is to refurbish the memories of his childhood. Moving from the scenes of a downtrodden boyhood in a worker's family presented in the first three chapters, Hayashi now evokes an almost idyllic life living close to the land and the people, but also one in which he is on the road to achieving the Meiji dream through the pursuit of his education. George Sipos has observed that most of the recognizable authors of *tenkō* literature turned to the trope of "family" to narrate their *tenkō* to others. Some, such as Nakano Shigeharu, Tokunaga Sunao, and Sata Ineko, wrote of returning to their family home and interacting with their parents to renew their will to write. Others like Murayama Tomoyo-

4. Hayashi, *Taiyō to Bara*, 110–111.

shi and Kubokawa Tsurujirō employed divorce as a metaphor in their fiction, exposing the failures of the organizational communist family. Sipos even notes that Hayashi's reintegration into the Japanese *kazoku kokka* (family-state) ideology manifests itself in his historical novel *Youth* as a variant of the same tendency to focus on family life in *tenkō* literature.[5]

The narrative in *Sun and Roses*, however, presents a more compelling example of this restructuring process, as Hayashi writes to realize the recovery of a happy family life, expressly to confirm the decisive "change of direction" in his own life. From Chapter 6, Takeo reconnects with the Japanese land as he works to reclaim part of the mountainside for farming. Along the way, any remaining doubt about his relationship with his father washes out with the sweat that both of them shed in the process of working together in the fields, with Takeo providing the knowledge and Tomitarō the strength for this common endeavor.[6] For the remaining chapters of the novel, Tomitarō is portrayed sympathetically, always ready to sacrifice for his son's and his wife's needs. In return, the peasants and his family embrace him, and the villagers welcome him back into their web of social relationships.[7] For Takeo's part, his opposition to parental authority also ends, resolving the antagonism between the two that spurred much of the conflict in the narrative of the first three chapters, which then turns into a strong father-son bond by the novel's end.

This fictitious transformation is difficult to reconcile with Hayashi's first-person description of his father in "With the Sea and the Offspring of the Flying Fish" from 1930. There, the first person narrator tells of his father's passing during the winter before he entered the university. He asks his mother if she felt better now that his father had passed away and she replies that she does feel relieved, but that she also pities his father for the miserable life he lived.[8] Nevertheless, in the context of Hayashi's political changes in 1938, he pushed those unhappy memories to the corners of his private library or removed them altogether. Ultimately, Hayashi must reward his mother's heroism and the sacrifices she made for her son. Thus, Hayashi's reworking of those memories was a process already under-

5. George Tiberiu Sipos, "The Literature of Political Conversion (*Tenkō*) of Japan" (Ph.D. diss., University of Chicago, 2013), 17–18.

6. Hayashi, *Taiyō to Bara*, 114–117.

7. Ibid., 126–128.

8. Hayashi, "Umi to Tobiuo no ko to," 6–8.

way by the end of the narrative in "With the Sea and the Offspring of the Flying Fish," and it eventually finds its conclusion in the narrative of *Sun and Roses.*

Still, one wonders if the key point here is the liberating role of the land and the people in removing Takeo from the political struggle with Kadoma and the principal as well as in extricating him from the childish antics of the pirate club. While Hayashi's desire to move his quest for social justice into the cultural nationalist form is evident here, the first step to accomplish this goal was to disassociate that quest from the political bounds of the proletarian literature movement and the ideology of the KOPF leadership. Next, he needed to separate his emotional call for social justice from the fictional form of the proletarian short story and restore it within the aesthetical confines of "pure literature" and the "cultural renaissance" movement. Hayashi attempted to accomplish this in *Sun and Roses* through the reconciliation between the factory girl's son Takeo and the industrial capitalist's daughter Mihoko. In Chapter 5, his reading of Lord Byron's 1814 work, *The Corsair,* from a classmate's library stirs Takeo to think of Mihoko again. We learn that she is attending a Women's College in Tokyo and that she has started studying French. Takeo thinks that Mihoko has none of the passion of the character Genevra in *The Corsair,* nor does he think that she possess Genevra's penchant for beastly cruelty.[9] Takeo continues to receive letters from Mihoko, but in the letters she exhorts Takeo to study harder and live up to his academic potential. Takeo dejectedly opines that it is becoming more difficult to keep up the fantasy that he and Mihoko might be a couple someday.

By Chapter 6, Takeo begins to view Mihoko as an "old miss." She is in the mountain resort town Karuizawa for the summer break, studying French at a language camp sponsored by the YWCA. She writes to him that while she is touched by the YWCA members' belief in God, she can only place her faith in human reason and in what she can touch and feel. For the young idealist Takeo, who is in the grip of the pirate club's romantic spirit of disobedience, the straight-laced Mihoko seems to fade out of existence in front of his eyes.[10] Takeo and Mihoko's relationship deteriorates during the fall and winter chapters only to revive itself when she

9. Hayashi, *Taiyō to Bara*, 101–103.
10. Ibid., 115–119.

confesses her love for Takeo in the spring chapter. In her letter, she reveals that her father had indeed taken out several mortgages from the Uramoto bank and that his incompetence in business affairs ultimately allowed the Uramoto family to seize control of the silk mill. The Horiguchi family was bankrupt and had lost everything. She then confesses her love to a shocked Takeo. He proceeds to break off his relationship with Uramoto Kuniko, the banker's daughter. In the last chapter, Takeo writes a love letter, commiserating with Mihoko's family situation and, eventually, declaring his love for Mihoko, hoping that the sun will soon shine on her and her family once more.[11]

In this way, Hayashi attempts to humanize Mihoko, allowing Takeo to identify with her through their shared experiences of financial difficulties within their families. Unlike the focus in the first three chapters, where Hayashi is intent on shedding light on the hardships experienced by the factory girls working in the Horiguchi Silk Mill, in the next seven chapters he highlights the reconciliation between the working class and the wealthy elite. The change in emphasis is evident in Takeo's interaction with several representatives of the industrial capitalist social classes: first, with Matsushita, the bookstore owner's son; Kōnō, the bureaucrat's son; and Minagawa, a relative of the Uramoto family from the pirate club; and then with Uramoto Kuniko; and finally with Horiguchi Mihoko, Misako, and Ichirō, the factory owner's children. Helping Takeo's family work on the mountainside to turn it into farmland, the pirate club members Matsushita, Kōnō, and Minagawa get their hands dirty working the land. However, they help his family only because Takeo refuses their invitation to join them at their summer retreat near the beach.

More importantly, with the financial failure of the Horiguchi Silk Mill, we learn why Mihoko had taken such a parental tone in her letters to Takeo. In essence, she has been the one taking care of her siblings and increasingly her parents, as her father's bad business dealings heightened the tensions between her father and mother. By the time we read Mihoko's confession in Chapter 9, both Takeo and the reader can empathize with the stress she has undergone throughout the story, which in turn helps explain her oddly obsessive behavior at the New Year's Day *karuta* party. Instead of the estrangement between Takeo and Mihoko that Hayashi led

11. Ibid., 191–195, 210–216.

the reader to expect at the end of "A Picture Book of Days Gone By," he ends *Sun and Roses* with Takeo's declaration of love for Mihoko. While we are not sure whether the two will come together, Hayashi does relieve the sense of unease that characterized Takeo's awkward relationship with Mihoko in the novel's first three chapters, replacing it with a sense of concern and yearning on Takeo's part.

In the context of his *tenkō* ideology, Hayashi disentangles Takeo from the external political struggles and confrontations that opened *Sun and Roses* and concludes with Takeo's internal emotional catharsis. Hayashi then shifts from the proletarian short story form to the sentimental bourgeois novel in his fiction, a move already supported by his earlier turn to the *shishōsetsu* style. If the measure of a *shishōsetsu* novel was how closely the narrative reflected the author's life, then Hayashi could metaphorically purge his political past as fiction, in this case as a transitory affair with socialism. In its place, he could then reproduce his childhood as one where his primary concern for love and for academic success took place within the beautiful natural world surrounding the village and finally within the harmonious social world of his family and the village.

Takeo's expression of his love for Horiguchi Mihoko in the final scene of *Sun and Roses* establishes the genuineness of his change from politics to literature. Preparing for his upcoming exams, he pulls out Mihoko's letter whenever he is tired and needs encouragement. He wants to believe that human striving is the defining force in this life. He then begins a letter to Mihoko so that he can express his gratitude to her for setting him on the right path again and rousing him from the insolence that jeopardized his studies. He must be maturing, he writes, since he is learning to distinguish between those base human desires that led to his delinquent behavior and the suitable aspirations that lead to success in life. From now on, he promises her that he will not act on these natural human passions without considerable deliberation. He wants to let Mihoko know that his first goal is entering higher school in order to continue his education, if possible, and to excel in his studies so that he can apply for a scholarship sponsored by the prefectural government. He wants to show her that through one person's efforts and hard work the two of them can build their own lives.[12]

12. Ibid., 209–111.

With Takeo's earnest statement of purpose here, Hayashi recovers his childhood as one guided by his wish to improve his own life and accordingly create a better future for himself and his family. In the last chapter of *Sun and Roses,* he substitutes the charming childhood of a budding writer and academic committed to literature in place of the destitute and anguished boyhood of a student radical dedicated to political change and social revolution. Moreover, he paints a glowing portrait of Mihoko to dominate the last wall of his private library. In *Sun and Roses,* Mihoko is placed on a pedestal and raised to the rarified level of an angel for Takeo; in this manner, her confession of love for him is transformative. Hayashi places this portrait of Mihoko across from his cherished memories of his mother, and together the light from these two memories proceeds to drive all other recollections to the background in Hayashi's memorial library of his youth.

Hayashi would not stop at rewriting his childhood, and his attempt to show positive support for the Japanese people and land in *Sun and Roses* reveals another piece in his *tenkō* ideology: the reversion to a humanist conception of life and living. Thus, during the writing of the last seven chapters of *Sun and Roses* from the summer of 1937 to the summer of 1938, we find Hayashi coming full circle in his intellectual approach to elucidating the causes of the social injustices evident in Japanese society. By the end of the novel, Takeo chooses to believe in the human effort as the defining force in life, and in so doing, he sets off this choice against two other universalistic intellectual approaches mentioned in the novel. In this way, we find Hayashi using his literature to convey a political message. Once again, he takes a swipe at the leadership of the proletarian literature movement, this time focusing on the leaders' insincerity in the practice of their socialist ideas.

In this fashion, Hayashi contrasts the authenticity of his *tenkō* to literature and cultural nationalism with what he perceives as the duplicity of KOPF's communist leaders. First, in Mihoko's letter from Chapter 6, she touches on the YWCA leaders' dedication to God's work, and then on how she cannot grasp why they would put their trust in Christian faith over human logic. Here, Takeo is unhappy with Mihoko's lack of youthful idealism, but later in Chapter 8, after Minagawa has left school and Matsushita and Kōnō are preparing for exams, Takeo recounts his experience with a Christian church in town. In this discussion, he remembers that when he was a small boy, at times, he used to attend the church on Sundays. He tells us that he used to play cricket and tennis with the missionaries' son Jack and other children until an altercation with Jack caused him to stop coming on Sundays. The last time he visited the church was for a Christmas party that winter, which the missionaries invited him to attend. Takeo was amazed by the festivities, but as the presents are handed out, he realizes that the wealthier kids receive nice toys, while the missionaries give the children from the poorer part of town only three small tangerines each.

A middle school student now, as he walks by the church Takeo is reminded of the disappointed look on the faces of the children. He notes that most middle school students dislike the word "God," and recalls Mihoko's rejection of the YWCA leaders' belief in God.[13] As such, Hayashi highlights the missionaries' unequal treatment of their flock—privileging the children from wealthier families over those from the poorer families attending the church. These representatives of Christianity perpetuate the social and economic inequalities of bourgeois Western society in Japan, despite preaching a religion where all are supposed to be equal under God.

In this way, we find Takeo dismissing Christianity and its proponents as advocates for social justice in Japan. Similarly, in the final chapter, he then moves to a similar conclusion in his talks with Kōnō about objective economic theory being the prime determining factor in life. We find him at the castle ruins in town, when Kōnō Sōichi comes upon him and surmises that he is waiting for Uramoto Kuniko. Takeo informs Kōnō that he is there to tell Kuniko goodbye so that he can focus on his studies once more. Kōnō skeptically counters that one cannot turn back the hands of time, to which Takeo responds that he has already overcome poverty and humiliation to reach this point. In the same way, he will surmount the depravity and senselessness around him now to finish his last two years of middle school. Kōnō then continues to tease Takeo. He asks what Takeo will do when he inevitably slips back into the degenerate behavior he picked up from the pirate club members. Ignoring him, Takeo remarks that Kōnō is a strange fortune-teller, particularly in predicting the Horiguchi Silk Mill's bankruptcy.

Earlier in the novel, while in their hideout overlooking the town, Kōnō points out to Takeo the construction of a massive new silk mill. He notes

---

13. Hayashi, *Taiyō to Bara*, 151–156.

that when completed, it will have room for 1,200 spindles, making it much larger than the three other silk mills in town. Most likely, Kōnō surmises, this new silk mill will put the other mills out of business. Kōnō asks Takeo if he has considered the ramifications of this development for his mother working in the Horiguchi mill, and for Mihoko, whose family will suffer once the Shinshū Mill goes into operation. Thus, in this meeting at the castle ruins, Kōnō is pleased to hear Takeo acknowledge the objective economic reality that led to the fall of the Horiguchi family. However, when Takeo tells Kōnō that he believes the real reason for the silk mill's ruin to be human failure, Kōnō is disappointed to hear Takeo blaming the Horiguchis' insolvency on what he refers to as subjective, humanist sentiments. Takeo, however, emphatically declares that a lack of human effort is always the determining factor in success or failure, not objective economic theory. As the two depart the castle grounds separately, neither happy with the other's interpretation of the causes for the Horiguchi Silk Mill's closure, the sound of a whistle from one of the town's factories reverberates across the town.[14]

Takeo not only rejects Kōnō's reliance on economic theory to predict the end of the Horiguchi Silk Mill and instead attributes its bankruptcy to human shortcomings, he also metaphorically discounts the Marxist intellectual approach to interpreting the social inequalities in Japanese society. In this manner, he criticizes the socialist intellectual's dependency on theory, not people, to interpret the movement of Japanese history. With this depiction of Takeo's insistence on human folly, not Socialist theory, causing the social problems in Meiji Japan, Hayashi now adds caricatures of Christianity, Socialism, and their supporters to the private memorial library of his boyhood. As expected, he symbolically hangs their likenesses beside the cartoonish representations of Kadoma, the principal, and the members of the pirate club from earlier in the novel.

Still, what does persist in the novel's last seven chapters is Takeo's preoccupation with finding an alternative means to explain the reasons for the social inequality around him, which in turn also reflects Hayashi's uncertainty. From his writing in *Sun and Roses*, the best answer to this problem promises to come from the organic relationship between the Japanese land and the Japanese people. Accordingly, in the novel we see Hayashi

14. Ibid., 204–209.

symbolically and very pragmatically recognizing the virtues of either complying with the punishment handed down by the representatives of state authority or making amends with the wealthy elite in the novel. Then, we witness the shift to a positive assertion of support for the land and people as a viable means of maintaining some semblance of a critical intellectual position on state-society relations. If Hayashi meant for Takeo's exaggerated declaration of his belief in human agency to Kōnō to mark a break with Marxism as a sustainable intellectual position, then Takeo's agreement with Mihoko on human reason over Christian faith also suggests the limitations of Christianity as a spiritual means to understand the social and economic forces shaping human life. Hayashi even admits in his afterword to the novel that, despite this autobiographical work being inspired by his reading of Goethe's *From My Life: Poetry and Truth*, it contains many more poems about his early life and personal experiences than truths. Furthermore, he encourages the reader to imagine these stories as conceivably happening in any small Japanese town.[15] As James Dorsey writes, "... the *tenkō* phenomenon ... brought forth ... a vision of, and keen dedication to, literary practice as a means to slip the ties that bind us to a modernity defined by the constellations and machinations of secular power."[16] These last seven chapters in *Sun and Roses* demonstrate that for Hayashi this meant the assertion of an apolitical narrative of his youth as a means of freeing himself from the dictates of the proletarian cultural movement's leaders, and at least temporarily, from the state's narrowing definitions of acceptable criticism.

Hayashi's cosmetic reshaping of the narrative of his youth is what led the writer and literary critic Kon Hidemi, in his harsh review of *Sun and Roses,* to compare Hayashi's fairy tale–like reflection on his youth to a bird warbling across a brilliantly blue, cloudless sky. Kon asserts that Hayashi's attempt at a romantic interpretation of his youth is straight out of nineteenth-century romantic literature, a place where no sorrow can exist. Moreover, it is a narcissistic work, since it creates a serene world

15. Hayashi, *Taiyō to Bara*, 217–218.

16. James Dorsey, "From Ideological Literature to a Literary Ideology: 'Conversion' in Wartime Japan," in *Converting Cultures: Religion, Ideology and Transformations of Modernity*, ed. Dennis Washburn and A. Kevin Reinhart (Leiden and Boston: Brill, 2007), 467.

where Takeo sails above the pain and the sorrow that prevail around him. Perhaps his mother truly is that kind of a saint to help him through life, Kon remarks, but in the end, he hopes in Hayashi's next autobiographical novel that he will move Takeo's story out of the realm of myth. At the very least, he hopes that Hayashi will write an epic poem; that way, the readers could experience the poetry in Takeo's life and witness the sadness and hardships he overcame to triumph in his childhood.[17]

Hence, Kon argues that the premise of Hayashi's *Sun and Roses* may have started out as an introspective piece meant to satisfy the author's desire to remember the highs and lows of his childhood. However, the intentionally selective portrait of his youth is designed to whitewash all the lows from his life, which leaves only the high points for others, including Hayashi himself, to see. Kon was one of the contributing writers to the Literary World group, but that did not stop him here from pointing out Hayashi's attempt to close the doors on these memories of his radical student youth. Encouraging Hayashi to reopen the album of personal experiences and restore those pictures from his time as a quintessential "Marx boy" from the 1920s, Kon argues that both the readers and Hayashi will benefit from the chance to witness the full range of poetry, if not the truth, from Hayashi's formative years.[18] Even so, Hayashi would not write any more short stories with factory workers, labor organizers, or student radicals as main characters. Nor would Hayashi revisit his childhood for material to write a sequel to *Sun and Roses*, instead preferring to draw on his immediate family life as husband and father during the postwar years for his popular novels. Thus, with the publication of *Sun and Roses* in 1938, as Kon emphasizes, Hayashi did attempt to put a coda to that time of his life, even as he laid the groundwork for his turn to ultranationalism in the 1940s by re-remembering his childhood with rose-colored glasses.

Written after Hayashi's trip to the Shanghai battlefront in the late summer of 1937, the last seven chapters of *Sun and Roses* also reflect the ongoing changes in Hayashi's life. Much as historian Andrew Barshay has noted in his study of Hasegawa Nozekan's *tenkō* in 1933, Hayashi's time as

17. Kon Hidemi, "Taiyō to Bara," *Bungakukai* 5, no. 12 (December 1938): 261–262.
18. Ibid., 262.

one of the first writers to tour an active battlefront and write about his trip seems to have been a life-changing experience for him.[19] Sponsored by the journal *Chūō kōron* (Central Review), Hayashi first reported on his trip in the October 1937 issue and then completed a book in December 1937 detailing his visit to the battlefront.[20] As observed elsewhere, Hayashi did make several critical remarks concerning the vulnerability of Tokyo, and Japan in general, to air raids, including a warning to Japanese citizens that the war against the Chinese would be protracted.[21] Hayashi also used his battlefield reports to highlight the good work of the Japanese military, government officials, and the Japanese residents he met in the Shanghai International Settlement as well as to admonish those pacifists at home. For Hayashi, the time had come to lay to rest the images of his own "Marxist boy" life. Thus, in reading the last seven chapters of *Sun and Roses*, this study argues that Hayashi attempted to prepare a highly selective and an undeniably romanticized record of his childhood memories so that he could move forward with his life. While he would take with him the Marxist legacy of dissent and his concerns with the disparity between the rich and poor in Japanese society at home, he would increasingly choose to express those concerns in the language and rhetoric of a chauvinistic ultranationalism during the wartime and postwar years.

EXPLAINING THE EARLY SHŌWA YEARS: A CONTENTIOUS DEBATE

From a historiographical perspective, the recent domestic and global interest in Japanese right-wing nationalism marks a significant turn in the scholarly reassessment of the Japanese right-wing leadership's intellectual and organizational activity through the early Shōwa years. Initial postwar

---

19. Barshay makes this point through reference to the Polish historian Andrzej Walicki's assertion about the development of Tolstoy's life and ideas in his work, *State and Intellectual in Imperial Japan: The Public Man in Crisis* (Berkeley, University of California Press, 1988), 203.

20. Hayashi Fusao, "Shanhai sensen," *Chūō kōron* 52 (October 1937), 437–463; and Hayashi Fusao, *Sensō no yokogao: bungakusha wa sensen de nani wo mita ka* (Tokyo: Shunjūsha, 1937).

21. Jeff E. Long, "The Japanese Literati and the 'China Incident': Hayashi Fusao Reporting the Battle of Shanghai," *Sino-Japanese Studies* 15 (April 2003): 39–40.

studies of the Japanese Right were driven largely by the need to explain the right-wing leadership's contribution to the militarism of the 1930s and 1940s. However, during the years of Japan's high-speed economic expansion, the focus shifted from the Right as scholars expanded their studies of the political milieu of interwar years to establish a broader base from which to examine Japan's road to war. With the end of the Shōwa era's phenomenal economic growth and the lingering Heisei (1989–) financial downturn in mind, however, two interrelated developments seem to be propelling a broader reconsideration of the complex influences, intellectual concerns, and historical impact of the Japanese right-wing leadership during the early Shōwa period.

On one side, recent controversy over Japan's secondary school history textbooks has fueled an intense exploration of the motives, aims, and influences on those groups pushing for textbook modification, specifically in light of the public's awareness of the neo-nationalist discourse accompanying this debate.[22] One work pushed to the forefront of this inquiry has been Hayashi Fusao's *Daitōa sensō kōteiron* ("In support of the Greater East Asian War, 1964, 1965"). A polemical work of the early 1960s, *In Support of the Greater East Asian War* advanced Hayashi's controversial thesis that the Pacific War culminated a hundred-year war against Western imperialism in Asia. His reaffirmation of Japan's role in the Pacific War was meant to counter early postwar assessments of what he labeled "liberal historians" who attributed the Japanese post-Occupation democratic and capitalist "successes" to the 1920s, neglecting Japan's "dark valley" of the 1930s and 40s.[23] His attempt to splice together the historical experiences of Shōwa Japan has shaped later generations' perception of the war and its place in Japanese history. Since

---

22. For example, see the coauthors' introductions in *Censoring History: Citizenship and Memory in Japan, Germany, and the United States*, edited by Laura Hein and Mark Selden (Armonk, NY: M.E. Sharpe, 2000), 3–50, and in *Perilous Memories: The Asia-Pacific War(s)*, edited by T. Fujitani, Geoffrey M. White, and Lisa Yoneyama (Durham: Duke University Press, 2001), 22–23; see also Akiko Hashimoto's discussion of this debate's influence on Japanese memory of these years in her work *The Long Defeat: Cultural Trauma, Memory, and Identity in Japan* (New York: Oxford University Press, 2015), 60–65.

23. Hayashi Fusao, *Daitōa sensō kōteiron* (Tokyo: Banchō shobō, 1964), 262. For more information on the historiographical influence of *In Support of the Greater East Asian War*, see Long 2000, pp. 7–9.

the 1960s, publishers have twice trotted out *In Support of the Greater East Asian War* during times of nationalist upswing among the Japanese people: first, in 1984 coinciding with the *Nihonjinron* (debate on Japanese national character) boom, and most recently in 2001, following the neo-nationalist "Liberal School of History" group's push for a more patriotic narrative of Japanese history in the Ministry of Education's officially sanctioned secondary school textbooks.[24] Still, Hayashi's presence in this debate regarding internal and external views of the Pacific War has not been limited to just this one work.

His ideological bearing on the Japanese Right has also been taken up among some contemporary scholars dealing with the age of Shōwa. Their theoretical attempts to comprehend the place of the Shōwa experience within Japan's modern capitalist development represent the academic side of this reexamination of the Japanese right-wing leadership, with such scholars increasingly advocating a transwar approach that treats the entire Shōwa period as a precursor to Heisei, including the later Shōwa years (1945–1989). In her essay written soon after the death of the Shōwa Emperor, Carol Gluck argues that a key theme in the study of modern Japanese history remains the awkward task of situating the Shōwa era (1926–1989) within Japan's modern experience. How were scholars to deal with Shōwa, cleaved between the temporal nodes of devastating total war and miraculous economic growth and the spatial grid of East and West?[25] Were they to continue with the theoretical dichotomy that had emerged, either disregarding the "dark valley" of early Shōwa for the economically prosperous later Shōwa or placing Shōwa within a longer timeframe to mitigate the uneasiness in giving purpose to the wartime years within Japan's modern development?[26] In the case of those intellectual historians taking a transwar approach to Shōwa, they have primarily concentrated on issues of modern Japanese identity, and the early Shōwa years have

---

24. Hayashi Fusao, *Daitōa sensō kōteiron*, Pocketbook edition, 2 vols. (Tokyo: Miki shobō, 1984) and Hayashi Fusao, *Daitōa sensō kōteiron*, Pocketbook edition, Hayashi Fusao Collection, no. 1 (Tokyo: Natsume shobō, 2001). See Rikki Kersten's article on this group's leadership, motives, and goals, "Neo-nationalism and the "Liberal School of History," *Japan Forum* 11, no. 2 (1999): 191–203.

25. Carol Gluck, "The Idea of Showa," in *Showa: The Japan of Hirohito*, ed. Carol Gluck and Stephen R. Graubard (New York: W.W. Norton & Company, 1992), 6–8, 18–20.

26. Ibid., 18–19.

taken on a new significance as a springboard for examining the intellectual history of later Shōwa and the Heisei years.

An unexpected consequence of this methodological development has been a renewed interest in the Japan Romantic School and its coterie from the mid-to-late 1930s. In particular, the contributions of its members to the Overcoming Modernity Symposium held in the summer of 1942 have been mined to understand how intellectuals from the 1960s, 1980s, and again at the turn of the century have reinterpreted those romantic nationalist ideas within the economic boom years of later Shōwa as well as the recessionary years of early Heisei. First and most prominent of these works in English was Kevin Doak's 1994 study of the five synchronic moments that he argues epitomized the Japan Romantic School's response to the modern condition. Doak frames these larger attempts to rethink the place of Shōwa within the evolution of Japan's modern identity.[27] Thus, his analysis has shaped how other works contextualize the predominant cultural leadership of the Japan Romantic School. For example, in 1998 Tetsuo Najita and Harry Harootunian study Japanese antimodernist and anti-Western thinkers from the early twentieth century, including those from the Japan Romantic School. [28] Harootunian went on to publish a book-length study in 2000 of the social and cultural impact of the antimodernist discourse during the interwar years.[29] Yumiko Iida's 2002 investigation of aesthetics in Japanese nationalism highlights the role of aesthetics as an alternative means of criticizing the state in prewar and postwar Japan.[30] Finally, Richard F. Calichman's 2008 deconstructionist introduction to his translation of the essays that Hayashi and others contributed to the Overcoming Modernity symposium of 1942 reveals the link between wartime nationalist propaganda and the current rise of neonationalism in Japan.[31]

---

27. Kevin M. Doak, *Dreams of Difference: The Japan Romantic School and the Crisis of Modernity* (Berkeley, CA: University of California Press, 1994).

28. Tetsuo Najita and H.D. Harootunian, "Japan's Revolt Against the West," in *Modern Japanese Thought*, ed. Bob Takashi Wakabayashi (New York: Cambridge University Press, 1998), 207–272.

29. H.D. Harootunian, *Overcome by Modernity: History, Culture, and Community in Interwar Japan* (Princeton: Princeton University Press, 2000).

30. Yumiko Iida, *Rethinking Identity in Modern Japan: Nationalism as Aesthetics* (New York: Routledge, 2002).

31. Richard Calichman, "Introduction: 'Overcoming Modernity': The Dissolution of

Doak includes Hayashi as the last of the Japan Romantic School's leading voices in his study,[32] and both Harootunian and Iida identify Hayashi as a leader of the Japan Romantic School. Harootunian and Iida also discuss Hayashi's ideas regarding the Meiji Restoration from the Overcoming Modernity Symposium in anticipation of his *In Support of the Greater East Asian War.*[33] In essence, their attempts to argue that Hayashi's ultranationalist views of Japanese historical development from the Symposium fed directly into his 1960s' neo-nationalist historiographical interpretation of Japan's war in Asia and the Pacific has contributed to a rather narrow portrayal of his intellectual development during the 1930s and 1940s. Namely, these studies argue that an extreme nationalist rhetoric characterized his literary production throughout the Shōwa years. Situated on the margins of both authors' efforts to reconsider the transition from the early to the later Shōwa years, neither author attempts to extricate the historical circumstances surrounding Hayashi's statements at the 1942 symposium. Moreover, Harootunian states early on in *Overcome by Modernity* that his focus is on how intellectuals collectively, from Japan and elsewhere, deliberated on the "experience of modernity" through the early twentieth century, rather than attempting to consider and relate the individual's social and economic experiences of the modern condition.[34] Doak, as well, centers his narrative on Hayashi's romantic voice to accent the Japan Romantic School's attempts to define multiple ethnic nationalist (*minzokushugi*) positions separate from the Japanese government's state nationalism (*kokkashugi*). As a result, he begins his analysis of Hayashi's romanticism from 1932, largely ignoring Hayashi's leadership roles in the Marxist student and literary movements

---

Cultural Identity," in *Overcoming Modernity: Cultural Identity in Wartime Japan*, Weatherhead Books on Asia: History, Society, and Culture, ed. Carol Gluck (New York: Columbia University Press, 2008), 1–41.

32. Doak, *Dreams of Difference*, xlii–xliii.

33. See Harootunian, *Overcome by Modernity*, 35, and Iida, *Rethinking Identity in Modern Japan*, 43, where each places Hayashi as a leader of the Japan Romantic School. For Harootunian's and Iida's link to Hayashi's *In Support of the Greater East Asian War*, see Harootunian, *Overcome by Modernity*, 35, and Iida, *Rethinking Identity in Modern Japan*, 52–56, 142–43. While Richard Calichman does acknowledge Hayashi as a member of both the Literary World group and the Japan Romantic School at the 1942 Symposium, he does so within the context of group representation at the Symposium, *Overcoming Modernity*, x.

34. Harootunian, *Overcome by Modernity*, xi.

of the early 1920s, and then quickly brushes aside his use of Marxism to concentrate on his romantic nationalism.[35] In dismissing Hayashi's individual experience of modern life before 1932, Doak sets the stage for Harootunian and others to accentuate Hayashi's ethnic nationalism and his participation in the Japan Romantic School as the defining elements in his intellectual growth.

Even so, viewed from the background of Hayashi's development as a writer in the 1930s, his association with the Japan Romantic School's coterie seems tangential at best. In practical terms, Hayashi's prior obligations to the journal *Bungakukai* that he helped to found in 1933 and his leadership position in its literary group did not allow him much time to associate with the Japan Romantic School. As Nakatani Takao, an original member of the school notes in his 1975 eulogy for Hayashi in *Yomiuri shinbun*, Hayashi participated in the coterie meetings as much as possible and often went drinking with members of the group. He encouraged them and criticized their works with his typically blunt yet insightful remarks (*hōgen*), but he published next to nothing in their journal, *Nihon Rōmanha* (Japan Romantic School).[36] Moreover, Iida following Doak structures Hayashi's move to ethnic nationalism and the Japan Romantic School within the 1930s as part of his leadership of the "cultural renaissance" period, typically dated from 1933 to 1937. She asserts that "the 'cultural renaissance' movement was by and large a safe means of reasserting literary freedom in the form of the depoliticization of culture." Drawing on Doak's analysis, she writes that for Hayashi "not only was literature to be freed from politics, but sociohistorical and material relations were seen as being absorbed into and subordinated to the subjective world of artistic creation." [37] The turn to literature was then a shift inward for Hayashi, Iida affirms, a way to reestablish some degree of control over his life and his writing. In this way, Iida seems to confirm what James

35. Doak, *Dreams of Difference*, 108–111.

36. Nakatani Takao's original obituary, "Hayashi Fusaokun wo itamu," appeared in the October 13, 1975, edition of the *Yomiuri shinbun*. It was then republished in *Tsuitō Hayashi Fusao* (Tokyo: Hayashi Fusao dainin tsuitō gyōji jikkō iinkai henshū iin, 1976), 27–28. Hayashi published only one poem, "Ikamahoshi Toho no kuni," in the July 1937 issue of *Nihon rōmanha*.

37. Iida, *Rethinking Identity in Modern Japan*, 36; 37. Iida utilizes Kevin Doak's analysis of the significance of the "cultural renaissance" period for Hayashi in *Dreams of Difference*, 108.

Dorsey has argued, that *tenkō* was a means for Hayashi to escape "ideological thinking" altogether.[38] Thus, as Dorsey has explained elsewhere, "*tenkō* was an epistemological revolution aimed at replacing a deployable social analysis with a personal, intuitive mode of cognition."[39] However, Hayashi's very public drive to separate politics from literature should not be accepted so uncritically, particularly for one as adept at the art of rhetoric as Hayashi. He began fostering the use of political techniques while writing short stories as a higher school student in Kumamoto and further refined those skills after moving to Tokyo and becoming a member of the proletarian literature movement in the mid-1920s. Thus, one of the main goals of this study has been to identify and trace the continually evolving ways that he employed literature to achieve a political objective, leading up and into the "cultural renaissance" period.

A HISTORIOGRAPHY OF THE *TENKŌ* EXPERIENCE AND HAYASHI FUSAO

While recent scholarship in the West has drawn attention to Hayashi's participation in the Japan Romantic School, well-known literary critic Isoda Kōichi in an earlier work points to a different intellectual context in which to read Hayashi Fusao's literature. Isoda queried in 1969: "Within the history of Shōwa literature, were any others surrounded by as much misunderstanding and scandal as Yasuda Yojūrō and Hayashi Fusao?"[40] While the source of controversy surrounding Yasuda dealt with his leader-

38. Dorsey, "From Ideological Literature to a Literary Ideology," 481. Here, Dorsey is referencing Hayashi's discussion of *tenkō* in one of his most polemical works from the spring of 1941, *Tenkō ni tsuite* (Yokohama: Shōfūkai, 1941), a work sponsored by the state and sent out to other *tenkōsha* to convince them to express their positive support for the state.

39. In this case and in his other works, Dorsey draws on Maruyama Masao's definition of *tenkō* as "an escape from the tensions of self-regulation imposed according to a theory (or formula); like the release of a tightly coiled spring, *tenkō* brought about an instantaneous return to a 'natural' world of inclusivity, blending, and conflation ..." *(Nihon no shiso;* Iwanami Shoten, 1961, 15), as quoted in James Dorsey's review of *War, Occupation, and Creativity: Japan and East Asia, 1920–1960*, ed. Marlene J. Mayo and J. Thomas Rimer with H. Eleanor Kerkham, *Monumenta Nipponica* 59, no. 1 (Spring 2004): 135.

40. Isoda Kōichi, "Hayashi Fusao, Dan Kazuo: sakka to sakuhin," in *Hayashi Fusao, Dan Kazuoshū*, ed. Itō Sei, vol. 66. Nihon bungaku zenshū (Tokyo: Shūeisha, 1969), 408.

ship of the Japan Romantic School, Isoda argues that the "misunderstanding and scandal" around and about Hayashi is due to his *tenkō* that marked his surrender to state power.

Summed up by the title of Tatsuo Arima's 1969 work *The Failure of Freedom*, early postwar scholars considering the Japanese intellectual community's relationship with the government during the early Shōwa years work from the assumption that Japanese intellectuals in different ways "failed" to protect and support the burgeoning democracy of the 1920s.[41] On the whole, scholars have often portrayed the *tenkō* phenomenon (*tenkō genshō*) of the early 1930s as a symbol of that failure, and they have treated writer and literary critic Hayashi Fusao specifically as a "poster boy" for the Japanese intellectual's turn to ultranationalism in the mid- to late 1930s. As Honda Shūgo observes in his study of *tenkō* literature, other literary works mark the beginning of *tenkō* literature, and there were many *tenkō* writers. Nevertheless, when other writers and members of the intellectual community consider the *tenkō* phenomenon's impact on Japanese literature, Honda asserts that Hayashi Fusao is always considered one of the first writers to have committed *tenkō*, and one of the leading *tenkō* writers of the 1930s.[42] Drawing on Hayashi's polemical writings and works of literature and literary criticism, scholars have looked to his example for lessons as to why Japanese intellectuals so willingly contributed to Japan's plunge into the "dark valley" of militarism.[43]

Historically, government efforts to obtain confessions and open renun-

---

41. Tatsuo Arima pointed to "the anticonstitutional strains among intellectuals" during the interwar years as the cause of this breakdown in his *The Failure of Freedom: A Portrait of Modern Japanese Intellectuals*, Harvard East Asian Series, no. 39 (Cambridge: Harvard University Press, 1969), viii. See also Robert O. Scalapino, *Democracy and Party Movement in Prewar Japan: The Failure of the First Attempt* (Berkeley, University of California Press, 1953); and George M. Beckmann, "The Radical Left and the Failure of Communism," in *Dilemmas of Growth in Prewar Japan*, ed. James William Morley (Princeton: Princeton University Press, 1971): 139–178 for a similar narrative on this period among party politicians and the Japanese communist movement.

42. Honda Shūgo, *Tenkō bungakuron*, 3rd edition (Tokyo: Miraisha, 1985), 196.

43. See Donald Keene's section on Hayashi as an example of a *tenkō* writer who "persisted in their right-wing views even after the war ended," in "Japanese Literature and Politics in the 1930s," *Journal of Japanese Studies* 2, no. 2 (Summer 1975): 236. Ben-Ami Shillony also mentions Hayashi as an example on an intellectual who "embraced nationalism and was released to become one of its main exponents" in his *Politics and Culture in Wartime Japan* (1981; repr., New York: Clarendon Press-Oxford, 1991), 120.

ciations of the Japan Communist Party and Leftist ideology became particularly evident with the mass arrests of suspected communists in March 1928 and April 1929 and continued with the 1931 public trial at the Tokyo District Court.[44] These efforts culminated in the early 1930s when two imprisoned leaders of the party, Sano Manabu and Nabeyama Sadachika, made use of the term *tenkō* to describe their break with the party and their denunciation of Soviet influence over the party.[45] Fukumoto Kazuo coined this expression during the 1920s in his dispute with Yamakawa Hitoshi over the ideological direction of the Japanese Communist Party. As a result, Sano and Nabeyama took the positive term *tenkō* that Fukumoto used to urge theoretical purity within the communist party leadership and modified the expression to denote the rejection of an ideology that was unsuited for the practical needs of Japanese society.[46] Sano and Nabeyama's joint *tenkō* statement of June 1933 initiated the *tenkō* phenomenon of the mid-1930s that ended with some ninety-eight percent of all those arrested for "thought crimes" (*shisōhanzai*) declaring a *tenkō* of some degree by 1945.[47]

As noted earlier, scholars examining the domestic developments of the 1930s in Japan have studied *tenkō* largely as a measure of how repressive Japanese society became during the early Shōwa years. Sociologist Patricia Steinhoff, in concentrating her analysis on the group and individual responses to state power and the integrative pull of personal relationships as much as or more than the physical pressure the state applied on the *tenkōsha* (those who underwent *tenkō*), emphasizes the human cost of these years in her 1969 dissertation.[48] Similarly, sociologist Kazuko Tsurumi uses six case studies of *tenkōsha* to examine how the state application of coercion affected their personalities as adults, and to consider how each *tenkōsha* adapted to the changes in Japanese society during the interwar period.[49] Historian Richard Mitchell, on the other hand, focuses on

44. Richard H. Mitchell, *Thought Control in Prewar Japan* (Ithaca: Cornell University Press, 1976), 99, 104.

45. Fujita Shōzō, "Shōwa hachi nen o chūshin to suru tenkō no jōkyō," in *Kyōdō kenkyū: tenkō* vol. 1, ed. Shisō no Kagaku no Kenkyūkai (Tokyo: Heibonsha, 1959), 33–35.

46. Fujita, "Shōwa hachi nen o chūshin to suru tenkō no jōkyō," 35.

47. Tsurumi Shunsuke, "Tenkō no kyōdō kenkyū ni tsuite," in *Kyōdō kenkyū: tenkō*, vol. 1, ed. Shisō no Kagaku no Kenkyūkai (Tokyo: Heibonsha, 1959), 23–24.

48. Steinhoff, *Tenkō*, 207.

49. Kazuko Tsurumi, "Six Types of Change in Personality: Case Studies of Ideological

the Justice Ministry's formation of its *tenkō* policy, underscoring the predominant role of state power and administrative planning in reintegrating political prisoners into Japanese society. Ultimately, he even argues for the relative leniency of the Japanese government's thought control system.[50] This stress on state power and the government's suppression of the Japan Communist Party and its supporting elements—such as the radical student movement, the labor unions, and the proletarian cultural movement—has frequently obscured and minimized the role of the *tenkōsha* in the *tenkō* process.

Both Steinhoff's and Mitchell's works drew upon Tsurumi Shunsuke's definition of *tenkō* in 1959 where Tsurumi defines *tenkō* as a "change in thought caused by the government's use of force."[51] His interpretation owes much to the early postwar work of political scientist Maruyama Masao, a fellow member of the Shisō no kagaku kenkyūkai (Institute for the Science of Thought). Maruyama's explanations of Japanese ultranationalism center on the Meiji period (1868–1912). He argues that Meiji elites permitted traditional social and cultural notions of public and private life being subsumed under the authority of the state to supersede external ideas such as the rule of law and the separation of church and state.[52] His view that traditional Japanese values overrode and eventually guided the development of Japan's "modern" institutions provides the intellectual construct for Tsurumi's assertion that it was natural for the Japanese people to submit to the government's political and moral authority when demanded. As literature scholar Moriyama Shigeo has pointed out, the problem with Tsurumi's conception of *tenkō* is that it dichotomized the responses between *tenkō* and *hitenkō*.[53] Thus, Tsurumi's definition emphasizes that one must either change one's ideas and beliefs or refuse to give up one's ideas and beliefs or, more to the point, surrender to state

---

Conversion in the 1930's," in *Social Change and the Individual: Japan Before and After Defeat in World War II* (Princeton: Princeton University Press, 1970), 29–79.

50. Mitchell, *Thought Control in Prewar Japan*, 190–193.

51. Tsurumi, "Tenkō no kyōdō kenkyū ni tsuite," 5. For Tsurumi's translation, see Shunsuke Tsurumi, *An Intellectual History of Wartime Japan 1931–1945*, Japanese Studies, ed. Yoshio Sugimoto (New York: KPI, 1986), 12.

52. Masao Maruyama, *Thought and Behaviour in Modern Japanese Politics*, expanded edition, ed. Ivan Morris (New York: Oxford University Press, 1969), 2–13.

53. Moriyama Shigeo, *Nihon Marukusushugi bungaku: bungaku toshite no kakumei to tenkō* (Tokyo: San'ichi shobō, 1977), 228–229.

power or resist government authority. Furthermore, Moriyama argues that identifying the concept of *tenkō* with the authorities led scholars to a study of the state and its application of force on the *tenkōsha*, instead of considering the creative, spontaneous response to the authorities by the *tenkōsha*.[54]

Even more troubling from the historical perspective of the 1930s is that Tsurumi's view of *tenkō* conveys the notion that the *tenkōsha* underwent a radical change of thought that forced them to abandon their analytical skills and disregard their personal experiences upon which they had based, thus far, their scholarly concerns and their intellectual approaches. In a much earlier work of the 1970s when Harootunian was more concerned with understanding and recovering the Japanese individual's experiences of modernity, he questions this interpretation of *tenkō* as useful in accounting for the intellectual development of Meiji writer Takayama Chogyū. He counters that perhaps "the deployment of *tenkō* really diverts historians from ever investigating the changes in a thinker as manifestations of earlier dispositions."[55] In the end, Harootunian insists that the *tenkō* experience might be thought of more fruitfully as "a dramatic turn in [a person's] consciousness of problems"—an epistemological change in what the Japanese often refer to as their "*mondai ishiki*" (their conception of the issues).[56]

In this way, Harootunian's assertion that Japanese intellectuals faced difficult, often ambiguous choices between politics and culture during the late Meiji (1890–1912) and Taishō (1912–1926) years underscores the varied responses of Japanese intellectuals to government authority. It also shifted the historiographical discussion away from the narrative of failure in the face of government oppression. Through the 1970s, 1980s, and early

---

54. Moriyama, *Nihon Marukusushugi bungaku*, 229. In English, see Tsuzuki Chushichi's essay on Marxist economist's Otsuka Kinnosuke that emphasizes Otsuka's choice to either convert or resist, "Tenkō or Teikō: The Dilemma of a Japanese Marxist between the Wars," in *Themes and Theories in Modern Japanese History: Essays in Memory of Richard Storry*, ed. Sue Henny and Jean-Pierre Lehmann (Atlantic Highlands, NJ: Athlone Press, 1988), 215–229.

55. H.D. Harootunian, "Between Politics and Culture: Authority and the Ambiguities of Intellectual Choice in Imperial Japan," in *Japan in Crisis: Essays on Taishō Democracy*, ed. Bernard S. Silberman and H.D. Harootunian (Princeton: Princeton University Press, 1974), 140.

56. Ibid., 140.

1990s, scholars increasingly characterized the narrative of the Japanese intellectual community's interaction with the state and society during the early Shōwa years as one of "crisis" and sought to examine in what ways Japanese intellectuals defined and confronted this sense of crisis as affecting their respective academic fields.[57] Individual studies by Henry Smith, William Miles Fletcher, Sharon Minichiello, Germaine Hoston, and Andrew Barshay as well as an edited volume by J. Thomas Rimer highlight the complex relationships between the state and Japanese thinkers. All of whom were attempting to contribute to the public dialogue on political, economic, social, and cultural issues regarding national identity and the fate of the nation's modern historical development.[58] Both Fletcher's and Barshay's criticism that early postwar scholars have stretched the concept of *tenkō* too thin to be of any use as a serious tool in comprehending the early Shōwa intellectuals' maturing thought processes reflects Harootunian's earlier dismissal of the *tenkō* concept as a means to assess Takayama's turn to Japanism. It has also inspired some current scholars to begin a reevaluation of the Japanese Left during the interwar years.[59] This recent reassessment also builds upon several other studies from the 1970s and 1980s focused on Marxist intellectuals in particular and that directly

57. As in Harootunian and Bernard S. Silberman's edited volume on the Taishō years, *Japan in Crisis: Essays on Taishō Democracy* (Princeton: Princeton University Press, 1974).

58. See Henry Dewitt Smith, II's *Japan's First Student Radicals*, Harvard East Asian Series, no. 70 (Cambridge: Harvard University Press, 1972); William Miles Fletcher's *Search for a New Order: Intellectuals and Fascism in Prewar Japan* (Chapel Hill: University of North Carolina Press, 1982); Sharon Minichiello, *Retreat from Reform: Patterns of Political Behavior in Interwar Japan* (Honolulu: University of Hawaii Press, 1984); Germaine A. Hoston, *Marxism and the Crisis of Development in Prewar Japan* (Princeton: Princeton University Press, 1986); Andrew E. Barshay, *State and Intellectual in Imperial Japan: The Public Man in Crisis* (Berkeley, University of California Press, 1988); and J. Thomas Rimer, ed., *Culture and Identity: Japanese Intellectuals during the Interwar Years* (Princeton: Princeton University Press, 1990).

59. William Miles Fletcher's *Search for a New Order*, 3–6; and Barshay, *State and Intellectual in Imperial Japan*, 23–33. For this reexamination, see Christopher Goto-Jones's study of Miki Kiyoshi's thought as opposed to Tosaka Jun's understanding of Marxism in "The Left Hand of Darkness: Forging a Political Left in Interwar Japan," and Rikki Kersten's explication of Asō Hisashi's political thought as the leader of the *Shakai Taishutō* (Socialist Masses Party) in "Painting the Emperor Red: The Emperor and the Socialists in the 1930s," in *The Left in the Shaping of Japanese Democracy: Essays in Honour of J.A.A. Stockwin*, ed. Rikki Kersten and David Williams (London: Routledge, 2006): 3–20; 21–41.

challenged the politically charged views of the *tenkōsha* as either committing "apostasy," hence betraying the political Left, or as undergoing an "ideological conversion" to some form of right-wing nationalism in response to state pressure.

As these scholars considering the *tenkō* phenomenon's influence on other Leftist intellectuals as part of this period of crisis have found, Hayashi's efforts to preserve his critical perspective following his 1932 *tenkō* in prison was not unusual. Germaine Hoston has shown in her studies of Sano Manabu that he endeavored to establish a theoretical position between Marxism and nationalism, even after his *tenkō* declaration in 1933.[60] Gail Bernstein in her intellectual biography of Kawakami Hajime notes his continued belief in communism and Marxism through the wartime years, even after Kawakami agreed not to participate in political activities after his subsequent release from prison.[61] In addition, Miriam Silverberg's study of fellow Marxist literati Nakano Shigeharu suggests that although the *tenkō* phenomenon called into question the USSR's power over the Japan Communist Party, Nakano did not give up his desire for change in Japanese society. For Nakano, Silverberg maintains, his *tenkō* in 1934 meant that he had "turned away from the institution [Japan Communist Party] but not the ideology [Marxism]. He remained an activist, revolutionary critic of the state."[62] On the contrary, for Hayashi Fusao, the Japanese state's crackdown on the Left cast doubt not only on the party's leadership over its affiliated cultural organizations but eventually also upon Marxist ideology as a viable method of social criticism. Hayashi then shifted to cultural nationalism as an alternative yet permissible means to continue his censure of the government for its treatment of the Japanese people and the national land.

Those researching the role of Hayashi's *tenkō* in his move away from the left-wing movement to ultranationalism have often done so to capture the emerging patriotic spirit of the 1930s. As part of the Institute for the

---

60. Germaine A. Hoston, "Tenkō: Marxism & the National Question in Prewar Japan," *Polity* 16, no. 1 (Fall 1983): 96–118.

61. Gail Lee Bernstein, *Japanese Marxist: A Portrait of Kawakami Hajime, 1879–1946*, Harvard East Asian Monographs, no. 152 (Cambridge: Harvard University Press, 1976; 1990), 163.

62. Miriam Silverberg, *Changing Song: The Marxist Manifestos of Nakano Shigeharu* (Princeton: Princeton University Press, 1990), 199.

Science of Thought's research on the *tenkō* phenomenon, Tsurumi Shunsuke studied the historical and biographical elements of the 1920s and 1930s surrounding Hayashi's *tenkō* to explain the move to militarism during the interwar years.[63] Writer Mishima Yukio was also fascinated by what he called Hayashi's "double image" of the same time.[64] Much as the 1930s was a time of crisis and indecision, Mishima singles out Hayashi as an example of those intellectuals caught between reason and emotion. Hayashi's *tenkō* in Mishima's estimation stands for the triumph of patriotic sentiment over intellect, and Mishima beautifies this image because it personified the 1930s and early 1940s for him, an image of noble failure that he admired. Both works provide insight into immediate interwar influences on Hayashi's *tenkō*, but each work is narrowly focused on elucidating the "radical or emotional transformation" of Hayashi's thinking.[65]

In contrast, Isoda Kōichi strives to situate Hayashi's *tenkō* within the greater context of his intellectual development. Surveying Hayashi's life and works from his childhood in Kyūshū through the postwar years, Isoda finds continuity in Hayashi's intellectual choices before and after his formal *tenkō* statement in 1932. Where Tsurumi and Mishima argue that Hayashi "converted" from Marxism to ultranationalism during this time, Isoda asserts that Hayashi's Marxist views and his ultranationalist position were largely similar.[66] Isoda's interpretation of Hayashi's *tenkō* reflects a perspective similar to Harootunian's observation concerning the conceptual effectiveness of *tenkō*. Isoda stresses that Hayashi did not "convert" to ultranationalism as much as the historical circumstances in which Hayashi found himself writing had changed fundamentally. As a result,

---

63. Tsurumi Shunsuke, "Kōki Shinjinkai'in," in *Kyōdō kenkyū: tenkō*, vol. 1, ed. Shisō no Kagaku no Kenkyūkai (Tokyo: Heibonsha, 1959), 127–134. Tsurumi illustrated the process of Hayashi's *tenkō* in quantifiable terms, organizing Hayashi's intellectual choices in three periods (1933–1937, 1938–1945, and 1946–1959). Tsurumi gave six reasons for Hayashi's *tenkō*, the first three personal and the latter three social: first, "a rise in his standard of living"; second, "his age"; third, "his consciousness of death"; fourth, "his frustration at not becoming a leader [of the socialist movement in Japan]"; fifth, "his evolving relationship with the leaders of greater Japanese society"; and sixth, "his overestimation of a parallel Japanese modernization process from his prison experience."

64. Mishima Yukio, "Hayashi Fusaoron," in *Mishima Yukio zenshū*, vol. 30. Hyōron, ed. Saeki Shōichi (Tokyo: Shinchōsha, 1975), 539.

65. Tsurumi, "Kōki Shinjinkai'in," 127–134; Mishima, "Hayashi Fusaoron," 509–535.

66. Isoda, "Hayashi Fusao, Dan Kazuo," 409.

Hayashi adapted his analytical framework to meet the political exigencies of the unsettled historical context of 1930s' Japan.

In moving away from interpreting Hayashi's *tenkō* as an emotional reaction to a judicious decision on Hayashi's part, Isoda builds on a near contemporary assessment of Hayashi's *tenkō* that emphasized his principled adjustment to the times. Hayashi's friend in Kamakura and well-known literary critic Kobayashi Hideo writing in the spring of 1941 maintains that Hayashi's *tenkō* was not a response to any perceived problems with Marxist theory (*riron*), nor was it an issue of his mental state (*shinri*). Rather, he argues that Hayashi's *tenkō* was a moral issue (*dōtoku*) for Hayashi, a matter of doing what was right.[67] Thus, in Hayashi's case, the Japanese state's attempts to silence the political Left forced Hayashi, in the wake of his *tenkō*, to modify his intellectual position. On the one hand, he articulated an intellectual position that drew inspiration from Marxist social criticism of the Taishō years, but he also expressed that position positively as a cultural nationalist concern for his country and the Japanese people in the early Shōwa years.

Still, while Kobayashi interprets this shift in the context of a patriotic decision to do what was best for his country at the time, Isoda argues that Hayashi's turn to cultural nationalism and a romantic interpretation of Japanese history and society was more an evolution in Hayashi's "conception of the issues" at hand. As such, it was a change in his intellectual approach to maintaining a critical position of the Japanese state's role in directing the nation-state's modern social and economic development. In this sense, Isoda's analysis suggests that Hayashi's *tenkō* was more than simply an emotional surrender to his multiple imprisonments and the police harassment he experienced. Neither was it merely a jingoistic concession to the rise of popular nationalism in the wake of the 1931 Manchurian Incident and war with China in 1937, as Kobayashi implies. Building on Isoda's argument, this monograph argues that Hayashi's *tenkō* was a rational, deliberate choice to find another, more admissible means of confronting the Japanese state. Moreover, Hayashi utilized the *shishōsetsu* style in

---

67. Kobayashi Hideo, "Hayashi Fusao ni tsuite," *Bungei shunjū* 19, no. 3 (March 1941): 329.

an attempt to infuse his "change of direction" with a sense of genuineness, following his departure from the proletarian literature movement.

Another set of objectives in this study has been biographical. First, to identify in what ways Hayashi's childhood experiences in rural Japan defined his "conception of the issues," shaping his scholarly concerns and intellectual interests. Then, second, to consider the changing ways in which Hayashi sought to accommodate these concerns and interests through a study of his proletarian short stories during the Taishō and early Shōwa years. These were stories that he defined as proletarian in content, but that originated from the concerns of Japanese society's samurai fringe in the early twentieth century. We noted that the political goal for many of Hayashi's proletarian short stories was the mockery of the leadership of the Socialist movement, which shifted to an outright denunciation of the KOPF leaders by the mid-1930s. His attack on the KOPF leadership suggests an emotional response in his *tenkō*, particularly a political desire for revenge, as Isoda observes in Chapter 1.[68] As such, this monograph builds on Dorsey's argument that Hayashi's *tenkō* represented a move from universal theories to a particular cultural understanding of Japan, but contends that this was less a "release from ideological thinking," as Dorsey surmises, and more a *repurposing* of ideological thinking for Hayashi (emphasis mine).[69] Thus, Hayashi relentlessly sought in his push for a "cultural renaissance," in his advocacy for the "return to Japan," and finally in his "service to the Emperor," which he promoted during the 1940s as an alternative means of expressing his "conception of the issues" based on his personal experiences. Concurrently, Hayashi also strove to repackage this latent desire for revenge as a dedication to literature, next as a spiritual concern for Japan's cultural traditions, and lastly as patriotic support for the preeminent wartime symbol of imperial Japan—its people, land, cultural habits and spiritual practices.

Accordingly, this work also hopes to contribute to the ongoing historiographical shift away from conceptions of "failure" and "crisis" to one of "competing modernities" that has influenced recent studies of Japanese state-society relations during the 1920s and 1930s. Published in 1998,

68. Isoda, "Hayashi Fusao, Dan Kazuo," 410.
69. Dorsey, "From Ideological Literature to a Literary Ideology," 481.

Sharon Minichiello's edited volume, *Japan's Competing Modernities*, expressly strove to highlight the new scholarship being conducted on issues of ethnicity, gender, class, and identity. This volume places that research within the greater tensions of "geographical and cultural space," "cosmopolitanism and national identity," and "diversity, autonomy, and integration" that characterized the multilayered and varied Japanese attempts to become "world citizens" during the early twentieth century.[70]

In the context of our study of *tenkō* and Hayashi Fusao, one result of this focus on the competing definitions of what being modern meant has been a restoration of some measure of agency to individuals during the period. Jennifer Cullen emphasizes this point in her innovative study of female *tenkō*. For scholars to focus mainly on personal and practical reasons to explain either Miyamoto Yuriko's defiance of state authority or Sata Ineko's decision to *tenkō*, she notes, diminishes the significance of their literature during the 1930s. It also reduces their intellectual choices to being determined by each author's different family circumstances.[71] Cullen argues that, for Sata in particular, her decision to *tenkō* reflected the tension she experienced between her public persona as part of the proletarian literature movement and her identity as an individual writer focused on empowering women in Japanese society, a more pressing issue for her. Ultimately, through a close reading of Sata's autobiographical literature, Cullen shows how over time Sata worked to separate and renegotiate the relative value she placed on literature as a means to encourage proletarian revolution versus her position as a writer working to inspire women to overcome the paternalism in Japanese society. Finally, Cullen concludes by pointing out that the multiple ways Sata presented her decision to *tenkō* at different times in the 1930s and the postwar period were an assertion of her right to determine the meaning of that *tenkō*. As an "active choice," she chose her role as author and her place as a woman in Japanese society over a particular class identity and the guidance of a particular political organization.[72] Similarly, Hayashi's *tenkō* would in-

70. Sharon A. Minichiello, "Introduction," in *Japan's Competing Modernities: Issues in Culture and Democracy, 1900–1930*, ed. Sharon A. Minichiello (Honolulu: University of Hawai'i Press, 1998), 14–18, 1.

71. Jennifer Cullen, "A Comparative Study of *Tenkō*: Sata Ineko and Miyamoto Yuriko," *Journal of Japanese Studies* 36, no. 1 (Winter 2010): 66–67.

72. Ibid., 76–84.

volve a negotiation and then reprioritization of his identity as a writer and his "core focus" on the detrimental impact of Meiji government social and economic policies on rural Japan over the demands for a particular form of writing made by the proletarian literature movement's leaders.[73] Thus, his decision to leave the Marxist cultural movement was a pragmatic attempt to find a space where he could redefine himself as an individual writer primarily so that he might then address his concerns regarding what he considered the ruinous changes in Japanese state-society relations.

Reassessing Hayashi Fusao's Tenkō Experience

Starting with the available literature that Hayashi wrote as a middle school student in 1918, this work has scrutinized his proletarian short stories primarily to explicate his maturing political responses to the social and historical circumstances surrounding his intellectual growth. We examined these responses from his time as a middle school and higher school student in Kyūshū, while a student at Tokyo Imperial University, and as a writer for various literary associations up to 1937, after he openly separated himself from the proletarian literature movement in spring of 1936. In uncovering Hayashi's political uses of his literature during these years, this monograph has highlighted the methods he employed to conduct his struggle against authority in Taishō and early Shōwa Japan. Ultimately, this monograph aims to shed light on his persistent attempts to maintain a critical position against the Japanese state through Marxist, cultural nationalist, and finally increasingly chauvinistic appraisals of the government's relationship with Japanese society.

As such, a historical study of writer Hayashi's turn to ultranationalism deemphasizes the emotional impact of the *tenkō* experience on his resolve to find another means to convey his intellectual concerns. Consequently, his *tenkō* was less a fervent patriotic or moral choice of allegiance, as Mishima and Kobayashi have asserted. Neither was it an explicit reaction to a spiritual crisis, which Patricia Steinhoff has argued animated most

73. See also Mats Karlsson's article on Hayashi, "An Alternative View of *Tenkō*: Hayashi Fusao's Popular Writings for *Shinseinen*," *Japanese Studies* 32, no. 1 (May 2012): 72–75, for his emphasis on an "unchanging core identity" that contradicts the idea that Hayashi underwent a radical intellectual transformation during early Shōwa years.

tenkō literature of the time, nor was it an exaggerated emotional response to state pressure, as Tsurumi has concluded.[74] Moreover, Yukiko Shigeto argues that Nakano Shigeharu's *tenkō* was much like writer Shiina Rinzō's assertion that his *tenkō* from the Japanese Communist Party in 1933 was a "falling" (*datsuraku*), or a moving away from the party with no particular destination.[75]

Unlike Nakano or Shiina, Hayashi's change of direction was purposeful. As Noriko Mizuno Lippit notes, Hayashi was one of those proletarian writers who wrote to show that their proletarian works were valuable as literature, not just as expressions of a political viewpoint. She writes, "The purity and legitimacy of their writings, therefore, had to be proven by presenting a new theoretical basis for writing proletarian literature without obvious political purpose."[76] Lippit asserts that the introduction of socialist realism into the proletarian literature movement during the 1930s allowed writers like Hayashi and others to move beyond "self-justification" in their works and that *tenkō* and the application of socialist realist theory to their writing meant "a new start as proletarian writers."[77] Ultimately, Hayashi's shift away from the proletarian cultural movement proved less "a new start" and more a bridge to a cultural nationalist critique of Japanese society. Following Isoda's line of argumentation, Hayashi's *tenkō* represents one in a number of increasingly difficult political choices he made to remain a writer engaged in a public analysis of Japanese state-society relations. What changed, then, were the methods and the means Hayashi employed during the Taishō and early Shōwa years first, to express his reservations concerning the modern social system

---

74. Patricia G. Steinhoff lists the spiritual *tenkōsha* as the fourth main archetype in her essay, "Tenkō and Thought Control," in *Japan and the World: Essays on Japanese History and Politics in Honour of Ishida Takeshi*, ed. Gail Lee Bernstein and Haruhiro Fukui (New York: St. Martin's Press, 1988), 91. See also her paper on the subject, Patricia G. Steinhoff, "Spiritual Tenkō and The Tenkō Bungaku Movement," *Proceedings of the Twenty-ninth International Congress of Orientalists*, 29 (July 1973), 139–142.

75. Yukiko Shigeto, "Tenkō and Writing: The Case of Nakano Shigeharu," *Positions* 22, no. 2 (2014): 519.

76. Noriko Mizuta Lippit, *Reality and Fiction in Modern Japanese Literature* (White Plains, NY: M.E. Sharpe, 1980), 178.

77. Ibid., 178. The other writers she mentions with Hayashi in this search are Tokunaga Sunao and Hirano Ken.

that emerged in the development of the Meiji state, and second, to recast his political as well as literary motives for writing.

Viewed in this way, a historical study of Hayashi's turn to Marxism and his political uses of literature through the 1920s and 1930s provide a much needed corrective lens through which to view his and other writers' and scholars' postwar attempts to paint his turn to ultranationalism as either a failure to support democracy or a spiritual crisis that led to a charged patriotic display. This monograph draws our attention to a number of Japanese intellectuals determined to remain involved in public matters during the early Shōwa years, no matter how strained their choices may seem to us now. Moreover, this historical study of Hayashi's political uses of literature also sets the stage for further analysis of Hayashi Fusao and his polemical use of *tenkō* as a way to reestablish his sincerity as a person and as a writer in transwar Japan. Hayashi represents an extreme example of an intellectual who committed *tenkō* in the 1930s and stood by his *tenkō* in the postwar years, refusing to issue a public statement abandoning his turn to wartime nationalism. In this way, Hayashi's confirmation of his prewar *tenkō* was an affirmation of Japan's part in what the Japanese government officially referred to as the Greater East Asian War. For Hayashi, this *tenkō* is what validated him as a person and his experiences as a writer. He would finally be able to sacrifice himself symbolically for his beliefs within the sea of public scorn and censure in the economically recovering Japan of the 1960s.

EPILOGUE

The Politics of Literature, The Politics of *Tenkō*

Hayashi Fusao's Search for Authenticity

> *Tenkō* is the ultimate reduction of politics to the human being, to the individual confronted with the freedom to choose with responsibility. Like other forms of decadence, *tenkō* brings the individual to a choice between either a total schizophrenic alienation or a fusion of body and mind wherein survival of the body is perceived as a contamination of the spirit. Thus it is that *tenkō* and *daraku* may be said to resonate with each other in the postwar, when individual Japanese who have survived must account for their survival when they might have / could have / should have died.
>
> —Alan Wolfe, "From Pearls to Swine"

> As one can tell from this episode, my youthful "communism" was built upon fanaticism (*kyōshin*) and illusion (*gensō*). The proletarian literature movement in which I got my start as a writer, as well, cannot be explained without referencing this simple, yet primeval zeal for revolution. We can't say that all writers who called themselves proletarian writers were zealots. Nevertheless, at the very least, fanaticism governed my youthful self.
>
> —Hayashi Fusao, "Bungakuteki kaisō"*

As Alan Wolfe observes, there are certain parallels between Sakaguchi Ango's postwar conceptualization of *daraku* (decadence) and the prewar *tenkō* phenomenon. In the quote above, Wolfe suggests a resonance between the two concepts as a form of survivor's guilt because in early Shōwa Japan, unlike in the West, the failure of communism pointedly called into question the authenticity of the individual. Ultimately, in the 1930s the Japanese

*Hayashi Fusao, *Hayashi Fusao chosakushū*, vol. 2 (Tokyo: Tsubasa shoin, 1969), 225.

populace expected the communists to martyr themselves for their ideas. Thus, in reading the *tenkō* literature of that period, both the popular audience and their fellow writers were unmoved by the *tenkō* writers' protestations of their commitment to Marxism and communism.[1] As an example, Wolfe focuses on the protagonist Benji in Nakano Shigeharu's best-known *tenkō* story "Mura no ie" ("The House in the Village") published in 1935. In this story, Benji argues that he has not lost the faith, but that he can no longer take the mental duress nor endure the physical pain of incarceration, and he signs the *tenkō* statement.[2] In Shimaki Kensaku's *tenkō* story "Rai" ("Leprosy") from 1934, he writes of the tubercular prisoner Ōta Jirō whom the authorities place in the prison wing for leprosy patients because he was a communist. There he finally meets his former comrade, Okada Ryōzō, who has contracted leprosy but who steadfastly refuses to commit *tenkō*. Ōta is more ambivalent than Okada, and while he does not commit *tenkō* in the story, it is obvious that he does not have Okada's mental or physical capacity to resist the authorities. His body eventually yields to the agony inflicted by his illness, and the story ends with Ōta being carried on a stretcher out of prison.[3] In such *tenkō* stories, Wolfe argues that the reading public anticipated the ultimate sacrifice of the person for their ideas as a show of sincerity. As a result, the readers were not interested in the main protagonist's expressions of weakness, nor were they sympathetic to the leading characters' explanations for their continued belief in communism, despite their *tenkō* statements.[4]

Tenkō was also "a rhetorical device" for Ango, Wolfe argues, one that in the postwar period he used to disarm the dominant militarist rhetoric of "transcendence" and "overcoming" of the prewar years by instead positing the need to rediscover, celebrate, and wallow in the imperfections of the

---

1. Alan Wolfe, "From Pearls to Swine: Sakaguchi Ango and the Humanity of Decadence," in *War, Occupation, and Creativity: Japan and East Asia, 1920–1960*, ed. Marlene J. Mayo and J. Thomas Rimer with H. Eleanor Kerkham (Honolulu: University of Hawai'i Press, 2001), 370–371. Mark Williams describes a similar sense of *tenkō* as survivor's guilt for the writer Shiina Rinzō in his article, "Shiina Rinzō: Imagining Hope and Despair in Occupation Japan," *Bulletin of the School of Oriental and African Studies* 66, no. 3 (2003): 444–447.

2. Wolfe draws on Brett de Bary's translation of "Mura no ie" in her translation, *Three Works by Nakano Shigeharu*, Cornell University East Asia Papers, No. 21 (Ithaca: China-Japan Program, 1979), 19–73, for this example.

3. Shimaki Kensaku, "Rai," *Bungaku hyōron* (April 1934): 130–170.

4. Alan Wolfe, "From Pearls to Swine," 371.

individual. This focus on human weakness was a way for Ango to sidestep the "totalizing tendencies" of both the prewar ultranationalists and the postwar communists in 1940s' Japan.[5] Wolfe asserts that Ango employed decadence as a means to challenge the individual to search inside himself or herself to free themselves from the universalistic truths that politicians, writers, and ideologues from both the Left and the Right were selling to the public, and to take responsibility for their own life decisions.

While Hayashi wrote the historical novel *Youth* as a *tenkō* story of reintegration with the family-state, it is in his proletarian short stories where we find him employing *tenkō* as "a rhetorical device" similar to Sakaguchi Ango's use of *daraku*. First, as observed in his proletarian fiction from Chapter 5, Hayashi strove to define the desirable personality traits of workers, organizers, and activists in his short stories. By writing short stories whose main characters modeled attitudes and behaviors of which he approved, he hoped to effect change in his comrades from the Marxist cultural movement. However, soon he realized that he could not influence KOPF's leadership group to think of literature outside of party dictates, which demanded the use of culture for propaganda and agitation purposes. In Chapter 6, we considered how at that point in his proletarian fiction Hayashi began recording and storing those moments that represented the highlights of the movement for him. Consequently, he employed his *tenkō* experience as a means to distance himself from the policies and leaders of the proletarian literature movement in the mid-1930s. Next, as demonstrated in Chapter 7, we find him writing a set of autobiographical stories to carve out a space for the now displaced legacy of dissent. Instead of declaring some form of support for left-wing ideology, however, we found him pondering the life events that fueled his anger and that eventually led to his participation in left-wing political and cultural movements. Lastly, in Chapter 8, we witnessed Hayashi eventually using the space that he produced for his dissent to create a replacement memory of his childhood sweetheart, their shared tribulations, and his bittersweet middle school days. The majority of the narrative in *Sun and Roses* becomes a sentimental substitute for the grittier depictions of his youth in his earlier proletarian short stories.

In this way, Hayashi's rhetorical use of his *tenkō* experience also

5. Alan Wolfe, "From Pearls to Swine," 369–370.

evolved during the late 1920s and throughout the 1930s. His formal *tenkō* statement in 1932 was the fulcrum for his escape from the political dictates of the left-wing literary theoreticians, and his public *tenkō* in the spring of 1936 solidified his turn to literature in the mid-1930s as a testament of artistic license to prioritize literature over the political concerns of the KOPF leaders. Hayashi gradually shifted the expression of his "conception of the issues" to a more permissible cultural nationalist analysis of the damage done to the Japanese land and people as set forth in Chapter 7. As James Dorsey notes in his study of the famed literary critic Kobayashi Hideo, Hayashi embraced Kobayashi's concept of *bungaku shugi* ("literary aestheticism") as a much-needed alternative to the Marxist understanding of social relationships. Referencing an August 1934 roundtable panel on the relationship between politics and literature, Dorsey then explains the difficulty Hayashi had in grasping Kobayashi's analysis of how the definition of politics was still in the process of changing over time. Moreover, Hayashi also struggled to grasp Kobayashi's argument that politics and literature were only becoming more intimately related as the Japanese state pushed for homefront unity in the wake of Japanese advances in Manchuria and China. Dorsey insists that Hayashi's belief in literature was an either/or choice and politics was its antithesis; thus, he could not bear any talk of a relationship between literature and politics, almost refusing to see the possibility of literature being influenced by politics.[6]

Ironically, Hayashi's reification of literature was a decidedly political act marking another rhetorical use of *tenkō*, this time as a means to remake his personal history through literature. In his chapter on Hayashi's place in the Japan Romantic School, historian Kevin Doak employs Western literary and cultural theory to explain the ways that Hayashi sought to redefine himself and thus produce a revived Japanese culture in wartime Japan without the baneful Western influences that had crept in since the Meiji period.[7] Doak argues that the "cultural renaissance" Hayashi envisioned was driven by an ethnic nationalism that ultimately led him during the wartime years to identify the emperor as the "locus of production," so

6. James Dorsey, *Critical Aesthetics: Kobayashi Hideo, Modernity, and Wartime Japan*, Harvard East Asian Monographs, 318 (Cambridge: Harvard University Asia Center, 2009), 155–158.

7. Kevin M. Doak, *Dreams of Difference: The Japan Romantic School and the Crisis of Modernity* (Berkeley, CA: University of California Press, 1994), 107–115.

that service to the emperor became the means to remake the self for him. Accordingly, Hayashi could re-create the romantic narrative of a timeless Japanese society, free from the historical taint of the Meiji modernizing process that produced the industrial capitalist society, which in turn victimized the Japanese people and land. Doak contends that Hayashi used this romantic understanding of history focused on the relationship between the emperor and the Japanese people to justify his active support of the war against the West from 1941. For him, this relationship was the means to produce a new Japanese culture and to push Japanese intellectuals to develop a new definition of imperial rule that would supplant the Western-influenced "modern" society established during the Meiji years.[8] In the end, Doak's goal is to include Hayashi Fusao as one of the formative voices of the Japan Romantic School. To accomplish this, Doak emphasizes the role of ethnic nationalism as the inspiration behind Hayashi's "new historicism"[9] and explains how Hayashi's decision to wrap himself in the patriotic cloak of the emperor cult became a significant part of the Japan Romantic School's cultural "revolt against the West."

Still, as our examination of his proletarian short stories, especially from the 1930s, has shown, Hayashi's clash with the communist leaders of the Writers' League also informed his revolt against the West. Hence, his stories were from the samurai fringe in the sense that his nationalist desire to address the victimization of the Japanese people and land that occurred during the Meiji years shaped his "conception of the issues" from his youth. Just as his personal experiences of watching his mother of samurai lineage suffer in the silk mill informed this consciousness, so did his work as a student radical, a labor organizer, and a writer in the proletarian literature movement. We have witnessed his involvement in the dispute against the communist leadership group of the Writers' League in the 1930s and examined how this struggle defined the subjects in his proletarian short stories through the publication of *Sun and Roses* in 1938. Thus, while Doak succeeds in illuminating how Hayashi attempted to introduce a cultural nationalist perspective in exchange for the Marxist legacy of dissent during the wartime years, he misses why filling this gap was so urgent for Hayashi, who in Dorsey's view was,

8. Kevin M. Doak, *Dreams of Difference*, 115–130.

9. Ibid., 131.

along with Kobayashi Hideo, so adamant that literature had to take the place of politics.

Hayashi's "revolt against the West" was, in essence, a search for authenticity.[10] On the one hand, his cultural nationalist critique drew on the social alienation his mother's family experienced with the shift to an industrial capitalist society during the Meiji and Taishō years. As such, employing *tenkō* as a rhetorical device in the 1930s became a means for him to continue his fight against the authority of the Japanese state. On the other hand, Hayashi's immediate sense of estrangement in the early Shōwa years was political. After all, the government had detained and imprisoned him three different times for his involvement in the left-wing movement, while concurrently KOPF's communist leadership had worked to marginalize his voice in the proletarian literature movement. They condemned his stance supporting the merit of maintaining an artistic perspective in writing politicized literature and, ultimately, called into question his sincerity as a writer for the proletarian literature movement in this debate.

Hayashi could carry out his revolt against the West within the cultural nationalist or ethnic nationalist idiom. However, in referring to the "West" in his writing of the 1930s, he meant communism and more specifically the Communist Party. Ultimately, his goal in turning to the ideology of "art for art's sake" in the 1930s was first to imagine and then to produce with his literature a memory of a Japan without the historical influence of communism and devoid of the historical presence of the Communist Party in Japan. Thus, his political opposition to the Writers' League and its communist leadership group was the fundamental driving force behind his rhetorical use of *tenkō* in the 1930s, but it had its limits. In the early 1940s, as the government narrowed the permissible expressions of dissent, Hayashi's cultural nationalist perspective was absorbed under the cloak of an emperor-cult ultranationalism. Once again, his rhetoric shifted to the larger anti-Western capitalism focus and he defined the "West" in terms of the adverse American influence on the Meiji state in his remarks as a participant in the Overcoming Modernity Symposium of 1942. This time,

10. Here I am borrowing the term used in Tetsuo Najita and H.D. Harootunian's "Japan's Revolt Against the West," in *Modern Japanese Thought*, ed. Bob Takashi Wakabayashi (New York: Cambridge University Press, 1998), 207–272.

however, returning to the theme of the social marginalization of his samurai roots did not have the desired outcome. For others, it only confirmed that Hayashi had become an ultranationalist ideologue for the Japanese imperial state.

Tenkō had "tainted" him personally during the prewar years, to use Wolfe's wording, calling into question his legitimacy as a writer. Moreover, his politics of *tenkō* would not remove that stigma during the wartime period, no matter how much he collaborated with the government or advocated service to the emperor.[11] His chance to redeem himself would not come until the postwar years. Only then, when he begrudgingly accepted defeat in occupied Japan but refused to renounce his *tenkō* to wartime nationalism, as many writers and intellectuals had done subsequently, was he able to accomplish what his prewar rhetoric of *tenkō* could not.

THE POLITICS OF *TENKŌ* IN OCCUPIED JAPAN

In his pioneering work, *Embracing Defeat*, historian John Dower succeeds in restoring a measure of agency to the Japanese people. Arguing that the Japanese populace did not simply accept the nearly seven-year occupation of their country, Dower asserts that the Japanese people made their seemingly national historical experiences their own.[12] Through a study of emerging social relationships, occupation subcultures, and the mindset of the Japanese people, Dower suggests that the breadth and magnitude of the popular revolution within Japan was a positive revolution of "embracing defeat" that shaped all Japanese lives to some degree.[13] In so doing, Dower has forged a path upon which we can begin to make some sense of the individual experiences of those Japanese who agonized over the ending of the war and the beginning of the peace.

One group who bounced back quickly from the war, Dower notes, was

---

11. As he did in his 1942 essay, "Kinnō no kokoro" (The Heart of Imperial Loyalty) translated in Richard Calichman's edited work, *Overcoming Modernity: Cultural Identity in Wartime Japan*, Weatherhead Books on Asia: History, Society, and Culture, edited by Carol Gluck (New York: Columbia University Press, 2008), 92–110.

12. John W. Dower, *Embracing Defeat: Japan in the Wake of World War II* (New York: W.W. Norton Press, 1999), 24.

13. Ibid., 25.

the Japanese intellectual community. Released from their largely obligatory support for the war effort, most members of the intelligentsia first repented for their failure to offer much if any principled resistance against the wartime state. Second, they moved away from the ultranationalist ideology associated with the wartime state and endeavored to reengage themselves with the Leftist and liberal ideas of the late Taishō years.[14] In this way, the intellectual community forgave themselves for suffering through the "dark valley" of the early Shōwa years and promptly lent their voices to the American-led "democratization" of their country with an air of assurance that Japan would surely "advance" now.[15] Much of the postwar work on the intellectual community has been concerned with how the postwar Japanese intellectuals and writers debated and defined the necessary problems to be overcome before "progress" in developing a "democratic" nation could be attained.[16] Moreover, most of the intelligentsia looked to Western models of Marxist or liberal democratic revolution to help them overcome the crises of personal, historical, and cultural identity that drove them to atone for their wartime failings.[17] However, Hayashi Fusao was one of those Japanese intellectuals who refused to follow this path and repudiate his support for the war.

Denounced as a "cultural war criminal" and forced into writing for "dreg magazines" in the early postwar years, Hayashi not only defended his wartime stance but also continued his early Shōwa use of fiction as a means of political commentary. As seen in his 1949 short story "Yotsu no moji" ("Four Characters"), this time he employed his literature to analyze the postwar Japanese state's acceptance of SCAP-led attempts to democratize Japanese society. Read autobiographically, Hayashi's character sketch of a Chinese official working for the Japanese collaborationist Nanjing government, who committed suicide after the war ended, reads as a lament for the lost ideals of loyalty and sacrifice. Even so, in tracing the motives behind the official's suicide, the narrator of "Four Characters" establishes a subject position that reveals the differences between those who "truly" were committed to the war effort in China and those who were not.

14. Ibid., 234.

15. Ibid., 235.

16. In particular, see J. Victor Koschmann's *Revolution and Subjectivity in Postwar Japan* (Chicago: University of Chicago Press, 1996) for more on this debate.

17. Dower, *Embracing Defeat*, 236–239.

This position calls into question Dower's argument that the Japanese during the early postwar years readily "embraced defeat" in the positive manner that he describes in his work. It also underscores Hayashi's political use of *tenkō* as a measure of commitment that he was determined to maintain at all costs, a means to recover his sense of authenticity as a writer.

Life as a "Cultural War Criminal"

One of SCAP's goals was to weaken those ultranationalist elements that supported the Japanese wartime government. To this end, Occupation authorities issued two purge orders on January 4, 1946: one order concerned ultranationalist organizations while the other pertained to individuals.[18] The directive targeting individuals, SCAPIN 550, included a "removal and exclusion" section that laid out seven categories of "undesirable personnel" from categories A to G, with category A denoting the most serious offenders.[19] Japanese government officials purged Hayashi Fusao under category G, "additional militarists and ultranationalists." Category G was a general classification that Japanese officials extended through their broad interpretation of the SCAP directive in March and May of that year to include those members of the Japanese literati who had promoted militarism or ultranationalism.[20] The Japanese government's March and May 1946 interpretations of this SCAP directive had the force of law; as such, it allowed Japanese authorities to screen and purge more than a thousand people before they promulgated the directive as an official ordinance a year later on January 4, 1947.[21] Of that number, Japanese government officials removed or excluded 458 persons as category G violators. As a result, this category became the principal means by which the Japanese

18. Ivan Morris, *Nationalism and the Right Wing in Japan: A Study of Post-War Trends* (New York: Oxford University Press, 1960), 9–10.

19. Supreme Commander for the Allied Powers, Government Section, *Political Reorientation of Japan: September 1945 to September 1948*, vol. 2 (Washington, D.C., 1949), 484–485.

20. Supreme Commander for the Allied Powers, Government Section, *Political Reorientation of Japan: September 1945 to September 1948*, vol. 1 (Washington, D.C., 1949), 21–22. For a complete transcript of the Japanese government's supplementary interpretation of category G, see SCAP, *Political Reorientation*, vol. 2, 516–528.

21. SCAP, *Political Reorientation*, vol. 1, 23.

government purged "the public information media" of ultranationalists and militarists.[22]

To understand the position in which this left Hayashi, we can trace how this categorization played out in his life. First, the purge order (*tsuihōrei*) affected his ability to make a living. In legal terms, the purge order simply meant that the government prohibited him from commenting on political affairs in the Japanese mass media. Staying at home in the Jōmyōji Takumagayatsu area of Kamakura (a small valley located behind the Hōkoku temple), he continued working on his biography of Saigō Takamori during the first months of the Occupation. However, once the government purged him in 1946, most of the major journals were either reluctant or they outright refused to accept his works.[23] To make ends meet, he had to borrow money from Utsunomiya Tokuma, a friend from his New Man Society days; and when literary critic Kobayashi Hideo asked him to join the editorial staff of the newly established afternoon daily newspaper *Shin'yūkan*, Hayashi took the job immediately. He did this despite the questionable background of the newspaper (it was the successor to Kodama Yoshio's and Iwata Fumio's right-wing newspaper, *Yamato shinbun*) and its director Kōgen Jūkichi (a trusted confidant of Kodama Yoshio, a man whom SCAP officials designated a category A war criminal).[24] Hayashi worked on the newspaper's editorial staff until it gained a stronger following and then he turned his editorial duties over to writer Nagai Tatsuo, opting to concentrate on writing the daily literary column for the newspaper and on writing his biography of Saigō.

Following his time on the editorial staff of the *Shin'yūkan*, he intensified his efforts to support his family. Starting in July 1947, he began writing a column for the *Yomiuri shinbun* called "Tōzai nanboku" ("In all directions"); he later changed the name of the column to "Memorabiriya"

22. See SCAP, *Political Reorientation*, vol. 1, 29, for a breakdown of the numbers of those purged under each category, and SCAP, *Political Reorientation*, vol. 1, 21–22, 23, for the use of this interpretation by the Japanese government against the mass media in Japan.

23. Hayashi Fusao, "Fu: Hayashi Fusao nenpu," in *Hayashi Fusao chosakushū*, vol. 1 (Tokyo: Tsubasa shoin, 1968), 458.

24. Hayashi Fusao, "Sengo no rirekisho," in *Hayashi Fusao chosakushū*, vol. 2 (Tokyo: Tsubasa shoin, 1969), 428–429; and Matsumoto Keiko, *Higanbana: miryoku aru otokotachi e no chinkonka* (Tokyo: Seiga shobō, 1989), 136.

("Memorabilia").[25] Writing the column under the pseudonym Shirai Akira, Hayashi commented on literary and political affairs despite the purge order. His column was so popular that *Yomiuri* retained it until the fall of 1950 when he finally dropped the pseudonym and quit writing the column. At that time, the Japanese government under SCAP's direction rescinded the purge order against the militarists and ultranationalists and began to remove suspected communists from public affairs instead. Hayashi could write freely using his original pen name again.

In addition to this literary column, he began to write light, entertaining stories for the public from 1947 well into the 1950s. During this time, he produced an incredible stream of these stories, serializing some of them in newspapers and others in what writers called *kasutori zasshi* ("dreg magazines"). The dreg magazines served a mass audience with what were usually poorly constructed stories that focused on the erotic or the nonsensical. Looked down upon by the members of the Japanese *bundan*, these magazines were popular for a period of three to four years after 1945. They earned the name *kasutori* because just as someone who drank "sake dregs" (*kasutori*) for three or four days would collapse, so these magazines would usually collapse after the public read three or four issues. He also published other stories as *chūkan* (middlebrow), *taishū* (popular), and *katei* (family) novels. He drew on his experiences with his own family as material for his *katei* novels while he used a wide variety of sources for his middlebrow and popular fiction. Japanese literary scholar Donald Keene notes that the difference between "middlebrow" fiction and "pure literature" often had as much to do with where the author published the short story as it did with the content of the story.[26] Since Hayashi was unable to publish his works in what most Japanese writers considered "respectable" journals, he published his stories in the "dreg magazines," in women's magazines (*fujin zasshi*), and in newspapers. He became very popular as a middlebrow novelist and could not keep up with

25. Nawa Kazuo, "Kaisetsu," in *Hayashi Fusao chosakushū*, vol. 2 (Tokyo: Tsubasa shoin, 1969), 464. Hayashi seems to have forgotten the first character of the title in his "Fu: Hayashi Fusao nenpu," 459.

26. Donald Keene, *Dawn to the West: Japanese Literature in the Modern Era*, Fiction, An Owl Book (New York: Henry Holt and Company, 1984), 834.

the demand for his short stories, producing close to two hundred of these during the late 1940s and early 1950s.[27]

Nevertheless, the strain from working under the purge order combined with personal problems and being overworked affected him mentally and spiritually. Just two days after Japan's surrender, Hayashi's friend and fellow writer from the Kamakura area, Shimaki Kensaku, passed away. Less than a month later, Hayashi's mother passed away at the age of sixty-four.[28] Besides these deaths, Hayashi faced the grim task of commuting every day through the charred ruins of downtown Tokyo to the Shinbashi district, where the newspaper rented out the third floor of a burned-out building for its offices. Shortly after he began working on the editorial staff for the *Shin'yūkan* in 1946, writer Mishima Yukio went to meet Hayashi Fusao for the first time. He noted that Hayashi had been drinking at the office and that he was already heavily intoxicated by the time they met. While exchanging their goodbyes, Mishima also recorded how zestfully Hayashi urinated out of a shattered window in the back of the office.[29]

Hayashi's lapse into such dubious behavior also showed up in the tone of his writing at that time. Starting with his historical novel *Youth*, he began to put out postwar editions of some of his previously published works in 1947. Sōgensha published what Hayashi called, in the new preface to the work, a "resurrected edition" (*fukkatsuban*) of *Youth*. In the new preface, he remained defiant and defended the stance he had taken during the wartime period, writing, "I take pride in the fact that *Youth* remains just as I wrote it ten years ago. I am overjoyed at being able to present a testament of proper Japanese ideals to the Japanese youth again. I, along with *Youth*, must resurrect the ideals of rescuing-the-nation (*kyūkoku*) and opening-the-country (*kaikoku*)."[30]

---

27. Hayashi, "Sengo no rirekisho," in *Hayashi Fusao chosakushū*, vol. 2 (Tokyo: Tsubasa shoin, 1969), 451.

28. Matsumoto, *Higanbana*, 135.

29. Mishima Yukio, "Hayashi Fusaoron," in *Mishima Yukio zenshū*, vol. 30, *Hyōron*, ed. Saeki Shōichi (Tokyo: Shinchōsha, 1975), 490.

30. Hayashi Fusao, *Seinen*, Resurrected edition (Tokyo: Sōgensha, 1947), 1. The National Diet Library in Japan holds the original text of this edition of *Seinen* and it has most graciously provided me with a copy of this rare work. All quotations that follow refer to this copy of the original text.

Hayashi's rebelliousness came at a desperate time in his life. Members of the Japanese literati—many had returned to Marxism and left-wing movements and many had turned to "democratic" literary movements (*minshushugi bungaku*) in the early postwar period—widely condemned him for his wartime stance. Both Mishima and writer Okuno Takeo attest to the bias and the animosity that most Japanese writers bore toward him during the immediate postwar period.[31] Many denounced him as a *senpan bunkajin* (cultural war criminal) and Mishima even confessed that one reason he initially approached Hayashi was to experience the thrill of a "dangerous liaison."[32] At that time, Mishima wanted to prove his disregard for the opinion of him held by the Japanese literary establishment and the Japanese media; thus, to provoke controversy, he went to meet and talk with Hayashi, someone whom both groups held in contempt.[33] As a result, although Hayashi attempted to maintain his optimistic outlook from the early Shōwa years, a sense of despondency tinged his idealism in the later Shōwa years, leading him to question himself and the changes occurring around him, as evidenced by his drinking and seclusion.

Literature from the Dregs: Hayashi Fusao's Acquiescence to Defeat

Nowhere is this inclination toward self-doubt and dissipation more evident than in his short story "Four Characters." Published in the December 1949 issue of *Shinshōsetsu*, the story is a brief character sketch of a Chinese official working for the pro-Japanese Nanjing government who committed suicide after the war ended.[34] Literary critic Oketani Hideaki has noted that Hayashi most likely based this story on the obituary of a Chinese official who did work in the pro-Japanese Nanjing government's civil service

---

31. See Mishima, "Hayashi Fusaoron," 491; and Okuno Takeo, *Sugao no sakka tachi: gendai sakka hyakusanjūni'nin* (Tokyo: Shūeisha, 1978), 148–150.

32. See Moroto Fu, "Hayashi Fusaoron: senpan bunkajin," *Bunka kakumei* 13 (1948): 22–23, for a common negative assessment of Hayashi in the early postwar years. The author of the article seems to have used an alias here, a play on the Russian political leader Vyacheslav Mikhailovich Molotov's name. Mishima writes of his initial reasons for meeting Hayashi in his "Hayashi Fusaoron," 490–491.

33. Mishima, "Hayashi Fusaoron," 491.

34. See Bungei Kyōkai, ed., *Bungei nenkan: 1950 ban* (Tokyo: Shinchōsha, 1950), 61, for the listing of "Yotsu no moji" being published in this journal.

department and who committed suicide the day after the war ended. Hayashi would have seen the official's obituary because it happened to be published next to the announcement of Shimaki Kensaku's funeral in the August 21, 1945, edition of the *Asahi shinbun*.[35]

Hayashi begins the story with a Japanese writer, the narrator in the story, reading the obituary of the Chinese official and wondering how he committed suicide. The narrator at first assumes that the official must have shot himself with a pistol, but after reassessing the official's character, he speculates that the official must have taken poison instead. Continuing, the writer explains that the difference between the two forms of suicide is that shooting oneself is a masculine, proactive way of ending things while taking poison is a feminine, negative means of suicide.[36] Thinking back on the many suicides at the end of the war, the writer maintains that most of them were "positive" (*yōsei*) because the Japanese who fought the war believed until the end that they would win it. In contrast, the writer concludes that the Chinese official believed that Japan would lose the war from the start; thus, he reveled in the daily pleasures of life, enjoying good food, wine, and women while the Japanese still occupied Nanjing. Nihilism ruled this official's hedonistic existence and outlandish behavior, the writer tells us.[37]

We then return to the time when the writer first met the Chinese official. Traveling through occupied China, the writer meets the official while in Nanjing, and the official invites him to have dinner at his home one night. At the dinner, the writer is intrigued by the official because he does not act like a typical politician; he discusses the finer points of food and wine instead of politics. In the same way, the official likes the narrator because he does not behave like a typical writer. He invites the narrator to accompany him the next day to a small restaurant out in the countryside. On the way there, the official stops at some train tracks near a small railroad station and he reveals to the writer that he had ordered the machine-gunning down along the train tracks of more than two hundred students who may or may not have been communists. He then adds that he, the

35. Oketani Hideaki, "Hayashi Fusao," *Seiron* 229 (September 1991): 376–377.

36. Hayashi Fusao, "Yotsu no moji," in *Hayashi Fusao, Yasuda Yojūrō, Kamei Katsuichirō, Hasuda Zenmeishū*, vol. 61, Gendai Nihon bungaku taikei (Tokyo: Chikuma shobō, 1970), 83.

37. Ibid., 83–84.

official, was also "killed" at that time.[38] With a loud laugh that chills the writer, they drive off and arrived at the restaurant. While eating at the restaurant, the writer remembers the previous night's dinner at the official's home. He also recalls how the official invited him alone up to the Japanese-style room on the fourth floor and showed him a small framed picture with four characters written in it.[39] Soon after, the writer returns to Japan and never sees the Chinese official again.

Having read about the Chinese official's suicide four years later, the narrator concludes the story by returning to the problem of how the official committed suicide. Considering the four characters that the official had written in the framed picture, the writer believes that the official had been preparing for death a long time. For the narrator such careful preparation means that the official must have committed suicide by taking poison. Finally, in the last paragraph of the story, the writer reveals the four characters:

> He [the official] was the only passenger who knew the fate of the fragile luxury liner that was [pro-Japanese] Nanjing government and still boarded it. He shared the fate of the ship, but from the start, he never intended to save the ship from its fate. As its passenger, he feared nothing and intended to savor every luxury the ship had to offer until its final moment, and this he did. He wanted to die, yet they say that he left these final words: "People will not judge me, heaven will." If we interpret this literally, his pious words meant that he intended to obey the will of heaven. However, I don't believe this for a minute. When did it happen, I wonder? When did he turn into the most treacherous type of politician: the devil's advocate, unafraid of heaven and a messenger of nihilism? He didn't die according to heaven's will; the son of a bitch killed himself. I can say one thing for sure. The four characters I saw that night in his Japanese-style room were 学我者死, follow in my footsteps, and you'll die (*ware o manabu mono wa shisu*).[40]

In this character sketch of the Chinese official, Hayashi projects the despair that he was feeling onto the character of the official. Mishima calls this work the best of Hayashi's postwar short stories, and he argues that the official who had given up on every ideal and form of thought from his

38. Hayashi Fusao, "Yotsu no moji," 88–89.
39. Ibid., 90.
40. Ibid., 90–91.

youth but still participated in the present represented the current situation in which Hayashi found himself.[41] Oketani evaluates Hayashi's present circumstance as one in which Hayashi was unable to adjust to the extreme changes that SCAP was demanding of the Japanese people.[42] Still, unlike many members of the Daitōjuku (Great East Institute), of which he had been a member, Hayashi did not commit ritual suicide following Japan's surrender to the allied forces. He lived on, so the question remaining was how to weather these years, particularly when history was denying everything in which he had believed during his youth. Unlike the official in the story, Hayashi had decided to let "heaven's will" decide his fate. As he must have expected, the interim Japanese government under SCAP's direction purged him and prohibited him from commenting on Japanese politics. With that now determined, he needed to choose how to live under these circumstances.

He could not become a Marxist or a proletarian writer again nor could he simply give up the militarist ideals that he had advocated during the war. For Hayashi, literary critic Isoda Kōichi asserts, writing became a secondary concern during this time as he lost his faith in literature.[43] Hayashi had seen Japan defeated. He had seen Marxist and liberal writers make a stunning comeback under the protection of the Occupation forces. From his standpoint in the late 1940s, he recognized that the younger generation of Japanese writers viewed him with disdain. In a literal sense, this group of younger writers were killing his literary career and forcing him into the "dregs" of Japanese literature. However, in "Four Characters" we also find the writer condemning the suicide of the official as the worst and most deceitful way out of the situation. If Hayashi felt himself to be an isolated and anachronistic presence in postwar Japan, he also seemed determined to make it through the difficult times ahead, though not without his share of self-doubt and anguish. In the end, the only way for him to restore his sense of authenticity as a person and as a writer was to maintain his commitment to his prewar *tenkō*. To do this, he needed to continue writing from that perspective, even though the world around him was changing rapidly and in ways that marginalized his voice even further

41. Mishima, "Hayashi Fusaoron," 545, 547–548.
42. Oketani, "Hayashi Fusao," 378.
43. Isoda, "Hayashi Fusao, Dan Kazuo," 420.

during the 1940s and 50s. Ultimately, Hayashi's new dawn came in the early 1960s when he found another means to reaffirm the rhetoric of his prewar *tenkō* and thus his sincerity in a new context: the emerging historiographical debate within Japan over the legacy of imperial Japan for the economic success of postwar Japan in the 1960s.

A NEW DAY DAWNS: HAYASHI FUSAO'S POLITICS OF WARTIME NATIONALISM IN POSTWAR JAPANESE SOCIETY

Although scholars link Hayashi's reemergence in postwar Japan to his taking charge of the *Asahi shinbun*'s literary column in 1963, Hayashi writes that a trip he took to Latin America in 1958 reawakened his desire to write. That year the *Yomiuri shinbun* organized a research group to explore the ancient Indian ruins in South and Central America. Requesting permission to accompany the group, Hayashi paid his way and left with the group in June for a three-month trip.[44] During his trip he visited several countries, including Peru, Bolivia, and Mexico. While the group searched for relics of the ancient Incan and Mayan kingdoms, Hayashi noticed that the scars of Spanish imperialism and colonialism on these countries' indigenous populations remained.[45] Exchanging the archaeological books that he had brought with him for copies of William Prescott's works on the subjugation of the Peruvian and Mexican people, he searched for answers as to why the native peoples in these countries still lived in such extreme poverty.[46]

Hayashi determined that Western imperialism was to blame. The United States was interfering in the politics of Latin American countries for its own benefit. Reconsidering the situation of the native peoples that he had encountered during his wartime trips to China and Southeast Asia, Hayashi began to think that what the imperial Japanese government

44. Hayashi, "Fu: Hayashi Fusao nenpu," 461.

45. Hayashi, "Sengo no rirekisho," 452.

46. Ibid., 452–453. See William H. Prescott, *History of the Conquest of Peru: With a Preliminary View of the Civilization of the Incas* (Philadelphia: J.B. Lippincott, 1863); and *History of the Conquest of Mexico: With a Preliminary View of the Ancient Mexican Civilization, and the Life of the Conqueror Hernando Cortez* (Philadelphia: J.B. Lippincott, 1868).

officially designated as the "Greater East Asia War" was not meaningless after all.[47] He came to believe that he was viewing the ongoing process of Western, particularly American, imperialism while traveling in Latin America. In his estimation, then, Japan's war in Asia and the Pacific was an attempt to arrest the spread of Western imperialism there. Thus, although Japan had failed in its attempt, Hayashi began to conclude that the continuing spread of American imperialism in Latin America vindicated Japan's attempt to halt Western imperialism in Asia and the Pacific. From his observations, he believed that American attempts to extend its dominance over Latin America showed that Western imperialism was still a major threat to the development of countries throughout the world.

However, following this awakening, Hayashi's weak physical condition prevented him from fully returning to his writing again. He suffered from altitude sickness during his trip to Latin America and needed more rest at home to recover. During the next few years, he cut back even more on his work and his drinking, and he spent most of his time either fishing or reading. He also wrote that reading the translation of historian Arnold Toynbee's *A Study of History* helped him to recover spiritually and mentally from the fatigue. More importantly, perhaps, reading Toynbee's attempt to develop a model to interpret the rise and fall of several world civilizations restored a new sense of purpose within him that he had not experienced since the end of the war.[48] While reading several volumes of Toynbee's masterpiece, Hayashi recounts that his desire for seclusion and his feeling of despair slowly subsided.[49]

Subsequently, when the editors of the *Asahi shinbun* asked him to take charge of its literary column from January 1, 1963, he readily accepted the one-year offer. That next month, writer Mishima Yukio published his extended essay examining Hayashi, his literary criticism, and his works of fiction, entitled "Hayashi Fusaoron" ("On Hayashi Fusao"), in the journal *Shinchō*. From that September on, Hayashi also began serializing his revisionist interpretation of the Asia-Pacific War, *In Support of the Greater East Asian War*, in one of Japan's leading monthly journals, the *Chūō*

47. Hayashi, "Sengo no rirekisho," 453.

48. Arnold J. Toynbee began his masterpiece in 1920 and finished the last volume of the work in 1954, *A Study of History*, 12 vols. (New York: Oxford University Press, 1962).

49. Hayashi, "Sengo no rirekisho," 454.

kōron.[50] Through this quick succession of events and publications, Hayashi reestablished himself within the Japanese media.

Moreover, his rhetoric of wartime nationalism struck a chord of support among the prewar generation suffering from a sense of dislocation in postwar Japan. While probing the causes behind the Security Treaty Crisis of 1960 that lasted until 1962, historian George Packard observes that the Japanese were more confident about their place in the world by then.[51] Brisk economic growth during the 1950s and an expanded role in world affairs (United Nations' members elected Japan to a seat on the Security Council in 1958 and Japan was preparing to host the Olympics in 1964) fostered a sense of accomplishment. Even so, the presence of foreign troops and U.S. bases on Japanese soil was a constant reminder that the Japanese were still dependent on others for their national security. Packard asserts that the security treaty that Japan signed with the United States came to symbolize a type of foreign domination for many Japanese. He also notes that one response to the treaty was an emerging nationalism from leftists, progressives, and conservatives alike: they hoped to revise the security treaty to gain greater autonomy for Japan, though each group had its own agenda and motives for revision.[52] Within this context of growing self-confidence and with a strong desire for treaty revision, scholars and students alike in the universities began to reconsider the meaning of the Asia-Pacific War for the Japanese.[53] Building on this trend, Hayashi affirms in *In Support of the Greater East Asian War* that although there was much to be ashamed of during the prewar and wartime years, the Japanese people had much to be proud of, such as Japan's attempt to prevent Western imperialism from dominating Asia. In 1963, eighteen years after the war, Hayashi found a receptive audience and intellectual climate in which to reassert his cultural nationalist vision of the Asia-Pacific War in the flow of Japanese history. Unlike the nearly universal condemnation in occu-

50. Hayashi Fusao, "Daitōa sensō kōteiron," *Chūō kōron* 78, no. 9 (September 1963): 294–307.

51. George R. Packard III, *Protest in Tokyo: The Security Treaty Crisis of 1960* (Princeton: Princeton University Press, 1966), 33–34.

52. Ibid., 34–41, 334.

53. Hayashi's *In Support of the Greater East Asian War* builds most prominently on Dōshisha University Professor Ueyama Shunpei's efforts, particularly his collection of articles entitled *Daitōa sensō no imi: gendaishi bunseki no shiten* (Tokyo: Chūō kōronsha, 1964).

pied Japan of his prewar *tenkō* stance, this time many Japanese embraced Hayashi's "affirmative view" of the war as a means to reconcile their post-war historical achievements, rapid economic growth, and increased involvement in world affairs with the militarism and ultranationalism of the 1930s and 1940s.

Hayashi's revival of wartime nationalism in his discussion of the Asia-Pacific War is significant for the three ways that it has shaped the succeeding generations' perception of and discourse on the war. First, as Packard and other scholars have observed, Hayashi was responsible for extracting the ongoing, positive reassessment of the Asia-Pacific War out of the academic setting and popularizing it in the mass media.[54] In 1969 historian George Wilson noted that "although not a trained historian and guilty of many errors of historical fact, Hayashi has attracted both interest and sympathy among a vast number of Japanese readers, who reflect the nation's increased pride and confidence in its new world role two decades after the war."[55] Nearly two decades later, and along the same lines, Japanese scholar Tsurumi Shunsuke affirms that *In Support of the Greater East Asian War* "received wide acclaim in the Japan of the sixties which was regaining confidence amid spectacular economic growth."[56] Thus, increasingly in the 1960s and 1970s, many Japanese came to associate Hayashi and *In Support of the Greater East Asian War* with the conservative position on the Asia-Pacific War.

Second, Hayashi's perspective on the war has become a polemical starting point for most current neonationalist discussion on the place of the Asia-Pacific War in Japanese history. Scholar Rikki Kersten, in her study of Tokyo University Professor Fujioka Nobukatsu and his "Liberal School of History" group's attempt to rethink the meaning of the Pacific War in Japanese history, shows how Fujioka first sought to differentiate his

54. Packard, *Protest in Tokyo*, 337. See also comments by Tetsuo Najita, "Nakano Seigō and the Spirit of the Meiji Restoration in Twentieth-Century Japan," in *Dilemmas of Growth in Prewar Japan*, ed. James William Morley (Princeton: Princeton University Press, 1971), 419; and see James William Morley's remarks regarding Hayashi, "Introduction: Choice and Consequence," in *Dilemmas of Growth in Prewar Japan*, 15.

55. George M. Wilson, *Radical Nationalist in Japan: Kita Ikki, 1883–1937*, Harvard East Asian Series, no. 37 (Cambridge: Harvard University Press, 1969), 166.

56. Shunsuke Tsurumi, *A Cultural History of Postwar Japan, 1945–1980* (London: KPI Ltd., 1987), 21.

position on the war from Hayashi's affirmation of the war.[57] Likewise, in a roundtable discussion among a group of well-known contemporary neo-nationalists, which included Kobayashi Yoshinori, Fukuda Kazuya, Saeki Keishi, and Nishibe Susumu, several members delineate their positions on the Asia-Pacific War by first relating their positions to Hayashi's *In Support of the Greater East Asian War.*[58] Perhaps the most telling evidence of Hayashi's association with an affirmative view of the war in the discussion was the usage of his name in adjective form to refer to a "Hayashi-Fusao-like" (*Hayashi-Fusao-teki*) support of the war. Other authors simply re-introduce the title of his work as *Shin Daitōa sensō kōteiron* (*A New In Support of the Greater East Asian War*), indicating an update to Hayashi's now "classic" work.[59]

Third, in addition to popularizing the "affirmative view" perspective in the Japanese media, and then having the Japanese people associate him with that position, *In Support of the Greater East Asian War* also encouraged the Japanese to reconsider their memories of the wartime years positively. Intellectual historian Andrew Barshay has argued that *In Support of the Greater East Asian* War played a meaningful role in repudiating the self-flagellation inspired by left-wing intellectuals during the early postwar years.[60] Hayashi intended his provocative historical arguments to assuage the Japanese people's feelings of shame over the war and help them overcome the Leftists' negative appraisals of the war during the Occupation years. However, historian Peter Duus has suggested that Hayashi's affirmative view of the war in the 1960s ended up contributing to the growth of cultural nationalism in the 1970s and 80s.[61] The expression of this new cultural nationalism, as Duus and other scholars have indicated,

57. Kersten, "Neo-nationalism and the 'Liberal School of History,'" 198.

58. Kobayashi Yoshinori, Fukuda Kazuya, Saeki Keishi, and Nishibe Susumu, *Kokka to sensō* (Tokyo: Hichō shinsha, 1999), 86–89.

59. Ibid., 39. See also Kersten, "Neo-nationalism," 198. See Tomioka Kōichirō's *Shin Daitōa sensō kōteiron* (Tokyo: Asuka shinsha, 2006), 22–58, for the section where he familiarizes his readers with Hayashi's original argument.

60. Andrew E. Barshay, "Postwar Social and Political Thought, 1945–90," in *Modern Japanese Thought*, ed. Bob Takashi Wakabayashi (New York: Cambridge University Press, 1998), 332–333.

61. Peter Duus, *Modern Japan*, 2nd ed. (New York: Houghton Mifflin Company, 1998), 332.

was the *Nihonjinron* boom in which Japanese authors devoted a tremendous amount of literature to congratulating themselves on Japan's achievements.[62] Thus, Hayashi's positive view of the war provided an alternate vision of the Asia-Pacific War for many Japanese during the 1960s. This alternative vision was significant because it played a pivotal, transitional role at that time. It encouraged the Japanese to work through the feelings of humiliation and shame that overwhelmed them during the immediate postwar years, and even allowed some of them to reassert their national distinctiveness in a mentally "healthier' way to the world community.

As we can see, one of the most difficult problems for the postwar Japanese nation-state has been handling the legacy of the Asia-Pacific War. The Japanese government has faced continued resistance from its Asian neighbors in its attempts to establish closer relations with them. This conflict originated from, among other reasons, these countries' lingering doubts as to Japan's attitude toward its wartime legacy. Beginning in the early 1990s, Asian women, predominately from Korea, who served as "comfort women" for the Japanese military during the Asia-Pacific War filed lawsuits and sought compensation from the Japanese government for the wrongs committed against them during the war. The end of the twentieth century brought a spate of books concerning the Nanjing Massacre of 1937 in China, which fueled the dispute over the historiography of the Massacre in the West and Japan.[63] Consequently, Japanese politicians have endeavored formally to mitigate the concerns of Asian countries since then, apologizing for the conduct of the Japanese military during the war;

---

62. See Duus's section on cultural nationalism in *Modern Japan*, 331–335; and see Ann Waswo's section on the 1970s and 1980s in *Modern Japanese Society, 1868–1994*, An OPUS Book (New York: Oxford University Press, 1996), 99–103, for examples of how the *Nihonjinron* boom swept across Japan. For an overview of the content and form of the *Nihonjinron* boom, see Harumi Befu's "Nationalism and *Nihonjinron*," in *Cultural Nationalism in East Asia: Representation and Identity*, ed. Harumi Befu, Research papers and policy studies, no. 39 (Berkeley: Institute of East Asian Studies University of California, 1993), 107–135.

63. See Iris Chang's *The Rape of Nanking: The Forgotten Holocaust of World War II* (New York: Basic Books, 1997); Honda Katsuichi, *The Nanjing Massacre: A Japanese Journalist Confronts Japan's National Shame*, trans. Karen Sandness (Armonk, NY: M.E. Sharpe, 1999); and Joshua A. Fogel, ed. *The Nanjing Massacre in History and Historiography* (Berkeley: University of California Press, 2000).

but unofficial comments by these same politicians have often invalidated their efforts.[64]

Hayashi Fusao, through his revived wartime nationalist interpretation of the Asia-Pacific War in *In Support of the Greater East Asian War*, grasped the chance presented him, not only to participate actively in the national debate over this problem of history but also to confirm the authenticity of his *tenkō* once again. Perhaps the section in Hayashi's afterword to *In Support of the Greater East Asian War* where he summarizes his nationalistic image of Japanese history in the 1960s best captures this attempt at his redemption as a national iconic figure. Here, he presents his reflections on the work of Mexican artist Diego Rivera (1886–1957) as a synecdoche for his own cultural nationalist project in *In Support of the Greater East Asian War*. Hayashi wrote:

> Several years ago when I visited Mexico, I saw a large mural portraying the history of the Mexican people by revolutionary and painter Diego Rivera. This work was from Rivera's youth when Marxism had deeply influenced him; still, the scene reproducing the splendor and prosperity of the empire that the ancient Mexicans, the Maya, and the Aztec peoples had built was more beautiful than the myths of any other country. The part depicting the Mexican Revolution [1910–1920] was more courageous and grand than any other war scrolls, and the final section illustrating the liberation of the workers and the farmers in the present resounded with hope for a bright future and an affection for the Mexican people now in a state of decline.
>
> Rivera was a revolutionary and an artist, but he was also an ardent patriot at the same time. Nothing separates these three attributes from each other. No matter how he criticized the present, resisted corrupt governments, or scorned the ugly turn of the Mexican people's history, it did not sully [the mural]. On the contrary, to a foreigner like myself, I felt the overwhelming beauty and power of the mural made history even more majestic. ... I am not a painter or a revolutionary, yet in hoping to combine the three qualifications of writer, historian, and patriot in perfect agreement, I want to learn from Diego Rivera's attitude toward Mexican history.[65]

It was an image and an interpretation grounded in Hayashi's prewar and wartime experiences. Much like Rivera who was a revolutionary and

64. See Mikiso Hane's *Eastern Phoenix: Japan since 1945* (Boulder, CO: Westview Press, 1996), 203–205, for a brief discussion of this topic.

65. Hayashi, *Daitōa sensō kōteiron*, 261–263.

a painter, Hayashi had been a student radical and a writer profoundly influenced by Marxism in the 1920s. After confronting the power of the state and struggling with the political changes in the proletarian literature movement, he searched for an alternative path through the politics of literature during the red decade between 1925 and 1935. As a result, he reconciled his Marxist views to the oppressive political situation of that decade, a pivotal time when the state began increasingly to integrate the intellectual community into its propaganda efforts.[66] He eventually rejected both the institutional expressions of Marxism and communism and even the Marxist worldview in 1941.[67] Despite this, the Marxist legacy of dissent did persist, and he endeavored to retain a critical position vis-à-vis the state through cultural nationalism, while still showing his support for the ordinary Japanese involved in the war effort during the 1930s. In a sense then, he strove "to combine the three qualifications of writer, historian, and *patriot*" in his discussion of Japanese history after that confrontation (emphasis mine). By the late 1930s and early 1940s, however, Hayashi's cultural nationalism gave way to ultranationalism as the state subsumed most expressions of patriotic fervor under its purview, and he steadfastly embraced the politics of his prewar *tenkō*. By the 1960s, and with Diego Rivera representing his perspective in this afterword, Hayashi celebrated the opportunity to wipe away the stain of insincerity and, through the writing of *In Support of the Greater East Asian War*, confirm his *tenkō* ideology and reclaim his place on the samurai fringe.

66. Sheldon Garon, "State and Society in Interwar Japan," in *Historical Perspectives on Contemporary East Asia*, ed. Merle Goldman and Andrew Gordon (Cambridge: Harvard University Press, 2000), 180–181.

67. Hayashi made this declaration in one of his most infamous polemical essays, Hayashi Fusao, *Tenkō ni tsuite* (Yokohama: Shōfūkai, 1941).

Bibliography

WORKS BY HAYASHI FUSAO (GOTŌ TOSHIO)

"Apples." In *For Dignity, Justice, and Revolution: An Anthology of Japanese Proletarian Literature*. Edited by Heather Bowen-Struyk and Norma Field. Translated by Jeff E. Long, 68–75. Chicago: University of Chicago Press, 2016.

"Arubamu." *Kaizō* 18, no. 10 (October 1936): 66–83.

"Baka." *Shinjin* 30, no. 12 (December 1925): 5–9.

"'Bungakukai' sōkan no koro." *Bungakukai: fukkokuban* 1, no. 1 (October 1933), 1. Reprint, Tokyo: Nihon kindai bungakukan, 1975

"Bungaku no tame ni." *Kaizō* 14, no. 7 (July 1932): 105–117.

"Bungakuteki jijōden." In *Rōmanshugi no tame ni*, ed. Bungakukaisha shuppanbu, 327–335. Tokyo: Bungakukaisha shuppanbu, 1936.

"Bungakuteki jijōden." *Shinchō* 32, no. 11 (November 1935): 60–68.

"Bungakuteki kaisō." In *Hayashi Fusao chosakushū*. Vol. 2, 222–410. Tokyo: Tsubasa shoin, 1969.

"Bungei jihyō." *Kaizō* 15, no. 2 (February 1933): 186–197.

"Chijō." *Shinchō* 26, no. 6 (June 1929): 55–77.

"Cocoons." In *The Cannery Boat and Other Japanese Short Stories*. [Edited and Translated by William Maxwell Bickerton.] New York: International Publishers, 1933. Reprint, AMS Press, 1970.

"Daishingun." *Bungei kōron* 2, no. 1 (January 1928): 155–159.

"Daitōa sensō kōteiron." *Chūō kōron* 78, no. 9 (September 1963): 294–307.

Daitōa sensō kōteiron. Tokyo: Banchō shobō, 1964.

Daitōa sensō kōteiron: zoku. Tokyo: Banchō shobō, 1965.

Daitōa sensō kōteiron. Revised edition. Tokyo: Banchō shobō, 1970.

Daitōa sensō kōteiron. Pocketbook edition. 2 vols. Tokyo: Miki shobō, 1984.

"Dominikku no byōki." *Shinjin* 30, no. 6 (June 1925): 52–53.

"E no nai ehon." *Shinshōsetsu* 31, no. 5 (May 1926): 11–28.

"Fu: Hayashi Fusao nenpu." In *Hayashi Fusao chosakushū*. Vol. 1, 446–462. Tokyo: Tsubasa shoin, 1968.

"Fune no kamisama." *Bungei sensen* 2, no. 5 (September 1925): 32–33.

"Gokuchūki." In *Hayashi Fusao chosakushū*. Vol. 3, 5–145. Tokyo: Tsubasa shoin, 1969.

"Hakudōka." *Ryūnan* 184 (December 1922): 80–87.

"Hakudōka." In *Rōgoku no Gogatsusai: Hayashi Fusao Sōsakushū*, 257–270. Tokyo: Shunyōdō, 1927.

Hayashi Fusao chosakushū. 3 vols. Tokyo: Tsubasa shoin, 1968–1969.

"The Heart of Imperial Loyalty." In *Overcoming Modernity: Cultural Identity in Wartime Japan*. Edited and Translated by Richard Calichman. Weatherhead Books on Asia: History, Society, and Culture, series edited by Carol Gluck, 92–110. New York: Columbia University Press, 2008.

"Hebi." *Ōita kōyūkai zasshi* 68 (September 1918): 51–53.

"Hitotsu no teian: puroretaria bungaku saishuppatsu no hōhō." *Bunka shūdan* 1, no. 6 (November 1933): 1–8.

"Hihyō ni tsuite." *Bungei sensen* 3, no. 12 (December 1926): 28–30.

"Ikamahoshi Toho no kuni." *Nihon rōmanha* 3, no. 5 (July 1937): 30–31.

Kanashimi no koto: Mishima Yukio e no chinkonka. Tokyo: Bungei shunjū, 1972.

"Kawabata Yasunari no utsukushisa." *Bungaku jidai* 1, no. 4 (August 1929): 128–129.

"Kimyōna moji Ein Mächen." *Kaihō* 4, no. 2 (November 1925): 104–105.

"Kindaiteki jōsei: ichimyō 'tōsei musume kishitsu.'" *Shinshōsetsu* 33, no. 2 (February 1927): 250–264.

"Kinema no gaidoku." *Bungaku jidai* 1, no. 6 (October 1929): 221–226.

"Kōen no aibiki." *Bungei sensen* 3, no. 4 (April 1926): 48–54.

"Kōjō no yūrei." *Kusari*, 45–60. Tokyo: Shunyōdō, 1928.

"Koibito: 'tsuki no monogatari,' sono san." *Shinjin* 30, no. 10 (October 1925): 27–28.

"Koi to yūrei." *Bungei kōron* 1, no. 7 (July 1927): 94–101.

"Kokuminteki eiyō: 'tsuki no monogatari,' sono ni." *Shinjin* 30, no. 9 (September 1925): 45.

"Kokusō." *Shinjin* 30, no. 8 (August 1925): 31–32.

"Kuzu." *Bungei shijō* 3, no. 2 (February 1927): 63–69.

"Mayone Yonekichi-shi no dōzō." *Kaizō* 12, no. 1 (January 1930): 127–136.

"Mayu." *Kaihō* 5, no. 7 (July 1926): 6–16.

"Mittei." *Senki* 1, no. 5 (September 1928): 8–28.

"Mukashi no ehon." *Kaizō* 19, no. 3 (March 1937): 1–21.

"Mura." *Ryūnan* 182 (July 1922): 1–26.

"Murasaki no tsuchi." *Ōita kōyūkai zasshi* 68 (September 1918): 44–49.

"Ori no naka no yonnin." *Senki* 2, no. 1 (January 1929): 38–47.

"Oriori no uta." *Ōita kōyūkai zasshi* 68 (September 1918): 70.

"Porii no yūutsu." *Bungei Nippon* 1, no. 5 (August 1925): 49–50.

"Puroretaria bungaku no saishuppatsu." *Kaizō* 15, no. 10 (October 1933): 167–178.

"Puroretaria dokusai ni kansuru hito kōsatsu." *Ryūnan* 184 (December 1922): 11–31.
"Ringo." *Bungei sensen* 3, no. 2 (February 1926): 44–48.
"Ringo." In *Bungei shinjin sōsho daisanpen: E no nai Eihon,* 84–97. Tokyo: Shunyōdō, 1926.
"*Robin Fuddo* jiken." *Shinchō* 26, no. 9 (September 1929): 2–16.
"Rōgoku no gogatsusai." *Bungei jidai* 3, no. 12 (December 1926): 22–42.
"Sakka kurabu no koto: puroretaria sakka no saidanketsu." *Bungaku hyōron* 2, no. 10 (September 1935): 118–119.
"Sakka toshite." *Shinchō* 29, no. 9 (September 1932): 57–65.
"Seinen." *Chūō kōron* 47, no. 8 (August 1932): 1–68.
Seinen. Chūō kōronsha edition. Tokyo: Chūō kōronsha, 1934.
Seinen. Authorized edition. Tokyo: Dai'ichi shobō, 1938.
Seinen. Resurrected edition. Tokyo: Sōgensha, 1947.
"Sengo no rirekisho." In *Hayashi Fusao chosakushū.* Vol. 2, 412–457. Tokyo: Tsubasa shoin, 1969.
Sensō no yokogao: bungakusha wa sensen de nani wo mita ka. Tokyo: Shunjūsha, 1937.
"Shakaishugi bungei undō: shasetsu (shizen seichō to mokuteki ishikisei, shakaishugi bungaku to geijutsu kachi)." *Bungei sensen* 4, no. 2 (February 1927): 6–9.
"Shanhai sensen." *Chūō kōron* 52, no. 10 (October 1937): 437–463.
"*Shinbirusukugō* jiken." *Kaizō* 11, no. 3 (March 1929): 41–52.
"Shin isoppu monogatari: gūwa saikō." *Shinshōsetsu* 31, no. 10 (October 1926): 28–48.
"Shinjidai tenbō." *Bungei sensen* 2, no. 3 (July 1925): 2–3.
"Shōnen." *Kaizō* 15, no. 7 (July 1933): 1–34.
"Shuhai." *Kaizō* 9, no. 5 (May 1927): 70–83.
"Shuju no kotoba." *Bungei sensen* 2, no. 4 (August 1925): 6–7.
"Shutsugokuki." In *Hayashi Fusao chosakushū.* Vol. 3, 146–181. Tokyo: Tsubasa shoin, 1969.
"Sodateru." *Kaizō* 15, no. 1 (January 1933): 200–228.
Taiyō to Bara: kakioroshi chōhen shōsetsu. Tokyo: Kawade Shobō, 1938.
Taiyō to Bara: kakioroshi chōhen shōsetsu. Tokyo: Toryō shoin, 1947.
Tenkō ni tsuite. Yokohama: Shōfūkai, 1941.
"Tēze ni kansuru gokai ni tsuite: Kajikun ni kotaeru." *Bungei sensen* 4, no. 3 (March 1927): 149–155.
"Tomoshibi ni atsumaru mushi." *Ryūnan* 183 (October 1922): 100–116.
"Tōshaban no kiseki." *Senki* 2, no. 4 (April 1929): 112–120.
"Umi to tobiuo no ko to." *Kaizō* 12, no. 8 (August 1930): 1–15.

"Unubore." *Ryūnan* 178 (July 1921): 17–28.

"Waga kuni ni okeru hokyū seikatsusha undō." *Marukusushugi* (March 1925): 45–58.

"Yamashita Monka no Menmen." *Shūkan asahi*, August 14, 1960, 76.

"Yotsu no moji." In *Hayashi Fusao, Yasuda Yojūrō, Kamei Katsuichirō, Hasuda Zenmeishū*. Vol. 61. Gendai Nihon bungaku taikei, 83–91. Tokyo: Chikuma shobō, 1970.

NEWSPAPERS

Miyako shinbun

Musansha shinbun

Teikoku daigaku shinbun

Tokyo Asahi shinbun

Tokyo nichinichi shinbun

Yomiuri shinbun

SOURCES IN JAPANESE

Asukai Masamichi. "Bunka undō ni okeru kyōsanshugi: senkyūhyaku nijūnana, hachinen wo chūshin ni." In *Nihon shakaishugi undōshiron*, ed. Watanabe Tōru and Asukai Masamichi, 281–306. Tokyo: San'ichi shobō, 1973.

———. *Nihon puroretaria bungaku shiron*. Tokyo: Aoki shoten, 1982.

Bungeika Kyōkai, ed. *Bungei nenkan: 1950 ban*. Tokyo: Shinchōsha, 1950.

Fujita Shōzō. "Shōwa hachi nen o chūshin to suru tenkō no jōkyō." In *Kyōdō kenkyū: tenkō*. Vol. 1, ed. Shisō no Kagaku no Kenkyūkai, 33–65. Tokyo: Heibonsha, 1959.

Heruminiya Tsuuru Myuuren. "Chiisai Pētā." Translated by Hayashi Fusao. *Bungei sensen* 3, no. 12 (December 1926): 90–98.

———. "Macchi hako no ohanashi: dōwa." Translated by Hayashi Fusao. *Shinjin* 29, no. 9 (September 1924): 60.

———. "Sekitan no ohanashi: dōwa." Translated by Gotō Toshio (Hayashi Fusao). *Shinjin* 29, no. 8 (August 1924): 49–53.

Hirano Ken. *Bungaku: Shōwa jūnen zengo*. Tokyo: Bungei shunjū, 1972.

——— et al., eds. *Tōron: Nihon puroretaria bungaku undōshi*. San'ichi shobō, 1955.

Honda Shūgo. *Tenkō bungakuron*. 3d ed. Tokyo: Miraisha, 1985.

Ishidō Kiyotomo and Tateyama Toshitada, eds. *Tokyo Teidai Shinjinkai no kiroku*. Tokyo: Keizai ōraisha, 1976.

Isoda Kōichi. "Hayashi Fusao, Dan Kazuo: sakka to sakuhin." In *Hayashi Fusao,*

Dan Kazuoshū. Vol. 66. Nihon bungaku zenshū, ed. Itō Sei, 408–422. Tokyo: Shūeisha, 1969.

Kagoshima Tatsuo. *Gendai Kamakura bunshi: yukari no shōsetsuka tachi*, Kamakura sōsho. Vol. 30, ed. Nuki Tatsuto. Kamakura: Kamakura shunjūsha, 1984.

Kaji Wataru. "Iwayuru shakaishugi bungei wo kokufuku seyo." *Musansha shinbun*, 5 February 1927.

———. "Kantan na okotae: nigatsugo, yongatsugo no zadankai wo yonde." In *Tōron: Nihon puroretaria bungaku undōshi*, ed. Hirano Ken et al. San'ichi shobō, 1955.

Kaneko Yōbun. "Dōnin zasshi ni miru shokubō subeki shinsakka." *Shinchō* 23, no. 10 (October 1926): 4–10.

Kamei Hideo. "Kamei Hideo no hatsugen: bungaku no naka no ringo." http://homepage2.nifty.com/k-sekirei/otaru/apple_06.html (accessed November 8, 2011).

Kawamori Yoshizō. "Hayashi Fusao den." In *Gendai Nihon bungakukan*. Vol. 28, ed. Kobayashi Hideo, 4–18. Tokyo: Bungei shunjū, 1969.

"Kenshō bungeihyō." *Ryūnan* 177 (March 1921): 228–244.

"Kenshō sōsaku saitenpyō." *Ryūnan* 178 (July 1921): 96–97.

Kikukawa Tadao. *Gakusei shakai undōshi*. Tokyo: Chūō kōronsha, 1931. Reprint, Kaiguchi shoten, 1947.

Kobayashi Hideo. "Sensō ni tsuite." *Kaizō* 19, no. 12 (November 1937): 218–223.

———. "Hayashi Fusao ni tsuite." *Bungei shunjū* 19, no. 3 (March 1941): 326–330.

Kobayashi Takiji. "Uyokuteki henkō no shomondai." *Puroretaria bungaku: fukuseiban* 1, no. 12 (December 1932): 22–40.

Kobayashi Yoshinori, Fukuda Kazuya, Saeki Keishi, and Nishibe Susumu. *Kokka to sensō*. Tokyo: Hichō shinsha, 1999.

Komori Kei, ed. *Shōwa shisō tōseishi shiryō: bekkan (ue) shisō tōseishi kenkyū hikkei*. Tokyo: Seikatsusha, 1981.

Kubokawa, Tsurujirō. Sakka kurabu ni tsuite no kansō." *Bungaku hyōron* 2, no. 12 (November 1935): 146–149.

Kubota Masafumi. "Sakuhin kaisetsu." In *Nihon gendai bungaku zenshū: puroretaria bungakushū*. Vol. 69, ed. Itō Sei, 398–405. Tokyo: Kōdansha, 1969.

Kurahara Korehito. "Geijutsuteki hōhō ni tsuite no kansō: kōhen (kaikyūteki bunseki ni tsuite, ikita ningen o egaku to yu koto, kiroku kara geijutsuteki gaikatsu e, ketsugo)." *Nappu* 2, no. 10 (October 1931): 52–77.

Kurata Michifumi. "'Mayu' 'Seinen' ni miru Hayashi Fusao no genzō," *Viento: Ōita no kaze* 3 (March 2004): 14–17, accessed January 10, 2007, http://www.pref.oita.jp/10400/viento/vol03/p14_17.html.

Kurihara Yukio. *Puroretaria bungaku to sono jidai*. Tokyo: Heibonsha, 1971.

Matsumoto Keiko. *Higanbana: miryoku aru otokotachi e no chinkonka*. Tokyo: Seiga shobō, 1989.

Matsuo Hiroya. "Kyoto Gakuren jiken: hatsudō sareta chian iji hō." In *Nihon seiji saiban shiroku: Shōwazen*, ed. Wagatsuma Sakae, 64–96. Tokyo: Dai'ichi hōki shuppan, 1970.

Mishima Yukio. *Hayashi Fusaoron*. Tokyo: Shinchōsha, 1963.

———. "Hayashi Fusaoron." In *Mishima Yukio zenshū*. Vol. 30. Hyōron, ed. Saeki Shōichi, 490–554. Tokyo: Shinchōsha, 1975.

Mizuno Yukiko, "Hayashi Fusao kenkyū: 'E no nai ehon' wo chūshin ni," *Shōwa Bungaku Kenkyū* 38 (March 1999): 1–13.

———. "Hayashi Fusao kenkyū: yōshōnenki saikentō," *Tsuru University Graduate School Review* 5 (2001): 50–64.

Mōri Toshio. "Hayashi Fusao no shōgai oyobi bungakuteki sōzō." *Tsurumi Daigaku kiyō: Dai'ichibu, Kokugo kokubungaku hen* 31 (March 1994): 131–184.

Moriyama Shigeo. *Nihon Marukusushugi bungaku: bungaku toshite no kakumei to tenkō*. Tokyo: San'ichi shobō, 1977.

Moroto Fu. "Hayashi Fusaoron: senpan bunkajin." *Bunka kakumei* 13 (1948): 22–23.

Naitō Yoshitada. "Bungaku-teki 'shinjitsu' no mondai: Nakano Shigeharu to Hayashi Fusao no tenkō." Paper and handout presented at *Tenkō* in Transwar Japan: Culture, Politics, History: An International Workshop, 1–6. Hinsley Hall, Leeds, UK, July 1, 2017.

Nakano Kōji, ed. *Kanagawa bungaku sanpoten: Kamakura, bungaku no Arukadeia*. Yokohama: Kenritsu Kanagawa kindai bungakukan, Zaidan hōjin Kanagawa bungaku shinkōkai, 1995.

Nakano Shigeharu. "Dokuritsu Sakka Kurabu ni tsuite." *Kaizō* 18, no. 4 (April 1936): 131–9.

———. "Keshō shitsutsuaru shōshiminsei." *Bungei sensen* 4, no. 3 (March 1927): 120–22.

———. "Kurabu e no kibō." *Bungaku hyōron* 3, no. 4 (April 1936): 102–105.

Nakatani Takao. "Hayashi Fusao no shigyō wo shinobite." *Yomiuri shinbun* 13 October 1975. Reprint, Tokyo: Hayashi Fusao dainin tsuitō gyōji jikkō iinkai henshū iin, 1976.

Nawa Kazuo. "Kaisetsu." In *Hayashi Fusao chosakushū*. Vol. 2, 459–466. Tokyo: Tsubasa shoin, 1969.

Noguchi Fujio. *Kanshokuteki Shōwa bundanshi*. Tokyo: Bungei shunjū, 1986.

Odagiri Hideo, ed. *Bungaku: Shōwa jūnendai wo kiku*. Tokyo: Keisō shobō, 1976.

Odagiri Susumu, ed. *Gendai Nihon bungei sōran: uemaki*. Tokyo: Meiji bunken, 1969.

———. "Kaisetsu." In *Bungakukai: fukkokuban* 1, no. 1 (October 1933): 28–33. Reprint, Tokyo: Nihon kindai bungakukan, 1975.

———. "Shōwa jūnendai bungaku-geijutsu nenpyō." *Bungaku* 29, no. 5 (May 1961): 594–624.

———. "Shōwa jūnendai no bungei zasshi." *Kokubungaku: kaishaku to kyōzai no kenkyū* 10, no. 7 (June 1965): 43–48.

Oketani Hideaki. "Hayashi Fusao." *Seiron* 229 (September 1991): 368–379.

Okuno Takeo. *Sugao no sakka tachi: gendai sakka hyakusanjūni'nin*. Tokyo: Shūeisha, 1978.

Satō Masaru. "Puroretaria bungaku no tenkai: Hayashi Fusao to Nakano Shigeharu." *Kokubungaku: kaishaku to kyōzai no kenkyū* 7, no. 10 (August 1962): 29–37.

Senkin Kanji. "'Dokuritsu Sakka Kurabu' setsuritsu shuisho: bijutsu undō no hōkō to, shakaishugi riarizumu ni kan shite." *Bungaku hyōron* 3, no. 1 (January 1936): 132–133. Quoted in Hirano Ken. *Bungaku: Shōwa jūnen zengo*. Tokyo: Bungei shunjū, 1972.

Shiga Naoya, "Kinosaki nite." *Shirakaba* 8, no. 5 (May 1917): 132–140.

Shimaki Kensaku. "Rai." *Bungaku hyōron* (April 1934): 130–170.

Shutō Motosumi. "Gokō no bunjin tachi: Hayashi Fusao." In *Kumamoto no bungaku II*, ed. Kumamoto daigaku gakusei bu, 133–148. Kumamoto: Kumamoto daigaku hōsō kōkai kōza, 1993.

———. "Hayashi Fusao: kindai no yōkōro." In *Kindai bungaku to Kumamoto: suimyaku no hirogari*, 94–109. Osaka: Izumi shoin, 2003.

———. "Hayashi Fusao oboegaki." In *Kumamoto no bungaku*. Vol. 3, ed. Kumamoto kindai bungaku kenkyūkai, 136–148. Tokyo: Banbisha, 1996.

Tanaka Tadao, ed. *Hayashi Fusao dainin tsuitō gyōji hōkokusho*. Tokyo: Hayashi Fusao dainin tsuitō gyōji jikkō iinkai, 1976.

Tsurumi Shunsuke. "Kōki Shinjinkai'in." In *Kyōdō kenkyū: tenkō*. Vol. 1, ed. Shisō no Kagaku Kenkyūkai, 114–149. Tokyo: Heibonsha, 1959.

———. "Tenkō no kyōdō kenkyū ni tsuite." In *Kyōdō kenkyū: tenkō*. Vol. 1, ed. Shisō no Kagaku no Kenkyūkai, 1–27. Tokyo: Heibonsha, 1959.

Ueyama Shunpei. *Daitōa sensō no imi: gendaishi bunseki no shiten*. Tokyo: Chūō kōronsha, 1964.

Yamada Seizaburō. *Puroretaria bungakushi: fūsetsu no jidai*. Vol. 2. Tokyo: Rironsha, 1954.

Yamada Seizaburō and others. "Hayashi Fusaoron: sayoku bundan shinsakkaron, ni." *Bungei sensen* 3, no. 11 (November 1926): 74–77.

Yamashita Etsuko. *Mazakon bungakuron: jubaku toshite no 'haha.'* Tokyo: Shinyōsha, 1991.

Yoshida Seiichi, ed. *Shōwa bungakushi*. Tokyo: Shibundō, 1959.

SOURCES IN WESTERN LANGUAGES

Anderson, Benedict. *Imagined Communities: Reflections on the Origin and Spread of Nationalism*, Revised Edition. New York: Verso, 1991.

Arendt, Hannah. "Introduction, Walter Benjamin: 1892–1940." In *Illuminations*, Translated by Harry Zohn, ed. Hannah Arendt, 1–55. New York: Schocken Books, 2007. Reprint, Harcourt, Brace & World, 1968.

Arima, Tatsuo. *The Failure of Freedom: A Portrait of Modern Japanese Intellectuals*. Harvard East Asian Series, no. 39. Cambridge: Harvard University Press, 1969.

Bakhtin, M. M. *The Dialogic Imagination: Four Essays*. Translated by Caryl Emerson and Michael Holquist, ed. Michael Holquist. Austin: University of Texas Press, 1981.

Barshay, Andrew E. "Postwar Social and Political Thought, 1945–90." In *Modern Japanese Thought*, ed. Bob Takashi Wakabayashi, 273–355. New York: Cambridge University Press, 1998.

———. *State and Intellectual in Imperial Japan: The Public Man in Crisis*. Berkeley: University of California Press, 1988.

Beckmann, George M. and Okubo Genji. *The Japanese Communist Party 1922–1945*. Stanford: Stanford University Press, 1969.

———. "The Radical Left and the Failure of Communism." In *Dilemmas of Growth in Prewar Japan*, ed. James William Morley, 139–78. Princeton: Princeton University Press, 1971.

Befu, Harumi. "Introduction." *Cultural Nationalism in East Asia: Representation and Identity*, ed. Harumi Befu, Research papers and policy studies, no. 39, 1–5. Berkeley: Institute of East Asian Studies University of California, 1993.

———. "Nationalism and *Nihonjinron*." In *Cultural Nationalism in East Asia: Representation and Identity*, ed. Harumi Befu. Research papers and policy studies, no. 39, 107–135. Berkeley: Institute of East Asian Studies University of California, 1993.

Benjamin, Walter. "Unpacking My Library: A Talk about Book Collection." In *Illuminations*, Translated by Harry Zohn, edited by Hannah Arendt, 59–67. New York: Schocken Books, 2007.

Bernstein, Gail Lee. *Japanese Marxist: A Portrait of Kawakami Hajime* 1879–1946. Harvard East Asian Monographs, no. 152. Cambridge: Harvard University Press, 1976; 1990.

Bowen-Struyk, Heather and Norma Field, eds. *For Dignity, Justice, and Revolution: An Anthology of Japanese Proletarian Literature*. Chicago: University of Chicago Press, 2016.

Calichman, Richard. "Introduction: 'Overcoming Modernity': The Dissolution of

Cultural Identity." In *Overcoming Modernity: Cultural Identity in Wartime Japan*. Weatherhead Books on Asia: History, Society, and Culture, edited by Carol Gluck, 1–41. New York: Columbia University Press, 2008.

Chang, Iris. *The Rape of Nanking: The Forgotten Holocaust of World War II*. New York: Basic Books, 1997.

Craig, Albert M. "Introduction: Perspectives on Personality in Japanese History." In *Personality in Japanese History*, ed. Albert M. Craig and Donald H. Shively, 1–28. Berkeley: University of California Press, 1970. Reprint, Michigan Classics in Japanese Studies, no. 13. Ann Arbor: Center for Japanese Studies at The University of Michigan, 1995.

———. "Kido Kōin and Ōkubo Toshimichi: A Psychohistorical Analysis." In *Personality in Japanese History*, ed. Albert M. Craig and Donald H. Shively, 264–308. Berkeley: University of California Press, 1970. Reprint, Michigan Classics in Japanese Studies, no. 13. Ann Arbor: Center for Japanese Studies at The University of Michigan, 1995.

Cullen, Jennifer. "A Comparative Study of *Tenkō*: Sata Ineko and Miyamoto Yuriko." *Journal of Japanese Studies* 36, no. 1 (Winter 2010): 65–95.

Dazai, Osamu. *No Longer Human*. Translation by Donald Keene. New York: New Directions Publishing Corporation, 1958. Reprint, Tokyo: Charles E. Tuttle Co. Publishers, 1984.

de Bary, Brett. "'Credo Quia Absurdum': *Tenkō* and the Prisonhouse of Language." In *Culture and Identity: Japanese Intellectuals during the Interwar Years*, ed. J. Thomas Rimer, 154–167. Princeton: Princeton University Press, 1990.

———. *Three Works by Nakano Shigeharu*. Cornell University East Asian Papers, No. 21. Ithaca: China-Japan Program, 1979.

Doak, Kevin M. *Dreams of Difference: The Japan Romantic School and the Crisis of Modernity*. Berkeley: University of California Press, 1994.

———. "Ethnic Nationalism and Romanticism in Early Twentieth-Century Japan." *The Journal of Japanese Studies* 22, no. 1 (Winter 1996): 77–103.

———. *A History of Nationalism in Modern Japan: Placing the People*, Handbook of Oriental Studies. Leiden and Boston: Brill, 2007.

———. "Nationalism as Dialectics: Ethnicity, Moralism, and the State in Early Twentieth-Century Japan." In *Rude Awakenings: Zen, the Kyoto School, & the Question of Nationalism*, ed. James W. Heisig and John C. Maraldo, 174–196. Honolulu: University of Hawai'i Press, 1994.

Dorsey, James. *Critical Aesthetics: Kobayashi Hideo, Modernity, and Wartime Japan*. Harvard East Asian Monographs, 318. Cambridge: Harvard University Asia Center, 2009.

———. "From Ideological Literature to a Literary Ideology: 'Conversion' in Wartime Japan." In *Converting Cultures: Religion, Ideology and Transformations of Modernity*, ed. Dennis Washburn and A. Kevin Reinhart, 465–483. Leiden and Boston: Brill, 2007.

———. Review of *War, Occupation, and Creativity: Japan and East Asia, 1920–1960*, ed. Marlene J. Mayo and J. Thomas Rimer with H. Eleanor Kerkham. *Monumenta Nipponica* 59, no. 1 (Spring 2004): 134–137.

Dower, John W. *Embracing Defeat: Japan in the Wake of World War II*. New York: W. W. Norton Press, 1999.

Duus, Peter. *Modern Japan*, 2d ed. New York: Houghton Mifflin Company, 1998.

Fletcher, William Miles. *Search for a New Order: Intellectuals and Fascism in Prewar Japan*. Chapel Hill: University of North Carolina Press, 1982.

Fogel, Joshua A., ed. *The Nanjing Massacre in History and Historiography*. Berkeley: University of California Press, 2000.

Fowler, Edward. *The Rhetoric of Confession: Shishōsetsu in Early Twentieth-Century Japanese Fiction*. Berkeley: University of California Press, 1988.

Freedman, Alisa. *Tokyo in Transit: Japanese Culture on the Rails and Road*. Stanford: Stanford University Press, 2011.

Fujitani, T., Geoffrey M. White, and Lisa Yoneyama, ed. *Perilous Memories: The Asia-Pacific War(s)*. Durham: Duke University Press, 2001.

Garon, Sheldon. *Molding Japanese Minds: The State in Everyday Life*. Princeton: Princeton University Press, 1997.

———. "Rethinking Modernization and Modernity in Japanese History: A Focus on State-Society Relations." *The Journal of Asian Studies* 53, no. 2 (May 1994): 346–366.

———. "State and Society in Interwar Japan." In *Historical Perspectives on Contemporary East Asia*, ed. Merle Goldman and Andrew Gordon, 155–182. Cambridge: Harvard University Press, 2000.

Gluck, Carol. "The Idea of Showa." In *Showa: The Japan of Hirohito*, eds. Carol Gluck and Stephen R. Graubard, 1–26. New York: W. W. Norton & Company, 1992.

Goto-Jones, Christopher. "The Left Hand of Darkness: Forging a Political Left in Interwar Japan." In *The Left in the Shaping of Japanese Democracy: Essays in Honour of J. A. A. Stockwin*, ed., Rikki Kersten and David Williams, 3–20. London: Routledge, 2006.

Hane, Mikiso. *Eastern Phoenix: Japan since 1945*. Boulder, CO: Westview Press, 1996.

Harootunian, H.D. "Between Politics and Culture: Authority and the Ambiguities of Intellectual Choice in Imperial Japan." In *Japan in Crisis: Essays on*

Taishō Democracy, eds. Bernard S. Silberman and H.D. Harootunian, 110–155. Princeton: Princeton University Press, 1974. Reprint, Michigan Classics in Japanese Studies, no. 20. Ann Arbor: Center for Japanese Studies at The University of Michigan, 1999.

———. *Overcome by Modernity: History, Culture, and Community in Interwar Japan*. Princeton: Princeton University Press, 2000.

Hashimoto, Akiko. *The Long Defeat: Cultural Trauma, Memory, and Identity in Japan*. New York: Oxford University Press, 2015.

Hein, Laura and Mark Selden, ed. *Censoring History: Citizenship and Memory in Japan, Germany, and the United States*. Armonk, NY: M.E. Sharpe, 2000.

Hirayama, Mikiko. "From Art without Borders to Art for the Nation: Japanist Painting by Dokuritsu Bijutsu Kyōkai during the 1930s." *Monumenta Nipponica* 65, no. 2 (2010), 357–395. doi: https://doi.org/10.1353/mni.2010.0011.

Honda, Katsuichi. *The Nanjing Massacre: A Japanese Journalist Confronts Japan's National Shame*. Translated by Karen Sandness. Armonk, NY: M.E. Sharpe, 1999.

Hoston, Germaine A. "Conceptualizing Bourgeois Revolution: The Prewar Japanese Left and the Meiji Restoration." *Comparative Studies in Society and History* 33, no. 3 (July 1991): 539–581.

———. "Emperor, Nation, and the Transformation of Marxism to National Socialism in Prewar Japan: The Case of Sano Manabu." *Studies in Comparative Communism* 18, no. 1 (Spring 1985): 25–47.

———. "*Ikkoku Shakai-shugi*: Sano Manabu and the Limits of Marxism as Cultural Criticism." In *Culture and Identity: Japanese Intellectuals during the Interwar Years*, ed. J. Thomas Rimer, 168–190. Princeton: Princeton University Press, 1990.

———. *Marxism and the Crisis of Development in Prewar Japan*. Princeton: Princeton University Press, 1986.

———. "Tenkō: Marxism & the National Question in Prewar Japan." *Polity* 16, no. 1 (Fall 1983): 96–118.

Iida, Yumiko. *Rethinking Identity in Modern Japan: Nationalism as Aesthetics*. New York: Routledge, 2002.

Iwamoto, Yoshio. "Aspects of the Proletarian Literary Movement in Japan." In *Japan in Crisis: Essays on Taishō Democracy*, ed. Bernard S. Silberman and H.D. Harootunian, 156–182. Princeton: Princeton University Press, 1974. Reprint, Michigan Classics in Japanese Studies, no. 20. Ann Arbor: Center for Japanese Studies at The University of Michigan, 1999.

———. "The Relationship between Literature and Politics in Japan, 1931–1945." Ph.D. diss., University of Michigan, 1964.

Kano, Fujio and Maurice Ward. "Socialism Is a Mission: Max Bickerton's Involvement with the Japanese Communist Party and Translation of Japanese Proletarian Literature in the 1930s." *New Zealand Journal of Asian Studies* 16, no. 2 (December 2014): 99–120.

Karlsson, Mats. "An Alternative View of *Tenkō*: Hayashi Fusao's Popular Writings for *Shinseinen*." *Japanese Studies* 32, no. 1 (May 2012): 61–76.

———. "Kurahara Korehito's Road to Proletarian Realism." *Japan Review* 20 (2008): 231–273. doi: 148.137.160.22.

Kasza, Gregory J. *The State and the Mass Media in Japan 1918–1945*. Berkeley: University of California Press, 1988.

Keene, Donald. *Dawn to the West: Japanese Literature in the Modern Era*, Fiction. An Owl Book. New York: Henry Holt and Company, 1984.

———. *Dawn to the West: Japanese Literature in the Modern Era, Poetry, Drama, Criticism*. An Owl Book. New York: Henry Holt and Company, 1984.

———. "Japanese Literature and Politics in the 1930s." *Journal of Japanese Studies* 2, no. 2 (Summer 1975): 236–244.

———. "The Shirakaba School." In *Dawn to the West: Japanese Literature of the Modern Era*, Fiction, An Owl Book, 441–505. New York: Henry Holt and Company, 1984.

Kersten, Rikki. "Neo-nationalism and the 'Liberal School of History.'" *Japan Forum* 11, no. 2 (1999): 191–203.

———. "Painting the Emperor Red: The Emperor and the Socialists in the 1930s." In *The Left in the Shaping of Japanese Democracy: Essays in Honour of J.A.A. Stockwin*, ed., Rikki Kersten and David Williams, 21–41. London: Routledge, 2006.

King, Lynda J. "Hermynia Zur Mühlen." *Dictionary of Literary Biography*. vol. 56, *German Fiction Writers, 1914–1945*, ed. James N. Hardin, 317–324. Detroit: Gale Research, 1987.

Koschmann, J. Victor. *Revolution and Subjectivity in Postwar Japan*. Chicago: University of Chicago Press, 1996.

Lippit, Noriko Mizuta. *Reality and Fiction in Modern Japanese Literature*. White Plains, NY: M.E. Sharpe, 1980.

Long, Jeff E. "Overcoming Marxism in Early Shōwa Japan: Hayashi Fusao's *Seinen* and the Turn to Ultranationalism." Ph.D. diss., University of Hawai'i, 2000.

———. "The Japanese Literati and the 'China Incident': Hayashi Fusao Reporting the Battle of Shanghai." *Sino-Japanese Studies* 15 (April 2003): 27–44.

———. "Songs That Cannot Be Sung: Hayashi Fusao's 'Album' and the Political

Uses of Literature during the Early Showa Years." *Japan Forum* 19, no. 1 (March 2007): 69–88.

Mackie, Vera. "Modern Selves and Modern Spaces: An Overview." In *Being Modern in Japan: Culture and Society from the 1910s to the 1930s*, ed., Elise K. Tipton and John Clark, 185–196. Honolulu: University of Hawai'i Press, 2000.

Mark, Ethan. "The Perils of Co-Prosperity: Takeda Rintarō, Occupied Southeast Asia, and the Seductions of Postcolonial Empire." *American Historical Review* 119, no. 4 (October 2014): 1184–1206.

Maruyama, Masao. "Introduction." In *Nationalism and the Right Wing in Japan: A Study of Post-War Trends*, xvii–xviii. New York: Oxford University Press, 1960.

Matsumoto, Tomone. "From Marxism to Japanism: A Study of Kamei Katsuichirō (1907–1967)." Ph.D. diss., University of Arizona, 1979.

Matsumura, Janice. *More Than a Momentary Nightmare: The Yokohama Incident and Wartime Japan*. Cornell East Asia Series, 92. Ithaca, NY: East Asia Program, Cornell University, 1998.

Minichiello, Sharon A. "Introduction." In *Japan's Competing Modernities: Issues in Culture and Democracy, 1900–1930*, ed. Sharon A. Minichiello, 1–21. Honolulu: University of Hawai'i Press, 1998.

———, ed. *Japan's Competing Modernities: Issues in Culture and Democracy, 1900–1930*. Honolulu: University of Hawai'i Press, 1998.

———. *Retreat from Reform: Patterns of Political Behavior in Interwar Japan*. Honolulu: University of Hawaii Press, 1984.

Mitchell, Richard H. *Censorship in Imperial Japan*. Princeton: Princeton University Press, 1983.

———. *Thought Control in Prewar Japan*. Ithaca: Cornell University Press, 1976.

Morley, James William. "Introduction: Choice and Consequence." In *Dilemmas of Growth in Prewar Japan*, ed. James William Morley, 3–30. Princeton: Princeton University Press, 1971.

Morris, Ivan. *Nationalism and the Right Wing in Japan: A Study of Post-War Trends*. New York: Oxford University Press, 1960.

Najita, Tetsuo. "Nakano Seigō and the Spirit of the Meiji Restoration in Twentieth-Century Japan." In *Dilemmas of Growth in Prewar Japan*, ed. James William Morley, 375–421. Princeton: Princeton University Press, 1971.

——— and H.D. Harootunian. "Japan's Revolt Against the West." In *Modern Japanese Thought*, ed. Bob Takashi Wakabayashi, 207–272. New York: Cambridge University Press, 1998.

Okudaira, Yasuhiro. "Some Preparatory Notes for the Study of the Peace Preservation Law in Pre-War Japan." *Annals of the Institute of Social Science*, no. 14 (1973): 49–69.

Olson, Lawrence. *Ambivalent Moderns: Portraits of Japanese Cultural Identity.* Savage, MD: Rowman & Littlefield Publishers, Inc., 1992.

Packard III, George R. *Protest in Tokyo: The Security Treaty Crisis of 1960.* Princeton: Princeton University Press, 1966.

Paulowich, Paul. "Dominick's Sickness." *The Young Workers* 2, no. 3 (March 1923): 17–18. https://www.marxists.org/history/usa/pubs/youngworker/v2n3-mar-1923-yw.pdf.

Perry, Samuel. *Recasting Red Culture in Proletarian Japan: Childhood, Korea, and the Historical Avant-Garde.* Honolulu: University of Hawai'i Press, 2014.

Pollack, David. *Reading Against Culture: Ideology and Narrative in the Japanese Novel.* Ithaca, NY: Cornell University Press, 1992.

Prescott, William H. *History of the Conquest of Peru: With a Preliminary View of the Civilization of the Incas.* Philadelphia: J.B. Lippincott, 1863.

———. *History of the Conquest of Mexico: With a Preliminary View of the Ancient Mexican Civilization, and the Life of the Conqueror Hernando Cortez.* Philadelphia: J.B. Lippincott, 1868.

Rimer, J. Thomas ed. *Culture and Identity: Japanese Intellectuals during the Interwar Years.* Princeton: Princeton University Press, 1990.

Scalapino, Robert O. *Democracy and Party Movement in Prewar Japan: The Failure of the First Attempt.* Berkeley, University of California Press, 1953.

Seidensticker, Edward. *Tokyo Rising: The City since the Great Earthquake.* New York: Alfred A. Knopf, Inc., 1990.

Shea, G.T. *Leftwing Literature in Japan: A Brief History of the Proletarian Literary Movement.* Tokyo: The Hōsei University Press, 1964.

Shigeto, Yukiko. "Tenkō and Writing: The Case of Nakano Shigeharu." *Positions* 22, no. 2 (2014): 517–540. doi: 10.1215/10679847-2413880.

Shillony, Ben-Ami. *Politics and Culture in Wartime Japan.* New York: Oxford University Press, 1981; Oxford: Clarendon Press, 1991.

Shimazaki, Tōson. *Before the Dawn.* Translated by William E. Naff. Honolulu: University of Hawaii, 1987.

Silverberg, Miriam. *Changing Song: The Marxist Manifestos of Nakano Shigeharu.* Princeton: Princeton University Press, 1990.

Sipos, George Tiberiu. "The Literature of Political Conversion (*Tenkō*) of Japan." Ph.D. diss., University of Chicago, 2013.

Smith II, Henry Dewitt. *Japan's First Student Radicals.* Harvard East Asian Series, no. 70. Cambridge, MA: Harvard University Press, 1972.

Starrs, Roy. "Writing the National Narrative: Changing Attitudes toward Nation-

Building among Japanese Writers, 1900–1930." In *Japan's Competing Modernities: Issues in Culture and Democracy 1900–1930*, ed. Sharon A. Minichiello, 206–227. Honolulu: University of Hawai'i Press, 1998.

Steinhoff, Patricia G. "Spiritual Tenkō and The Tenkō Bungaku Movement." *Proceedings of the Twenty-ninth International Congress of Orientalists*. 29 (July 1973), 139–142.

———. *Tenkō: Ideology and Social Integration in Prewar Japan*, Harvard Studies in Sociology. New York: Garland Publishing, 1991.

———. "Tenkō and Thought Control." In *Japan and the World: Essays on Japanese History and Politics in Honour of Ishida Takeshi*, ed. Gail Lee Bernstein and Haruhiro Fukui, 78–94. New York: St. Martin's Press, 1988.

Storry, Richard. *The Double Patriots: A Study of Japanese Nationalism*. Chatto & Windus, Ltd., 1957. Reprint, Westport, CT: Greenwood Press, Publishers, 1976.

Supreme Commander for the Allied Powers, Government Section. *Political Reorientation of Japan: September 1945 to September 1948*. 2 vols. Washington, D.C., 1949.

Tansman, Alan. *The Aesthetics of Japanese Fascism*. Berkeley: University of California Press, 2009.

———, ed. *The Culture of Japanese Fascism*. Durham: Duke University Press, 2009.

———. "Images of Repose and Violence in Three Japanese Writers." *Journal of Japanese Studies* 28, no. 1 (Winter 2002): 109–39.

Tipton, Elise. *Japanese Police State: The Tokkō in Interwar Japan*. Honolulu: University of Hawaii Press, 1990.

Torrance, Richard. "*The People's Library*: The Spirit of Prose Literature versus Fascism." In *The Culture of Japanese Fascism*, ed. Alan Tansman, 56–79. Durham: Duke University Press, 2009.

Toynbee, Arnold J. *A Study of History*. 12 vols. New York: Oxford University Press, 1962.

Tsurumi, Kazuko. "Six Types of Change in Personality: Case Studies of Ideological Conversion in the 1930's." In *Social Change and the Individual: Japan before and after Defeat in World War II*, 29–79. Princeton: Princeton University Press, 1970.

Tsurumi, Patricia E.. *Factory Girls: Women in the Thread Mills of Meiji Japan*. Princeton: Princeton University Press, 1990.

Tsurumi, Shunsuke. *A Cultural History of Postwar Japan. 1945–1980* London: KPI Ltd., 1987.

———. *An Intellectual History of Wartime Japan 1931–1945*. Japanese Studies, ed. Yoshio Sugimoto. New York: KPI, 1986.

Tsuzuki Chushichi. "Tenkō or Teikō: The Dilemma of a Japanese Marxist between the Wars." In *Themes and Theories in Modern Japanese History: Essays in Memory of Richard Storry*, ed. Sue Henny and Jean-Pierre Lehmann, 215–29. Atlantic Highlands, NJ: Athlone Press, 1988.

Ward, Max. "Crisis Ideology and the Articulation of Fascism in Interwar Japan: The 1938 Thought-War Symposium." *Japan Forum* 26, no. 4 (2014): 462–485.

Waswo, Ann. *Modern Japanese Society, 1868–1994*, An OPUS Book. New York: Oxford University Press, 1996.

Williams, Mark. "Expedient Conversion? *Tenkō* in Transwar Japanese Literature." In *Routledge Handbook of Modern Japanese Literature*, ed. Rachael Huchinson and Leith Morton, 141–153. New York: Routledge, 2016.

———. "Shiina Rinzō: Imagining Hope and Despair in Occupation Japan." *Bulletin of the School of Oriental and African Studies* 66, no. 3 (2003): 442–455.

Wilson, George M. *Radical Nationalist in Japan: Kita Ikki, 1883–1937.* Harvard East Asian Series, no. 37. Cambridge: Harvard University Press, 1969.

Wolfe, Alan. "From Pearls to Swine: Sakaguchi Ango and the Humanity of Decadence." In *War, Occupation, and Creativity: Japan and East Asia, 1920–1960*, ed. Marlene J. Mayo and J. Thomas Rimer with H. Eleanor Kerkham, 360–379. Honolulu: University of Hawai'i Press, 2001.

Yamazaki, Masakazu. "The Intellectual Community of the Showa Era." In *Showa: The Japan of Hirohito*, ed. Carol Gluck and Stephen R. Graubard, 245–264. New York: W. W. Norton & Company, 1992.

Zur Mühlen, Hermynia. *Was Peterchens Freunde erzählen: Märchen.* Berlin: Malik-verlag, 1921.

DICTIONARIES AND ENCYCLOPEDIAS

Brown, Sidney DeVere. "Shizoku." In *Kodansha Encyclopedia of Japan*. Vol. 7, ed. Itasaka Gen. Tokyo: Kōdansha, 1983.

Jidai betsu Nihon bungakushi jiten henshū iinkai, ed. *Jidai betsu Nihon bungakushi jiten: gendaihen*. Tokyo: Tokyo tōshuppan, 1997.

Odagiri Susumu, ed. *Gendai Nihon bungei sōran*. 4 vols. Tokyo: Meiji bunken, 1969.

——— et al., ed. *Nihon kindai bungaku daijiten*. 6 vols. Tokyo: Kōdansha, 1977.

Rin Shukumi. "Puroretaria bungaku no kaitai." In *Jidai betsu Nihon bungakushi jiten: gendaihen*, ed. Jidai betsu Nihon bungakushi jiten henshū iinkai. Tokyo: Tokyo tōshuppan, 1997.

Shakai Mondai Kenkyūkai, ed. *Uyoku jiten: minzokuha no zenbō*. Tokyo: Futabasha, 1970.

Shiota Shōbē et al., ed. *Nihon shakai undō jinmei jiten*. Tokyo: Aoki shoten, 1979.

Tōgō Katsumi. "Bungei fukkō no mosaku." In *Jidai betsu Nihon bungakushi jiten: gendaihen*, ed. Jidai betsu Nihon bungakushi jiten henshū iinkai. Tokyo: Tōshuppan, 1997.

Wilson, George M. "Ultranationalism." In *Kodansha Encyclopedia of Japan*. Vol. 8, ed. Itasaka Gen. Tokyo: Kōdansha, 1983.

Index

About the Author

Jeff E. Long is Professor of Asian History in the Department of History at Bloomsburg University of Pennsylvania. His research focuses on the role of *tenkō* (ideological/political conversion) in the writings of Hayashi Fusao and Shimaki Kensaku from the 1930s.

Professor Long received his Ph.D. in History from the University of Hawaii, Manoa, where his doctoral studies focused on the role of tenkō (ideological/political conversion) in the thought and literature of Hayashi Fusao (1903–1975) and Shimaki Kensaku (1903–1945). His publications include "Songs That Cannot Be Sung: Hayashi Fusao's 'Album' and the Political Uses of Literature during the Early Shōwa Years" in *Japan Forum* (March 2007) and a translation of Hayashi Fusao's short story "Apples" in *For Dignity, Justice, and Revolution: An Anthology of Japanese Proletarian Literature*, edited by Norma Field and Heather Bowen-Struyk (University of Chicago Press, 2016).

CORNELL EAST ASIA SERIES

4 Fredrick Teiwes, *Provincial Leadership in China: The Cultural Revolution and Its Aftermath*
8 Cornelius C. Kubler, *Vocabulary and Notes to Ba Jin's Jia: An Aid for Reading the Novel*
16 Monica Bethe & Karen Brazell, *Nō as Performance: An Analysis of the Kuse Scene of Yamamba.* Available for purchase: DVD by Monica Bethe & Karen Brazell, "Yamanba: The Old Woman of the Mountains"
18 Royall Tyler, tr., *Granny Mountains: A Second Cycle of Nō Plays*
23 Knight Biggerstaff, *Nanking Letters, 1949*
28 Diane E. Perushek, ed., *The Griffis Collection of Japanese Books: An Annotated Bibliography*
37 J. Victor Koschmann, Ōiwa Keibō & Yamashita Shinji, eds., *International Perspectives on Yanagita Kunio and Japanese Folklore Studies*
38 James O'Brien, tr., *Murō Saisei: Three Works*
40 Kubo Sakae, *Land of Volcanic Ash: A Play in Two Parts,* revised edition, tr. David G. Goodman
44 Susan Orpett Long, *Family Change and the Life Course in Japan*
48 Helen Craig McCullough, *Bungo Manual: Selected Reference Materials for Students of Classical Japanese*
49 Susan Blakeley Klein, *Ankoku Butō: The Premodern and Postmodern Influences on the Dance of Utter Darkness*
50 Karen Brazell, ed., *Twelve Plays of the Noh and Kyōgen Theaters*
51 David G. Goodman, ed., *Five Plays by Kishida Kunio*
52 Shirō Hara, *Ode to Stone,* tr. James Morita
53 Peter J. Katzenstein & Yutaka Tsujinaka, *Defending the Japanese State: Structures, Norms and the Political Responses to Terrorism and Violent Social Protest in the 1970s and 1980s*
54 Su Xiaokang & Wang Luxiang, *Deathsong of the River: A Reader's Guide to the Chinese TV Series* Heshang, trs. Richard Bodman & Pin P. Wan
55 Jingyuan Zhang, *Psychoanalysis in China: Literary Transformations, 1919–1949*
56 Jane Kate Leonard & John R. Watt, eds., *To Achieve Security and Wealth: The Qing Imperial State and the Economy, 1644–1911*
57 Andrew F. Jones, *Like a Knife: Ideology and Genre in Contemporary Chinese Popular Music*
58 Peter J. Katzenstein & Nobuo Okawara, *Japan's National Security: Structures, Norms and Policy Responses in a Changing World*
59 Carsten Holz, *The Role of Central Banking in China's Economic Reforms*
60 Chifumi Shimazaki, *Warrior Ghost Plays from the Japanese Noh Theater: Parallel Translations with Running Commentary*

61 Emily Groszos Ooms, *Women and Millenarian Protest in Meiji Japan: Deguchi Nao and Ōmotokyō*
62 Carolyn Anne Morley, *Transformation, Miracles, and Mischief: The Mountain Priest Plays of Kyōgen*
63 David R. McCann & Hyunjae Yee Sallee, tr., *Selected Poems of Kim Namjo*, afterword by Kim Yunsik
64 Hua Qingzhao, *From Yalta to Panmunjom: Truman's Diplomacy and the Four Powers, 1945–1953*
65 Margaret Benton Fukasawa, *Kitahara Hakushū: His Life and Poetry*
66 Kam Louie, ed., *Strange Tales from Strange Lands: Stories by Zheng Wanlong*, with introduction
67 Wang Wen-hsing, *Backed Against the Sea*, tr. Edward Gunn
69 Brian Myers, *Han Sōrya and North Korean Literature: The Failure of Socialist Realism in the DPRK*
70 Thomas P. Lyons & Victor Nee, eds., *The Economic Transformation of South China: Reform and Development in the Post-Mao Era*
71 David G. Goodman, tr., *After Apocalypse: Four Japanese Plays of Hiroshima and Nagasaki*, with introduction
72 Thomas Lyons, *Poverty and Growth in a South China County: Anxi, Fujian, 1949–1992*
74 Martyn Atkins, *Informal Empire in Crisis: British Diplomacy and the Chinese Customs Succession, 1927-1929*
76 Chifumi Shimazaki, *Restless Spirits from Japanese Noh Plays of the Fourth Group: Parallel Translations with Running Commentary*
77 Brother Anthony of Taizé & Young-Moo Kim, trs., *Back to Heaven: Selected Poems of Ch'ŏn Sang Pyŏng*
78 Kevin O'Rourke, tr., *Singing Like a Cricket, Hooting Like an Owl: Selected Poems by Yi Kyu-bo*
79 Irit Averbuch, *The Gods Come Dancing: A Study of the Japanese Ritual Dance of Yamabushi Kagura*
80 Mark Peterson, *Korean Adoption and Inheritance: Case Studies in the Creation of a Classic Confucian Society*
81 Yenna Wu, tr., *The Lioness Roars: Shrew Stories from Late Imperial China*
82 Thomas Lyons, *The Economic Geography of Fujian: A Sourcebook*, Vol. 1
83 Pak Wan-so, *The Naked Tree*, tr. Yu Young-nan
84 C.T. Hsia, *The Classic Chinese Novel: A Critical Introduction*
85 Cho Chong-Rae, *Playing With Fire*, tr. Chun Kyung-Ja
86 Hayashi Fumiko, *I Saw a Pale Horse and Selections from Diary of a Vagabond*, tr. Janice Brown
87 Motoori Norinaga, *Kojiki-den, Book 1*, tr. Ann Wehmeyer
88 Chang Soo Ko, tr., *Sending the Ship Out to the Stars: Poems of Park Je-chun*
89 Thomas Lyons, *The Economic Geography of Fujian: A Sourcebook*, Vol. 2
90 Brother Anthony of Taizé, tr., Midang: *Early Lyrics of So Chong-Ju*
92 Janice Matsumura, *More Than a Momentary Nightmare: The Yokohama Incident and Wartime Japan*
93 Kim Jong-Gil tr., *The Snow Falling on Chagall's Village: Selected Poems of Kim Ch'un-Su*
94 Wolhee Choe & Peter Fusco, trs., *Day-Shine: Poetry by Hyon-jong Chong*

95 Chifumi Shimazaki, *Troubled Souls from Japanese Noh Plays of the Fourth Group*
96 Hagiwara Sakutarō, *Principles of Poetry (Shi no Genri)*, tr. Chester Wang
97 Mae J. Smethurst, *Dramatic Representations of Filial Piety: Five Noh in Translation*
99 William Wilson, *Hōgen Monogatari: Tale of the Disorder in Hōgen*
100 Yasushi Yamanouchi, J. Victor Koschmann and Ryūichi Narita, eds., *Total War and 'Modernization'*
101 Yi Ch'ŏng-jun, *The Prophet and Other Stories*, tr. Julie Pickering
102 S.A. Thornton, *Charisma and Community Formation in Medieval Japan: The Case of the Yugyō-ha (1300–1700)*
103 Sherman Cochran, ed., *Inventing Nanjing Road: Commercial Culture in Shanghai, 1900–1945*
104 Harold M. Tanner, *Strike Hard! Anti-Crime Campaigns and Chinese Criminal Justice, 1979–1985*
105 Brother Anthony of Taizé & Young-Moo Kim, trs., *Farmers' Dance: Poems by Shin Kyŏng-nim*
106 Susan Orpett Long, ed., *Lives in Motion: Composing Circles of Self and Community in Japan*
107 Peter J. Katzenstein, Natasha Hamilton-Hart, Kozo Kato, & Ming Yue, *Asian Regionalism*
108 Kenneth Alan Grossberg, *Japan's Renaissance: The Politics of the Muromachi Bakufu*
109 John W. Hall & Toyoda Takeshi, eds., *Japan in the Muromachi Age*
110 Kim Su-Young, Shin Kyong-Nim, Lee Si-Young; *Variations: Three Korean Poets*; trs. Brother Anthony of Taizé & Young-Moo Kim
111 Samuel Leiter, *Frozen Moments: Writings on* Kabuki, *1966–2001*
118 Mae J. Smethurst and Christina Laffin, eds., *The Noh* Ominameshi*: A Flower Viewed from Many Directions*
112 Pilwun Shih Wang & Sarah Wang, *Early One Spring: A Learning Guide to Accompany the Film Video* February
113 Thomas Conlan, *In Little Need of Divine Intervention: Scrolls of the Mongol Invasions of Japan*
114 Jane Kate Leonard & Robert Antony, eds., *Dragons, Tigers, and Dogs: Qing Crisis Management and the Boundaries of State Power in Late Imperial China*
115 Shu-ning Sciban & Fred Edwards, eds., *Dragonflies: Fiction by Chinese Women in the Twentieth Century*
116 David G. Goodman, ed., *The Return of the Gods: Japanese Drama and Culture in the 1960s*
117 Yang Hi Choe-Wall, *Vision of a Phoenix: The Poems of Hŏ Nansŏrhŏn*
119 Joseph A. Murphy, *Metaphorical Circuit: Negotiations Between Literature and Science in Twentieth-Century Japan*
120 Richard F. Calichman, *Takeuchi Yoshimi: Displacing the West*
121 Fan Pen Li Chen, *Visions for the Masses: Chinese Shadow Plays from Shaanxi and Shanxi*
122 S. Yumiko Hulvey, *Sacred Rites in Moonlight: Ben no Naishi Nikki*
123 Tetsuo Najita and J. Victor Koschmann, *Conflict in Modern Japanese History: The Neglected Tradition*
124 Naoki Sakai, Brett de Bary, & Iyotani Toshio, eds., *Deconstructing Nationality*
125 Judith N. Rabinovitch and Timothy R. Bradstock, *Dance of the Butterflies: Chinese Poetry from the Japanese Court Tradition*

126 Yang Gui-ja, *Contradictions*, trs. Stephen Epstein and Kim Mi-Young

127 Ann Sung-hi Lee, *Yi Kwang-su and Modern Korean Literature:* Mujŏng

128 Pang Kie-chung & Michael D. Shin, eds., *Landlords, Peasants, & Intellectuals in Modern Korea*

129 Joan R. Piggott, ed., *Capital and Countryside in Japan, 300–1180: Japanese Historians Interpreted in English*

130 Kyoko Selden and Jolisa Gracewood, eds., *Annotated Japanese Literary Gems: Stories by Tawada Yōko, Nakagami Kenji, and Hayashi Kyōko* (Vol. 1)

131 Michael G. Murdock, *Disarming the Allies of Imperialism: The State, Agitation, and Manipulation during China's Nationalist Revolution, 1922–1929*

132 Noel J. Pinnington, *Traces in the Way: Michi and the Writings of Komparu Zenchiku*

133 Charlotte von Verschuer, *Across the Perilous Sea: Japanese Trade with China and Korea from the Seventh to the Sixteenth Centuries*, tr. Kristen Lee Hunter

134 John Timothy Wixted, *A Handbook to Classical Japanese*

135 Kyoko Selden and Jolisa Gracewoord, with Lili Selden, eds., *Annotated Japanese Literary Gems: Stories by Natsume Sōseki, Tomioka Taeko, and Inoue Yasushi* (Vol. 2)

136 Yi Tae-Jin, *The Dynamics of Confucianism and Modernization in Korean History*

137 Jennifer Rudolph, *Negotiated Power in Late Imperial China: The Zongli Yamen and the Politics of Reform*

138 Thomas D. Loooser, *Visioning Eternity: Aesthetics, Politics, and History in the Early Modern Noh Theater*

139 Gustav Heldt, *The Pursuit of Harmony: Poetry and Power in Late Heian Japan*

140 Joan R. Piggott and Yoshida Sanae, *Teishinkōki: The Year 939 in the Journal of Regent Fujiwara no Tadahira*

141 Robert Bagley, *Max Loehr and the Study of Chinese Bronzes: Style and Classification in the History of Art*

142 Edwin A. Cranston, *The Secret Island and the Enticing Flame: Worlds of Memory, Discovery, and Loss in Japanese Poetry*

143 Hugh de Ferranti, *The Last Biwa Singer: A Blind Musician in History, Imagination and Performance*

144 Roger des Forges, Minglu Gao, Liu Chiao-mei, Haun Saussy, with Thomas Burkman, eds., *Chinese Walls in Time and Space: A Multidisciplinary Perspective*

145 Hye-jin Juhn Sidney & George Sidney, trs., *I Heard Life Calling Me: Poems of Yi Sŏng-bok*

146 Sherman Cochran & Paul G. Pickowicz, eds., *China on the Margins*

147 Wang Lingzhen & Mary Ann O' Donnell, trs., *Years of Sadness: Autobiographical Writings of Wang Anyi*

148 John Holstein, tr., *A Moment's Grace: Stories from Korea in Transition*

149 Sunyoung Park in collaboration with Jefferson J.A. Gatrall, trs., *On the Eve of the Uprising and Other Stories from Colonial Korea*

150 Brother Anthony of Taizé & Lee Hyung-jin, trs., *Walking on a Washing Line: Poems of Kim Seung-Hee*

151 Matthew Fraleigh, trs., with introduction, *New Chronicles of Yanagibashi and Diary of a Journey to the West: Narushima Ryūhoku Reports from Home and Abroad*

152 Pei Huang, *Reorienting the Manchus: A Study of Sinicization, 1583–1795*

153 Karen Gernant & Chen Zeping, *White Poppies and Other Stories by Zhang Kangkang*

154 Mattias Burell & Marina Svensson, eds., *Making Law Work: Chinese Laws in Context*

www.ingramcontent.com/pod-product-compliance
Lightning Source LLC
Chambersburg PA
CBHW030642270326
41929CB00007B/169

* 9 7 8 1 9 3 9 1 6 1 9 0 1 *